Long Island

THE GOLDEN ISLE

• • •

PRODUCED IN COOPERATION WITH THE
LONG ISLAND ASSOCIATION
80 HAUPPAUGE ROAD
COMMACK, N.Y. 11725
516/499-4400

Photo by Lisa Meyer.

Long Island
THE GOLDEN ISLE

• • •

BY PAULA HARTMAN COHEN

CORPORATE PROFILES BY DORIS MEADOWS

FEATURING THE PHOTOGRAPHY OF BRUCE BENNETT STUDIOS

Community Communications, Inc.
Publishers: Ronald P. Beers and James E. Turner

Staff for *Long Island: The Golden Isle*
Publisher's Sales Associates: Constance Ledgett and William McAllister
Executive Editor: James E. Turner
Managing Editor: Mary Shaw Hughes
Design Director: Camille Leonard
Designer: Rebecca Carlisle
Photo Editors: Mary Shaw Hughes and Rebecca Carlisle
Production Manager: Corinne Cau
Editorial Assistant: Katrina Williams
Sales Assistant: Annette Lozier
Proofreader: Opal Banish
Accounting Services: Sara Ann Turner
Printing Production: Frank Rosenberg/GSAmerica

Community Communications, Inc.
Montgomery, Alabama

James E. Turner, Chairman of the Board
Ronald P. Beers, President
Daniel S. Chambliss, Vice President

Photo by Scott Levy.

LONG ISLAND: THE GOLDEN ISLE
PART I

A Legacy of Innovation

Long Island is a region rich in history, a home to more innovators and inventors than perhaps any other two counties in the country. Many colonial-era homes are still standing, trees trained as fencing still grow along the roadside, and many villages, streets and boundaries have not changed appreciably since they were set up by early settlers more than 300 years ago.

Abundant Resources

Suffolk County, the eastern-most county on Long Island, leads the state in agriculture market value. Yet, it is the 49th county in the state in terms of acres farmed. That's because fishing is still one of the most important agricultural industries in New York, and Long Island is the base for that industry.

The Good Life, Then & Now

Long Island's Gold Coast is famous for its string of mansions, where the Vanderbilts, the Whitneys and other of America's wealthiest families made their summer homes. Today thousands of families live here because of the good life. On Long Island, that means one centering around outdoor activities along the water, excellent schools, good health facilities, proximity to airports and other means of transportation, a high standard of living and the beauty of small towns and suburban communities.

A Diverse & Generous People

Long Islanders are generous people. Although many are relative newcomers, Long Islanders are known to help each other in emergencies with a large outpouring of work and donations. A rich network of non-profit organizations keeps this area among the top in the nation in terms of funds raised for national charities and numbers of people participating in volunteer activities.

Health & Wisdom

When it comes to quality health care, Long Island patients can choose from small community hospitals with individualized service, to large teaching hospitals offering the latest technology and clinical trials. One reason the region is blessed with superior health care facilities is its ability to attract the most talented providers. And one of the main attractions is Long Island's top quality education, available at all levels. Long Island's schools are well known for being some of the best-funded and best-equipped in the nation.

Water, Water Everywhere

This is a place surrounded by water. If you're not one of the thousands who live along the Island's 1,000 miles of shoreline, you probably live a short drive from the beach. You may walk its uninterrupted beach for relaxation and exercise. County government and parks departments make good use of Long Island's resources, while protecting it for generations to come.

A Precious Environment

Convinced a healthy environment promotes a healthy economy, the environmental forces on Long Island include both the tourism and agriculture industries, The Nature Conservancy, the Pine Barrens Preservation Society, the LI Greenbelt Trail Conference, the New York State Office of Parks, Recreation and Historic Preservation, and many business groups. They appreciate the fact that the Island's environment is precious, not only to those who live here now and will live here in the future, but also to the nation as a whole.

The Promise of Tech Island

Major technology companies have paved the way for expansion in fields using technical applications. Long Island is heading in the direction of becoming a high-technology center, with new biotech and software companies starting every month, and with world-class research centers introducing the concepts and technology that will be necessary to bring us into the 21st Century.

LONG ISLAND ENTERPRISES
PART II

FOREWORD

• • •

LONG ISLAND. THE RHAPSODIC VERSE OF WALT WHITMAN touched upon its natural beauty. F. Scott Fitzgerald captured the disillusionment of the Jazz Age against the backdrop of its renowned Gold Coast. Artist William Sidney Mount depicted the region's diverse 19th-century communities, while contemporary artist Joseph Reboli finds the East End to be a prolific source of subjects for his paintings.

Many authors and artists have borrowed Long Island as a place in which to set their works. But those who live and do business here know that it is more than just a place. In the story you are about to read, Long Island plays the role of the protagonist: a solid, steady presence in the lives of those around it, yet a community continuously undergoing growth and evolution of its own.

Like the fable of the six blind men who tried to describe the elephant standing before them, Long Island can seem to be many things, both to the people who live here and to those who visit. And, as in the fable, Long Island always turns out to be more than the sum total of its parts.

We have taken great care to capture that sum total, and more, in the following pages. And we hope that in reading *Long Island: The Golden Isle* you capture a sense of Long Island as more than just a place. It is a disposition, a feeling, a way of life.

Long Island is a great place to live, to work, and to do business. But most of all, Long Island is a place simply to enjoy.

Matthew T. Crosson
President
Long Island Association

Southhampton Campus of Long Island University. Photo by Scott Levy.

LONG ISLAND • 9

PREFACE

. . .

I N THE FAR REACHES OF MY HALL CLOSET, THERE sits a small bag that was moved but never unpacked some 20 years ago, because I never expected to remain on Long Island. We had stopped off here on the way to someplace else, on the road to that elusive, perfect little town where a person could enjoy a full and productive life while raising a child. Needless to say, that town was here. We sank roots deep into the sand, becoming part of the ebb and flow of a coastal environment. Twenty years later, the child is grown and has moved to another town. I've outlived several careers, and every time I considered moving on, I realized that would require cleaning the garage.

In the mid-1990s, I faced the possibility of moving again, and the idea of going "off Island" was intriguing: it would mean I could drive an unlimited distance in any direction without running out of land. I would possibly pay less for housing and utilities but, after a while, I would miss my little house deep in a stand of oaks, the well-stocked neighborhood library, a world-class daily newspaper, and my morning walk on the beach.

In one of poet William Heyen's magnificent books, he has a dream sequence in which he pictures his son opening a clamshell found in Smithtown Harbor, not far from my home. Inside is a note saying, "We left these here for you." That haunting image has stuck in my mind for 15 years, leaving me at once grateful and mindful of my own obligations to this fragile spit of land, as Walt Whitman called it.

Those of us who come here from somewhere else never get over that first moment when we saw the water, or felt the sea breeze, or smelled the salt air. Every time I think I'll move on, I have to ask myself why.

The task of gathering information for this project involved months of research and interviews of more people than I can ever thank for their time and interest. Certainly the most important has been Daniel Cohen, my son and research assistant, as well as a writer in his own right. My special thanks to him and to the following people and organizations for their generous assistance:

Bruce Hartman/Dilworth, Paxson, Kalish & Kaufman; Paul Hartman, Harryet Hartman; Lanning Likes/PPPI; Arthur Belli, Jr./Laikin Agency; Brad O'Hearn/Brad O'Hearn Associates; Matilda R. Cuomo/HELP; John Renyhart/The Museums at Stony Brook; Gloria Rocchio/Stony Brook Community Fund; Joseph Gergela/Long Island Farm Bureau; Kenneth Schmitt/Schmitt Bros. Farms; Maria Cinque/Cornell Cooperative Extension Service of Nassau County; Emerson Hasbrouck/Marine Program, CCE of Suffolk County; George Gorman, Jr./NYS Office of Parks, Recreation and Historic Preservation, LI Region; Michael Davidson/Long Island Convention and Visitors Bureau; Roger Tollerson/New York Seafood Council; Jack Van de Wetering, Nate Corwin/Ivy Acres.

Hon. Steven Englebright/NYS Assembly, 4th District; Pres. David Steinberg, Christine Hendriks, Corrie Ferger/Long Island University; Pres. James Shuart, Michael DeLuise, Dr. Barbara Kelly/Hofstra University; Pres. Shirley Strum Kenny, Vicky Penner Katz, Sue Risoli/State University of New York at Stony Brook; Dr. Elizabeth D. Blake/Suffolk County Community College; Linda Howard Weissman/Touro College, Jacob D. Fuchsburg Law Center; Dr. Ward Deutschman, Dr. Dorothy Germano/Briarcliffe College.

Matthew Crosson, Valerie Scibilia/Long Island Association; Richard Bravman, Nancy Tully, Dixie Scovel, James Garvey/Symbol Technologies; Peg Mancuso, Peter Dorogoff, Barbara Shea, Mary Ann Skinner, Dave Smukler/Newsday; Francis "Pat" Hession/Long Island High Technology Incubator; Diane Greenberg/Brookhaven National Laboratory; Bob Buchmann, Paul Fleishman/WBAB-FM; Michael Jacobchek/Riverhead Attractions Committee; Suffolk County Police Department, Public Relations Office; Ed Grilli/Office of the District Attorney, Nassau County; Pat Macri/Millennium Communications; Frank Becher/Olympus America, Inc.; Hilary Hartung/Nassau Veterans Memorial Coliseum; Pat Calabria/New York Islanders; Debbie Ross/Bruce Bennett Studios.

Michael Rodzenko, Christine Hendriks, Linda Berman/South Nassau Communities Hospital; Michael P. Quane/Mercy Medical Center; Lori Gluckman, Phyllis Abrams/Winthrop-University Hospital; Carol Hauptman, Ellen Mitchell/North Shore-University Hospital; Ellen Barohn/University Medical Center, SUNY Stony Brook; Guide Dog Foundation for the Blind; Wendy O'Neill/St. Francis Hospital; Sue Fragale, Tracey Gittere/Long Island Random Acts of Kindness; Diane Valek/Make-A-Wish Foundation of Suffolk County.

Stan Brodsky; Elise Ross/Hospice of the South Shore; Joan Convery/Community Development Corporation of Long Island; Gerald Nichols/Suffolk Cooperative Library System; Smithtown Public Library; Middle Country Public Library; Grace Shen/The Long Island Arts Council at Freeport; Rev. Reginald Tuggle/Memorial Presbyterian Church; Abby Kenigsberg/Long Island Coalition for Fair Broadcasting; Billy Joel; Noel Gish/Hauppauge High School; Nora Lynch/Diocese of Rockville Centre; Kathy Day/Staller Center for the Arts; Teddy Bookman/Friends of the Arts; Hilary Hartung/Nassau Veterans Memorial Coliseum; Lillian Barbash/Islip Arts Council; Mindy Newton/Clarity Editing; Tony Doyle/Gonsalez Internet Consulting; Suffolk County Historical Society; Jerome Seckler/Nassau County Office of Cultural Development; Nassau Library System; Stephen M. Levy/NSFRE.

Special thanks to Mark Becker, D.O.; John Dervan, M.D.; John Fiore, M.D.; Daniel Seigel, M.D.; Robert Scher, M.D.

— *Paula Cohen*

Photo by Lindsay Silverman.

PART I

THE GOLDEN ISLE

Photo by Deborah Ross.

THE OLD HOOK MILL
OPEN
Friday Saturday Sunday
10 to 5

INTRODUCTION

• • •

LONG ISLAND

• • •

East Hampton. Photo by David Giacopelli.

WHAT LOOKS GREEN FROM ABOVE, IS 120 miles long, and found in the North Atlantic? No, it's not an American version of the Loch Ness monster, but Long Island, New York. Although it's home to 2.6 million people, you will be hard-pressed to find it named on any map. That's because it is an invention, a "golden isle" if you will, carved out of a real island called Paumanok to the Indians, but Long, today. The geographic Long Island includes four counties, two of which are New York City boroughs and two generally considered the region we call Long Island. All of which may explain, in part, why the place is so misunderstood by those off-Island.

Completed in 1796, the Montauk Point Lighthouse is the oldest lighthouse on Long Island and in New York State. (left) Photo by John Giamundo. (below) Photo by Scott Levy.

Newcomers find Long Island much greener and prettier than expected and are often surprised by the treed neighborhoods. (left) White Post Farms in Melville. Photo by Bruce Bennett. (above) Along Route 25A. Photo by Martha Leider. (right) Autumn in Garden City. Photo by Deborah Ross.

On Long Island, you can feel the America of the past and the future. (above) Photo by Lindsay Silverman. (right) The Old First Presbyterian Church of Huntington was built in 1665, then dismantled and rebuilt in 1715. During the Revolutionary War, the British used it as a stable and storehouse. Photo by James McIsaac.

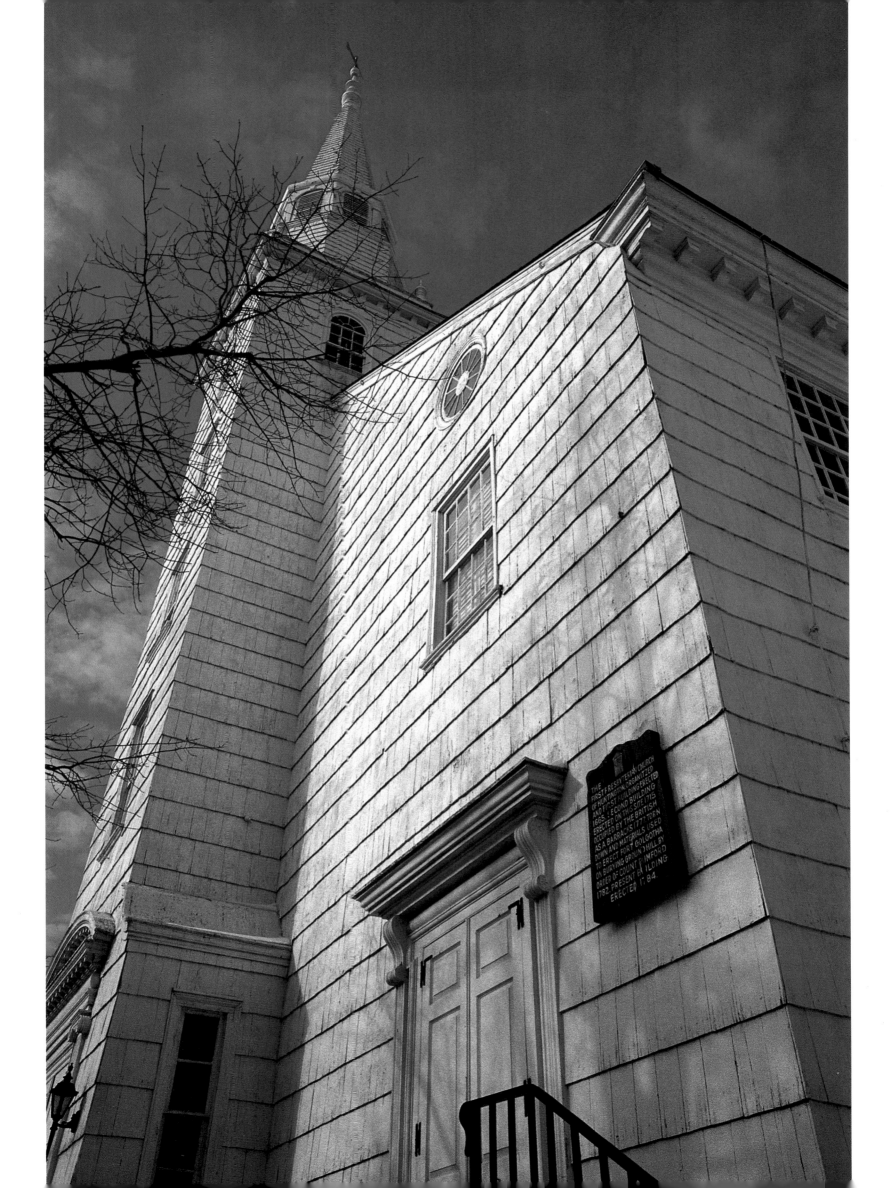

THE
FIRST PRESBYTERIAN CHURCH
OF HUNTINGTON, ORGANIZED
AND FIRST BUILDING ERECTED
1665. SECOND BUILDING
ERECTED ON THIS SITE 1715
OCCUPIED BY THE BRITISH
AS A BARRACKS 1777, TORN
DOWN AND MATERIALS USED
TO ERECT FORT GOLGOTHA
ON BURYING GROUND HILL BY
ORDER OF COUNT RUMFORD
1782. PRESENT BUILDING
ERECTED 1784.

Long Island has a certain style and flair that sets it apart from other suburban areas. (above) Bethpage State Park Golf Course. Photo by David Giacopelli. (left) Southhampton home. Photo by James McIsaac.

**Equestrian activities are popular pastimes on Long Island.
(above) Horse barn in Old Westbury. Photo by Bruce Bennett.**

Newcomers find it much greener and prettier than they expected. Although it's well-peopled, Long Island still has open space and gentle, treed neighborhoods. The schools, libraries, hospitals, and most town services are excellent. Although it's not hard to find the usual commercial strips that line most of the nation's highways, it's just as easy to turn off a main road, wind through some back roads, and trip over something that's downright beautiful.

Crime is among the lowest of any suburban area in the country and water purity rated among the highest. You can get as friendly with your neighbors as you want, or if you covet your privacy, you can maintain it without fanfare. Weather is generally temperate, with constant ocean breezes. Best of all, the beach is captivating, and if you can't stand the peace and quiet, the "city that never sleeps" is close enough.

Can such a rich and interesting place really be the home of the infamous "Lawn Guylander" of sitcom jokes? That caricature, coupled with the abundance of stories in the tabloid press, belies the reality of this place. Some say it's the price we pay for being convenient to New York City.

Long Island is both serene and energetic, rural and sophisticated. (left) Interior of home in East Hampton. Photo by Bruce Bennett. (above) Historic Roslyn Park. Photo by Deborah Ross.

The Long Island beaches are captivating at any time of the day. (above) Yacht racing off Mt. Sinai Harbor. Photo by Lisa Meyer. (right) Robert Moses State Park on Fire Island. Photo by James McIsaac.

(left) The Big Duck, a former duck farmer's poultry store, is now a center for tourist information. Photo by Brian Winkler.

Long Islanders take special pride in preserving history. (right) The steeple of Hempstead Town Hall is being refurbished. Photo by Deborah Ross.

(left) Winter on Long Island has its own special brand of charm. (below) A view of Cold Spring Harbor homes. Photos by Deborah Ross.

Many of Long Island's wineries have reputations well beyond the area. (left) Banfi Vintners, Old Brookville. Photo by Deborah Ross. (above) Photo by Martha Leider.

In 1919, millionaire William R. Coe built himself a 65-room house and named it Planting Fields, the original Indian name for the area. Today, the arboretum's greenhouses, flower shows and concerts attract visitors year-round. Its majestic trees, sweeping lawns and landscaped gardens have also been the backdrop for numerous wedding photos, like the one pictured above. Photo by Deborah Ross.

Long Islanders love to eat out. Many go to local diners, where they know the waitresses by name and the menu by heart. Glen's Dinette in Babylon is one of many. Photo by Deborah Ross.

On the contrary, Long Islanders are an energized mix of middle managers and storeowners, writers and artists, teachers and engineers, salespeople, government workers, pilots and corporate executives, social workers, secretaries and computer programmers, farmers, college students, and retired couples. Most emigrated from the city as children and have fond memories of a New York City that once was. Those who are third and fourth-generation Long Islanders have a hearty feistiness about them reminiscent of (perhaps mythical) Vermonters. And there are enough people from other parts of the world to remind you this is a gateway to a global community.

While they're a worldly, sophisticated bunch, it's true that some Long Islanders border on the provincial. Many are convinced they have the best of all possible worlds, even though they grouse as much as people do anywhere else. At least, they have some of everything, and all within easy reach.

For instance, many who live here see no point in going away on vacation. They are within a short driving distance of the beach or Broadway. Others see this as the ideal place for a second home. The Hamptons are full of them. Most regions that draw tourists are

(above) Seen from a hilltop on the mansion grounds, boats seem to glide past Coindre Hall's gothic-styled boathouse on the shore of Huntington Harbor. On their way out to the Long Island Sound, weekend sailors often pass working baymen because the harbor is a popular base for western Suffolk clamming. Coindre Hall was once a mansion and later a military academy, but now houses the Museum of Long Island's Gold Coast. Photo by Lindsay Silverman.

(right) Built in 1648, the Old Halsey House is the oldest English frame house in New York. Photo by James McIsaac.

practically unlivable, but that's not the case here. And most places that are built to provide for the generations would be uninteresting to the daytripper. Wrong, again.

This is a place with its own hair, dress, and music styles, as recognizable as California's to the aficionado. Tastes in food tend to revolve around the ethnic and the marine; people here eat out a lot. Not surprisingly, they rank fourth in the United States in spending on food outside the home, which means there are lots of choices for those who don't like to cook. And Islanders have their own slang, their own idiosyncrasies in language, some of which are more often communicated through body language than words.

Long Islanders are generous people. In fact, they top the ranks of people in metropolitan areas for the amount of dollars they spend yearly in contributions, giving almost twice the national average to charities. Yet, the urban upbringing of many Long Islanders makes them cautious in their everyday dealings with people, leading most outsiders to misunderstand them.

The roads here follow paths built to take farmers to market, and some days it seems like everyone is out, going to the same fire sale.

There is a wide range in size and style of homes throughout Long Island's neighborhoods. (above) Long Island is known for its Levitt homes, many of which have been expanded over the years. A number of the original houses, like the one above, still stand in Levittown, one of the nation's first suburban communities. Photo by Deborah Ross. (left) Photo by Bruce Bennett.

Cars are newer and more expensive than what you find on the road in some parts of the country. Houses are big, with plenty of crossover between the inside and outside, and always designed with a certain flair, with some little style statement setting them apart from other suburban areas, something that says, "We're on an island and like it that way."

This book will introduce you to our Island, where you'll find the America of the past and the future. Bruce Bennett's photography will show you Long Island is both serene and energetic, rural and sophisticated, rooted in history and poised on the cusp of the future. And Doris Meadows' corporate profiles will give a hint of what's here and what's to come. You'll find that there's a strange energy to this place. Neither country nor city, it has the friction produced when the two get too close to each other, producing an energy almost harnessable. Anything can happen here, and probably will.   •••

Not surprisingly, salt-water fishing is one of Long Islanders' favorite leisure activities. With more than 1,100 miles of coast line, there's plenty of surf fishing and dozens of party boats to take groups out to the ocean or the sound. (left) Surf fishing at Horton's Point on the North Fork. Photo by James McIsaac. (above) Captain Ben's in Freeport. Photo by Scott Levy.

Fire Island stretches out along 75 miles of the South Shore of Long Island, protecting the main island from the Atlantic Ocean. The 168-foot Fire Island Lighthouse in the Fire Island National Seashore, was the first light seen by many early immigrants sailing into New York Harbor. Photo by Scott Levy.

(right) Sailboats docked at Stony Brook Harbor. Photo by Deborah Ross.

(above) Built by John S. Phipps for his English bride, the Manor House of Old Westbury Gardens is elegantly furnished and surrounded by one of the great gardens of the Western world. Photo by Lindsay Silverman.

(left) Visitors can't leave Long Island without a deep sense of the Island's history. The mill in Roslyn Park is one of several working mills in the area. Photo by Gary Fox.

(on the following page) Sunset over Eaton's Neck. Photo by Scott Levy.

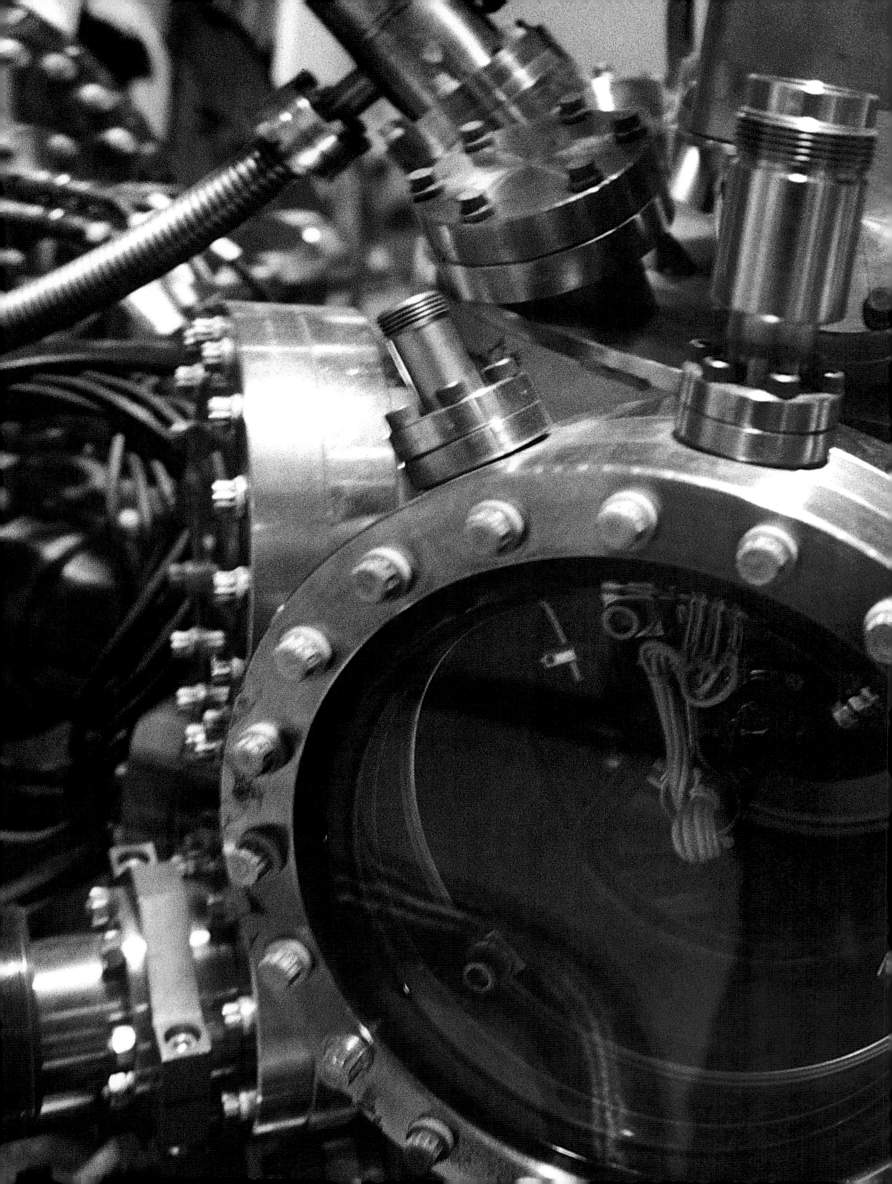

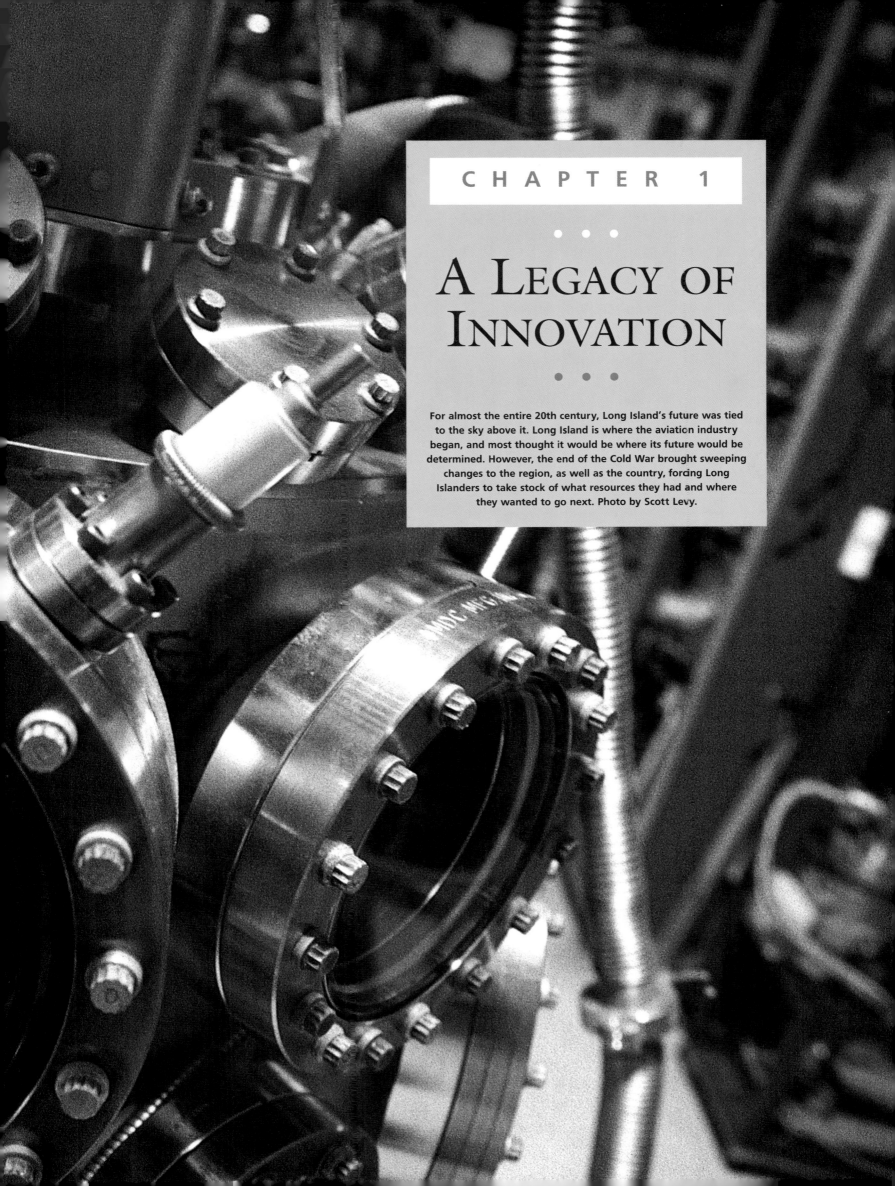

CHAPTER 1

A LEGACY OF INNOVATION

For almost the entire 20th century, Long Island's future was tied to the sky above it. Long Island is where the aviation industry began, and most thought it would be where its future would be determined. However, the end of the Cold War brought sweeping changes to the region, as well as the country, forcing Long Islanders to take stock of what resources they had and where they wanted to go next. Photo by Scott Levy.

HISTORY SHOWS US THAT THIS COUNTRY, and the Long Island region in particular, has always been resilient. A quick look at history proves that Long Island is fertile ground for innovation and ingenuity, claiming an inordinate number of "firsts." As Shirley Strum Kenny, president of SUNY at Stony Brook says, "This place has a lot of fizz." With that in mind, there's reason to believe more pivotal ideas will be born here, taking us into areas we cannot even imagine.

Those on the very edge of innovation, artists and inventors, have long loved this area. Its geography, horizon, and abundant light make it a favorite for painters. And inventors of some of the world's most important technology, as well as scientists uncovering the basic structure of the universe, have found inspiration and acceptance here. After all, this was the summer hideaway of Einstein and the birthplace of the lunar landing module.

INNOVATORS IN THE ARTS

According to Stan Brodsky, a well-known Huntington-based painter who spent 20 years exploring color and light in tide pools, "Since it's so easy to see water every day, you really feel connected to it. It imprints itself on your memory. You see the changes that take place at the water's edge all the time. Artists on Long Island are involved in that kind of visual material, intimately involved with tides and light reflecting off the water, day after day."

Modern painters such as Willem de Kooning have been moved by the light, or the horizon, or the shoreline, or all three to see the world from a different perspective, a requirement of any innovative thinking. And Brodsky is one of many contemporary artists whose work has been impacted by life on the Island. Others, like Northport painter Stanley Twardowicz, the late Long Island University (LIU) professor and sculptor Alfred Van Loen, Roslyn painter Nola Zirin, environmental construction artist Barbara Roux, and the innovative young Huntington sculptor Mark Kuhn, have drawn on their relationship with the easily available light and the sky—two things hard to find in the urban landscape of New York City.

One of the first truly American painters, William Sydney Mount of Setauket, used local scenes as backdrops for his paintings of colonial

(left) Larry Rivers: *Boy in Blue Denim*. Photo by Noel Rowe, courtesy of the Parrish Art Museum.

(below) Photo of Stan Brodsky by Scott Levy.

William Merritt Chase: *The Bayberry Bush.* **Photo by Noel Rowe, courtesy of the Parrish Art Museum.**

The Walt Whitman House in Huntington Station is the birthplace of one of America's most famous poets. Photo by Martha Leider.

life. Mount is one of the first American painters to use the common people as subjects, leaving a rich legacy of images of life in the early 19th century on the North Shore. He was one of the first painters to represent black people with dignity, as in *Eel Spearing at Setauket* (1845). Relatives of some of his portrait subjects still live in and around Setauket. The Museums at Stony Brook has a large collection of his work in the permanent collection as a result of purchases made by the museum's and the village's benefactor, Ward Melville.

The first series of sporting lithographs produced in American art, done by Currier & Ives, feature Long Island hunting scenes. One, titled *Catching A Trout: We Hab You Now, Sar*, depicts Daniel Webster catching a record trout at the Mill Pond on the Carmans River. The print was made in 1827.

Equally important was Childe Hassam (1859-1935), the most talented of "The Ten," a group of American artists dedicated to the French Impressionist style. Another one of the group, William Merritt Chase, is well-known for his Long Island landscapes. In this century, the Ashcan School of Art, famous for finding beauty in the commonplace, found a home in Bellport in the 1920s. Further east in the Hamptons, controversial artists Jackson Pollock, Willem and Elaine de Kooning, Roy Lichtenstein, Larry Rivers, and Robert Rauschenberg set the standard for much of what has been produced since the 1960s. Their presence drew more painters, turning the Hamptons into an artist colony, which in turn, attracted television and movie stars, writers, musicians, and other creative people.

American literature was equally impacted by Long Islanders.

In-laws of *The Last of the Mohicans* author James Fenimore Cooper were part of prominent society on Shelter Island, a place Cooper visited often. From there, he got to know the surrounding East End villages and later used them as settings in several novels. Parts of *The Sea Lions* are set in Orient and Shelter Island, and the setting of *The Water Witch* is presumed to be Sag Harbor, where Cooper liked to stay at the Fordham Inn. Today's American Hotel on Main Street has a Cooper room, containing a desk he supposedly used to write one of his novels. About 100 years later, Pulitzer Prize-winning novelist John Steinbeck lived in the same town and used it as a backdrop for *The Winter of Our Discontent*.

Jupiter Hammon, America's first black poet and the first black American to have his writing published, was a slave in the 18th century on the Lloyd Manor, in what is now called Lloyd's Neck, across the harbor from Huntington. And Huntington, actually West Hills, was birthplace to Walt Whitman, perhaps America's first truly revolutionary poet. Whitman's controversial work turned poetry upside down and put America on the map, in an artistic sense. Even today, *Leaves of Grass* engenders controversy and discussion. Again, his work elevated the common person, the human animal, the coarse and the ordinary, to a position of beauty and note.

F. Scott Fitzgerald may be the writer most associated with Long Island. His novels of the excesses of life on the North Shore in the 1920s gave name to an era, while breaking new ground in American literature. Who can forget the fictional "West Egg" and "East Egg" in *The Great Gatsby*, which were loosely based on his memories of

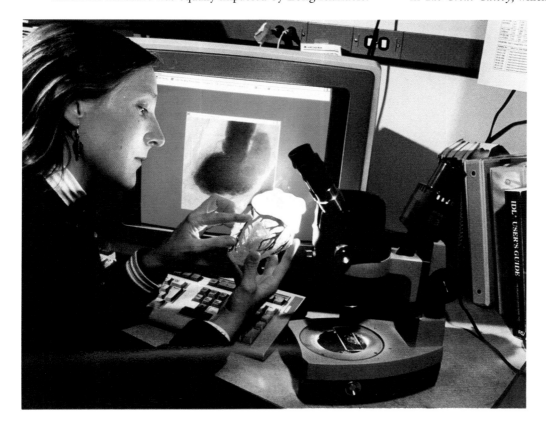

Transvenous angiography is a pioneering development in the battle against heart disease at BNL. Photo courtesy of the Brookhaven National Laboratory.

(above) Cold Spring Harbor Laboratory may be best known as the home base of DNA discoverer James D. Watson. Photo by Scott Levy.

(right) Budding scientists enjoy the "walk of life" at the DNA Science Center. Photo by Bruce Bennett.

THE WALK OF LIFE

GLYCINE

CYSTEINE

CYTOSINE

ADENINE

GUANINE

CYTOSINE

URACIL

GUANINE

URACIL

GUANINE

When Americans first set foot on the moon, Long Islanders took special pride in the achievement because the astronauts' vehicle was a Grumman-made lunar module, the LEM. Photo courtesy of the Cradle of Aviation Museum, Mitchel Field.

Great Neck Estates and Sands Point? The Fitzgeralds we e the nucleus of a mini-salon of writers in the Great Neck area, which included Ring Lardner, Will Durant, and P.G. Wodehouse.

Beatnik guru Jack Kerouac lived in Northport, hung out in the bars and on the town dock, and left a legacy of existential excess. His "On the Road" launched a generation of poets and novelsts, then was resurrected in the late 1960s as the inspiration for the adolescent rite-of-passage: driving across the country in search of America.

By the 1950s and 1960s, the Hamptons had become the full-or part-time home of Truman Capote, Mary Roberts Rinehat, journalist A.J. Leibling, novelists Norman Mailer and Budd Schulbe g, all innovators in their own right. Today, the Island is home to as many highly respected writers, including poets Louis Simpson, David Ignatow, Vince Clemente, and the youthful Cornelius Eady; award-winning historical novelist Thomas Flanagan (*The Year of the French*, *Tenants of Time*), and novelists Peter Maas, E.L. Doctorow, and Kurt Vonnegut.

(right) When Charles Lindbergh made the first solo trans-Atlantic flight in 1927, the point of origin was Roosevelt Field on Long Island. Photo courtesy of the Cradle of Aviation Museum, Mitchel Field.

(below) The proposed Cradle of Aviation Museum renovation rendering, courtesy of the Museums at Mitchel Center.

The Cradle of Aviation Museum houses restorations and replicas along with memorabilia chronicling important aviation events. Photos by Scott Levy.

IMPORTANT SCIENTIFIC DISCOVERIES AND TECHNOLOGICAL ADVANCEMENTS

Few would guess, but Long Island played a significant role in the birth of telecommunications. Croatian inventor and electrical engineer Nikola Tesla conducted some of his first wireless transmissions from a huge tower he built near Shoreham. Tesla is credited with developing alternating-current electrical power. Among other things, he laid the theoretical basis for radio communications as early as 1892, although that feat was claimed by Guglielmo Marconi, who conducted the first FM radio transmission from a shack along Montauk Highway in Babylon.

In 1951, Brookhaven National Laboratory (BNL) completed a much-anticipated trial using atomic energy in cancer therapy for the first time in medical history. This first step in boron neutron capture therapy opened the door for modern radiation treatment and other forms of nuclear medicine.

Brookhaven National Laboratory, one of nine multipurpose labs built to develop a peaceful use of atomic energy, has been the site of research for four Nobel Prizes and has produced countless innovations, such as mag-lev transportation technology, zinc-phosphate coating to make cars rust-resistant, a variety of noninvasive techniques for medical imaging, and procedures used to measure the impact of various energy sources on health.

This is where L-dopa was first discovered in the 1960s, opening the door for treatment, but not the cure, for Parkinson's disease. Other BNL medical research has yielded radioisotopes used in diagnosis of many diseases and disorders. Several years ago, project FISHNET linked doctors at both Stony Brook University Hospital and Brookhaven via fiber-optic cable, allowing them to observe a cardiac catheterization in progress, the first step in opening doors for doctors in remote places or on battlefields to have first-rate assistance from off-site medical professionals, in real time. Meanwhile, the BNL biology department is working to improve sequencing techniques for the human genome project, which began as a result

The Bayport Aerodrome Society preserves the Long Island tradition of aviation. Photo by Scott Levy.

Stony Brook was the world's first planned community designed around a village center set up specifically for the automobile. (on the previous page) The lovely village center was featured in a story in National Geographic Magazine, with this staged photograph depicting its early days. Photo courtesy of National Geographic Society. (above) Stony Brook Post Office eagle flaps its wings on the hour. Photo by Deborah Ross.

of work done at Cold Spring Harbor Laboratory.

Brookhaven Lab has also been a place for innovations in technology for energy conservation. In the 1970s, its well-known passive-solar model home was a unique example of the fusion of technological and commercial construction methods, offering ideas such as heat-gathering interior walls and the careful use of color and texture in interior design and decoration. The Brookhaven House, as it was called, was the focus of many magazine and newspaper articles.

Long Island's other think tank, Cold Spring Harbor Laboratory, may be best known as the home base of one of the discoverers of

DNA. CSHL Director James D. Watson and Dr. Francis H.C. Crick of England shared the 1962 Nobel Prize for isolating and revealing the significance of the molecular structure of deoxyribonucleic acid, the basic genetic material of living cells. Their work was actually done at Cambridge, and their book, *The Double Helix*, turned their scientific inquiry into a mystery story for the general reader. The discovery of the master code for protein synthesis in cells led to the eventual development of numerous uses of genetic material, from the fledgling gene therapy in medicine to genetic cloning, which has tremendous commercial and medical promise.

Dedicated to basic research but committed to the understanding and conquest of cancer, in 1981 CSHL scientists isolated the gene that turns a healthy cell into a cancer cell, a watershed moment in medical history. And, in 1988, an international team of scientists, building upon the work of Watson and Crick, began a project to construct a map of the human genome, to complete the circle of genetic knowledge gleaned over the last 30 years.

In 1970, Dr. Barbara McClintock of CSHL was awarded the National Medal of Science and, in 1983, the Nobel Prize for physiology of medicine, the first woman ever to win an unshared prize in that category. In the 1940s and 1950s, the maverick McClintock disputed the thinking of the times, saying she thought chromosomes could break off and recombine to create unique genetic combinations. The importance of her findings was not recognized for many years, but today the genetic research community considers her one of the most important figures in the history of genetics, alongside Gregor Mendel and Hunt Morgan. McClintock died in Huntington in 1992.

Another award winner, Chinese-born American theoretical physicist Chen Ning Yeng, is professor of physics at the State University of New York at Stony Brook. In 1957, Yang was awarded the Nobel Prize for physics with Tsung-Dao Lee for research done at BNL in particle physics that disputed one of the universal laws of symmetry in physics. Their work demonstrated that parity is violated when elementary particles decay; in other words, the physical world is not symmetrical in all aspects, as once believed. If it were, you could run physics backward or forward and it would be the same, but it's not, according to the findings of Lee and Yang.

THE CRADLE OF AVIATION

Perhaps because it has always relied on machinery to connect it to the mainland—either rails, ships, telecommunications, or aircraft—Long Island has always been a generator of new aviation technology.

Lacking the heights needed for falling water to power turbines, inventive Long Islanders focused their energies on technology that would take them up and away, or over ground faster, making the need for electric power less important.

Called the "cradle of aviation," Long Island may not have given birth to the flight, but it nurtured it from infancy into its adolescence and beyond. Not long after the Wright brothers made the first successful man-carrying, engine-powered, heavier-than-air flight at Kitty Hawk in 1903, Glenn Curtiss of upstate Hammondsport and others began using the flat, open Hempstead Plain in Nassau County to test similar machines. By 1909, Curtiss had perfected his equipment and flying technique enough to take his Golden Flyer a record 47.8 miles, winning the first international air meet in Reims, France, and setting a world record. Curtiss later became an aircraft manufacturer and went on to build the world's first seaplanes.

By 1911, the first U.S. airmail service started taking off from Roosevelt Field, an airstrip that would launch hundreds of important flights before being turned into a shopping mall and center for commerce and education later in the century. In 1922, Lt. James H. Doolittle left Garden City to make a historic flight to California, the first to traverse North America in less than 24 hours.

But, perhaps the most famous flight originating at Roosevelt Field was that of the Spirit of St. Louis in 1927, when Charles Lindbergh made the first solo trans-Atlantic flight, a feat that captured the imagination of the entire world. Lindbergh's 33 1/2-hour adventure opened the door for the development of the airplane as a viable instrument for commerce and warfare, and the fact that it started in Hempstead put Long Island on the map as a center for both experimental and commercial aviation.

More historic flights followed. Two years later, Doolittle made the first demonstration of "blind" flight, using navigational instruments developed by Long Island's Sperry Gyroscope. In 1931, Wiley Post and Harold Gatty were the first to fly around the entire globe. They took their Lockheed monoplane on a 15,477-mile, 14-stop, 8-day, 15-hour-and-51-minute jaunt from Roosevelt Field and back, once again bringing attention to Long Island. And, on July 10,

The Stony Brook Grist Mill has undergone an extensive restoration so that visitors can see the millers grinding grain. Photo by Bruce Bennett.

1937, Howard Hughes and his crew flew a Lockheed 14 around the world from Long Island, breaking Post's and Gatty's record, covering 14,971 miles in 3 days, 19 hours, and 8 minutes.

Not surprisingly, this region became a center for aircraft manufacturing and navigational development between the wars. By the start of World War II, Grumman Aircraft Engineering Corporation, the Fairchild Camera and Instrument Corporation, Republic Aviation Corporation, Sperry Gyroscope, and Liberty Aircraft Products Company were producing defense and commercial aviation products for the U.S. market and abroad. Among them, they employed almost 90,000 people at the height of defense-equipment production during the war. In its glory days, Grumman alone employed 26,000 Long Islanders. One in every six Long Island families depended upon Grumman for its income.

In July of 1969, the whole world watched as the dream of a nation unfolded on color television: an American was the first to set foot on the moon. Long Islanders took special pride in the achievement because astronauts Neil Armstrong and Edwin Aldrin got there in a Grumman-made lunar landing module. Their LEM resembled a large spider made from curtain rods and aluminum foil, hardly the instrument you would expect to carry 20th-century explorers to their first extraterrestrial body. But that lightweight, reflective, and compact vehicle also carried the Apollo 13 crew safely back to Earth when an engine problem left their craft floundering on the far side of the moon. During the frightening voyage of Apollo 13, Grumman employees were brought back to work in the middle of the night to assist the NASA team in devising a safe return for the three astronauts.

Later, when digital technology enhanced the production and navigation of aircraft and marine craft, related companies sprang up on Long Island. Gould, AIL, and Unisys, among others, brought the

Long Island is the birthplace of the environmental movement, due in large part to the work of Robert Cushman Murphy. (above) Rushes grow along the edge of Captree Island. Photo by Deborah Ross. (right) Photo by Scott Levy.

industry to sophistication by developing instruments and systems for aircraft and marine craft. By the 1960s and 1970s, Long Island was known for its fighter-plane development and by the 1980s, as a center for defense communications and navigational systems. By the time of its demise in the 1990s, Long Island's aircraft and defense industry had grown, matured, and spun off numerous cutting-edge industries for this region as well as the rest of the country.

FERTILE GROUND FOR SOCIAL CHANGE

Nassau and Suffolk counties have spawned some important social movements that have a profound impact on the way we live today, the way we treat each other, and the way we look at the world around us.

For example, the Three Village area on the North Shore of Suffolk County is home to both the real estate and legal arms of the modern environmental movement. Stony Brook village, a sleepy, run-down fishing village before it was turned into the living artifact it is today, could be called the birthplace of environmentally sensitive urban planning. It was here that wealthy developer Ward Melville incorporated the natural landscape into a gigantic period piece and succeeded in building a village that's still thriving, still a tourist attraction as well as a favorite place for people from neighboring towns to stroll on a summer Sunday.

The modern Stony Brook is the world's first planned community designed around a village center set up specifically for the automobile. It was built 15 years before Levittown, but unlike Levittown, which was built on potato fields, this project incorporated existing buildings, vegetation, ponds, land contours, and ambiance into a new town. By the 1960s, it was a robust community, with a shopping center, a university, houses of worship, a waterfront area, accommodations for tourists, and many historic sites. When it was completed, Melville protected his artifact under the aegis of a nonprofit organization, the Stony Brook Community Fund, which still manages the property and the town.

Melville didn't live in the village, but down the road in Oldfield next to Flax Pond. It is one of the two most studied salt marshes in the world, due largely to the interest of Melville's neighbor, Robert Cushman Murphy, a naturalist and ornithologist. In 1938, Murphy was named president of the National Audubon Society, one of the only activist environmental groups of its time.

Robert Cushman Murphy, a scientist at the American Museum of Natural History in New York, was one of the world's first preservationists devoted to halting the degradation of the ecosystem by unrestrained and poorly planned development, especially along the coast and in wetland areas. In the 1940s, he and a small group of scientists put forth the radical idea that part of the world should be set aside for preservation for long-term ecological studies. It is largely attributed to them, and their friend Ward Melville, that New York State's master planner and builder, Robert Moses, preserved the land that is now the

America's first supermarket was opened by the Cullen family in 1930. Their stores are found throughout the region. King Kullen photos by Deborah Ross.

Fire Island National Seashore. Flax Pond was one of the first sites to be purchased by The Nature Conservancy, the world-renowned group that developed out of that same band of activist scientists.

In the late 1960s, Suffolk County was besieged by gypsy moths. The county decided to do massive aerial spraying, much to the dismay of a group of scientists at the new state university set up on Ward Melville's property in Stony Brook. These scientists enlisted the help of locals and held a meeting in the community room over the Stony Brook post office, at Melville's invitation. They called themselves the Environmental Defense Fund and soon applied to the Rockefeller Foundation for money to launch a legal attack on the spraying. They lost in the courts, but won the public's interest and eventually became the most important legal arm of the modern environmental movement.

Activism was not limited to environmental issues. In 1963, Betty Friedan came out with *The Feminine Mystique*. That book by Friedan, now a Sag Harbor resident, is credited with being the catalyst for a movement that changed the lives of the people of this country.

If that's not enough innovation, consider this: Long Island may be one of the first places in America where swords were literally beaten into plowshares after World War II. The first place where the fledgling United Nations set up offices was in Lake Success, on the site of Sperry Gyroscope's bombsight factory. And Camp Upton in eastern Suffolk was transformed from a place to train foot soldiers for war into Brookhaven National Lab, which would go on to do research into the peaceful use of atomic energy.

A FEW BUSINESS FIRSTS

Long Island has produced numerous institutions and systems we take for granted as part of the business and commercial scene today. In light of its history of innovation and leadership, it should be no surprise that much of the transition that occurred as the nation moved from rural to an urban/suburban economy, happened here first. Many of the institutions associated with suburban living we recreated here. Consider the following:

The Vanderbilt Long Island Motor Parkway was the first limited-access tollroad built in America. Originally designed as a private speedway for the Vanderbilts and their friends, it remains a scenic east-west route today, although it is open to all.

The Northern State and Southern State Parkways, designed and built by Robert Moses while he was president of the Long Island State Parks Commission in the 1920s to 1930s, set a standard for

Newsday, the leading local daily newspaper for Island residents, has been publishing since 1940. With a circulation of over 500,000 daily, it is the seventh-largest daily newspaper in the United States. (above) Photo by Scott Levy.

On September 3, 1940, Alicia Patterson started the presses in a garage in Hempstead to run off the first 15,000 copies of *Newsday*, one of the first suburban tabloids. By 1990, the newspaper had moved to state-of-the-art headquarters in Melville and was printing almost a million papers a day.

Newsday, Copyright, 1940.

Sag Harbor resident Betty Friedan is generally credited with signaling the start of the woman's movement with her book, *The Feminine Mystique*. Photo by Bruce Bennett.

(on the following page) Photo by Scott Levy.

being cultivated on Long Island, including vast potato farms running down the middle of the island. Moving west to east, the Golden Nematode, a wormlike parasite brought in from Europe, infested potato fields one at a time, until the land in some parts of Nassau was unsuitable for the crop. The land is considered quarantined to this day, necessitating special attention from Cornell Cooperative Extension and other agriculturists. Farmers who didn't want to diversify were quick to put up their land for sale, and developers such as William Levitt were ready to buy.

The turning point came in May of 1947. Returning World War II veterans and their families were unable to find affordable housing. Levitt, who had already built a few small-scale rental developments in the South near military bases, had a plan for a huge community of Cape Cod homes that would rent for $60 a month and sell for about $7,000. The stumbling block was a town ordinance prohibiting houses built without basements.

Newsday, the local daily newspaper started in 1940, led a campaign to get the local town code changed. *Newsday*'s backing helped Levitt pack the town board meeting with almost 1,000 veterans demanding the town ease restrictions to allow for the creation of affordable housing. By October of that year, the first families were moving in, and *Newsday*'s circulation was gaining by the hour.

The Levitt business model was to use concrete slabs, pre-cut and standardized materials, radiant heat, non-union labor, and mass purchasing of appliances and material, all of which allowed for quick and cheap construction. On some days, as many as 35 houses went up. At completion, Levittown contained almost 18,000 homes, 500,000 trees, and enough room for 83,000 people.

Newsday itself was and is a pioneer. Newspapers usually grow out of established markets, not the reverse. The paper started publishing a year before Pearl Harbor, when the population was still fairly small and scattered. Virtually all respectable newspapers of the time were broadsheets, but Miss P, as Patterson was called, chose a tabloid format to simulate a daily magazine for the suburban housewife and her commuter husband. *Newsday* went on to reap many awards for journalism and public service, and has long been recognized as an innovator in an industry that's built on creating a new product every day.

What is it, the water? How can one little, fairly isolated place produce so many inventions, so many authors, daredevils, entrepreneurs, mavericks in the arts, industry, and science? It must be the water.   •••

suburban highways. They limited traffic to automobiles while providing woodland scenery to delight drivers and passengers. These limited-access roads are now important parts of the region's suburban transportation system taking commuters to the city and back, or to important commercial locations on the Island.

America's first supermarket was built by the Cullen family of Point Lookout, founders of the King Kullen chain. The first of their many stores opened in Queens in 1930, but soon expanded into and throughout Long Island. By 1995, King Kullen was the region's eighth-largest non-government employer, with 4,500 full-time employees.

Long before the food industry modernized its delivery systems, Long Island served as an important provider of fish, fruits, and vegetables to the southeastern corner of New York State. Not surprisingly, the state's first farm cooperative started out as the Riverhead Town Agricultural Society. It held an annual fair, attracting locals and dignitaries from near and far, even President Theodore Roosevelt, Governor Alfred E. Smith, and showman P.T. Barnum. The group later became known as the Long Island Farm Bureau, still a major influence in Island business and government.

One of the nation's first large-scale suburban planned towns, Levittown, is situated in the middle of Nassau County on land that once produced most of the potato crop for southern New York and the Middle Atlantic states. A synonym for suburban development, Levittown and its successes were replicated across America throughout the 1950s and 1960s, bringing the advantages of suburban living to middle-class families. Ironically, the modern suburban town owes its existence to two things: a parasite and a watershed town board meeting.

Just after World War II, there were 120,000 acres of farmland

CHAPTER 2

ABUNDANT RESOURCES

Photo by Deborah Ross.

FROM THE MERLOT GRAPES HARVESTED IN
Mattituck to the flounder unloaded on the Freeport
dock, Long Island's natural resources are surprisingly
rich and productive. In fact, its varied agricultural
products—fin and shellfish, corn, potatoes, cauliflower and specialty vegetables, table fruit, and wine grapes—make
the region the state leader in market value. With fewer than 40,000
acres under cultivation, Long Island's two counties still outrank the
rest of New York State's 62, generating a whopping $1 billion in
revenue annually.

In a state known for its wine, apples, cheddar cheese, and lush
rolling upstate farmland, most people are shocked to learn it's Long
Island's two counties that lead the state in wholesale value of crops.
Suffolk County leads the state in cantaloupe and pumpkin production, and is ahead of most counties in berries and other fruits and
vegetables. Nassau has 33 farms devoted to nursery stock, making it
fifth in the state. And it's Long Island that produces more than half
of the state's nursery and greenhouse products, valued at $300 mil-
lion wholesale. The 600,000 gallons, or 3 million bottles of wine
coming out of Long Island each year, are worth another $30 million.
The combination of crops, farm stands, poultry, horticulture, nurseries, viticulture, and fishing makes up 5 percent of the region's
economy, employing well over 10,000; up to 30,000 if you count
ancillary occupations, according to Joseph Gergela III, executive
director of the Long Island Farm Bureau.

"Agriculture is bigger on Long Island than people realize," adds
Gergela. Most of Long Island has been heavily developed, but
enough land has been kept in production to maintain a strong agricultural community, which is strengthened by the internal support
systems farmers, fishermen, nurserymen, and other growers have
forged with the Farm Bureau and Cornell Cooperative Extension.
Nonetheless, progress and development have had an impact on the
rich resources of the Island.

Twenty years ago, Long Island potatoes, Long Island duckling,
and Long Island clams were readily available in grocery stores across
the country and considered among the finest a shopper could buy.
Thousands of acres were planted in potatoes, using the flat, open
contour of the land and the sandy soil to advantage. Even in 1982,
19,000 acres were used for potatoes. But the golden nematode
undermined that crop, and the land became more valuable for housing than for a crop that could barely support the land it grew on. In

Suffolk County leads the state in pumpkin production and is ahead of most counties in berries and other fruits. (left) Photo by James McIsaac. (below) Photo by Bruce Bennett.

1992, only 6,500 acres were dedicated to the vegetable. The water surrounding the Island grew less hospitable to clams and lobsters, but shellfishing has shown resiliency in recent years, bringing the catch up to record pounds in 1993. All in all, the agricultural markets changed, and people want different products from fishermen and farmers than they did a decade ago. In order for local families to stay in agriculture and fishing, they had to change, as well.

"Long Island's agricultural economy is thriving today because those involved have changed with the times, diversified crops, and used technology to its fullest. We produce here what the people want—fresh produce, poultry, flowers, fruit," adds Gergela.

During the summer, open-air markets pop up in eastern Nassau and several South Shore and North Shore towns in Suffolk, brimming over with local produce. Family-run farm stands seem to be everywhere. Drive through the East End on a Saturday in late summer and you will see farm stands along Sound Avenue stocked with the harvest of berries, eggplant, red and white cabbages, cauliflower, a host of squashes, bicolor or tricolor corn, all kinds of tomatoes, lettuces, and herbs. Often, you'll find pies, jellies, and other homemade delicacies using a grower's product. By October, they have added pumpkins, apples, and cider, plus bright fall blooms and dried flowers for the table.

Ornamental horticulture is big business on Long Island. (above) Annual seedlings are planted in the spring in cell-packs with the aid of robotics technology at Ivy Acres Greenhouses in Calverton. Photo by Scott Levy. (above right) The flowers are cultivated in the greenhouse and shipped to nurseries around the state. Photo by Deborah Ross. (below right) Photo by Scott Levy.

In the last decade, many farmers in this area have shifted from traditional crops to high-value, specialty crops to meet the demand placed on them by local customers and tourists. More and more acreage is being sown in arugula, basil, baby corn, baby eggplant, and other miniatures, as well as fennel, dill, and oriental vegetables. These delicacies satisfy the needs of the region's gourmet cooks, while they keep precious farmland planted with salable products instead of shopping centers.

"The land is only worth what it can bring in as crops or as real estate," says Ken Schmitt, one of the owners of Schmitt Bros. farms in Melville and Riverhead. He and his relatives are some of the last of the western-area farmers. Some of their fields are now smack up against office buildings, parking lots, and new homes. The Schmitt farm stand and its neighbors still working in the Route 110 corridor draw the lunchtime crowd from surrounding offices, as well as school-children on field trips out to pick strawberries and pumpkins.

The area's ornamental horticulture industry is equally impor-tant. With about 350 acres under glass, Long Island grows 60 per-cent of the state's greenhouse and nursery stock. The area has been

a leader in greenhouse production for years and is known as one of the few places in the United States that can rival the Netherlands in the amount of glass it uses. And, like the Dutch, Long Island producers have used high technology to make their greenhouses even more efficient.

In Calverton, Jack Van de Wetering has built one of the first fully computerized greenhouse farms in the United States. Nestled between some of the area's oldest family farmland and a golf course carved out of former fields, Van de Wetering's Ivy Acres moves one million seedlings a day by using robotics to do most of the work. Plugs of tomato, begonia, and impatiens seedlings are grown and they are shipped in the spring to many of the nurseries and garden centers around the state.

Of all the new developments in the Island's agriculture, the wine industry may be the most significant. Wine grapes have been cultivated along the coast since the English and Dutch settlers first started

Wine grapes have been cultivated along the coast since the English and Dutch settlers first started farming here. (above) Herodotus Damianos, MD, founded the renown Pindar Vineyards in Peconic in 1981. Photo by Scott Levy. (right) Picking grapes at Peconic Bay Vineyards in Cutchogue. Photo by Bruce Bennett.

farming, but today's industry began in earnest two decades ago with the opening of the Hargrave family vineyards in Cutchogue. Now it seems to expand by the week. Some of the wineries—such as Banfi, Pindar, Bedell, Palmer, Lenz, Le Reve, and Hargrave—have reputations well beyond Long Island. Most offer tours; some have tasting parties, poetry readings, even parties on terraces overlooking the vines. Today, there are about 20 working wineries on the Island. Although only 2 percent of the state's wine grapes are grown here, they are used for 90 percent of New York's premium wines.

Why Long Island? Because of the long growing season, the relatively mild weather due to the Gulf Stream, the flat and sandy soil, the breezes and the salt air, the number of sunny days. It is said that the growing conditions on Long Island are the closest one can get to those in the best wine regions in France, which is why some of France's highest-quality grapes are being planted here. And, because of the Island's high standard of living and the wine country's proximity to the summer playground of the rich and famous, the Hamptons, Long Island's vineyards have become equally important as tourist attractions.

Tourists flock here to see what remains of the East Coast's fishing industry, as well. American waters, in general, have not been able to support fishing the way they did in our grandparent's time, but

The Long Island commercial fishing industry is doing well, with the annual catch amounting to 50 million pounds. Photos by Deborah Ross.

the Long Island fleet continues to reap the riches of the sea, with the added advantage of being close to market. And, since most of the Island's coastline has been reserved for parks and housing, the fishing industry, to a great extent, has been insulated from some of the pollution other coastal areas have suffered. For a time in the 1980s, the water surrounding the Island grew less hospitable to clams and lobsters, but shellfishing has shown resiliency in recent years, bringing the catch up to record pounds in 1993.

The commercial fishing industry is suffering north and south of Long Island, but doing well here, according to Emerson Hasbrouck, cooperative extension agent for marine environmental issues and fisheries management of Cornell Cooperative Extension. In fact, Long Island landings, as the catch is called, have remained relatively stable in the last 10 years, amounting to 50 million pounds a year, bringing in more than $55 million a year to the area, according to the National Marine Fisheries Service. And, unlike other industries that export the bulk of their product, Hasbrouck points out, most of the money made fishing stays at home.

Long Island's two counties bring in more fish than the entire states of Connecticut, Maryland, South Carolina, Alabama, or Mississippi. (above) Robert Moses State Park. Photo by James McIsaac. (above right) Photo by Scott Levy. (below right) Bay of Fundy, near Freeport. Photo by Martha Leider.

About 90 percent of the state's landings are in Long Island waters, which means the Island's two counties bring in more fish than the entire states of Connecticut, Maryland, South Carolina, Alabama, or Mississippi, or all of the Great Lakes states combined. In 1993, that meant a catch of almost 400,000 pounds of bluefish, 3 million pounds of tilefish, and 10 million pounds of whiting, along with almost 2 million pounds of lobster, 17 million pounds of clams, and almost 9 million pounds of squid.

Although they share the same ocean, there are several reasons why Long Island fishermen have been relatively insulated from the woes of their Gloucester, Massachusetts, or Delmarva peninsula counterparts, but the overwhelming advantage is their location on the coastline. Long Island straddles two distinct ocean regions, brushed by the Gulf Stream on its southern shores, and by the Block Island Sound and the North Atlantic on its northeastern-most tip. That puts it at the northern end of the range for middle-Atlantic species and the southern limits of the northern specie range. So,

while species in both regions have declined in the last 20 years, Long Island fishermen have been able to harvest from the two groups.

A second and equally unique geographic advantage is the Island's proximity to one of the best markets, New York City, and a major international airport for foreign export.

"Our fishermen can, literally, catch a fish in the morning, get it to JFK (International Airport) in the afternoon, and it will be served in a restaurant within hours in Madrid, Paris, or Tokyo," says Hasbrouck. Surprisingly, Long Island fish might be easier, and therefore cheaper, for foreign restaurateurs to purchase than the same species from their own distributors, just because the lines of transportation are in place and smoother.

It's often the high-end, top-quality fish that are exported—usually tuna, fluke, summer flounder, or whiting—and many times it is exported live, according to industry reports. Butterfish, sea bass, fluke, and blackfish may be kept alive for freshness, so diners can choose their entrees, or so they can be prepared as sushi.

The Fulton Fish Market, the largest wholesale market in the United States, is only three hours from the most remote docks on the

The potato has been a staple in the Long Island agricultural industry for many years. (left) Photo by Bruce Bennett. (above) Photo by James McIsaac.

Island and less than an hour from the Nassau fleet. Most Long Island fishermen who use the market ship it on consignment, knocking out the need for a middleman, so they get more money for the same fish.

Across Long Island, there are places where fish are sold off boats to local seafood lovers, who may be the luckiest diners of all. Many Long Islanders live close enough to fishing communities that they can buy fresh fish right off a town dock, race home and fry it up within the hour for a family gathering. Of course, the myriad of seafood restaurants up and down the shoreline serve the same purpose for those who don't want to cook it themselves.

A third reason why the Long Island fishing industry has remained strong is that it has not been afraid to use new technologies or marketing strategies. In order to compete in the global market, technology had to be developed to reduce the length of time

between a fish's demise and its preparation as a meal. To accomplish this, refrigeration techniques were developed on large boats using sea water that lowers the fish's temperature, but keeps it alive, allowing it to arrive at its destination fresher and worth more than its frozen cousin. In fact, the export business has allowed producers to make as much or more money marketing smaller numbers of live fish than they did with larger numbers of dead fish. And, by establishing their own foreign trade contacts, the Long Island commercial fishing community has built a firmer base for the future, making it easier to justify the expansion of the airfreight opportunities out of JFK or elsewhere.

The shellfish industry has evolved along parallel lines. Some species are down; others enjoy good years, then bad, due to over-fishing, brown tide, or other natural disasters. Once again, the location of the waters and the savvy of those who work them have kept the overall harvest stable. According to industry experts, most of the

Long Island continues to reap the riches of the sea, with the added advantage of being close to the market. (left) Photo by Lindsay Silverman. (below) Photo by Scott Levy.

recent catch has shifted from the solitary baymen to the large boats, because they can follow the catch into deeper water and can adapt more readily to a changing industry, while taking advantage of the wide range of species throughout the region. It's the more traditional, in-shore fisher who has been impacted most by the reduction in species.

On the other hand, lobstering is good these days, according to Hasbrouck, and although the market fluctuates, a bayman can still make a living trapping the prized marine crustacean. That's not the case, in general, with hard clams, bay scallops, striped bass, or anything brought in by gill netting or seining, both of which have suffered in the last 15-20 years. Some areas, such as Huntington and Oyster Bay, have seen a resurgence of hard clams lately, while the Great South Bay has lost many of its clam beds.

Far from predicting its demise, Joe Gergela sees slow and steady growth in agriculture and fishing in the next decade, with continued expansion of viticulture, the use of more high-level technology throughout farming and fishing, diversification of crops and products, and closer ties to tourism and related businesses. • • •

The Cold Spring Harbor Fish Hatchery and Aquarium houses New York State's largest collection of native freshwater fish, reptiles, and amphibians. Visitors can feed the newly hatched trout or fish in an adjacent pond. (left) Photo by Martha Leider. (above) Photo by Scott Levy.

(on the following page) Cornfield photo by Bruce Bennett. Greenhouse photo by Scott Levy.

Peatmoss 4 cubic ft. 9⁹⁹
2 cubic ft. 6⁹⁹
1 cubic ft. 4⁹⁹
Pinebark Nuggets 3 cubic foot 5⁹⁹
5/26⁰⁰
Mini Nuggets 3 cubic foot 5⁹⁹
5/26⁰⁰
Mulch 3 cubic foot 5⁹⁹
5/26⁰⁰
Cedar Mulch 3 cubic foot 5⁹⁹
5/26⁰⁰
Cocoa Mulch 2 cubic foot 5⁹⁹
5/26⁰⁰

Top soil 40 lb ··
Cow Manure 40 lb composted dehydrated
Pro-Mix 3.8 cubic ft. 32⁵⁰
The Mix 2 cubic ft. 14⁵⁰
20 Qt. 6⁵⁰
Lime 50 lb 3²⁹
Pelletized Lime 40 lb ·· ·

Top Soil
$3.²⁹
4/$11.⁰⁰
40 lb bag

CHAPTER 3

The Good Life, Then & Now

Photo by Brian Winkler.

LONG ISLANDERS HAVE LIVED "THE GOOD life" for centuries, but that term has been interpreted many ways. To some, the good life has been measured in acres. For others, it has been dollars. For most, it has meant the opportunity to live in a safe, attractive, and comfortable neighborhood, with schools, a top-notch volunteer sports program, and the opportunity to partake of a rich and varied cultural life. All in all, Long Islanders today have a lifestyle about as close to the suburban ideal as one can get anywhere in this country.

THEN

As early as the 1660s, Long Island was a hunting and fishing area for city dwellers. One of the first horse racetracks already had been built on the Hempstead Plain by that time, setting the foundation for a sport still popular today. By the 1860s, Long Island's recreational riches had been featured in art and literature by no less than William Cullen Bryant and Currier & Ives. Hempstead Harbor and Oyster Bay were established areas for racing yachts. August Belmont, and others of his sports club, had purchased property along the Carmans River that is now parkland used by thousands of local families.

Hobbies were drawing the leisure class out of a city, mucked up by relentless construction, to the relatively pristine countryside. The recreational paradise to the east was even more convenient by 1834 when the Long Island Rail Road (LIRR) was completed, connecting Manhattan to distant Greeport to facilitate steamship traffic to the north and south. When the LIRR built interim stops, it opened the whole Island to the development of more permanent second-homes

(left) Old Bethpage Village is a pre-Civil War farm village with original structures moved from other parts of the Island. Photo by Lindsay Silverman.

(below) A visit to Old Westbury Gardens is like stepping into an English landscape. Photo by Lindsay Silverman.

and entire communities built around providing diversion for the rich and famous.

Between 1840 and 1940, more than 900 estates were built on Long Island. In 1902, the *New York Herald* reported "Country homes, with their mile-long driveways are continuous for a hundred miles...Long Island is rapidly being divided up into estates of immense acreage...beyond all precedent of American country life."

Many of those homes are still standing. Some have been taken over by the state for parkland, such as the Marshall Field estate in Caumsett State Park on Lloyd Neck. Others were easily adapted to academic settings, like the Pratt estate in Glen Cove housing the Webb Institute of Naval Architecture; LaSalle Military Academy in Oakdale, based in the Frederick Gilbert Bourne estate, the largest mansion ever built on Long Island; and the Walter O. Chrysler estate in Kings Point, now the U.S. Merchant Marine Academy. One, Sagamore Hill in Oyster Bay, served as the unofficial White House when President Theodore Roosevelt was not in Washington.

Long Island's famous country houses varied in size and accoutrements from austere farmhouses, like W.R. Grace's estate in Great Neck, to elaborate, fanciful castles built by William Randolph Hearst, J.P. Morgan, William K. Vanderbilt, Vincent Astor, and Harry Payne Whitney, among others. It's hard to name a major figure involved in America's 19th-century expansion and industrial development who did not own property or spend leisure hours on Long Island, America's first playground.

Following close behind, modest hotels and inns, as well as clubs and summer colonies for the growing middle class, began to spring up along the north and south shores in Sea Cliff, Oyster Bay, Massapequa, and finally farther out in Bay Shore and Patchogue. Drawing from the ranks of the agricultural community and the thousands of immigrants entering the country through New York City, outlying communities sprung up to provide permanent homes for those who cooked at, maintained, and ran the resorts and tourist sites up and down Long Island's coasts. The foundation for Long Island's modern tourism industry had been set.

So by 1940, when there were a little more than a half-million people spread out from the city line to Montauk Point, two very distinct heritages were in place: the persistent remains of an agricultural society dating back to the founding fathers and the more contemporary and mutually dependent service and leisure classes, growing out of the establishment of dozens of vacation communities taking

Early in June, Belmont Park overflows with excitement as fans from all over the world gather to witness the Belmont Stakes. Photos by Deborah Ross.

The Long Island Rail Road is the most-traveled railroad in North America and the oldest commuter rail line in the world. Chartered in 1834, the LIRR carries an average of 256,000 passengers each weekday on 740 daily trains, reaching 134 stations from one end of the Island to the other. It has just completed a 10-year, $2.1 billion investment in improvements in stations and infrastructure. (left) The LIRR station in Long Beach. Photo by Deborah Ross. (above) An antique caboose. Photo by Gary Fox.

advantage of good transportation, cheap land, cheap labor, and great views. Some were so good, in fact, they warranted the destruction of whole communities, such as Lattingtown, to provide uninterrupted vistas for the very rich. But the wealth that destroyed also preserved, giving Long Islanders a whopping 93 documented Tiffany windows that are still in place, along with 275 buildings or districts currently listed in the National Register of Historic Places, and a tradition of cultural and historic preservation.

It was into this milieu that William Levitt and company arrived with a plan to provide solid, inexpensive housing for returning veterans of World War II, built on languishing potato fields. Housing developments like his own Levittown went up quickly and provided the country with a model for suburban living, a model that has been perfected over the last 50 years in that same spot as well as other parts of Long Island and the country. By 1950, the region's population was up to almost a million, and by 1970, it had skyrocketed to 2.5 million.

Now

The neighborhoods of Long Island still retain much of the cohesiveness of the original settlements, as well as the grand traditions of the Gatsby era. Since Long Island has more owner-occupied housing than most regions, communities tend to be stable and well-maintained. Although it may be hard for outsiders to tell where one community ends and another begins, natives are fiercely loyal to their home communities, and there are many of them.

What is called "Long Island" is only part of the geographic entity that contains it. Nassau and Suffolk counties actually share a stretch of land east of Manhattan: a long, fish-shaped island sitting out in the North Atlantic with Queens and Brooklyn, two of New York City's boroughs. In the part known as "Long Island," there are 2 counties, 13 towns or townships, 94 incorporated villages, 2 cities, and 127 school districts. Within those 13 towns, there are 334 separate communities, all distinct even if they are close together, emphasizing the small-town atmosphere. They center, for the most part,

around school districts, houses of worship, shopping areas, cultural institutions, health care, or recreational facilities. No neighborhood is more than 10 miles as the crow flies from water, or more than an hour or two from New York City. Yet, it is a world apart from the city and unlike any other place in the United States.

If it were not for the proximity of New York City, Long Island probably would be better known for its rich cultural and arts heritage. With 2 major concert halls and 34 other theaters, several nationally known outdoor concert series, 4 world-class art museums, a superior regional historical museum and 2 of the nation's most unusual reconstructed villages (Old Bethpage Village Restoration and the working village of Stony Brook), top playhouses, and a renowned philharmonic orchestra, Long Islanders have plenty to keep them

Long Island still has numerous Tiffany stained glass windows, such as this beautiful example found at All Saints Episcopal Church in Great Neck. Photo by Deborah Ross.

busy. In fact, every Friday, *Newsday*, the area's largest daily news-paper, runs eight pages of listings of the upcoming week's arts and cultural offerings.

Tilles Center, located on the campus of the C.W. Post Campus of Long Island University in Old Brookville, is the home of the Long Island Philharmonic and Friends of the Arts and is an important stop for every major touring orchestra. 'With a quarter of a million tickets sold through its box office last year, it is the most successful cultural center of its kind in the country," according to Dr. David Steinberg, president of LIU. As the largest concert hall on Long Island, it accommodates more than 2,000 music lovers who come to enjoy great orchestras, jazz, opera, and dance.

Its Suffolk counterpart, the Staller Center for the Performing Arts on the campus of State University of New York at Stony Brook, has a theater, recital hall, and an art gallery. Home of the annual

Mansion at Banfi Winery and stained glass window detail. Photos by Deborah Ross.

(above) Buster and the Soul Brothers at the "Blues and Brew" concert at Bald Hill. Photo by James McIsaac.

(left) The Westbury Music Fair is the nation's leading presenter of top name entertainers for theaters seating under 3,000 patrons. With its unique in-the-round configuration, Westbury Music Fair offers concert-goers an intimate atmosphere for seeing entertainers as varied as Huey Lewis, Dan Fogelberg, Tony Bennett, Gladys Knight, Vince Gill, Julio Iglesias, or Jay Black & the Americans. Photo courtesy of Westbury Music Fair.

(above left) Exterior of the Tilles Center. Photo by William Baker, courtesy of the Tilles Center. (below left) Interior of the Tilles Center. Photo by Bruce Bennett.

The Shinnecock Pow Wow, which takes place on the Shinnecock Reservation, is a celebration of spirit and beauty. (above) Photo by Bruce Bennett. (left) Photo by James McIsaac.

Bach Aria Festival in June and an important cinema series every year, Staller has established itself in a little less than two decades as an important regional cultural institution.

Friends of the Arts, based in Locust Valley, provides a rich mix of popular and classical music at Tilles as well as other smaller venues in the cold months and in an outdoor setting in summertime on the grounds of the Planting Fields Arboretum in Oyster Bay. Its Long Island Jazz Festival, held in late July, draws top jazz artists and spectators from around the country. Hosting an annual Beethoven Festival, plus such headliners as Judy Collins, Michael Feinstein, the Preservation Hall Jazz Band, and others, FOA has given Long Island the closest thing to Tanglewood right in its own backyard.

Westbury Music Fair, founded in the 1950s, was one of the country's first theaters-in-the-round. Originally set in a tent, this building now comfortably seats almost 3,000 people, each with the

African-American dance troupe DIATA DIATA performs at the African-American Museum in Hempstead. Photo by Deborah Ross.

best seat in the house, enjoying revivals of Broadway musicals and some of the top pop artists of the day.

On a hot summer night, what could be better than listening to music right at the beach? At Jones Beach Amphitheater, the stage backs up to the Atlantic Ocean and faces 11,000 bathing-suited fans catching the ocean breeze while they listen to their favorite rock and pop groups.

Every summer, hundreds of town parks on the Island hold free, outdoor concerts showcasing community bands. Also, tens of thousands of families pack picnics and go to Bald Hill Cultural Center in Farmingville or Eisenhower Park in East Meadow, where music and entertainment are on the agenda every weekend and many summer days.

There are nearly 100 museums on Long Island. They house historical artifacts, fine art, crafts, and science exhibits. In Nassau, a museum-hopper has a choice of many, including the African-American Museum in Hempstead dealing with contributions to American life made by Long Island's African-Americans; the exciting, interactive Long Island Children's Museum near Roosevelt Field

Shopping Mall in Garden City; the Sands Point Preserve, where one can marvel at reproductions of 16th-century architecture and furnishings; the Nassau County Museum of Art in Roslyn, built on land once owned by William Cullen Bryant, housing an impressive permanent collection of paintings and sculpture by some of the world's most loved artists; or Old Bethpage Village Restoration, the impressive restoration of a typical 18th-century village complete with a farm, craft shops, a schoolhouse, and a general store, and site of the annual Long Island Fair, an old-fashioned Fourth of July celebration, and candlelight evening programs at Christmas.

Their Suffolk neighbors can marvel at interactive science exhibits at the Science Museum of the Brookhaven National Laboratory in Upton; look at the stars at the Vanderbilt Planetarium in Centerport; contemplate Whitman at the poet's birthplace, a farmhouse tucked

Visitors can watch Gerry Holzman, above, and other craftspeople, sculpt figures for the Empire State Carousel at a studio in Islip. When completed, the structure will feature carvings of New York State animals, birds and historic figures. More than 800 people have volunteered time to the project over the last decade. Photo by Deborah Ross.

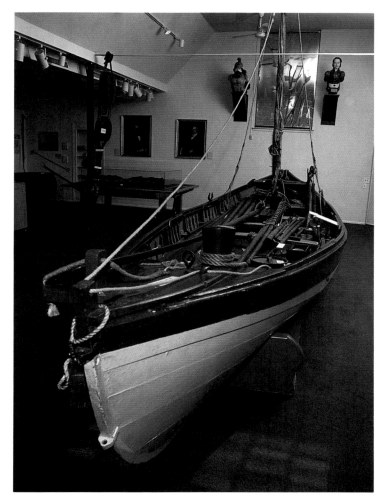

behind a shopping center in South Huntington; watch craftspeople create the Empire State Carousel at Brookwood Hall Park in Islip; or buy penny candy at the St. James General Store, the nation's oldest continuously operated general store.

Suffolk County is home to a particularly rich tapestry of art and historic museums. The Cold Spring Harbor Whaling Museum celebrates the region's past maritime importance while the Carriage Museum, part of the Museums at Stony Brook, houses one the nation's finest collections of historic carriages. The Heckscher Museum of Art in Huntington and the Parrish Museum in Southampton each have notable collections of 18th- and 19th-century American landscapes among their permanent collections holdings. Both the Heckscher and the Parrish offer ambitiously eclectic schedules of changing exhibitions and educational programs for adults and

There once were many whaling ports on the Island. (right) A whale boat from the collection of the Cold Spring Harbor Whaling Museum. Photo by Deborah Ross.

Cold Spring Harbor Whaling Museum features historical boats, ship models, whaling tools, scrimshaw, and documents. Photo by Scott Levy.

children. The Art Museum of the Museums at Stony Brook has extensive holdings of the works of William Sidney Mount, an important 19th-century artist of the region. Guild Hall in East Hampton frequently showcases the works of contemporary artists, especially those who are identified with the important East End art community.

If your passion is aviation, you're in luck. Long Island has three museums devoted to flight. The biggest, although not completed, is the Cradle of Aviation Museum at Mitchel Field in Garden City. It houses a vast collection of some of the most important historic planes in this country, outside of the Smithsonian Institution. There is a smaller sampling at the Bayport Aerodrome, which also hosts occasional vintage aircraft fly-ins, and a fine collection of photos and memorabilia at the Long Island Aero Museum in Westhampton Beach, open only by appointment.

All that museum-hopping can make a person hungry, and, luckily, one of Long Islanders' favorite pastimes is eating. There may be more

Constructed in 1884 by President Theodore Roosevelt, this 23-room Victorian mansion was his "summer White House." Photo by Lindsay Silverman.

pizza parlors, delis, and fast-food restaurants on Long Island than anywhere in the United States, or maybe it just seems that way. And that's not counting the famous Long Island diner, which has inspired whole tomes. With menus longer than some phone books, the diners of Long Island may be the most important local institution. And, for those with more refined tastes, there are hundreds of fine restaurants on the Island, including many that are world-class.

Long Island is a shopper's paradise. Accustomed to a panoply of possibilities, shoppers have no trouble locating the most exotic trinket or the most popular item of the day in one of thousands of stores found in shopping malls, town centers, or neighborhood shopping centers. The malls are big and well-stocked. Several are multileveled;

(above) Children of all ages enjoy the hands-on experience offered by the Long Island Children's Museum in Garden City. Photo by Bruce Bennett.

(left) The greenhouses at Planting Fields Arboretum feature tropical plants and special seasonal displays. Photo by Deborah Ross.

(left) Philanthropist August Heckscher commissioned "Youth Eternal" by Evelyn Beatrice Longman as a permanent installation for the Heckscher Museum of Art, the museum he built and donated to the people of Huntington in 1920. Photo courtesy of the Heckscher Museum of Art.

Many of Long Island's premier designer boutiques line the Manhasset area known as the "Miracle Mile." Photos by Scott Levy.

(above right) Long Island has a diverse array of shopping opportunities. Photo by Deborah Ross.

(below right) In continuous operation since 1857, the St. James General Store offers 19th-century-style merchandise, candies, preserves, and handicrafts. Photo by Brian Winkler.

Sunshine or snowfall, Long Island has an activity for everyone to pursue. (above) The Long Island Marathon is held every year on the first Sunday in May. (right) Old Bethpage State Park is perfect for cross-country skiing. Photos by Bruce Bennett.

(above) Golfing at the Indian Island Country Club in Riverhead. Photo by Brian Winkler.

(left) Jones Beach has a 6-mile stretch of ocean beach, 2-mile boardwalk, bay beach, pool, golf, bandshell, and concerts at the famous outdoor Marine Theater. Photo by John Mohr.

one has a huge food court built around a colorful mobile made by Alexander Calder; another has 66 outlet shops.

Long Island has major department stores, specialty shops, outlet malls with convenience features for serious shoppers, and a dozen major malls, each containing from 45 to 200 stores anchored by some of the best-known names in retail, including Macy's, JC Penney, Bloomingdales, Stern's, and Sears. At the Americana Shopping Center in Manhasset, which is referred to as shopping's "Miracle Mile," a clotheshorse will find several dozen of the world's most exclusive designer clothing and furnishings stores. The new, expanded Roosevelt Field Mall, the fifth largest in the country, has valet parking, a huge food court, and world-class stores.

For those who prefer more leisurely excursions, there are a number of quaint villages with quality boutiques worth exploring. The elegant downtown of Garden City is home to small-size major department stores that still offer some of the amenities you probably thought had disappeared a generation ago. Bustling downtown Huntington has lots of specialty shops, a wonderful bookstore, plus a lively nightlife. Port Jefferson's Main Street starts right at the water,

welcoming tourists as they get off the ferry from Connecticut. Nearby Stony Brook village has more than 30 shops in a colonial setting, including antiques and gift shops, centered around an unusual post office with a decorative eagle that flaps its wings on the hour. Southampton and East Hampton contain the tony, upscale stores New Yorkers adore, even when away from home, while Sag Harbor's bookstores cater to a cerebral crowd.

The quality of the shopping on Long Island reflects the quality of the consumer. With 53 of their communities having median family incomes over $100,000, Long Islanders live in some of the highest

(left) There are many opportunities for elegant dining on Long Island. Photo by Scott Levy.

The North Shore of Long Island, sometimes called its Gold Coast, is dotted with hundreds of mansions left by the rich and famous of the late 19th and early 20th centuries. The 56-room, Beaux Arts-style Woolworth mansion in Glen Cove was built in 1916 and now is a private conference center. Its elaborate marble staircase is considered one of the most expensive ever built. Photo by Bruce Bennett.

income zip codes in the nation. More than 59 percent of the households earned over $50,000 in 1994, in comparison to 31 percent nationally, making it the top area in median household effective buying income. That reflects a total disposable income of a whopping $58.7 billion in 1994 in just two counties, the sixth-highest suburban district in a ranking of metropolitan areas, most containing many more than two counties.

GOOD, CLEAN FUN

The vast number of golf courses, tennis clubs, beaches, and other sports facilities indicate the importance leisure and spectator sports plays in Long Island life. Almost 50 public links dot the Island, in addition to even more private golf courses. The open land, soft landscape, and prominence of water make this a perfect place for golf. It's no surprise that nearly one-fifth the population consider themselves golfers, or that the first formal golf club in the United States, the Shinnecock Hills

(above) Ballet photo by Scott Levy, courtesy of Nassau BOCES Cultural Arts Center, Syosset.

(right) Located in the heart of the Gold Coast, the Nassau County Museum of Art presents continually changing world-class exhibitions. Photo by Deborah Ross.

Golf Club, was built here and remains one of America's premier sites.

Long Island is home to some of the most important pro and amateur tournaments in the golf world. In 1995, the U.S. Open was held at Shinnecock, and it will return to the Island in 2002 at Bethpage's famous public Black Course, designed by A.W. Tillinghast. The Northville Long Island Classic, held at the Meadow Brook Club in Jericho, is an important stop on the senior pro tour and a big fund-raiser for Long Island charities. The annual Long Island Golf Classic in Bethpage State Park attracts many wannabee-

pros, and the Garden City Golf Club is the site of the prestigious Travis Memorial, one of the country's oldest amateur competitions.

Tennis players are equally at home here, with outdoor and indoor courts available at more than 70 places offering a total of 500 indoor and outdoor courts. Every summer, it's only a short ride to the U.S. Open in nearby Queens, where a tennis lover can study the moves of some of the world's best players. And, every year, thousands attend the Waldbaum's Hamlet Open in Commack, or watch it on television.

Water sports are, of course, the big draw here. Smith Point, Robert Moses, and Jones Beach State Parks have a fair number of regular surfers working their waves, surrounded by hundreds of thousands of swimmers and beachgoers every season. Of course, the beaches are open for walking all year-round. Thousands of scuba divers explore the aquatic life found along the shore or around shipwrecks in coastal waters. It's safe to say that the Island's estimated

Polo Matches are held every Sunday from May to November at Bethpage State Park. (above) Photo by James McIsaac. (right) Photo by Bruce Bennett.

80,000 sailors, windsurfers, canoeists, and power boaters can't find a better place to enjoy the water.

Jones Beach, of course, is more than simply one of the greatest beaches in the world for swimmers and sunbathers. It also contains waterfront restaurants, an outdoor theater, an outdoor dance area, fitness trails, fishing piers, a miniature golf course depicting local sites, basketball courts, ballfields, and a huge swimming pool. Many of these areas are connected to the beach by a world-class boardwalk.

This is horse country. There are more pleasure horses living here than there are people in some small cities (60,000), along with 12,000 stately thoroughbreds. With more than 20 horse clubs and 150 registered horse shows held every year, including the world-famous Hampton Classic, horse trailers sometimes fill the roads on summer weekends.

The 34-mile Suffolk Greenbelt Trail, stretching from Sunken Meadow State Park on Long Island Sound to Heckscher State Park on the Great South Bay, offers hikers and bird-watchers unspoiled beauty from coast to coast. Nassau's 22-mile trail extends from Cold Spring Harbor to Massapequa. Plus, there is a 20-mile trail on Fire Island that takes hikers from Davis Park to Smith Point State Park, through some extraordinary coastal environments.

For children, there are amusement parks, miniature golf centers, a great big water park full of slides and thrills, an aquarium, whale-watching cruises, and miles and miles of the best beaches in the world. Special events for children abound in this family-centered region. Parents can check listings in numerous guides, including the calendar put out by the Long Island Arts Council at Freeport.

To keep their kids fit and strong, many parents enroll them in some of the hundreds of teams that make up the vast sports network that cover the Island. Most of these programs are run by parent-volunteers, but some, like summer sports camps, involve retired professionals or school coaches. The Special Olympics, an important Long Island program, involves hundreds of volunteers and athletes at its June and October events.

Soccer rules on Long Island. There are more college soccer and lacrosse players coming out of this area than from any other part of the state. Of course, there are also Little League, Boy's and Girl's Clubs, PAL, YM/YWCA/HA, town leagues and pools, ice skating

(above and right) The Nassau Veterans Memorial Coliseum is home to the New York Islanders hockey team, New York Saints indoor lacrosse team, and host to concerts, trade shows, and the circus. (right) Photo by Deborah Ross. (above) Photo by Bruce Bennett.

Suffolk County Vietnam Veteran's Memorial, Long Island's highest attraction, is a memorial to those who gave their lives, as well as a tribute to the survivors. Photo by James McIsaac.

rinks, and many other volunteer networks providing recreation for thousands of children all year.

For those who want to let someone else do all the work while they watch, there are quality spectator sports to fit every taste. You can catch NASCAR racing on summer weekends at the quarter-mile Riverhead Raceway, enjoy the grace and excitement of horses at Belmont Park racetrack or surfers at the annual New York State Surfing Championships in October. Watch the New York Jets practice at their summer training camp at Hofstra University, or go to a collegiate football game at any of four campuses on a fall Saturday afternoon.

The area's professional hockey team is the New York Islanders, based at Nassau Veterans Memorial Coliseum. Four-time Stanley Cup champs and active in many local charities, the Islanders are loved by the local fans, even when they don't have a winning season.

If that's not enough, the Mets, Yankees, Knicks, Nets, Rangers, Devils, Jets, and Giants are all within a short drive, along with some of the best museums, restaurants, nightclubs, and theaters in the world. Long Islanders have the advantage of having New York City at their backdoor, without having to actually live there.

And just who lives here? Besides doctors, lawyers, and Indian chiefs, just about any famous clothing designer, author, television personality, or musician you can think of. Jerry Seinfeld, Mariah Carey, Madonna, Billy Crystal, and Eddie Murphy all grew up here. So did

The Long Island Fair at Old Bethpage gives visitors a chance to step back in time. (above, left, and above right) Photos by Martha Leider.

(below) Participants and observers enjoy a bit of history during the Civil War reenactment on Long Island University's C.W. Post Campus. Photo by Lisa Meyer.

Billy Joel, who has made himself part of the fabric of the Island by getting involved in many charities and by espousing the cause of baymen in his hit song "Down Easter, Alexa." Plenty of athletes grew up here, too, including Carl Yastremski, Boomer Eliason, Gerry Cooney, and John McEnroe. Those who have adopted Long Island as their summer or permanent residence include Alan Alda, James Garner, E.L Doctorow, Barbara Walters, Woody Allen, and a list too long to mention, which is just fine with many on it because they moved here so they could live relatively normal, small-town lives. •••

The New York Islanders, four-time winners of the prestigious Stanley Cup, play home games at the 16,000-seat Nassau Coliseum. (right) Photo by John Giamundo. (below) Photo by Bruce Bennett.

From baseball to barrel racing, Long Island's got it all. (above) A Little League game at Plainview-Old Bethpage Community Park. Photo by Bruce Bennett. (left) The Islip Horsemen's Association annual competition. Photo by Lisa Meyer.

(on the following page) Roosevelt Field Mall photo by Scott Levy.

CHAPTER 4

• • •

A Diverse & Generous People

• • •

Photo by Deborah Ross.

M ANY OF LONG ISLAND'S OLDEST communities can trace their roots to the years when this country was settled by those escaping religious persecution and civil war in Europe. Others were founded more recently on less-lofty grounds. Places such as Oakdale, Babylon, Glen Cove, and Old Westbury, for instance, probably owe more to the insatiable desires of the extremely rich looking for recreation sites. No matter how they were founded, all of the 300-plus communities of Long Island reflect the diverse population of this country today, and each plays a role in the region's spirit of community and generosity.

Shortly after the official birth of America, Long Island's two counties were home to about 27,000 souls. By the time of the American Bicentennial, that figure had increased a hundredfold.

The pattern of settlement is interesting; the areas we now consider remote were settled first. The areas most heavily populated today were the last to be built up. The first European settlers came

(far left) There was a time when nomadic Indian tribes roamed the woods in the center of the Island. Photo by James McIsaac.

(above and left) The Hofstra Dutch Festival celebrates the culture of some of the earliest settlers in the area. Photos by Lisa Meyer.

here by boat and stayed close to shore. Nomadic Indian tribes roamed the woods in the center of the Island, and the settlers may have wanted to keep their distance. Today, there are more people living in the middle of the Island than along the shores; there are many people here who came as immigrants or whose parents did; and there still are a few Native Americans.

The coastal towns of Southampton and Southold were the first developed in New York State, and the south shores of Hempstead

Town and the northern coast of Oyster Bay were the first in Nassau County. While the English settlers built communities in north-western and eastern Suffolk, Dutch settlers moved eastward from Manhattan to open up what is now Nassau County. In 1673, the Dutch claimed jurisdiction over all Long Island, but a year later the English overturned them.

Over the next 250 years, thousands landed in New York City and many of them pushed eastward. In the early 1800s, the huge German migration brought people hungry for the opportunity to farm their own land to areas of Queens that are now part of Nassau. Later, Irish immigrants moved to the coastal towns of Seacliff, Huntington, and Amityville to work in the booming resort industry. Polish settlers came to Glen Cove, Smithtown, Port Jefferson, and Riverhead. Many Italian families lived in the city first, then moved out to the country where they eventually were joined by Jewish immigrants before and after World War II.

By the time Europeans started emigrating to Long Island in great numbers in the 20th-century, there was already a sizable African-American population on Long Island. This was an important stop on the Underground Railroad, although it was also home to some slaves until at least 1830. There is a burial ground in Orient where 20 African slaves and their owners rest. Greenport, Manhasset, Setauket, and other port villages were embarkation points for slaves running by land or sea from the South, or moving further North. It's still possible to find houses and churches scattered across the Island with hidden rooms designed to house slaves enroute to freedom. One of the first communities build by former slaves was Success, today's Lake Success, where the AME Zion church was founded in 1832 by African-American families and Matinecocks from Long Island's East End.

These, then, are the groups that formed the basis of the great suburban expansion of Long Island after World War II, leaving most

Long Island is truly a melting pot of diverse communities. (left) Martin Luther King celebration. Photo by Deborah Ross. (above) Students at the Mid-Island Y Jewish Community Center in Plainview celebrate Hanukkah. Photo by Deborah Ross. (right) Long Island Islamic Center. Photo by Scott Levy.

Riverhead is home to many descendants of Polish settlers. The St. Isadore Roman Catholic Church on Pulaski Street (left) is at the center of the community. (above) Shop window detail. Photos by Deborah Ross.

of the bi-county population between 1945 and 1975 descendants of Irish, Italian, Jewish, German, or Polish immigrants.

In the second half of this century, smaller groups of immigrants from other countries settled here, sometimes bypassing the cities entirely. Often, members of several families from the same village emigrated together, with the encouragement of relatives who already had found homes here. In many cases, they remained a cultural unit in their new villages: the Portuguese in Mineola and Selden, Russians in Long Beach, Iranians in Great Neck, Salvadorans in Brentwood and Central Islip, South Americans in Westbury, Haitians in Huntington Station, and Greeks in Glen Cove. In the

late 1970s, a strong wave of Central Americans increased the size of several communities. And, between 1985 and 1990, tens of thousands of new immigrants replaced a declining native population and brought new skills and traditions, plus new needs, to schools, jobs, and the marketplace.

Through all of this, a small number of Native Americans remained on Long Island. Descendants of the original Montauketts and Matinecocks, who lost their ancestral lands on the South Fork to the English and Dutch settlers, are scattered through Sag Harbor, East Hampton, Manhasset, Amityville, and Smithtown. On the other hand, the Shinnecock have maintained a small but viable identity on their 600-acre reservation in the heart of Southampton. Their neighbors down the road on the Poospatuck reservation in Mastic are what is left of the Unkechaugs. All told, there are about 500 Native Americans living on the two reservations and several hundred others within the general population.

Obviously, those who bemoan the homogeneity of suburban life have not looked closely at Long Island. This region more closely resembles the melting pot of New York City than not. Today, one in nine Long Islanders is an immigrant, according to *Newsday*. In some Nassau communities, such as Great Neck, Elmont, South Floral Park, and Thomaston, a quarter of the population is foreign-born. According to the 1990 U.S. Census, one-tenth the populations of Amityville, Brentwood, North Bay Shore, Holbrook, Huntington Station, Stony Brook, and Montauk were born outside the country. In 1994, Long Island was the 16th most popular destination for newcomers, according to the U.S. Immigration and Naturalization Service.

From 1985 to 1990, about 80,000 immigrants settled on Long Island, with the largest number coming from Asia, specifically China, India, and the Philippines. The second-largest group was from Central America, mostly from El Salvador, whose long war prompted massive emigration in the late 1980s. The third-largest group came from Europe—mainly from Britain, Poland, and Ireland—and that fairly small group was made up of predominantly middle-aged and senior relatives of established Long Islanders. Almost as many came from the Caribbean, with smaller numbers emigrating from South America, Africa, and Canada.

The large influx of immigrants in the 1980s and 1990s made a dramatic impact on Long Island's schools. Declining school populations of the 1970s bounced back, requiring the expansion of programs and even a few new buildings. In 1995, several

(far left) The Fall Festival at Captree State Park. Photo by Deborah Ross. (above) Storefront in Cold Spring Harbor. Photo by Scott Levy. (left) On the boardwalk at Jones Beach. Photo by Bruce Bennett.

In 1979, Abby Kenigsberg noticed New York City radio and television news shows were ignoring Long Island. In response, she founded a not-for-profit, nonpartisan citizen's group, the Long Island Coalition for Fair Broadcasting, to let them know that part of their licensed obligation included Nassau and Suffolk counties. Since then, New York television and radio stations have added news bureaus on Long Island and have increased their coverage of Island issues, news, and events. Photo by Scott Levy.

school districts offered courses in Farsi and Mandarin to meet student demand. It was not unusual for students in a single school to speak as many as 40 languages among themselves. The county library systems found it necessary to increase purchases of foreign language books, adding to their Creole, Serbo-Croatian, and other collections that, 20 years earlier, had few readers. Such diversity brought new meaning to social studies curricula, not to mention changes in cafeteria menus and teenage clothing fads.

Immigration also has brought religious diversity to the Island, as a natural consequence. Some groups found no appropriate religious community when they arrived, so they established their own. As was the case for so many groups in past centuries, the religion that held

There is no stereotypical Long Islander. (below left) Photo by Deborah Ross. (above) Photo by Bruce Bennett. (above right) Photo by Deborah Ross. (right) Huntington named a park for hometown celebrity Billy Joel. Photo by Scott Levy.

them together in their homelands served as an anchor in their adopted country, giving their children an ethnic identity and offering a concrete way to keep traditions alive. Many times, groups shared space with existing houses of worship; in others, they built their own. Iranian Jews forged a tight-knit religious community in Great Neck. A group of Koreans built a huge Methodist church in Dix Hills. A Sikh community opened a temple in Plainview.

In 1995, the religious map of Long Island looked like this: Roman Catholics were by far the largest group, with 1.3 million

Enjoying the outdoors in Freeport (above) and Cold Spring Harbor (right). Photos by Deborah Ross.

members in the Diocese of Rockville Center, including all of Long Island and parts of Brooklyn and Queens. The second-largest group consisted of Conservative Jews, with 150,000 members. Another 30,000 were estimated to be members of Reformed, Orthodox, Reconstructionist, or Lubavitch congregations, bringing the entire Long Island religious Jewish population to a little under 200,000.

Protestant churches showed much smaller numbers, with the Episcopalians having the largest membership (75,000, which includes Brooklyn and Queens), Lutherans at 60,000, and Presbyterians at 15,000. There are about 30,000 Methodists here and an additional 13,000 tied to the African Methodist Episcopal Zion church. But, unlike many other suburban regions, Protestants are the minority here.

The numbers fall dramatically after that. Ethical Humanists counted 300 members at their Garden City site, the Unitarian-Universalists had 1,600 followers, and the Church of Latter-Day Saints had a surprising 3,000 affiliated with their Plainview church. In addition, there were 10,000-15,000 Muslims in 11 mosques, plus Hindus, Buddhists, Baha'is, Seventh-Day Adventists, Christian Scientists, and Quakers worshiping each week.

Not all immigrants, or all Long Islanders, are formally connected to a religious community, but religious values and traditions form a large part of the fabric of their lives. The region abounds with ethnic and cultural festivals, many rooted in the religious calendar, which complement traditions perpetuated by tight-knit families.

Whether it's the Feast of San Rocco, St. Patrick's Day, or Succoth, Islanders join together in community after community to keep traditions alive. Like many melting-pot areas, intermarriage has made multi-ethnic families more the rule than the exception, building a rich texture of diversity into the population. And, since Long Islanders live in America's largest cul-de-sac, there are few transients to befriend, making the family the basis of their social as well as cultural life.

Paralleling the strength of the religious community, nonprofit organizations, including charities, educational institutions, and public health facilities, are extremely important to the quality of life on Long Island. One in three Islanders does volunteer work, participating in some activity that makes life better for everyone in the region. Without the huge volunteer community, many of the museums, hospitals, and helping organizations would be hard-pressed to provide services. And Islanders have managed to maintain that high quality of life during periods of deep budget cuts because they've made up the difference with their own time and energy.

Whatever your roots may be, Memorial Day is a wonderful time for a celebration. Picnic at Silver Lake in Baldwin. Photo by Deborah Ross.

Some of the most enduring start-up businesses have been non-profit institutions designed to help people live better lives. For example, the Helen Keller National Center for Deaf Blind Youths and Adults in Sands Point, named for the famous deaf and blind woman who overcame her handicaps, was started in New Hyde Park in 1969. In 1995, the nationwide operation chartered by the U.S. Congress served 5,200 students through 10 regional offices and 40 affiliates. Recently, a vegetable garden for the blind was built at the Sands Point site, enabling students to experience the pleasures and perils of working outdoors in a protected environment.

Nonprofits employ fully 10 percent of the overall work force and 35 percent of the service industry work force. The largest non-governmental employer in 1995 was the Diocese of Rockville Centre with a total of 12,500 workers. North Shore University Hospital was second at 7,250 employees. Nonprofits generate almost $3 billion in income and expenses on Long Island each year, according to the National Society of Fund Raising Executives.

The mid-1980s and early 1990s brought a number of natural and man-made disasters to the United States. The response of Long Islanders to the victims of Hurricane Andrew in Florida, the 100-year floods in the Midwest, and the bombing in Oklahoma City was extraordinary. Long Island volunteers were among the first to arrive on the scene at each site. Specially trained people from volunteer fire companies went to Oklahoma City, along with New York City police officers and police dogs, to assist in the location of casualties. Truckloads of clothing, household items, and food rolled down the LIE the day after Hurricane Andrew flattened Homestead, Florida. And Pet Savers, an animal welfare organization connected to the North Shore Animal League, worked to locate and treat pets injured in the California earthquakes of 1993 and 1994.

Fortunately, Islanders are generous people. *American Demographics* magazine cites the Nassau-Suffolk region at the top of the list in terms of contributions made to charities. The national average is $1,200 per household per year, but Long Island families gave $2,010 in 1993.

From the elegant to the everyday, all Long Islanders are proud to call this place "home." (far left) The Mirabelle Restaurant in St. James. Photo by Scott Levy. (above) The Baldwin Volunteer Fire Department in a Memorial Day Parade. Photo by Deborah Ross. (left) Enjoying a slice of pizza in Plainview. Photo by Bruce Bennett.

(above) The North Shore Animal League in Port Washington is one of the nation's largest animal rescue and adoption organizations. Photo by Lisa Meyer.

(right) One of the New York chapters of the Guide Dog Foundation for the Blind is located in Smithtown. Photo by James McIsaac.

In the years 1980-1995, volunteers built more than a dozen homes for homeless families in Nassau and Suffolk through local chapters of Habitat for Humanity. They fed thousands at 325 sites stocked with food by Long Island Cares (LIC), a group started by the late singer/songwriter Harry Chapin. LIC takes private donations, government surplus, and food from national food banks, then sorts, packs, and delivers it to food pantries, soup kitchens, homeless shelters, and day care and senior centers around the Island. They prepared 3,000 meals a day at 21 soup kitchens run by the Interfaith Nutrition Network, based in Hempstead. And they helped hundreds of needy families through the year-end holidays by contributing $500,000 to *Newsday's* annual Adopt-A-Family appeal.

And some very special charities are based here, which can't be a coincidence. One of the only New York chapters of the Guide Dog

(above) Teaching the next generation about environmental concerns is Okeanus Research Foundation's business. Photo by John Giamundo.

(left) The nationally-known God Squad, Msgr. Tom Hartman and Rabbi Marc Gelman, are regulars on Telicare, their hometown religious cable channel. Photo courtesy of Telicare.

Foundation for the Blind is located in Smithtown, where it trains dogs and their prospective owners to make the best use of their acute senses. Dogs are raised by local volunteer families, then put through a rigorous training period before being given away.

The Okeanos Ocean Research Foundation, Inc., based in Montauk, studies marine life and looks for ways to protect the habitat of marine mammals, in particular. Many Islanders have learned about marine life on their whale-watching cruises or at their Riverhead aquarium, while others have answered Okeanos' call to volunteer to clean the beaches, look for dolphins, or take care of sick animals.

Telicare, a local cable television network for religious programming, has its studios and headquarters in Uniondale. One of its most popular programs features "The God Squad," as hosts Msgr. Tom Hartman and Rabbi Marc Gelman call themselves. The two, who often act as commentators on broadcast network shows as well, look for common ground in their different backgrounds in discussions of current events and social trends.

Stony Brook was the birthplace of the Environmental Defense Fund, throwing the area into the spotlight at the start of the environmental movement. For years, Suffolk County led the nation in

(right) The Mary Brennen Interfaith Nutrition Network in Hempstead serves many meals every day. Photo by Deborah Ross.

(below) Many organizations participate in Habitat for Humanity projects around the Island. Photo by Scott Levy.

Island were tinderboxes, which sparked into dozens of fires. The most dangerous, dubbed the Sunrise Fire because it jumped the six-lane Sunrise Highway, burned 6,000 acres of forest right up to the edge of small villages and heavily populated areas. More than 2,000 volunteer firefighters fought the blaze for days, while they slept in tents or in the halls of classroom buildings on the eastern campus of Suffolk County Community College.

The Sunrise Fire was the biggest forest fire in the state's history. Governor George Pataki asked President Bill Clinton to declare it a national emergency, allowing for help from the National Guard and professional firefighting teams. When it was all over, everyone was amazed at what our local heroes had accomplished: only a handful of homes was lost, there were no lives lost due to the fire, and injuries were kept to a minimum. To show their appreciation, Long Islanders prepared thousands of meals, donated bedding, tents, and telephones and anything else they could spare, then feted all volunteer fire-fighters and their families to a big party in October. •••

(above) Rev. Reginald Tuggle was sent by the governing body of the church to dissolve the Memorial Presbyterian Church in Roosevelt. Instead, he stayed and built the largest Presbyterian church in New York State. Photo by Deborah Ross.

(right) The golden cock weathervane has been resting on the steeple of Saint George's Church in Hempstead for more than 250 years. During the Revolutionary War, continental soldiers used the weathervane for target practice. Sixteen bulletholes can still be seen. Photo by Deborah Ross.

(on the following page) Photo by Bruce Bennett.

protecting its water supply by restricting the use of detergents and certain household chemicals. Although some of those restrictions have been rescinded, the general mission remains, prompting overwhelming support of environmental legislation at the county and state levels, in an otherwise politically conservative electorate. The drinking water coming from the aquifer below the Long Island Pine Barrens is considered some of the purest in the world.

The summer of 1995 was one of the driest in recent history. By the end of August, the dwarf pine forests on the eastern end of the

CHAPTER 5

• • •

HEALTH & WISDOM

• • •

Students in Old Bethpage. Photo by Bruce Bennett.

ST. FRANCIS HOSPITAL

WITH A MEDIAN HOUSEHOLD INCOME of more than $62,000, Long Islanders spend more on education than people in comparable suburban areas, but save money on health care. That's according to an examination of the 1990 U.S. Census done by *American Demographics* magazine in 1996. Although it is the metro area with the highest disposable income in the nation, it has high-quality, almost bargain health services when adjusted for the cost of living, with providers generally coming in under the national average. Still, average households pay a little more for services than the $1,800 national average for average services, but less than they would pay in many areas of Florida or even Pittsburgh.

Long Island's 33 hospitals employ more than 45,000 people, a sizable chunk of the work force. If medical offices, rehabilitation centers, home health care providers, and other health services are included, Long Island has 108,000 jobs at 6,786 Long Island firms and institutions, paying an average of $32,950 a year.

With occupancy rates averaging over 75 percent, hospitals in the two counties operate quite efficiently, while they provide some of the best health care available in the Northeast. Long Island's proximity to a host of major medical schools in the metropolitan area makes this a prime area for training tomorrow's doctors and nurses and Long Islanders are living longer as a result of the growing health care industry. In fact, in 1995, 1,300 interns and residents trained at 15 of Long Island's hospitals.

When it comes to quality health care, what do Long Island patients have to choose from? Everything from care in small community hospitals with individualized community service, to large teaching hospitals offering the latest technology and clinical trials.

Nationally known North Shore University Hospital in Manhasset expanded recently to include a network of seven hospitals, two nursing homes, a world-class research center, and ambulatory programs and services at sites throughout Long Island, all under the

(left) St. Francis Hospital, The Heart Center, in Roslyn. Photo by Lisa Meyer.

(below) The Brentwood Legion Ambulance is one of many EMT units that provide a valuable service to area residents. Photo by Scott Levy.

North Shore University Hospital in Manhasset. Photo by Lisa Meyer.

umbrella of the North Shore Health System. The Manhasset facility contains 720 beds in 11 medical buildings on 56 acres, and serves as both an academic and clinical campus for the New York University School of Medicine. It is one of three Level 1 trauma centers on Long Island, has intensive care services for medical, cardiac, surgery, pediatric, and newborn patients, and is the cornerstone of the North Shore Health System.

In addition, the network includes North Shore University Hospital at Glen Cove, North Shore University Hospital at Plainview, Huntington Hospital, Franklin Hospital Medical Center in Valley Stream, Syosset Community Hospital, LaGuardia Hospital in Queens, and more than 20 other satellite sites.

Its Suffolk counterpart is a state hospital, University Hospital of the University Medical Center at Stony Brook, the only tertiary-care hospital in the county. In 1993, the hospital cared for 23,000 inpatients and 210,000 outpatients, while its emergency room handled 42,000 cases. University Medical Center is Suffolk's only academic medical center, serving as a training site for 366 residents in 45 residency programs, 97 fellows in 25 fellowship programs, and the 2,000 students enrolled in SUNY's five health profession schools during the 1993-1994 academic year.

Stony Brook is a major research and grant center, garnering grants of more than $43 million in 1993 alone. It is one of a dozen sites chosen from around the country for the National Institutes of Health Women's Health Initiative Program, is home to part of the Long Island breast cancer study, and conducts world-class research on many other timely medical concerns. The hospital contains one of the nation's major Lyme disease centers, is a state-designated trauma center providing backup to every hospital in Suffolk County, is one of the region's top burn centers, has the only neonatal, pediatric, and cardiovascular intensive care units in the county, and coordinates all of the organ transplants done on Long Island. Stony Brook recently built a child abuse clinic where law enforcement, the court system, social workers, and medical professionals can handle child abuse cases in concert, with minimum trauma to the child.

The St. Francis Hospital in Roslyn boasts the nation's second-busiest cardiac program. Almost 2,300 open heart procedures, 6,200 catheterizations, and 2,000 balloon angioplasties were performed in 1995. Another leader in cardiac care is Winthrop-University Hospital in Mineola. Winthrop is ranked one of the top 10 cardiac centers in New York State, based on its open heart surgery success rate and

The University Hospital and Medical Center at Stony Brook photo by Deborah Ross.

other criteria. More than 5,000 babies are delivered at Winthrop each year in a setting that is known for handling high-risk pregnancies and offering midwifery services.

Nassau County Medical Center, in the heart of the county it serves, is also a tertiary care and trauma center. A helicopter pad allows it to receive patients with life-threatening injuries from miles away. The A. Holly Patterson Geriatric Center, in nearby Uniondale, is an extension of its services for seniors.

Mercy Medical Center in Rockville Centre expanded its oncology and cancer care services in 1995 to form The Long Island Cancer Institute. The core is the Bishop McGann Center for Oncology and Imaging, opened in 1996. Mercy was the first hospital on Long Island to offer a hospice program for terminally ill patients. There now are eight separate hospices serving communities throughout the Island and four other palliative care programs run by hospitals for their patients.

Neighboring South Nassau Communities Hospital in Oceanside was named one of the most cost-efficient hospitals in the United States in 1995, while it offered some of the newest medical equipment and quality education to its family practice residents. South Nassau offers hometown care in a quality setting to many patients living in southern and western parts of Nassau County. Additional Nassau hospitals are Hempstead General Hospital, Long Beach Medical Center, and Massapequa General Hospital. Long Island Jewish Medical Center based at the nearby Queens/Nassau border is not considered a Long Island hospital by the Nassau-Suffolk Hospital Council, but with 829 beds and a full range of services, it is a major health care provider for the region.

West Islip's Good Samaritan has 425 beds and 2,500 employees, making it the fourth-largest hospital in the region. Situated next to a state parkway, it receives serious accident patients from all over Suffolk. Nearby Southside Hospital in Bay Shore has 451 beds and a full range of services.

To the north, St. John's Episcopal Hospital in Smithtown recently purchased Community Hospital of Western Suffolk, adding an ambulatory surgery facility and substance abuse center to its many offerings. St. Charles Hospital and Rehabilitation Center and John T. Mather Memorial Hospital, both in Port Jefferson, also serve Suffolk's North Shore, offering a wide range of services.

Eastern Long Island is served by Brookhaven Memorial Hospital Medical Center in Patchogue, Central Suffolk Hospital in Riverhead, Southampton Hospital, and Eastern LI Hospital in Greenport. Among them, they offer more than 800 beds to patients in six towns.

In addition, Long Island has four state psychiatric centers, two private psychiatric hospitals, a large veteran's hospital, and 66 certified nursing homes able to serve more than 13,000 patients at a time. More nursing homes are under construction.

EDUCATION

If the region is blessed with superior health care facilities, it is because it has been wise enough to attract the right amount of the most talented providers to the area. Besides natural beauty, one of the main attractions for people relocating to Long Island is the quality of education available at all levels and the highly skilled and educated labor force. Long Island's schools are some of the best-funded and

A helicopter pad allows Nassau County Medical Center in East Meadow to receive patients with life-threatening injuries from miles away. Photo courtesy of Nassau County Medical Center.

Southside Hospital in Bay Shore. Photo by Deborah Ross.

best-equipped in the nation. Long Island has 127 school districts employing almost 30,000 teachers to educate roughly 400,000 public school students. Another 50,000 students attend 211 private schools.

In 1995, New York State ranked first with 16 of the 40 finalists in the prestigious Westinghouse Science Foundation Award competition, and six of those were from Long Island. California ranked second with 6 finalists. In 1994, Long Island alone produced 31 semifinalists and 9 finalists.

Is this an accident? Local educators would say "no." It's the result of superior schools producing top-notch students for tomorrow's world. The Island's population is ranked among some of the highest educated in the nation, so parents put a premium on the schooling their children receive.

On Long Island, the average teacher/student ratio is slightly under 20:1, with more than half of graduating students going on to four-year colleges and a full 85 percent pursuing some form of higher education. Almost half of those undergrads will stay here, while the other half is recruited by off-Island schools to supplement their enrollments. Long Island is known to college recruiters as fertile ground for some of the best students, and best student athletes, on the East Coast.

If the people who live here seem preoccupied with their schools, there is a reason. Often, the school board election is the most important election in the community, because in many cases the school district is the main thread unifying neighborhoods.

Long Island students have a wide range of extracurricular activities and sports available to them. In addition, special programs are run by the Board of Cooperative Education Services, a state-created but locally funded and operated institution designed to offer schools the benefits of shared services. Nassau and Suffolk BOCES offer more than 200 programs on Long Island, including vocational programs at one of their tech centers, teacher training, Saturday programs, and summer workshops for students. Since students live in a coastal environment, BOCES offers special enrichment programs in marine studies

Nassau and Suffolk BOCES offer more than 200 programs on Long Island. Photos by Scott Levy, courtesy of Nassau BOCES Cultural Arts Center, Syosset.

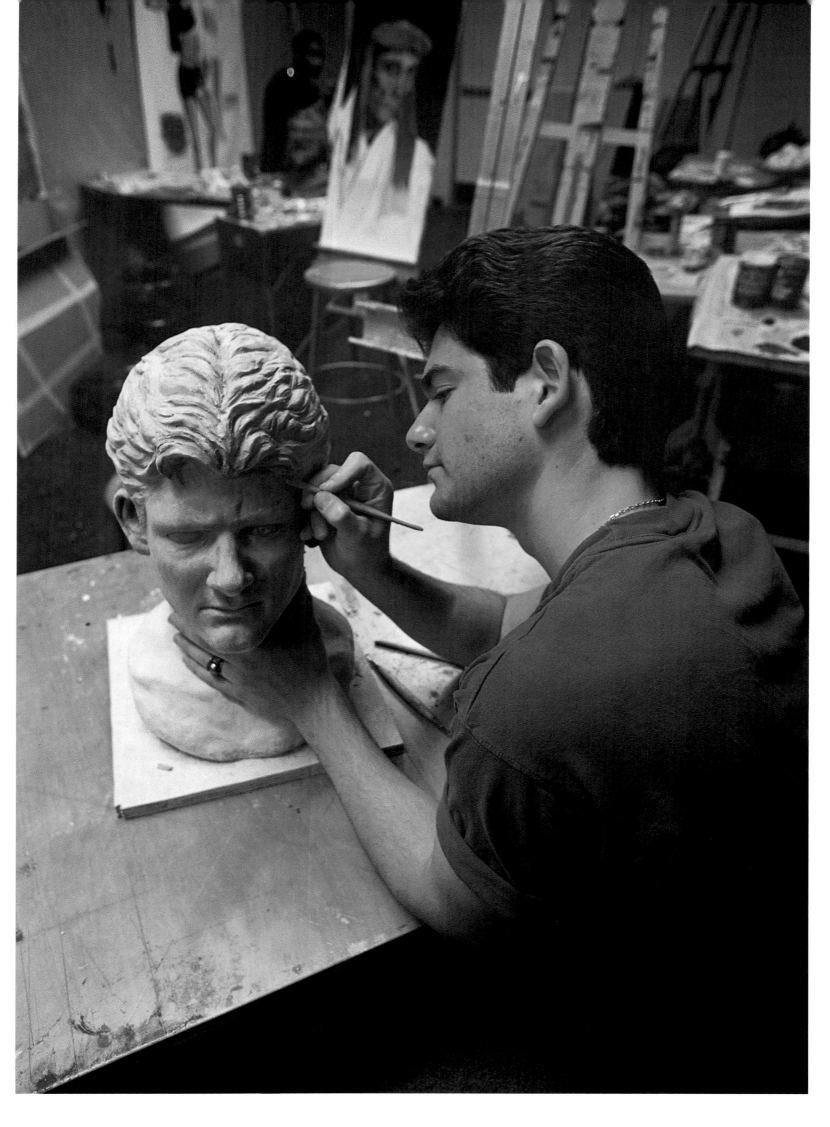

Adelphi University in Garden City has built a strong reputation on liberal arts. Photo by Lisa Meyer.

for elementary students. Proximity to New York City has allowed performing and fine arts students to be mentored by artists, musicians, and dancers while they prepare for the rigorous New York State Regents diploma at the Nassau BOCES Cultural Arts Center in Syosset. Students find they are well served by the higher education offerings available in their own backyard, but like students everywhere, many want to try their wings away from the nest. Those who choose to stay, an impressive 137,000, are rarely disappointed, perhaps because, in addition to excellent schools, they have the beach, the city, the mall, and their parents' refrigerators close at hand.

There are 21 colleges in Nassau and Suffolk counties. They run the gamut in offerings, but one thing is constant: many people come from far away to attend them. For instance, SUNY at Stony Brook attracts students from around the world to its excellent biology, physics, engineering, computer science, and math programs. Hofstra University and the two main local campuses of Long Island University, C.W. Post Campus and Southampton College, draw students from near and far, as does the highly rated Polytechnic University and U.S. Merchant Marine Academy in Kings Point. Although none of the colleges can be

pigeonholed, several programs stand out at each. Hofstra has rounded out its multidimensional resources with a world-class business college, a law school, and scholarly conferences of national note. It is home to the most up-to-date television production facility of any nonprofit organization in the Northeast, employing state-of-the-art editing and broadcasting equipment. Its campus is carefully planted in the tradition of its Dutch founders and serves as a national arboretum, a treasure locals appreciate.

Polytechnic University in Farmingdale was once the training ground for the Island's high-tech industry. Poly grads are highly prized recruits at the region's high-tech companies, and far beyond Long Island. In fact, in the 1995-1996 academic year, the college promised placement of graduates within six months of graduation.

C.W. Post's Palmer School of Library and Information Science, one of the few in the Northeast, is a leader in information

Hofstra University's 288-acre campus in Hempstead was officially designated an arboretum in 1985. Photo by Lisa Meyer.

St. Joseph's College in
Patchogue offers acceler-
ated weekend courses for
those who can't attend
weekday classes. Photo
by James McIsaac.

technology. And Post's cooperative education program for undergrads pairs thousands of students every year with local businesses
for real-life training in some of the most promising career paths.
Tilles Center for the Performing Arts, a landmark of the Post campus, offers worldclass cultural events. The beautiful campus draws
many visitors, especially in the spring, for the Renaissance Fair.

Adelphi University in Garden City has built a reputation on liberal arts and its flexible programs for working students. It offers a
popular Master of Social Work program and two doctoral programs.

Right in the heart of Nassau's Gold Coast, SUNY Old
Westbury provides important training for many of the Island's
teachers and business leaders. Old Westbury offers degrees in sciences, visual arts, education, and labor studies, among other fields.
Its library contains special collections focusing on women's and
African-American studies, reflecting the college's commitment to
addressing the needs of nontraditional students and minorities.

SUNY College of Technology at Farmingdale has switched from
concentrating on developing leaders for the region's agriculture

Students can earn a law degree at Touro College in Huntington. Photos by Scott Levy.

industry, to strengthening its tech base. It now offers two-year and four-year degrees in a variety of areas, including visual communications, aeronautical science, and electrical engineering technology.

Dowling College in Sayville has a small, friendly campus. Situated on a cove of the Great South Bay on the grounds of a Vanderbilt summer estate, Dowling offers liberal arts studies as well as transportation and aviation programs. The college recently opened the country's first National Aviation and Transportation Center, training students in all areas of aviation as a resource for the implementation of NAFTA and other international business partnerships.

St. Joseph's College in Patchogue is a small but important component of the area's higher education community. It has accelerated

weekend courses for those who can't attend weekday classes, leading to degrees in health administration or human resources management. It also has a number of business, education, and sociology majors, as well as liberal arts.

Those who know just what they want to do might choose one of the campuses of the New York Institute of Technology for engineering or computer science, or its highly acclaimed culinary arts institute on the Central Islip campus. Many people who live close to the school cherish memories of gourmet meals they "tested" at special programs open to the public, and with such a large restaurant industry in the area, culinary arts students are in high demand.

Musicians might consider Five Towns College in Dix Hills, which specializes in preparing people for jobs in the music industry. Students can master instruments, or study technical and business methods used in New York's important recording industry. Another unique school, Webb Institute in Glen Cove, specializes in naval

With a 400-acre campus noted for its beauty, the C.W. Post Campus of Long Island features Tudor-style buildings and the gracious estate house built for Marjorie Merriweather Post and E.F. Hutton in 1921. Post's horse barn (above) and Kumble Hall (right). Photos by Lisa Meyer.

architecture and marine engineering. Since the school is set on the waterside, it's easy for students to translate theory into practice, right at their doorstep.

One possibility for the nontraditional student is the SUNY Empire State College, operating out of the campus of SUNY Old Westbury. Empire follows an independent study approach, allowing great flexibility for students with busy lives. It is possible to attain an A.A., B.A./B.S., or M.A. degree from Empire by attending evening or summer courses and completing much of the work off campus with the help of an adviser.

Molloy College in Rockville Centre offers two-year and four-year degrees in health-related areas, as well as business and liberal arts, and an M.S. in nursing.

Briarcliffe College for Business and Technology has three campuses providing training in computers and computer graphics, business administration, legal assisting, and telecommunications. Katherine Gibbs School in Melville has 500 business students, and the Barry Z. Levine School of Health Sciences has as many students studying to be physician assistants or physical therapists, among other health vocations. Levine is part of the Manhattan-based Touro College system, which also has its law campus in Huntington.

Dowling College in Oakdale features a magnificent campus situated on the historic Vanderbilt estate, along the Connetquot River. Dowling photos above and right by James McIsaac.

SUNY College of Technology at Farmingdale develops leaders for the agriculture industry, aeronautical science, electrical engineering, and visual communications. Photo by Deborah Ross.

Long Island high schools provide a full range of extracurricular activities for all students. (above and right) Photos by Lisa Meyer. (far right above and below) Photos by Scott Levy.

There also are 12 trade and technical schools offering everything from court reporting to real estate appraisal, truck driving to labor relations studies. These schools serve 8,000 students a year.

Most students need some time to try out study areas before they commit to a major. Tens of thousands of them each year go to one of the two local community colleges. Nassau Community College in Uniondale has 22,000 students in dozens of associate degree and continuing education programs. It is a prime stepping-stone to all of the upper-level colleges of the State University of New York system— as is its counterpart, Suffolk County Community College, with 23,000 students spread across three campuses. Both Suffolk and Nassau work closely with the business community to develop programs that lead to real jobs.

For those with a B.A., there are two law schools (Hofstra University Law School and Touro Law Center), two medical schools (SUNY Stony Brook School of Medicine and NY College of Osteopathic Medicine of NYIT), a dental school (School of Dental Medicine at Stony Brook), and programs for advanced degrees in everything from art to mechanical engineering. More than 3,000 students are enrolled in these professional programs.

(above) Merchant Marine Academy in Kings Point. Photo by Bruce Bennett.

(left) Old Bethpage Grade School. Photo by Bruce Bennett.

(above) LaSalle Military Academy. Photo by James McIsaac.

(left) WLIW-TV Channel 21, the local public television affiliate, has studios near the Long Island Expressway in Plainview. Photo by Brian Winkler.

(on the following page) Photo by Scott Levy, courtesy of BOCES Cultural Arts Center, Syosset.

Higher education doesn't stop at age 22, however. All of Long Island's colleges are extremely involved in providing continuing education programs for the Island's work force, through specially targeted course offerings and on-site training developed in conjunction with area employers. Numerous seminars, special events, and libraries have been developed specifically for the business community, as the two communities find new ways to provide for each other while they build a stronger community. As Dowling President Victor Meskill said at a recent conference, "Colleges used to feel the need to 'publish or perish.' Today, colleges realize they have to 'partner with business or fail to prosper.'" •••

CHAPTER 6

• • •

WATER, WATER EVERYWHERE

• • •

Photo by Lisa Meyer.

I'VE SAID THIS SO OFTEN,
but have said nothing,
but there's still more:
except for gulls
that floated like prayers of white paper;
except for billions of lives
beating in their shells, sheathes, and scales
beneath me, I worked alone.
I rocked those waves alone.
And later, packing chowders
back along the same path where none
but stars and white wild roses held
the evening air,
I knew that everything I'd ever bless, or be,
would come to this.

— "Tonging at St. James Harbor," by William Heyen

from *Long Island Light: Poems & a Memoir,* Vanguard Press, Inc.,
1979. Reprinted with permission from the author.

EELING, CRABBING, FISHING, AND CLAMMING with or without tongs, have been the birthright of Long Island children for as long as families have lived here, which may be one reason why their parents have made waterfront living the ultimate symbol of the Long Island lifestyle. With more than 1,000 miles of coastline, there are plenty of places to build that dream house, tie up that treasured boat and drop that crabpot.

(left) Eeling in Baldwin Harbor. Photo by Deborah Ross.

(below) Robert Moses Causeway. Photo by John Giamundo.

Start at any point in Nassau or Suffolk counties, and you can't drive for more than 15 miles north or south without running into water. On the north, you may have to look at the bottom of a craggy cliff to find it, but on the south shore, it will be lapping at an open, sandy beach. And, if you follow an east-west route, you'll hit water eventually, as well. In between coasts, you'll find canals, ponds, lakes, wetlands, harbors, bays, and other configurations of water as easily as you can find shopping centers in other parts of the country.

In fact, the only way on or off Long Island is across, through, or underwater. It is, after all, an island. To go to Manhattan or the continental United States, you must first wind your way through Queens or Brooklyn and cross a bridge or two, or go underwater via a tunnel.

Long Island offers walkers and rowers a host of possibilities. (above and below right) Photos by James McIsaac. (above right) Photo by Deborah Ross.

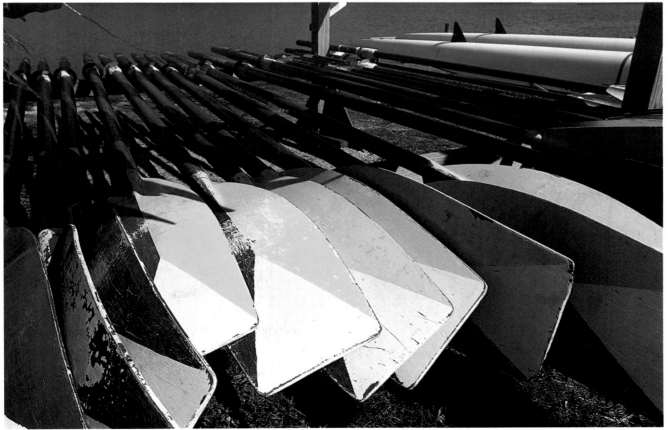

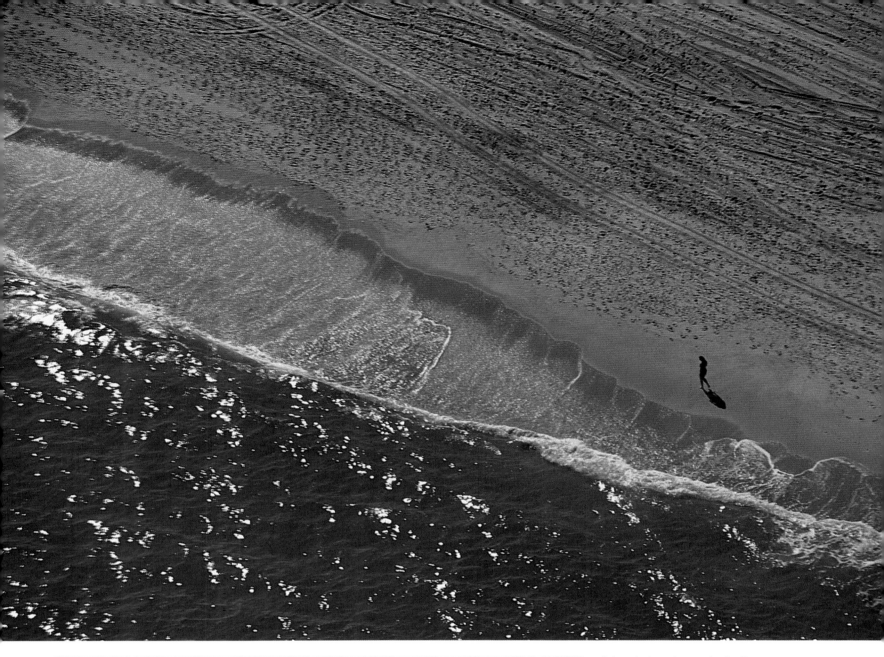

(above) Photo by Frank Abadie.
(left) Photo by Deborah Ross.

(left) The current 166-foot brick tower on the Fire
Island Lighthouse was illuminated November 1, 1858.
Photo by Lindsay Silverman.

Captain Ben's is a popular spot in Freeport. Photo by Deborah Ross.

To go to Connecticut and north, you have several options: You can take a bridge across eastern Queens to the Bronx and then continue around the west coast of the Long Island Sound, eventually heading east. Or, you can jump, with or without your car, onto a ferry at Port Jefferson to go to Bridgeport, or get on one in Orient to go all the way out to New London, which puts you on the road to scenic Mystic, Boston, or Cape Cod. For the adventurous, there are hydrofoil ferries to Wall Street, and there is talk of building ferries to New Jersey, to hasten the trip to Atlantic City for the optimistic. Of course, there's always the Long Island Railroad or Long Island MacArthur Airport. Or, your own boat.

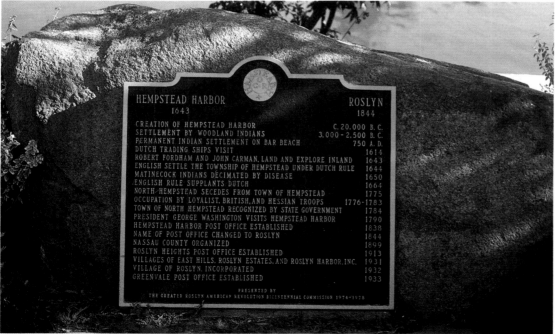

(above) Dry-docking in Freeport. (left) Historic marker in Roslyn Park. Photos by Deborah Ross.

(left) The Shinnecock Canal is the gateway to the Hamptons. It connects the Peconic Bay to the Shinnecock Bay, which opens into the Atlantic at the Shinnecock Inlet. (above) Long Island is a family place as well as a resort getaway. Peconic Bay jetties. Photos by Brian Winkler.

Perhaps it is this isolation that makes this place so unique. You are inclined to stay here and make the most of it—which could be why Long Islanders have created so many recreational and cultural attractions, so many ways to enjoy the water, and so many reasons to stay here.

Newcomers to the Island are quick to notice the constant wind, rarely less than 12 mph, and the visceral tug of the tides and seasons. Since one is always surrounded by water with no protection from geography, the breeze coming in off the water is tinged with salt and a smell reminiscent of the beach on a sunny day, no matter what the season. Gulls hover over roads and sit on light poles. Bits of shell and sand line the roads after a rain. The sky is brighter here on a sunny day than it is other places, or at least it seems to be, probably because there is so much reflected light bouncing around off the water.

By and large, real estate falls into two categories: property on the water and all other property. Even with the threat of flood or hurricane, home buyers yearn for a water view, or better yet, their own little piece of the beach. There's nothing quite like waking up to or going to sleep to the sound of water lapping up against the beach or a dock. And, since the coastline is either on the north or the south, everyone gets a little bit of sunset or sunrise reflected on their water surface.

There are many places here to live on the water, and they fit a variety of pocketbooks. For the well-to-do, there are exotic beach houses on the South Shore in Southhampton, Fire Island, and West Hampton. These areas offer unrivaled ocean vistas and a certain amount of privacy, as there is no street parking allowed, discouraging daytrippers, gawkers, and beachgoers from beyond the neighborhood. Or there are the more settled, stately areas along the North Shore, like Sands Point, Lloyd Harbor, Nissequogue, Oldfield, and Belle Terre, where the woods meet the water and offer picturesque protection from civilization.

Between the Civil War and 1940, more than 900 estates, or country houses as they were called, were built on Long Island. Many

With more than 1,000 miles of coastline, there are plenty of places to build that dream house. (above left) Canals meander through Oakdale. Photo by James McIsaac. (below left) Swan at Twin Lakes in Wantagh. Photo by Deborah Ross. (above) Gracious home on Stony Brook Harbor. Photo by Deborah Ross.

of those homes are still standing, some used as museums, some as college campuses, others as clubhouses for yacht clubs, golf courses, and botanical gardens. Some estates have been divided and sold as unspoiled property for late 20th-century mansions.

For the young or the up-and-coming, there is the famous Fire Island, a delicate strip of sand lying between the ocean and most of the South Shore. Accessible only by boat, Fire Island contains communities catering to a myriad of personalities and lifestyles. Houses tend to be huddled together, as if they are fending off the North Atlantic, which only occasionally lets its strength be known. Since there are no roads or cars on Fire Island, it's the perfect place for children, seniors, walkers, and well-behaved dogs. Which brings up

the subject of rules: There are many, as would be expected in such a delicate environment. This doesn't seem to discourage the thousands who come here, summer after summer, for a week or a season to enjoy the beach and casual lifestyle. All supplies must be brought in by boat and moved to homes in little wagons, which residents leave at the docks or general store.

That's not to say there are no residents who stay year-round. Several hundred people live on the western end of Fire Island, schooling their children in a small, one-room school on the island and only going off-island for emergencies. Many of these families are connected to the U.S. Coast Guard Station, or other facilities connected to one of the state parks on the barrier island.

Outside of Fire Island, there are other places people can live on or near the water. For the average family, there are Cape Cods on canals in Amityville, contemporary canal homes in Merrick with connecting boathouses, townhouses in Copiague with decks and skylights taking advantage of the spectacular views, and suburban split-levels in the various Islips perfect for parents who want to raise their children near the water. Or, there are the well-maintained fishing villages of Babylon, Sayville, Bayport, and Bellport. Or the more urban Freeport, with its many recreational facilities and dockside restaurants. On the north, the colonial villages of Roslyn, Stony Brook, Cold Spring Harbor, and Sag Harbor all share quiet marine views, but are near to their more raucous cousins Port Washington,

(above) Bellmore Creek. Photo by Gary Fox. (left) Freeport fishing station. Photo by Deborah Ross.

(right) Rowing on Twin Lakes Preserve, Wantagh. Photo by Melanie Bennett.

Shinnecock Inlet (above and right) is a favorite fishing spot. Photos by Bruce Bennett.

(above) Montauk sunset photo by Brian Winkler.
(right) Photo by Lindsay Silverman.

It's hard to decide if boat or automobile is the best mode of transportation. This ferry takes people from Port Jefferson to Bridgeport, CT. (left and right) Photos by Ken McIsaac.

(below) Danford's Inn overlooks Port Jefferson Harbor. Photo by Ken McIsaac.

Huntington, and Port Jefferson, which have nightlife to offer along with everything else.

All of these towns have marinas, fishing docks, and beaches. Most have waterside parks or shops. Some have museums and historic buildings. At least one has a deepwater dock; another, a robust arts community. Most are fairly small and have strict rules governing the maintenance of their attractive Main Street. All have excellent schools, libraries, and upscale shopping.

But, even young couples and those with more love of water than bank accounts can find something close to the shore. In communities like Long Beach, Lindenhurst, Bay Shore, and Patchogue on the South Shore, or Kings Park, Rocky Point, and Sound Beach on the

north, there are affordable bungalows, many updated from summer to year-round living.

Several waterfront towns are undergoing facelifts and revitalization efforts that should make them the "hot" towns of the future. According to oldtimers, Bay Shore, Patchogue, and Riverhead in Suffolk County have the potential for being the new desirable locations of the next decade, and Long Beach, Freeport, and Glen Cove in Nassau County are well under way to becoming sought-after waterfront locations in the west. In each case, a strong town government and the influence of the tourism or arts community have made the difference, bringing visitors, new business, and home buyers into the area.　　　•••

(left and above) Jones Beach photos by Lindsay Silverman.

(on the following page) Mill Neck, after an ice storm.
Photo by Deborah Ross.

CHAPTER 7

• • •

A PRECIOUS
ENVIRONMENT

• • •

Photo by Deborah Ross.

ROBERT CUSHMAN MURPHY'S LEGACY TO Long Island and the world goes beyond the founding of the Environmental Defense Fund and his activism in other environmentally focused organizations. Long Islanders, in particular, have him to thank for laying the groundwork leading up to the passage of the Long Island Pine Barrens Protection Act of 1993, as well as the preservation of beach that is part of federal and state parkland.

In 1933, shortly after regional planner Robert Moses' masterpiece, Jones Beach State Park, was opened to the public, Murphy suggested setting aside the pristine pine forests at the ocean's edge for permanent preservation. Murphy and some of his colleagues wanted the state to act on saving the beach "as soon as possible

before vandalism and development have destroyed the natural features," to allow generations of Americans the opportunity to enjoy what Long Islanders took for granted. By 1965, Murphy's dream was realized when the Fire Island National Seashore project set aside 5,000 acres of barrier beach as a national treasure. Today, thousands

(left) Rising 15 feet above the ground, Manhasset's Shelter Rock offered protection from wind and rain to generations of native people and early settlers before it was set aside as a historical monument. Photo by Gary Fox.

(below) Long Islanders are committed to preserving the environment for future generations. Apple picking at Wickham's Fruit Farm in Cutchogue. Photo by Bruce Bennett.

use the park annually, in all seasons, making Fire Island and its lighthouse the symbol of Long Island to many.

When development swept the Island in the 1960s and 1970s, it was partly because of what was perceived as an endless stretch of "scrub" pine wastelands available in Suffolk County. Not suitable for crops, this land attracted the contempt of residents and the interest of builders on the lookout for cheap land. In 1978, *Newsday*'s important series, Long Island at the Crossroads, targeted pine barrens areas for aggressive development. At roughly the same time, a movement to set aside 27 percent of the state of New Jersey as a reserved "pinelands" drew the attention of naturalists on Long Island, who already had determined that Long Island's pigmy pine forests were unlike New Jersey's, although they both shared the plant association of pitch pine, bearberry and pink moccasin flower, and a number of similar bird and animal species.

In 1978, the conflict between developers and naturalists intensified over a plan to expand the old Suffolk County Airport into the surrounding dwarf pine plains of Southampton, the same area hit by wildfires in 1995. This conflict eventually led to the birth of the Long Island Pine Barrens Society, which felt the piecemeal development of the pine barrens was unwise management of the county's

Long Island has a legacy of environmentally focused organizations that actively work to preserve the precious coastline. (below) Aerial view of Fire Island. Photo by Frank Abadie. (right) Photo by James McIsaac.

Fire Island
National Seashore

United States Department of the Interior
National Park Service

Fire Island stretches 32 miles from Robert Moses State Park to Smith Point Park. Several parts are managed by the National Parks Service as part of the Fire Island National Seashore. Visitors will enjoy the hardwood groves and spotting wild geese, long-legged herons, and an occasional deer. (above) Photo by Deborah Ross. (left) Photo by Martha Leider.

(right) Photo by Scott Levy.

largest watershed. Lawsuits were filed, development was slowed then further halted by the national recession in the 1980s. Finally, the Long Island Association stepped in to play a key role in negotiating a compromise among builders, environmentalists, and government. By Earth Day, 1991, the state had a comprehensive ecological vision for eastern Long Island leading to the Central Pine Barrens Comprehensive Land Use Plan in 1995 that protects 55,000 acres of the core forest, making it the third-largest forest preserve in New York State, and delineates the limits of development in the region.

Okeanus Research Foundation in Riverhead offers lectures and other instructional opportunities to learn more about ecological balance. Photo by John Giamundo.

Everyone can take an active part in Long Island's preservation. Planting Fields Arboretum. Photo by Deborah Ross.

What is left of this, the oldest forest in New York State, still covers 100,000 acres of eastern Suffolk County. Its miles of greenery act as sentinel to four trillion gallons of high-quality drinking water sitting in the Island's largest aquifer. While the pine barrens provide unique recreational resources for fishing, hiking, and bicycling, they also are home to the most diverse collection of plants and animals anywhere in the state.

In 1991, The Nature Conservancy named eastern Long Island one of a dozen "Last Great Places" in the Western Hemisphere. The Long Island Chapter of the Conservancy, another Murphy legacy, is committed to protecting as much as possible of the Peconic Bioreserve, an area stretching from the headwaters of the Peconic River in central Brookhaven to the Peconic Bay in Riverhead, and reaching out to include the North and South Forks and all the islands in between. This area provides habitats for the highest concentration of New York's rarest plants and animals, all relying on the waters of the bay, the river, or its tributaries. So far, the Conservancy has helped protect more than 25,000 acres within the 41 preserves it manages inside the boundaries of the bioreserve, an investment of $125 million, mostly from local contributors.

At the far eastern end of the bioreserve, the South Fork Shelter Island Chapter maintains the Mashomack Preserve, 2,000 acres of salt marsh and oak woods on Shelter Island. The site is home to the ruby-throated hummingbird, muskrat, fox, harbor seal, terrapin, owl, osprey, great blue heron, glossy ibis, and other wildlife. Close to the south ferry slip, this lovely preserve is a favorite of photographers and amateur naturalists. On the western end of the Island, several environmentally sensitive areas have been protected as well. The Takapausha

Once a year, employees from local businesses volunteer to spend a day sprucing up public places. All photos of Robert Moses State Park. Photos by Deborah Ross.

Long Island's environment is precious to those who live here now
and will live here in the future. (above) Twin Lakes Preserve in
Wantagh. (right) In-line skating along Wantagh State Parkway.
Photos by Bruce Bennett.

Preserve, 80 acres maintained by Nassau County on the South Shore, includes a wildlife sanctuary and the largest stand of white cedar trees in the region. The park was named after a sachem, or chief, of the Massapequa tribe. On the North Shore, Nassau County's Muttontown Preserve includes six distinct habitats in its 550 acres, plus a mansion and other buildings currently used for cultural programs. The area is home to opossums, bats, foxes, snapping and box turtles, red-backed salamanders, and other amphibians. The nearby Saint John's Pond Preserve, another Conservancy project, offers a picturesque refuge for flying squirrels, raccoons, and endangered ospreys.

Naturally, interest in protecting the environment doesn't stop at the shoreline. When waste-disposal practices changed and landfills started closing in the 1980s, some of the fallout landed on beaches up and down the East Coast. The public was outraged, prompting

tighter controls on all types of waste products and on the purity of the water in swimming and recreation areas. Now all landfills on the Island are closed, garbage and most trash is hauled off to mainland landfills, and recycling is required in most areas. Plus, Long Island's beaches are carefully monitored in summer months, usually on a daily basis. Areas around the beaches are noticeably cleaner than they were 20 years ago, due mainly to the vigilance of the towns and counties that line them.

The quality of the water in the Long Island Sound and on the Atlantic beaches is a concern to everyone on the Island. The federal government and the governments of the areas surrounding the Sound—including Nassau and Suffolk counties, Queens, the Bronx and Westchester counties in New York, and the state of Connecticut—have joined forces to clean up the water to the Island's

Wetlands are an important piece of the environmental puzzle. (above and right) Oceanside Marine Nature Study Area. Photos by Deborah Ross.

(far right) Pine forests make up large tracts of land in eastern Long Island. A conflict between developers and naturalists led to the birth of the Long Island Pine Barrens Society. Photo by Deborah Ross.

north, committing years to the planning of the multibillion-dollar project. Since there is little or no heavy industry along the coastline on both the North Shore and South Shore of the Island, runoff is usually generated by agriculture and lawn residue, or sewage. Measures have been taken to control both. However, industrialization along the shores of New York City, Westchester, and Connecticut contribute to the Sound's pollution problems.

The Federal Clean Air Act has prompted the use of special gasoline in metropolitan-area cars in summer months, when pollution is

more of a problem than in cooler seasons. The constant 9-13 mph winds sweeping the Island take care of some of the problem, but the sheer number of cars used here requires special precautions. Additional lanes have been added to the Long Island Expressway, including 13 miles of High Occupancy Vehicle lanes, with more under way. All of this is to increase traffic flow, thereby reducing pollution caused by tens of thousands of cars idling in the summer heat.

Convinced a healthy environment promotes a healthy economy, the environmental forces on Long Island include both the tourism and agriculture industries, The Nature Conservancy, the Pine Barrens Preservation Society, the LI Greenbelt Trail Conference, the New York State Office of Parks, Recreation and Historic Preservation, and many business groups. They appreciate the fact that the Island's environment is precious, not only to those who live here now and will live here in the future, but also to the nation as a whole. •••

The Nature Conservancy named eastern
Long Island one of a dozen "Last Great
Places." Photos by Deborah Ross.

(on the following page)
Photo by Scott Levy.

CHAPTER 8

THE PROMISE OF TECH ISLAND

· · ·

LILCO switching equipment. Photo by Scott Levy.

THE LAST FEW YEARS OF THE 20TH CENTURY promise to bring significant change to Long Island. The region prospered as a result of its specialized industries during the Cold War: Fully one-third of the state's high-technology manufacturing firms were located here, the fastest-growing area in New York for much of the 1980s. As a consequence, Long Island was one among the first to feel the full force of the defense cuts. But, as of early 1996, having regained nearly one-third of the lost jobs, the region has begun the slow and steady process of rebounding and repositioning itself for the next millennium.

The 1990s brought numerous attempts at finding the key to realizing the promise of Tech Island, but no business group invested as much time and effort into economic development as the Long Island Association (LIA). Among other things, the LIA organized a health insurance purchasing cooperative for small business, lobbied to phase out the state's petroleum business tax, promoted the extension of the Long Island Expressway's fourth lane to facilitate interstate transportation, and backed the strengthening of tourist services and environmental conservation.

"The LIA is committed to reestablishing the strength of our manufacturing jobs in order to maintain the strength of our economy," said Matthew Crosson, president of the LIA. In 1994, the LIA organized the first Long Island Summit, a convention of representatives from higher education, major industries, unions, government, and small business, brought together to find common directions in a plan for economic development. A number of issue-specific coalitions was formed, based on needs shared by formerly opposed factions. According to Dr. Pearl Kamer, chief economist for the LIA, "The Long Island Summit sensitized people to the need for change."

The Summit's resulting document, the Long Island Action Plan, contained more than 250 ideas for ways to stimulate the economy, involving all sectors. Some of the ideas were implemented quickly, such as the successful effort of one coalition to lobby the New York State Senate for passage of the bill requiring all school budget elections to be held on the same day. Others will take years to accomplish. Perhaps the most important legacy of the Summit is that the pendulum has swung in the direction of reducing or maintaining tax levels, according to Crosson, and the Long Island Action Plan has increased pressure to consolidate some of the Island's 1,000 tax districts. These two trends alone are bound to offer some relief to

(left) Cold Spring Harbor Laboratory's DNA Learning Center photo by Bruce Bennett.

(below) Symbol Technologies photo by Bruce Bennett.

homeowners and businesses without disrupting the ready access to the governments imposing those taxes that Long Islanders have come to expect.

A number of long-term initiatives was spawned, as well, including Project Long Island. This required a year's research of existing business to determine which Long Island high-tech manufacturing industries merited special attention to stimulate growth. Careful not to repeat the mistakes of the past by putting "all their eggs in one basket," planners decided to optimize their chances by spreading their energies across five industries: emerging electronics, biotechnology and bioengineering, medical imaging and health care information systems, graphic communications, and computer software.

The goal of Project Long Island (PLI) is to create 28,300 new manufacturing jobs for the region by the turn of the century. If those jobs can be created, they in turn will generate more jobs in collateral supplier industries, service industries, and other segments of the economy. All told, PLI's goal is to create close to 65,000 jobs in 10 years, making up for the 60,000 manufacturing jobs that were lost between 1988 and 1995 as a result of cutbacks in the defense industry. The LIA is trying to position the region for jobs that, by and large, will pay more than those lost in the 1980s, ones that require specialized education and those with good chances for survival

through evolution with the technical industries. These jobs are essentially information-based, changing the whole concept of manufacturing, according to Crosson.

By building partnerships among related businesses and promoting the concept of "buy on Long Island," the LIA hopes to enrich existing industries. And, by encouraging public schools and colleges to train students for specific fields that will be useful to these industries, the region can build continuity in the work force, along with opportunities for area young people. Briarcliffe College, for example, has started a degree program aimed at preparing people for jobs in the graphics communications industry.

Each target industry has a base of impressive companies in place on which to build a network of complementary and collateral businesses. Each group contains a few large companies as well as some of the 10,000 small and medium-sized technology companies on the Island. Among the large companies, some are world leaders—such as Computer Associates International, the largest independent software company in the world; Symbol Technologies, inventor of the bar code

Computer Associates International in Islandia is a giant in the software industry. Photo by James McIsaac.

scanning system, which saw its stock value increase by 70 percent in 1995; Bennett X-ray, maker of some of the world's most advanced radiographic equipment; and Olympus America, an international leader in optical technology for business, medical, and consumer markets.

The biotech component may be the most established, with more than 50 companies and 2,200 employees, making Long Island the nation's fourth-largest biotech center, according to the LIA. It also holds out hope for high salaries to match the required skills and education. Planners see growth in companies involved in new drug delivery systems, new drug discovery partnerships, and new methods for diagnosing genetic and infectious diseases.

Spinning out of technology developed at the major research centers are Collaborative Laboratories of Setauket, the country's largest maker of liposomes for the cosmetic industry and a major supplier to Estee Lauder in Melville; Oncogene Sciences, Inc. of Uniondale, a national leader in the development of cancer tests and treatments using genetic engineering and molecular biology; Enzo Biochem of Farmingdale, a genetic-product manufacturer; and Melville Biologics, Inc., a pharmaceutical manufacturer using blood plasma.

Cold Spring Harbor Laboratory is developing plans to commercialize its gene-based research. Photo by Scott Levy.

Medical imaging technologies owe a lot to this region. Scientists at Brookhaven National Laboratory (BNL) found a use for thallium-201 in cardiovascular testing, now called the thallium stress test, among other diagnostic tools developed there. Fonar Corporation of Melville, whose founder won the first patent for using MRI technology for cancer testing, employs 350. And Bennett X-ray makes the world's most advanced mammography equipment at its Copiague plant.

As part of the rapid expansion of the systems development industries spawned in the late 1980s, a concentration of companies evolved to provide specialized computer applications for the health care and medical fields. These include Medical Connections of Hicksville; Datamatic Corp. in Hauppauge; and Strategic Marketing Information of Nesconset. Drawing on the large number of software developers and systems engineers in the area, plus the potential coming out of Stony Brook, Polytechnic, NYIT, and Farmingdale, among other colleges,

health information promises to be a good bet for growth. The LIA is projecting 3,000 new jobs in this field by the year 2000.

Project Long Island is estimating the start of 12,000 new jobs in electronics fields, employing former defense industry engineers and others. They see the new jobs more closely tied to applications springing from the computer industry. Computer hardware manufacturers and software developers alike will need specialized electronics to blend the two technologies as the world gets more wired. Symbol Technologies, for example, is a major success story for Long Island. Its founder, Gerald Swartz, invented the concept of the hand-held bar code scanner, which miniaturized the technology and made bar coding appealing to many businesses besides retailing. Another local success story shows the ingenuity available to make the switch from defense to civilian markets. Frisby Airborne Hydraulics of Freeport, started out as a family-owned airplane parts manufacturer, then diversified to develop ways to stabilize temperatures in electronic components used in computer products.

Frisby Airborne Hydraulics made the switch from defense to civilian markets. Photo by Charles Orrico, courtesy of Frisby Aerospace.

Long Island is home to several major computer software companies serving a global market, so it is no surprise that Project Long Island expects that sector to expand. Recently, 40 local software companies surveyed by KPMG Peat Marwick forecast revenue growth of 38 percent in 1996. And, drawing on the record of revenue growth in the industry in 1995 and projections for 1996, forecasters see continued expansion in software industries for the remainder of the century.

Unlike so many large companies facing downsizing, the major players in the software field have expanded in recent years, taking risks along the way and giving back to the community. The giant Computer Associates (CA) International, maker of Unicenter and Unicenter TNG network management software, has had a major impact on the Island's economy. According to industry analysts, its annual revenues may reach

$4 billion in 1996. Acclaim Entertainment, the highly successful computer game developer, put its headquarters in the heart of Glen Cove, giving a welcome boost to that city's downtown. And Cheyenne Software added 30 new employees per quarter through 1995, when it moved to a facility in Lake Success. The unique new headquarters was designed to facilitate employee telecommuting, freeing up road space and helping Long Island meet clean-air standards.

With neighboring New York City the advertising and publishing capital of the nation, it was only natural that Long Island's graphic design and production businesses would flourish. Because they have cheaper rent and a highly skilled work force, more than 700 small and medium-sized printers, artists, package designers, marketing professionals, and publishers employ 11,000 people, making Long Island one of the nation's largest print markets. Several companies have done well, such as Konica Imaging USA in Glen Cove, PTN Publishing in Melville, and First Impressions of Plainview, by specializing in electronic delivery of graphic material. Advertising agencies, such as Erin/Edwards of Glen Head, embraced the World Wide Web by incorporating design groups to gain entree into the new Internet-savvy market. Other more traditional printers, such as Cedar Graphics, which employs 175, use high-tech equipment to get superior results in printing posters, brochures, magazines, and books. Chyron Corp. makes the industry-standard equipment for television graphics and text. It employs 165 people at its Melville facility.

It would be wrong to assume that Project Long Island is the only effort in place to promote economic development on Long Island. In addition to LIA, organizations and agencies such as Long Island Forum for Technology (LIFT), Regional Center for Economic Development, the Long Island Regional Planning Board, Action Long Island, Advancement for Commerce and Industry, Sky Island Club, the Long Island Farm Bureau, Long Island Convention and Visitors Bureau, and others, have worked for the betterment of all Islanders for years. In addition, there are a number of collateral initiatives already at work and already successful at nurturing original ideas coming out of local efforts. These include entirely new networks built among existing institutions, the expansion of established research and business alliances, and the short-term infusion of expertise to jump-start businesses.

It took several years to get the Long Island High Technology Incubator (LIHTI) on the campus of SUNY Stony Brook up and running, for example, but now its principles are being replicated at other sites. Without waiting for a single industry to come forward as the next focus for the region, the incubator opened in 1992, built on a base of biomedical research already in place at the university and beyond.

The incubator's goal is to provide a safe haven for entrepreneurs to take ideas being developed in academe and turn them into profitable businesses. The 40,000-square-foot site offers fledgling businesses affordable space, supportive services, expert advice, use of

Millenium Communications is known for its web page development. Photo by Bruce Bennett.

the university's licenses, and networking opportunities with others in similar situations. Some of its more impressive "graduates" include Moltech, Curative Technologies, Collaborative Laboratories, and Olympus Biomedical, all of which have generated more than 500 jobs and annual revenues of over $50 million.

According to LIHTI Executive Director Francis P. Hession, Long Island is ripe for development of high-technology products, perhaps more than anywhere else in the United States. He attributes this, at least in part, to the downturn of the defense industry, which left thousands of highly trained engineers and researchers available and anxious to take on new projects. Hession sees plenty of potential on Long Island for entrepreneurs interested in biotech, materials development, software, computing, and multimedia products .

Meanwhile, the success of the LIHTI at Stony Brook has spurred state officials and others to replicate the concept. A similar incubator is being built on the campus of SUNY Farmingdale. Cold Spring Harbor Laboratory is working on a plan to put one in an existing industrial park to create an environment to commercialize its gene-based research. North Shore University Hospital and New York University Medical Center have begun a similar project in Manhasset, based on their medical research.

The Long Island Research Institute, a collaboration of the four major research centers in the region—Cold Spring Harbor Laboratory, the Brookhaven National Laboratory, SUNY at Stony Brook, and the North Shore University Hospital—offers a technical base for tech transfer industries. The concentration of so much knowledge, "so much creativity, so much fizz," according to Stony Brook President Shirley Strum Kenny, is one of the factors adding to the tremendous potential for significant growth. Couple that energy with venture capital, and the possibilities are staggering.

For example, Brookhaven National Laboratory's Computing and Communications Division collaborated with Cablevision Systems Corporation, the former Grumman Data Systems, and SUNY Stony Brook to implement the Fiber-Optic, Island-Wide Super High-Speed Network, or FISHNet, one of the first high-speed, fiber-optic systems in the nation to incorporate asynchronous transfer mode, or ATM, technology. In 1994, an experiment involved several of the LIRI members testing what was then a state-of-the-art technology, but adapting it to medical use. Several applications were demonstrated using ATM for research, including one that linked researchers and physicians at the University Medical Center at Stony Brook with BNL's National Synchrotron Light Source Department to view transvenous angiography images simultaneously. Such technology could provide fast, accurate diagnosis and treatment for patients when their doctors are separated from one another geographically, but connected digitally. According to BNL's William Thomlinson, "The time, expense, and travel required to participate in an imaging session could be sharply reduced," which could make a big difference in whether a patient survived or not.

There were good reasons why Long Island became a playground for the titans of business in the late 19th century, the cradle of aviation in the early 20th, and the hope of returning veterans after World War II. The Island's open space, clean air and water, the beach, the natural beauty, the quality of the schools, and the diversity of its people all worked together to make it attractive to the visionaries who came here. There is good reason, as well, to expect watershed inventions, industries, and coalitions to come from the same fertile environment to strengthen today's and tomorrow's economy and lifestyle. •••

(far left) Acclaim Entertainment is a highly successful computer game developer. Photo by Scott Levy.

Cardiologist John P. Dervan, M.D., is director of interventional cardiology at the Stony Brook School of Medicine and director of the University Hospital and Medical Center Cardiac Catheterization Laboratory. Stony Brook's cath lab is one of several state-of-the-art diagnostic centers on Long Island, which is known for the quality of its health care facilities. Photo by Scott Levy.

(left) The Relativistic Heavy Ion Collider (RHIC), now under construction at Brookhaven National Laboratory in Upton, will allow scientists to study phenomena that have not occured in the natural universe since the original "Big Bang." BNL is an internationally renowned scientific research institution, attracting thousands of visiting scientists each year to perform research at its facilities and attend conferences. Photo by Scott Levy.

(right) Olympus America is an international leader in optical technology for business, medical, and consumer markets. Photo by Frank G. Becher, courtesy of Olympus America, Inc.

Aerial view of Brookhaven National Laboratory (BNL), showing the ring for RHIC. Photo courtesy of BNL.

(on the following page) Master builder Robert Moses initiated construction of a highway stretching across the spine of Long Island from Manhattan to Hauppauge in 1954, expecting it to be sufficient for many years. By 1972, the Long Island Expressway had been extended to Riverhead and already was the busiest commuter highway in America. To alleviate congestion, service roads and high-occupancy vehicle lanes have been added in recent years, making it, at some points, a 12-lane superhighway. Photo by Vincent Pugilese.

THIS ISLAND
• • •

LOW TIDES, EARLY MORNINGS,
I'd walk the mud flats for nothing,
saying, as reeds bowed, straightened,
and bowed again in the brine wind,
or an eel or flounder startled
a cloudy trail through low water,
know you have forever, now,
know you have forever.

The Sound fallen back, this Island
risen, I kneel, touch my head
like a reed to the mud home of the crab,
wash my face in a gull's shadow,
knowing I have forever, now,
knowing I have forever.

— by William Heyen

from *Long Island Light: Poems & a Memoir*, Vanguard Press, Inc., 1979. Reprinted with permission from the author.

Photos by Deborah Ross.

Photo by Deborah Ross.

(above) Photo by Deborah Ross.

(left) Photo by Scott Levy.

Photos by Deborah Ross.

(above) Photo by Scott Levy.

(left and above) Photos by Deborah Ross.

Photos by Deborah Ross.

CHAPTER 9

· · ·

NETWORKS

· · ·

Photo by James McIsaac.

BROOKLYN UNION
Energy Leadership for the Next Century
• • •

FOR MORE THAN A CENTURY, BROOKLYN UNION has played a leading role on the great stage of New York City, spurring urban change and growth and evolving right along with the city it serves. Today, as it looks toward its second century as one of the nation's largest gas distribution companies, Brooklyn Union is at the cutting edge of the energy industry. That Brooklyn Union envisions a future of great expansion was made clear by the company's Chairman and Chief Executive Officer, Robert B. Catell, who said: "Growth, customer satisfaction, competitive pricing, and employee excellence are the initiatives by which we will realize our corporate vision of becoming the premier energy company in the Northeast."

Brooklyn Union was founded just over a century ago. At that time, Brooklyn was a thriving port and center of commerce whose growth was symbolized by the opening in 1884 of the Brooklyn Bridge. The gas industry was a rough-and-tumble business, with companies fighting furiously—employing street crews known as "gas-house gangs"—for territory and customers. But in 1895, the seven largest companies combined to form The Brooklyn Union Gas Company. In 1896, Brooklyn Union's board of directors, including William Rockefeller of the Standard Oil family, gave command of the company to James Jourdan, former Civil War general and president of the Fulton Municipal Gas Company.

General Jourdan shaped Brooklyn Union. It was his task to establish territories for the newly-consolidated company and secure new markets for manufactured gas, which was at the time used primarily for lighting rather than heating fuel. Brooklyn Union faced the challenge of adapting to a changing market. Electricity was taking over the lighting business. Coal and coke competed with gas for the cooking, water-heating, and industrial markets.

From 1896 to 1910, Brooklyn Union purchased six more gas companies, including four in Queens. Emphasizing modernization, it tripled gas manufacturing capacity and quadrupled storage. Its customer accounts increased from 108,000 to 387,000.

Gas lighting virtually disappeared between 1910 and 1926, but Brooklyn Union's annual sales doubled, due in large part to population growth in Brooklyn and Queens. In 1914, the company built a new headquarters on Remsen Street in Brooklyn Heights. This remained the company's main address until 1962, when it moved to a new building on Montague Street, just a block away from Brooklyn Borough Hall.

In 1950, the completion of a 1,840-mile pipeline brought natural gas, which had twice the heating value of manufactured gas, from the Southwest to Brooklyn Union's territory.

The successful establishment of a delivery system was the beginning of the great drama of introducing natural gas to Brooklyn Union's customers. Brooklyn Union had more than 850,000 customers using gas for heating, cooking, and industrial operations. To properly utilize the new fuel, Brooklyn Union had to convert all two million appliances in its territory. During the months from March through September of 1952, Brooklyn Union completed the transformation of its entire gas delivery system.

In the 1960s, Brooklyn Union placed ever greater emphasis on the revitalization of the neighborhoods it served. Since 1966, the company's Cinderella program has provided grants to renovate many of Brooklyn's magnificent brownstones. Over the years, the program has grown to include the refurbishment of commercial establishments as well as residential buildings.

Brooklyn Union has long recognized that its own growth is

The growing use of natural-gas-powered vehicles is helping New York City to improve the quality of its air.

Brooklyn Union's headquarters, center foreground, symbolizes the renewal of downtown Brooklyn and the vital role the company plays in the economic future of New York City.

dependent upon the health of the communities it serves. Therefore a priority at Brooklyn Union has been to create and implement strategies for local economic development. Many of these initiatives have been carried out through the company's Area Development Fund. The Fund assists business start-ups, relocation, and expansion, as well as housing development, by providing the kinds of financing most difficult to obtain from conventional lending institutions: equity investments, site acquisition loans, loan guarantees, and loan packaging. Through administration of the Fund, Brooklyn Union develops partnerships committed to revitalizing neighborhoods in the company's service territory. This approach to community reinvestment has received national acclaim. The Area Development Fund was the model for The Utility Network For Community-Based Development, a consortium of utilities and trade associations formed to explore how utilities could play a larger role in fostering investment in low- and moderate-income housing.

Through the 1980s, Brooklyn Union became an ever stronger advocate for commercial development. The company takes an aggressive approach to retaining and attracting businesses in and to its core territory of Brooklyn, Queens, and Staten Island, and works closely with city and state authorities, as well as with local community and financial organizations, to develop programs to improve the economy.

The company was in the leadership of promoting the economy of its territory when it spearheaded the development of MetroTech, an 11-building academic and commercial complex in downtown Brooklyn. Working with Polytechnic University, Brooklyn Union envisioned MetroTech as a center in which companies that used or developed advanced information technology would come together and exchange ideas. In 1991, Brooklyn Union moved its headquarters into MetroTech, joined by other prestigious tenants such as Chase Manhattan Bank and Bear Stearns and Company. Today, MetroTech stands as the centerpiece of the renaissance of the downtown Brooklyn area.

Brooklyn Union also supports a wide range of cultural programs that enhance the quality of life for its customers. The Queens Museum, Queens Botanical Gardens, Brooklyn Public Library, Staten Island Zoo, and Snug Harbor Cultural Center are among the organizations that benefit from Brooklyn Union support. With social responsibility a strong company tradition, company executives are active in the area's leading cultural and educational institutions. Brooklyn Union employees are counted among the volunteers for such community service organizations as the Boy and Girl Scouts, United Way, March of Dimes, Muscular Dystrophy Association and "Meals on Heels."

As part of its commitment to the future of its community, Brooklyn Union has developed a corporate agenda for education. The company has created a variety of programs to promote academic excellence in New York City schools. An advocate for educational reform, Brooklyn Union supports efforts by the educational community to enhance the ability of students to make positive choices for their future and to help educators respond to workplace needs and

(above) The Iroquois pipeline transports natural gas from Canada to markets in the Northeastern United States.

A gas well in the Gulf of Mexico, where Houston Exploration Company, a Brooklyn Union affiliate, has exploration and production interests.

Canada to the Northeastern United States. The Iroquois Gas Transmission System began service along its entire 370-mile route in 1992, and was by early 1993 delivering as much as 700 million cubic feet of gas per day to the Northeast.

In 1986, Brooklyn Union formed a new subsidiary, Gas Energy Cogeneration, Inc., to take advantage of electric-power shortfalls in the Northeast by participating in ventures to construct, own, and operate cogeneration plants. That year, Brooklyn Union's exploration and production affiliate, Fuel Resources Inc. (FRI), expanded and formed a subsidiary, Brooklyn Union Gas Exploration Company (now called Houston Exploration Company), to participate in ventures along the Gulf Coast. Another FRI company, Brooklyn Interstate Natural Gas Corporation (BRING) was formed to take advantage of new regulatory conditions and broker gas throughout the United States.

The bold leadership set by General Jourdan and the spirit of aggressive competition which marked the birth of Brooklyn Union continues to the present day as the company operates in a deregulated business environment in which independent marketers, brokers, and producers can compete for business within Brooklyn Union's established territories.

The course for the Brooklyn Union company of the future is being charted by Robert Catell, who became the company's President and Chief Executive Officer in 1991. Mr. Catell has noted that one effect of deregulation has been to expand a process that he saw developing as far back as the 1970s: that of Brooklyn Union's becoming more than a utility. As he says, "anticipating change is a guiding principle at Brooklyn Union."

Brooklyn Union has already set out on the path of its next century through initiatives such as the New York Market Hub, formed

expectations. In collaboration with the New York City Board of Education, the company created "Energy Choices: The Challenge," a segment of the New York City ninth-grade science curriculum.

The early 1980s were a time of continued growth in traditional residential apartment house, commercial, and industrial markets. In 1985, the Federal Energy Regulatory Commission further opened up the marketplace by, among other things, allowing local distribution companies to negotiate directly with suppliers. The gas-supply contract that Brooklyn Union and the Enron Corporation signed in 1987 was the first long-term arrangement between a local distributor and a major supplier.

Brooklyn Union also became the largest shareholder among 15 Northeastern utilities in a consortium called Boundary Gas, which began to import natural gas by pipeline displacement from Canada in late 1984. The company then initiated the formation of a partnership to construct the first major pipeline to transport gas from

Brooklyn Union works day and
night to answer the energy
needs of its customers.

The KIAC cogeneration plant supplies electricity, heating, and cooling to John F. Kennedy International Airport.

to offer flexible, reliable and competitively priced supplies of natural gas throughout the Northeastern United States. In 1996, the company launched a new marketing subsidiary, KeySpan Energy Services, headquartered in Stamford, Connecticut. KeySpan buys and sells gas, and provides transportation and related services to commercial and industrial customers in Brooklyn Union's traditional service area as well as throughout the greater New York metropolitan region. Mr. Catell said that KeySpan strengthens Brooklyn Union's "commitment to meet the challenges of a deregulated industry."

As it enters its second century of service, Brooklyn Union has reorganized itself, submitting to the New York State Public Service Commission a plan to form a holding company, of which Brooklyn Union would be the major subsidiary. Through this new holding company structure, the company expects to enhance its ability to compete effectively against other energy suppliers and have the organizational flexibility to act quickly to take advantage of timely market and investment opportunities.

Historically a forward-looking company, Brooklyn Union began to arm itself for the competitive demands of deregulation more than a decade ago when it set out to become what it called a new kind of company growing in different ways; one that would be more sharply focused on the wants and needs of its customers and one that also would reach out beyond its traditional boundaries. Where deregulation presents a threat to Brooklyn Union's established territories, it also presents the challenge of opportunities beyond those territories.

As part of Brooklyn Union's ongoing efforts to face the challenge of deregulation, in May of 1996, Mr. Catell was named Chairman and Chief Executive Officer, Craig G. Matthews was named President and Chief Operating Officer, and Helmut W. Peter was named Vice Chairman.

As Brooklyn Union enters its second century of service, it is operating in a vastly altered marketplace that presents daunting challenges—and exciting opportunities. Focusing on these opportunities of the company's evolving future, Brooklyn Union has adopted the motto: "It's not just where we've been—it's where we're heading." •••

Brooklyn Union aggressively seeks new markets and applications for natural gas, such as the YORK Triathlon heating/cooling system.

NEWSDAY
Linking Long Island Together
• • •

NEWSDAY, LONG ISLAND'S HOMEGROWN newspaper, links together the diverse chain of communities along this long, thin island. At the same time, its reputation has grown beyond the boundaries of the island. *Newsday* has become one of the top 10 newspapers in the country. In size and in editorial quality, *Newsday* ranks as a world class daily.

In the more than 55 years since *Newsday*'s birth, the newspaper has reached deep into the heart of Long Island communities by offering a rich variety of content and photographs and a deep commitment to serving as a leader addressing the critical issues faced by the island's communities.

Reaching beyond Long Island, *Newsday* has covered wars, genocide, disease, famine, and major political trends throughout the world. Some of these stories have included Pulitzer Prize-winning coverage of "ethnic cleansing" in Bosnia, coverage of contagious viruses around the world, and of a year in the life of parishoners of a Long Island Catholic Church. Today's readers can get the complete international, national, and local story in their own hometown paper.

Newsday was founded by newspaper family member Alicia Patterson in 1940, just prior to the years of extraordinary growth Long Island experienced in the post-WW II era. The newspaper grew as Long Island matured from a bedroom community dependent on New York City to an independent economic and cultural market. Many *Newsday* articles and editorials defined and spurred that growth.

Newsday, guided by Patterson until her death in 1963, started in a former automobile showroom in Hempstead, moved on to a plant in Garden City, and then in 1979, established its present home in Melville. Patterson's widower, Harry Guggenheim, and the Patterson heirs sold *Newsday* to Times Mirror Company, the owner of the Los Angeles Times and several other major urban newspapers. Today,

The *Newsday* Editorial Board meets regularly to discuss editorial page policy. The newspaper plays a vital leadership role in the communities of Long Island by suggesting solutions and offering its analysis and opinions of important international, national and local issues. From left are Phineas Fiske, editorial writer; Jim Klurfeld, editor of the editorial page; Publisher Raymond A. Jansen; Carol Richards, deputy editorial page editor; Alvin Bessent, editorial writer; Jim Lynn, editorial writer, and Adrian Peracchio, editorial writer.

Newsday is the second-largest newspaper in the Times Mirror group and the seventh largest in the country.

The heart and soul of *Newsday*, the news operation, under the direction of veteran reporter and editor Anthony Marro, gives readers depth as well as the broad scope of the news. From prize-winning international and national coverage, to top-flight sports stories and features, to neighborhood news of weddings and bicycle thefts, its coverage is unparalleled. *Newsday*'s coverage of important local, national, and international issues has garnered the paper more than a dozen Pulitzer Prizes as well as countless other prestigious awards.

Newsday's news coverage brings to readers discussion of critical issues affecting their lives. Major local stories have delved into Long Island's traffic bottlenecks, garbage congestion, taxation problems, breast cancer, political trends, education issues, race relations, and breaking news such as raging fires in eastern Long Island. In addition, the newsroom covers news and trends in New York City and Washington and several foreign countries. Through in-depth editorials,

Newsday staff member Gloria Sandler shows students on a tour of the newspaper how a news story is stored in *Newsday*'s vast computerized files.

At the end of a long night, newspapers come off a conveyor from the press, already folded and ready to be trucked to readers. Pressroom employees check the quality of the papers to make sure customers get good copies.

Newsday explores the significance of news issues and events to the everyday lives of its readers and points to solutions.

Newsday seeks dialogue with its readers. By phone, by letter, in person, in on-line electronic services, or in print, *Newsday* readers share their thoughts with the paper's staff. Publisher and Chief Executive Officer Raymond Jansen works closely with the editorial page editor, James Klurfeld, and the editorial board in *Newsday*'s efforts to educate, lead and stimulate decision makers and voters.

Newsday continuously seeks ways to expand that dialogue. The highly interactive Student Briefing Page draws the interest and enthusiasm of young readers who learn about current events in a lively exchange. *Newsday*'s Research Department regularly sponsors focus groups to find out what readers most enjoy and expect of their newspaper. Readers converse with the newspaper regarding questions about delivery, content, and services.

In another initiative to reach out to readers, *Newsday* inaugurated *Newsday* Direct, an on-line service which provides an electronic version of the daily newspaper on the computer screen along with extensive information on communities and access to years of *Newsday* stories.

Newsday also reaches out to Long Island through its speakers' bureau. Reporters, editors and other *Newsday* personnel visit nonprofit organizations, schools, and other community-based groups to speak on topics of interest to their members. In turn, many community groups tour *Newsday* for a firsthand glimpse of how the paper is produced. Groups and individuals visit *Newsday* to meet with the publisher and editorial board to present *Newsday* with their points of view or to attend one of the publisher's ongoing meetings with community groups.

Because of these and other activities, *Newsday* is an integral part of its community and is particularly committed to improving Long Island's economic and cultural quality of life. Reflecting the changing community it serves, *Newsday*'s editorial content is the product of a staff that is increasingly diverse. The paper is written and edited by people of many ethnic and cultural backgrounds. Reflecting other societal changes, *Newsday* is now completely a morning newspaper, available to its readers on the newsstands or at home before household members leave for their day's activities.

Also mirroring a society in which readers must receive diverse information in diverse ways, *Newsday*, through its subsidiary, Distribution Systems of America, improved its system for efficient delivery of preprinted materials and product samples to homes from the East River to the East End.

In 1985, *Newsday* decided to build on its strong readership foundation in Nassau and Suffolk counties and part of Queens. The New York *Newsday* edition was launched. Over the 10 years of its evolution, it brought the same type of in-depth coverage to the neighborhoods of New York City as the Long Island edition did to its neighborhoods. Because of its emphasis on comprehensive reporting of local news in addition to its commitment to sports, entertainment, and national and international news stories, New York *Newsday* created a new standard for urban coverage.

New York *Newsday* developed a devoted following of readers. However, by mid-1995 it became clear that the newspaper market in New York City could no longer sustain the paper's necessary growth. As a result, *Newsday* closed the New York edition and rededicated and refocused itself on its home territory of Nassau, Suffolk, and Queens counties.

Looking toward its future, *Newsday* continues to build on its already strong commitment to the kind of local, national, international, sports, and feature news coverage that its readers have come to rely on over the 56 years since Alicia Patterson embarked on her remarkable enterprise. Readers of *Newsday*, now and in the years to come, will experience new sections, improved delivery times and even more efficient, responsive customer services.

Newsday will continue to be a newspaper that changes with the communities it serves and provides the people in those communities with the information essential to their daily lives.   •••

Newsday reporters Bill Keeler, left, and Laurie Garrett celebrate upon learning they had won 1996 Pulitzer Prizes. Keeler won the Pulitzer Prize for Distinguished Beat Reporting for his series of a study of the religious life of a parish of St. Brigid's, a Roman Catholic Church in Westbury. Garrett won the Pulitzer Prize for Explanatory Reporting for her reports from Zaire on the outbreak of the deadly Ebola virus.

THE LONG ISLAND RAILROAD

Going Your Way

• • •

THE LONG ISLAND RAILROAD IS THE BUSIEST commuter railroad in the United States, and is an integral, and essential part of the Long Island economy. Every day, over 70 percent of commuters from Long Island to Manhattan take the railroad, making the Long Island Railroad (LIRR) critical to the mobility of everyone who lives in the region.

Every morning, between 6 and 10 AM, 100,000 passengers arrive in Manhattan's Penn Station aboard LIRR trains, the rough equivalent of a Boeing 747 unloading every 30 seconds. On an annual basis, the LIRR provides 73.6 million rides, and handles through Penn Station as many people as John F. Kennedy and LaGuardia Airports, combined.

The railroad's history and development are intimately tied to the history and development of Long Island. Similarly, its future, and its ability to adapt to the changing transportation needs of Long Islanders, will play a key role in the future of Long Island. Under the leadership of Thomas F. Prendergast, President, the LIRR is in the midst of a 5-year, $1.1 billion capital improvement program. The program is designed to improve the reliability and efficiency of the LIRR, to improve service for existing riders, and to enable the LIRR to expand its capacity to carry even more commuters.

ONLY 11 1/2 HOURS TO BOSTON

The Main Line of the LIRR was completed in 1844, long before even the idea of a suburb had been contemplated. It was designed, in fact, to be a new and faster way of traveling to Boston from Brooklyn. The new railroad terminated in Greenport, where travelers boarded a steamboat to cross Long Island Sound, and then another train for the rest of the trip to Boston. Total time: 11 1/2 hours.

During the railroad-building era that followed, there were several competing railroads on the Island, like the South Side Railroad, and the Flushing Railroad. There were fare wars, excess trains, bankruptcies and foreclosures until the railroad was finally unified in the early 1880's. The locations of stations were dictated by which land was donated by local communities. The dream of service into Manhattan finally became reality in 1910, after the Pennsylvania Railroad constructed a tunnel under the East River. Completion of this link, and nearly simultaneous electrification, spurred the development of real estate along the branches of the railroad, in turn leading to the LIRR's role as a commuter railroad.

In the 1950's, New York State took the first steps toward government ownership of the railroad. In 1968, the Metropolitan Transportation Authority was created, and today, the LIRR is an MTA agency.

"Now, the LIRR brings suburban residents safely to and from jobs in New York City, and takes city dwellers to the beautiful beaches and attractions of Long Island," says President Prendergast. "We look forward to playing a major role in Long Island's continued prosperity and development."

THE "ONE-SEAT RIDE" & OTHER IMPROVEMENTS

As everyone who lives on Long Island knows only too well, getting around is not easy. Over half of all vehicle delays in New York State, measured in vehicle hours, occur on Long Island. Part of the LIRR's on-going mission is to contribute to the economic well-being of Long Island, and to its quality of life, by offering a convenient, economical alternative to driving.

Thanks to federal and state funding, the LIRR has completed, and is still at work on projects to significantly improve its service. One major project has been the renovation of the Penn Station terminal, at a cost of $190 million. Riders now enjoy climate-controlled, well-

A New Front Door. The LIRR's new 34th St. entrance in Manhattan has won numerous design awards. Built to be functional as well as attractive, the entrance pavilion neatly disguises climate control workings for the station. Photo credit: Mike Kamber

Friendly Faces. LIRR conductors are happy to answer customer questions. These commuters are waiting for a train at the Railroad's recently completed Ronkonkoma Hub station, where coordinated bus service is readily available. Photo credit: Ilene Kaufman Messina

Sunrise on the LIRR. As the day dawns in Mineola, early morning commuters on the Port Jefferson Branch can relax, read the morning paper or catch up on their sleep as the LIRR's new Dual Mode engines and bi-level coaches express their way to Manhattan. Photo credit: Ilene Kaufman Messina

lighted waiting areas. Electronic sign boards, located throughout the station, make it easy to find trains. A new entrance from 34th street, as well as new stairways escalators, and many other amenities, have received high marks from riders.

The LIRR has also involved commuters in another major improvement: replacement of its aging diesel fleet. Beginning late in 1997, the LIRR will begin taking delivery on 114 new bi-level coaches that will feature interiors designed with the help of commuters. They will have wider aisles, more comfortable seats, and better lighting. On the Port Jefferson branch, six new dual-mode locomotives will offer commuters a "one-seat ride"—no need to change trains to board an electric for the finish of the commute to Manhattan. The Montauk and Oyster Bay branches will also offer the dual-mode locomotives.

Because the usage of Penn Station is nearly at capacity, the LIRR is also studying the possibility of adding another Manhattan terminal, on the East Side. By using the existing, but now empty, 63rd Street tunnel, the LIRR could add another 8 to 10 million rider trips per year, and offer added convenience to customers who work on Manhattan's East Side.

At the same time, the LIRR has been working to revitalize its freight business. A recently-completed study recommended privatization as the best way to grow the business and make it more competitive with trucking.

REVERSE COMMUTING & OFF-PEAK TRAVEL

While west-bound commuters rely heavily on the LIRR, those commuting to the East in the morning are often unable to find a convenient train. This situation exists because of the physical limitations of the LIRR's track capacity. Within these limitations, however, the LIRR has worked with local bus operators to coordinate timetables and maximize its schedule of reverse-commute service.

The LIRR has also developed innovative marketing programs to attract riders on weekends and during non-peak commutation times. A Family Fare lets kids between ages 5 and 11 ride for only 50 cents; kids under age 5 ride free. Tickets purchased from the LIRR for major attractions in Manhattan such as Radio City Music Hall and the Ringling Brothers Barnum & Bailey Circus include free round-trip service on the train.

Comfortable parlor cars take weekend pleasure seekers to the Hamptons and Montauk Point. New York City residents bound for Jones Beach and Robert Moses State Park can pick up coordinated bus service from nearby railroad stations. Tourists can use the LIRR for tours of Long Island that are guaranteed free of traffic jams. Long Island vineyards, museums, and famous homes and gardens can be toured via the LIRR. •••

Heading East. An LIRR engineer operates a diesel train through Queens toward Long Island, leaving behind Manhattan and its dramatic skyline. Photo credit: Ilene Kaufman Messina

LONG ISLAND LIGHTING COMPANY
Fueling Long Island's Economic Growth
• • •

THE LONG ISLAND LIGHTING COMPANY (LILCO) IS widely known as the source of the natural gas and electricity that powers the region's homes, schools and businesses. LILCO's more than one million customers are in Nassau and Suffolk Counties and on the Rockaway Peninsula in Queens County, a service area of 1,230 square miles with a population of 2.7 million. A customer-driven organization, LILCO's more than 5,000 employees are dedicated to providing Long Island with the best possible electric, gas and consumer-based programs.

What is perhaps less known is the role the utility plays as a partner to Long Island's business community by initiating, developing and administering economic development programs for local businesses.

According to Bruce E. Germano, LILCO's manager for major accounts and electric business services, the company's overall goal in its economic development initiatives is to maintain the competitiveness of the Long Island business environment and to work with others in the economic development community to assist in the development of current and future businesses.

Recognizing the importance of manufacturing to any regional economy, LILCO has put programs in place that work to maintain Long Island's core manufacturing base. The central issue addressed by many of LILCO's programs, said Germano, is "the effective use of energy and its importance to the bottom line." Through

these energy programs, LILCO identifies a company's energy usage needs and then packages its products and services in a way that will fulfill the company's energy needs at the lowest possible cost. But Germano emphasized that LILCO brings more to the table than abatements and rate incentives. He explained: "We bring our energy skills and expertise to keep their costs as low as possible so that the company can increase its competitiveness and profitability."

Working in partnership with the economic development community—agencies on the state, county and town levels—LILCO offers a broad-based range of services that constitute a one-stop shopping facility for companies that are seeking programs of energy conservation or working capital to diversify or expand.

Among the tools offered by LILCO are rate incentives for companies who complete New York State's Industrial Effectiveness Program. Germano noted that this program was designed to help companies, most particularly manufacturers, become more competitive by assisting them to institute more cost-effective operations. At the invitation of a local business, a NYS/LILCO team conducts an organizational assessment, identifying areas to be improved. According to Germano, "we provide the remediation steps, then work with the manufacturer to develop these steps and provide the working capital through state grants." Additionally, LILCO also offers these businesses abatements on their electric rates.

Energy assessments for new construction projects are among LILCO's many services to Long Island's businesses.

A LILCO high-voltage crew member prepares to extend a transmission line.

Of the more than 200 Long Island companies which have participated in various LILCO programs, Germano cited one, Dayton T. Brown, an environmental testing organization tied to the defense industry. According to Germano, the company successfully increased its market share as a result of participating in a LILCO program.

The NYS Industrial Effectiveness Program, along with LILCO's other programs to serve business and industry, operate under the umbrella of the Long Island Partnership. The Partnership is an Island-wide organization that was formed to provide full service to businesses seeking to remain or expand on Long Island as well as to companies from other regions which may be exploring relocation to Long Island.

With its stress on building programs that stimulate Long Island's business growth, LILCO examines how it can best assist companies to diversify in the face of shrinking markets. Defense and manufacturing, once core strengths of the Long Island economy, have greatly diminished in recent years. Therefore, LILCO looks toward how the strengths that remain, especially Long Island's high-tech community and well-educated labor force, can serve as the springboard for both the diversification of present businesses and the development of future business sectors.

One of LILCO's economic development partners, the Long Island Development Corporation, is a quasi-public body that assists defense related companies to diversify. The Corporation administers the Small Business Authority (SBA) loans that allow for expansion and diversification. Other LILCO diversification efforts are centered around Long Island's fishing industry in the face of new legislation which displaces many of those in the industry.

Another role LILCO plays is that of the facilitator. Companies relocating to Long Island find that they can turn to LILCO to organize the crucial contacts among banks, real estate companies and telecommunications services that will get them up and running as a part of the local business community.

LILCO further facilitates contacts through its Business Resource Guide which lists sources of funding for businesses. Among those sources are the small business development centers, industrial development agencies, the Long Island Development Corporation, and various university-based business assistance centers.

LILCO is an active participant in revitalizing the region's disadvantaged areas through the programs available for businesses located in designated Economic Development Zones in North Bellport, Central Islip and Far Rockaway. Businesses in communities so designated are eligible for a range of programs that have been designed to aggressively stimulate economic growth. Among these programs are energy rate abatements, wage tax credits and investment tax credits.

In conjunction with the incubators at Stony Brook and Brookhaven, LILCO is a partner in programs planned to assist start-up businesses. Once a given start up "graduates" from its incubator status, LILCO provides electric rate reductions and guides the company toward other programs that serve to nurture its growth.

LILCO works with companies that range from these small start ups right through the spectrum to major Long Island corporations such as Symbol Technologies, Nature's Bounty and Acclaim Entertainment. While "there's no company we wouldn't try to assist," Germano did stress that "there are criteria for identifying companies that LILCO assists in seeking out grants."

Describing the nature of LILCO's comprehensive range of economic development initiatives, Bruce Germano said that "all these programs reflect LILCO's awareness of the diverse type of community we operate in, the sophisticated needs of our business community, and our commitment to providing these businesses with the tools for economic growth on Long Island."   •••

NEW YORK POWER AUTHORITY
Hidden Competitive Edge for Long Island Business
• • •

POWER. SOME OF NEW YORK'S LOWEST-COST power. Power for world-class, Long Island-based companies to compete.

That's what the New York Power Authority (NYPA) offers a growing number of businesses. On Long Island today, some 35 companies receive low-cost power from NYPA, helping to create or preserve about 20,000 jobs. Overall, NYPA supplies more than 20 percent of the Island's electricity needs. Some of the electricity flows to the Long Island Lighting Company (Lilco) for resale, without profit, to its customers. Community-owned electric systems in Freeport, Greenport and Rockville Centre are other recipients.

NYPA is the nation's largest non-federal public power organization and unique among New York electric utilities. Without a franchise territory or "captive" customers, NYPA has to be a low-cost provider to attract and keep customers. Providing about a quarter of the state's electricity, NYPA operates 12 generating plants—from Holtsville in Suffolk County to the Niagara Frontier—and more than 1,400 miles of transmission lines. A non-profit, public-benefit corporation, NYPA does not use tax revenues or state credit. It funds construction of its projects through sale of bonds to private investors and repays the bonds with revenues from operations.

NYPA has always been operated as a disciplined private sector business, well prepared to compete in a regulated market now moving rapidly in the free market direction taken by the telephone companies a decade ago.

Gov. Franklin D. Roosevelt and the state Legislature created the New York Power Authority in 1931 to harness the hydroelectric potential of the St. Lawrence River. Its founders envisioned that NYPA would provide a benchmark for measuring the prices and services of the private utilities.

Today, NYPA continues to ensure that the state gets the maximum return from its resources, while meeting legislative requirements for the sale of power. Under those guidelines, NYPA sells electricity to job-producing businesses, encouraging them to locate, expand or retain their New York State operations; to government agencies, including the City of New York and the Metropolitan Transportation Authority; to the state's 7 investor-owned utilities; to New York's 51 municipal and rural cooperative electric systems; and to 7 neighboring states, as required by federal law.

POWER TO COMPETE

NYPA awards companies lower-priced electricity in exchange for pledges to create or preserve specified numbers of jobs. Statewide, NYPA power helps to keep more than 150,000 New Yorkers on the job.

Among Long Island companies receiving its electricity:

• Software leader Computer Associates International (CAI), which moved 900 employees from three sites in Garden City to its new Islandia world headquarters, constructed in the early 1990s, and today employs 1,500. The power allotment, which saves the firm more than $1,750,000 annually, was a major factor in CAI's decision to build its headquarters on Long Island.

• B. Dalton Bookseller, Inc., was encouraged by a NYPA allocation to relocate its financial operations from Minnesota to Westbury in 1991, bringing some 300 jobs to Long Island.

• In May 1996, Upton-based Brookhaven National Laboratory received an increased allocation of electricity to energize expansion projects and create up to 500 new jobs through the year 2000. The prestigious national research facility, a NYPA customer since 1982, currently employs more than 4,000 at its sprawling 5,200-acre Suffolk County complex. The new allotment is for development of the laboratory's Relativistic Heavy Ion Collider, which will be one of the world's premier nuclear physics research facilities when commissioned in 1999.

• Melville-based Newsday Inc. committed in 1992 to preserving more than 2,400

Bright overhead lights match the mood in a third grade reading class at East Patchogue's Verne Critz Elementary School. Installed under NYPA's High Efficiency Lighting Program (HELP) in more than 300 Long Island public schools, the new lights are noticeably brighter and can save up to 25 percent on lighting costs—or more than $175,000 annually—for Critz Elementary and six additional district schools.

Natural gas-generated power from NYPA's Richard M. Flynn Plant in Holtsville flows to the Long Island Lighting Co. for resale, without a profit, to its customers. The 135,600 kilowatt facility will help ensure adequate power for Nassau and Suffolk counties well into the next century.

jobs in return for a power allocation that has since saved Long Island's daily newspaper about $340,000 annually. The following year, Newsday received an additional allocation to power a new data processing center, protecting existing jobs and creating 51 new positions.

- General Instrument Corp. (GIC) of Westbury received an allotment in 1993 in return for creating 19 new positions and investing $2.5 million to expand its production of silicon materials for electronics equipment. GIC employs 44 people in Westbury.

- Nature's Bounty Inc. of Bohemia, a vitamin and dietary supplement manufacturer, added 30 positions to an existing base of 705 jobs in return for a 1994 allotment.

- A 1995 allocation induced Olsten Corporation, an international leader in providing temporary health care and office staffing services, to keep its world headquarters on Long Island and create jobs. As part of its agreement with NYPA, Olsten consolidated three facilities into its Melville headquarters, saving more than 160 jobs and setting a course for job expansion.

FLYNN PLANT—COMPETITIVE BY DESIGN

Some of the NYPA electricity serving Long Island is home-grown. NYPA's Richard M. Flynn Power Plant in Holtsville, which began operation in May 1994, is the first generating facility constructed under a New York State program requiring utilities to solicit competitive bids for new plants. Winning the construction contract against 20 other entrants, NYPA negotiated a 20-year pact to supply the plant's electricity to Lilco. The combined-cycle facility primarily uses natural gas, by far the cleanest fossil fuel, and recovers the hot exhaust normally lost to generate 50 percent more power. The Flynn

Scientists inspect a 2 1/2-mile-circumference Relativistic Heavy Ion Collider (RHIC) under construction at Upton's Brookhaven National Laboratory, a NYPA customer since 1982. A cornerstone of the U.S. nuclear physics program, the RHIC will create matter believed present at the beginning of the universe. Lower-cost NYPA electricity helps keep Brookhaven one of Long Island's largest employers.

plant is Long Island's most fuel-efficient generating unit.

SOUND STRATEGY: SOUND CABLE

NYPA's Sound Cable Project, running beneath Long Island Sound from Westchester County to Long Island, increases energy supplies, stabilizes rates and helps create and keep jobs on Long Island. The 26.3-mile underground-underwater transmission line nearly doubled the capacity of Long Island's transmission ties to neighboring electric systems, creating a path for up to 600,000 kilowatts of less-expensive power from upstate New York and Canada. In keeping with its good-neighbor tradition, NYPA provided more than $1 million in grants for community improvements along the cable's route. Uses of the grants ranged from purchasing emergency rescue equipment to funding production of educational videotapes about the Sound for school use.

HELP FOR SCHOOLS, GOVERNMENTS, HOSPITALS

Through its nationally recognized High Efficiency Lighting Program (HELP), NYPA helps public schools and other government facilities on Long Island reduce their electricity bills and energy use. HELP will save Long Island recipients more than $13 million annually when the program's lighting, air-conditioning and other improvements are fully implemented. Projects have been completed, are under way or are planned at more than 300 of the Island's public schools; Nassau and Suffolk community colleges; SUNY campuses at Farmingdale, Westbury and Stony Brook; state office buildings in Massapequa and Happauge; and the Village of Garden City.

POWER TO COMPETE TOMORROW

As the electric utility industry advances toward open competition, NYPA has adopted flexible new strategies and services tailored to individual user needs to meet the challenges of a new electricity market. Whatever the shape of the energy future, it is certain that NYPA will continue to work in partnership with Long Island businesses to build a stronger, more resilient regional economy. •••

CABLEVISION SYSTEMS CORPORATION
A History of Quality and Innovation
• • •

FOUNDED ON LONG ISLAND IN 1973, CABLEVISION Systems Corporation is one of the world's leading telecommunications companies. Now headquartered in Woodbury, this multi-faceted company is poised for growth into the 21st Century in all areas of television and communications technology.

Led by the father-and-son team of Chairman Charles F. Dolan, and Chief Executive Officer James L. Dolan, Cablevision is the nation's sixth largest operator of cable television systems. The company serves nearly 3 million cable television customers in 19 states, with major operations clustered in the Boston, Cleveland, and New York Metropolitan areas.

Cablevision Systems Corp. was established by the senior Mr. Dolan, who built the country's first urban cable television system in New York City during the early 1960's. After selling that Manhattan operation, Mr. Dolan began constructing the Long Island cable television system which has grown to serve more than 650,000 customers, and today stands as the second largest single cable system in the nation.

**Charles F. Dolan, Chairman, (left)
and James L. Dolan, Chief Executive Officer
Cablevision Systems Corporation**

Through its subsidiary Rainbow Programming Holdings, Inc., Cablevision owns and manages some of the most valued and critically acclaimed television program networks, including American Movie Classics, Bravo, and the SportsChannel Regional Network. These networks are offered not only to Cablevision customers, but through affiliation agreements with other television service providers in the U.S. and abroad.

More than 7,000 Cablevision employees today implement the company's original guiding vision: to use telecommunications systems to bring consumers quality television programming and a choice of value-added services unmatched by its competitors.

Cablevision has been responsible for numerous industry landmarks, including:
• Launching the nation's first

24-hour local cable news service—News 12 Long Island in 1986;
• Creating the first regional sports network—SportsChannel;
• Creating the first network exclusively devoted to films by independent producers—The Independent Film Channel;
• Establishing on Long Island the first local exchange telephone company owned by a cable television system operator, Cablevision Lightpath, Inc.

Cablevision Lightpath, a subsidiary of Cablevision Systems Corp., currently offers a full array of telephone services to business customers on Long Island.

Cablevision's strategic approach to the new age of convergence of the telephone, personal computer and television is to bring customers everything they use and enjoy on their television, computer and telephone in the fastest and most appealing way possible.

Cablevision has also focused on the unique value that local programming holds for its customers, and offers geographically distinct local news services through separate News12 operations serving Long Island, Westchester, Connecticut and New Jersey. A further refinement of the concept is Neighborhood News 12, which focuses on a single town's news information, and is currently offered in townships and villages in Nassau County, as well as EXTRA HELP, an interactive educational channel devoted to fostering self-help and lifetime learning for adults and children.

In partnership with ITT Corp., Cablevision owns and operates the Madison Square Garden Properties, which include the arena complex as well as the NBA New York Nicks, the NHL New York Rangers and the MSG television network.

Cablevision has set its sights on the future, ensuring that customers on Long Island and beyond will enjoy the very best in telecommunications choice into the 21st century. • • •

TRIGEN-NASSAU ENERGY CORPORATION
The Right Energy, The Right Company
• • •

THE TRIGEN-NASSAU ENERGY CORPORATION, WITH its parent company, Trigen Energy Corporation, is the largest independent owner, operator and developer of Community Energy Systems in North America. From its operation in Mitchel Field, Trigen-Nassau provides clean, efficient heating and cooling to multiple buildings, and sells electricity to the Long Island Lighting Company. All of these operations are part of a "trigeneration" process that offers significant financial and environmental benefits not only to its customers and Nassau County, but to all Long Islanders as well.

In addition, Trigen-Nassau offers hospitals, universities and large industrial complexes the opportunity to out-source their energy facilities operations and management. After a study, Trigen will offer to purchase, upgrade and automate a potential customer's energy facilities, and then to sell back the total energy at a reduction from what the facility had been spending, totally eliminating future capital expenditures, all part of a long-term agreement. Trigen takes on ownership responsibilities for the energy facilities, allowing the customer to concentrate on their core business.

Trigen-Nassau Energy Corporation was formed in 1987 to take over the operation of Nassau County's Central Utility Plant, which the County had built to supply district heating and cooling services to Mitchel Field properties.

Trigen's proposal was consistent with its corporate mission, which is to "heat and cool multiple buildings (and industrial processes) using one half or less of the fuel and producing one half or less of the pollution associated with conventional energy conversion."

In 1991, at a cost of $85 million on the site of the Central Utility Plant, Trigen-Nassau completed construction of a 57 megawatt, gas-fired cogeneration facility. This produces electricity sold to LILCO and is the energy source for the cooling and heating supplied to the Long Island Marriott Hotel, Nassau County's Medical Center and Correctional Facility, the Nassau Veteran's Memorial Coliseum and Nassau Community College. To reach the medical and correctional centers, Trigen-Nassau constructed a 2.7 mile steam pipe and return pipe for condensate. Trigen-Nassau also took over operation of the power plant at the Medical Center.

CLEANER AIR FOR LONG ISLAND

Trigen-Nassau's fully-automated operations eliminate the need to burn 17 million gallons of oil or oil equivalent annually by combining electric generation, thermal and chilled water generation. This substantially reduces emissions of carbon dioxide, and since the plant's fuel is natural gas, another major pollutant, sulfur dioxide, is virtually eliminated as well.

Trigen-Nassau Energy Corporation at Mitchel Field.

The plant is staffed 24 hours per day by at least 2 trained operators, and backed up by a management team of power plant specialists. The plant has consistently delivered steam, hot water or chilled water to its thermal customers, and its electric generation has been available 95 percent of the time.

Trigen-Nassau Energy Corporation and its relationship with Nassau County is a successful example of outsourcing and privatization. In a study performed by Ernst & Young in 1990, it is estimated that the county will save $90 million over the life of its 25-year contract with Trigen-Nassau.

Trigen-Nassau's parent company, Trigen Energy Corp., has annual sales in excess of $200 million, and is publicly-traded on the New York Stock Exchange (Symbol: TGN). It has operating companies in 12 cities besides Nassau County, and serves more than 1,500 customers.
• • •

Trigen-Nassau Energy Corporation's cogen/central utility plant cogenerates steam and electric energy, supplying heating and cooling to its customers through a network of underground pipes.

PREMIER CAR RENTAL
Where Service is Everything
• • •

WHEN GEORGE WRIGHT, ALAN HERZOG AND Lynn Dutney founded Premier Car Rental on Long Island, they didn't anticipate being number 61 on *Inc. Magazine's* "500 Fastest Growing Privately Owned Companies in America" in only six years. But as a result of vision-ary management, industry experience, and strategic financing, that is exactly what happened.

"You know who was number 61, ten years ago?" asked Wright. "Microsoft."

ABOUT THE INDUSTRY

Premier Car Rental specializes in the insurance replacement portion of the automobile rental indus-try, and succeeds by establishing solid relationships with insurance agents, car dealers, corporate accounts and body shops. It provides them with replacement vehicles for individuals whose cars are temporarily off the road because of accidents, break-downs, or manufacturer-ordered repairs.

Now nationwide, Premier operates on Long Island out of 14 prime locations with 1,500 vehi-cles. It rents a wide variety of makes and models including vans and sport utility vehicles of such manufacturers as General Motors, Ford, Nissan, Toyota and Chrysler. Every car is less than 14 months old and is delivered to, and picked up from the customer personally by Premier's professional staff.

"Our focus on providing exceptional customer service has made us what we are today," said Wright. "Our managers' hands-on, shirt-sleeve attitude, and the teamwork of the entire office, are critical."

"An entry level position with Premier is manager-trainee," contin-ued Wright. "Therefore, all of our employees learn this business from the ground up, and are always on the front line with customers. We emphasize training and use incen-tive programs to motivate, and we recruit individuals from colleges and universities who are energetic, hard-working and career-oriented."

George Wright
Sr. Vice President and Co-Founder
Premier Car Rental

THE ELEMENTS OF SUCCESS

Controlled, stable growth has been an important ingredient of Premier's success. The company now has an overall fleet of 10,000 cars and expects that figure to increase to 15,000 by 1997, when sales should also top the $100 million mark.

"All without a significant investment in advertising," added Wright, a native Long Islander who graduated from Hofstra University (Hempstead). "Word-of-mouth is our chosen advertising strategy, relationship marketing is our strength, and customer satisfaction is definitely our hallmark."

Continued Wright: "Dealers, agents and corporate accounts depend on us to keep their customers happy, and that's our ultimate objec-tive. One person tells another about how well Premier treated them, and when that friend needs a rental, they call us first—and last."

That philosophy brings not only cus-tomers, but high quality personnel to Premier as well. Because of its effective training pro-gram, and the potential career opportunities offered by the firm, Premier's managers are highly motivated to achieve.

Offices open daily at 7 AM, and the company is opening new markets constantly with at least 100 cars each time. Premier pro-motes from within when it opens new offices, and with its aggressive expansion schedule, managers who prove themselves can advance rel-atively quickly.

In addition, as soon as employees are promoted to area man-agers, they receive stock in the company; on other levels, bonus-es are granted based on growth and profit.

Who did you say provided your rental car? From now on make it Premier. •••

Premier soars under the lead-ership of (Left to Right): Lynn Dutney, Vice President and CFO; Alan Herzog, President and CEO; and Wright.

LONG ISLAND MACARTHUR AIRPORT
The Island's Convenient Air Travel Gateway
• • •

LONG ISLAND MACARTHUR AIRPORT IS THE ONLY airport in Nassau and Suffolk Counties that provides year-round commercial flights on major airlines. More than one million leisure and business travelers a year take advantage of its convenient location, ample parking and intimate terminal to fly non-stop to Florida, Washington D.C., Chicago, Boston, Philadelphia, Pittsburgh, and Albany, and to make connections to most other major U.S. cities.

Located on Veteran's Memorial Highway, the Airport and the Foreign Trade Zone on its site have also been a "magnet for industrial and economic growth" according to Bill Mannix, Islip Town's Economic Development Director. The Bohemia/Ronkonkoma area where the Airport is situated is one of the Island's top employment centers.

As of the last census, 26,000 people were employed there, working in offices that comprise one-quarter of all the office space in Islip. Of the Island's 10 industrial parks with more than 1 million square feet of space, two—Airport International Plaza and MacArthur Center—are located near the airport. Another five parks with more than 250,000 square feet of space each are also located nearby.

The Airport came into being in 1942, when a Resolution by the Islip Town Board named it in honor of General Douglas MacArthur. The Airport was built originally for under $1 million, and the present terminal was completed in 1966. Under the leadership of manager Al Werner, also the Town of Islip's Commissioner of Transportation and a board member of the Metropolitan Transportation Authority, the Airport terminal building is about to undergo a major renovation that will improve the baggage claim area, airline counters, concession and other operational areas.

Each day, 100 commercial flights use the Airport's four runways, two of which are lighted, and one of which is both lighted and equipped with an instrument landing system. Commercial airlines serving the airport include American, Business Express (Delta Connection/Northwest Airlink), Carnival, United Express and USAIR.

Surveys have shown that for businesses located nearby the Airport offers an important advantage. Enterprises that require heavy business travel by their sales representatives and executives, or who receive frequent visits from customers, clients or business associates, find the easy access to the Airport important in avoiding loss of productive time. Sixty-eight percent of nearby businesses use the Airport more than four times a year, and 41 percent use it more than once a month.

Adding to the Airport's appeal to businesses is its Foreign Trade Zone. Just one hour by car from New York City, the Zone has 435,000 square feet of office, warehouse and industrial space on 52 acres of land. It is outside the jurisdiction of the United States Bureau of Customs. That means considerable cash flow benefits for importers and exporters, since duties are paid only on goods sold on the domestic market, and only after the goods actually leave the Zone.

Among the major companies located near the Airport and Zone are Nature's Bounty and Twin Labs, both of which make natural vitamin supplements, and Symbol Technologies, the world's leading designer and manufacturer of bar code scanners. • • •

Photo courtesy of Aerographics Corporation.

CHAPTER 10

MANUFACTURING
& DISTRIBUTION

Photo by Scott Levy.

OLYMPUS AMERICA INC.
Touching Lives in Many Ways
• • •

Sidney Braginsky, President of Olympus America Inc.

FOR CONSUMERS OLYMPUS America is widely known for its handy, easy-to-use 35 mm cameras. But in the scientific, industrial and medical communities, Olympus is esteemed for its endoscopic products and high-tech digital information equipment. As evidence of how far Olympus has traveled from its one-time core business of cameras and microscopes, Sidney Braginsky, President of Olympus America, noted that fully two thirds of the company's business is now in healthcare products. It is Olympus innovations in endoscopy that have enabled rapid advances in minimally invasive surgical techniques. For patients, replacement of the scalpel with slender fiber-optic tubes by Olympus translates to less painful post-operative recoveries, shorter hospital stays, and lower medical costs. Although Olympus is the world's leading manufacturer of cameras, endoscopes and microscopes, few are aware of the depth and breadth of the company's diverse lines of products and complete systems.

Olympus America Inc. is the Western Hemisphere business center for Olympus Optical Co., Ltd. of Tokyo. The parent company was founded in 1919 as a manufacturer of microscopes. Subsequently, Olympus entered the visual, medical and information processing fields. Today, under the global leadership of Masatoshi Kishimoto, Olympus Optical is a leader in the development of optic, opto-electronic, opto-mechatronic and precision technologies. Major products manufactured and marketed by Olympus include 35 mm cameras. Microcassette recorders, medical and industrial endoscopes, microscopes and clinical analyzers. The company also produces magneto-optical disk data storage systems, ion deposition printers, and environment-friendly cleaning solvents and chemical cleaning systems.

The history of Olympus in the United States dates back to 1968 when the Tokyo company sent some of its top executives over to study the feasibility of establishing an American subsidiary. Lured to Long Island by its educated and well-trained workforce, cosmopolitan culture and pleasant living conditions as well as the region's excellent air and sea transportation links and proximity to New York City's financial markets, Olympus Corporation of America was established in Lake Success to sell and service scientific equipment, microscopes and endoscopes. In 1978 Olympus Camera Corporation was established as a second subsidiary in Woodbury to sell, market and service 35 mm cameras. Five years later the two subsidiaries combined to form Olympus Corporation. To herald the unified mission and identity of all Olympus business interests in the United States, Canada and Latin America, Olympus Corporation changed its name to Olympus America Inc. on April 1, 1993. The corporate management and management of all of its divisions were brought together in 1995 when Olympus America moved into its new 270,000 square foot corporate headquarters in Melville. In addition to the modern Melville headquarters, Olympus maintains a 94,000 square foot distribution center in Woodbury and a major repair center in San Jose, California as well as ten customer service offices

Olympus America's New Image Cafe.

Dining out on the Patio of the New Image Cafe.

throughout the United States.

As Olympus settled into its Long Island home, the company began to make clear that it intended to be a responsible corporate citizen. Reflective of the Olympus global philosophy that stresses the importance of integrating the company into society and sharing its values, Mr. Braginsky said that Olympus becomes involved in "whatever will position us as a good neighbor." He cited education, healthcare and culture as among the company's major philanthropic interests. Mr. Braginsky serves as chairman of the Long Island Association's committee on high technology.

Olympus sponsors internships with many local colleges and universities and is an active supporter of the proposed Long Island Museum for Science and Technology. Under the banner of Long Island Volunteer Enterprise, Olympus employees have been involved in community betterment projects such as the cleaning of the beachfront at Target Rock Wildlife Preserve and the painting of living quarters at the Little Flower Children's Center.

Other organizations which have received support from Olympus or its employees include the Association for Handicapped and Retarded Children, the Interfaith Nutrition Network, the American Heart Association, the American Cancer Society, the March of Dimes, and St. Charles Hospital.

In 1996 Olympus reorganized its present divisions into two new groups: The Scientific Products Group which encompasses health care systems and industrial systems, and the Digital & Image Systems Group which incorporates the consumer products division and Olympus Image Systems, Inc. Additionally, Olympus established a new division to serve Latin America.

SCIENTIFIC PRODUCTS GROUP

Within the Scientific Products Group is the Olympus endoscope business. In 1968 the world's first gastrocamera with fiberscope was introduced by Olympus into the United States. Today Olympus is the world leader in endoscopy, holding an 80 percent market share globally for flexible endoscopes.

Olympus strengths in video imaging, flexible fiberoptic and rigid telescopes technology have provided integrated systems for non-invasive endoscopic diagnostic and surgical procedures. As the country's only full-line supplier of instrumentation for minimally invasive surgery, gastrointestinal endoscopy, bronchoscopy, computer networking systems and medical software, Olympus is on the leading edge of containing health care costs by providing the products and methods that reduce the number of conventional surgeries and the length of hospital stays.

And there's far more on the horizon. According to Masatoshi Kishimoto, President, Olympus Optical Co., Ltd., Olympus intends "to take minimally invasive surgery to a new level" He explained: "We are researching and developing micro machines in tandem with virtual reality technology that will revolutionize and expand the scope of minimally invasive surgery procedure to accomplish what can only be done through open surgery today."

Olympus endoscopic products also play a significant role in the diagnostic capability of physicians to detect early cancers. For instance, Olympus sigmoidoscopes have been critical in achieving a 14 percent decrease in colorectol cancers since 1979.

By aggressively expanding into new areas such as plastic surgery, ENT, and cardiovascular surgery, Olympus has maintained its place at the forefront of advances in medical technology.

The first fiberscope in space—the Olympus Industrial Fiberscope—was used by the crew of the Space Shuttle Atlantis for on-board maintenance. Today, remote visual inspection equipment by Olympus is the most frequently used method for pre-flight safety inspection for both commercial and military aircraft.

Olympus Family Day.

screening of more than 85 percent of North America's blood supply. Within the Scientific Products Group the Clinical Instrument business unit manufactures and markets automated high speed blood typing machines, fluid chemistry

Within Industrial Systems, the Endoscope Division fulfills the inspection needs of many industries. This group's products permit internal or remote visual inspection of machinery, power turbines, aircraft, vital pipelines, manufactured parts and structures without disassembly.

The United States Customs Service and the U.S. Coast Guard use Olympus industrial fiberscopes and videoimagescopes to search for drugs and contraband. The automotive industry initially utilized Olympus borescopes as a research tool and today has expanded their use as a valuable diagnostic tool for many local dealers and repair shops. For the motorist the use of Olympus diagnostic products serves to reduce and even eliminate some repair expenses.

Microscopes and histology products are the specialty of the Olympus Precision Instrument unit, part of the Scientific Products Group. Three-quarters of a century ago, microscopes were the parent company's first product. Today's compound microscopes and steroscopic microscopes are the result of giant leaps in this technology by Olympus. More hospitals in the United States use Olympus microscopes in their clinical laboratories than any other brand. Olympus microscopes are also used in fertility clinics to study in vitro fertilization, cell fusion, electrophysiogical and genetic research. Whether used for biological or industrial purposes, these precision optical instruments can be light microscopes or the laser scanning type.

Olympus is also America's largest supplier of student microscopes for colleges and universities. Although just recently introduced, the company's highly sophisticated, motorized and automated photo-research microscope has already gained significant market share.

The Olympus line of histology products includes microfomes and forges for drawing micropipettes.

So predominant is the Olympus line of histology products that the company's instrumentations are utilized in the analysis and

analyzers, and a complete line of chemistry reagents. The market for these products are hospitals, clinics, research and commercial laboratories, as well as the Department of Defense. Each year more than one billion clinical chemistry tests are performed on Olympus chemistry analyzers. These include chemistry panels, thyroid panels, therapeutic drug monitoring and assays for abused drugs.

Olympus clinical analyzers are known for their reliability, efficiency and cost effectiveness. They serve to reduce the cost of medical diagnostics by lowering expensive labor costs in the laboratory. Further, as the manufacturer of the chemical reagent systems used in these analyzers, Olympus is deeply involved in bio-medical research and is positioned to incorporate the newest procedures and diagnostic discoveries into its systems for reliable, rapid-response testing.

DIGITAL & IMAGE SYSTEMS GROUP

Now part of the new Digital & Image Systems Group, the Consumer Products business unit is a leading supplier of high- quality photographic and consumer electronic products. The 35mm cameras, binoculars, Microcassettes tape recorders, transcribers and dictation equipment produced by Olympus are valued for their compact size, light weight and award-winning designs.

A pioneer in the development of easy-to-use cameras, Olympus products have made possible the capturing of visual memories and the widespread enjoyment of photography. The company's Infinity Stylus series, the most popular, fully-featured series of cameras available today, has sold more than six million units worldwide. The Infinity Stylus Zoom, the Infinity Stylus Zoom 105, the Super Zoom 3500, the IS-3 and the IS-10 have won particular favor with consumers. Olympus holds the number one market share in two point-and-shoot categories: Autofocus and Zoom.

The new corporate headquarters of Olympus America.

ITS Information Technology Services at Olympus America.

General offices at Olympus America.

In 1969 Olympus invented the Microcassette audio recording format that is the basis for so much communication in today's homes and offices. Tape recorders, dictation equipment and telephone answering machines are some of the currently widely used products that resulted from the Microcassette audio recording format. This Olympus innovation is used in the company's Pearlcorder compact tape recorders, transcribers and dictation equipment as well as telephone answering machines produced by other manufacturers.

The space age technology that characterizes the Scientific Products Group at Olympus also guides the Digital & Image Systems Group. The company's newly introduced Olympus Infinity Optics Binoculars incorporate more than 75 years of optical design and precision expertise. Another recent development by this division is a digital camera that doesn't use film but instead captures images internally on a special miniature storage disk. The digitally stored images can be instantly retrieved on a high-resolution computer screen and can be printed out in full color. Since the images are stored in a computer, they can readily by transmitted via modem to friends, relatives or business associates.

THE PAST AND FUTURE OF OLYMPUS

From its inception, Olympus has been involved in imaging of one type or another. As Olympus America Inc. president Sidney Braginsky explained, imaging is "the use of light to create images or a reaction on a sensor." And imaging is central to the company's vision of its future as well. Breakthroughs on the horizon are micromachines for endoscope industrial uses and developments in robotics that will have implications for endeavors as diverse as sample handling to surgical procedures.

Mr. Braginsky emphasized that the business of the future for Olympus is in developing its imaging core in terms of digital information "whereas in the past we were creating analog images." Focusing on the continued development of high-tech digital information, Mr. Braginsky expects that Olympus endoscope innovations in the years to come will allow increased flexibility, ease of use and will be able to operate in different environments. As Olympus increasingly produces digital products, predicted Mr. Braginsky, "there will be greater synergy across all products." •••

MARCHON EYEWEAR, INC.
Supplying Frames Worldwide from Long Island
• • •

WHO SAYS YOU CAN'T HAVE FUN WHILE building a big business? Certainly not the three co-presidents of Marchon Eyewear, Inc. Alfred Berg, Larry Roth, and Jeff White—known around the office as "the boys"—have built a privately held company that this year is edging toward the $180 million sales mark. And they're clearly having a ball doing it.

Marchon is a wholesale distributor of exclusive brands of eyeglass frames and sunglasses. The company is the exclusive representative for 14 collections, including important designer lines by Calvin Klein, Fendi, Alexander Julian, and Disney. These lines are manufactured for Marchon in Italian and Japanese factories.

The company's 30,000 United States customers, with another 3,000 in Canada and others in Western Europe, Australia, Mexico, and Central and South America, range from independent opticians and specialty shops to major chains and department stores.

Marchon operates out of a stylish, state-of-the-art 110,000-square-foot office facility and worldwide distribution center located in Melville. The unusual nature of triumvirate leadership is perhaps best reflected in the company's main conference room. Shaped like a triangle, the room is dominated by a triangular table. Each of the three co-presidents thus gets to sit at the "head" of the table.

Also at the Melville facility, Marchon maintains an in-house advertising agency. The agency's many awards, including rows of coveted BOLIs (Best on Long Island), are proudly displayed along the walls of a conference room.

Prior to the founding of Marchon, Berg, Roth, and White worked together at Avant-Garde Optics, White's family business. Berg and White were friends from childhood; Roth is White's brother-in-law. When Avant-Garde was sold, the three banded their skills and talents to form the new company. How they landed their first factory alliance portrays something of the brash entrepreneurial spirit that has guided this company from the outset.

Berg, Roth, and White decided that they should be the exclusive U.S. distributor for the Italian manufacturer Marcolin. The fact that Marcolin already had a U.S. distributor didn't hold them back for a moment. Together, they journeyed to Italy and through force of personality managed to convince Marcolin to switch distributors. The fledgling company was now in business!

![Marchon founders and co-presidents (l to r) Alfred K. Berg, Jeffrey J. White, and Laurence Roth.]

Marchon founders and co-presidents (l to r) Alfred K. Berg, Jeffrey J. White, and Laurence Roth.

The highly visible, hands-on management style practiced by Berg, Roth, and White is apparent everywhere at Marchon. At Christmas time, the three presidents suit up as Santa, dispensing presents left and right. Summer days may find them outdoors at the barbecue, preparing lunch for the staff. Acknowledged micromanagers, the triumvirate has also demonstrated unusual skill at long-range planning.

When Marchon's current telephone system was designed some eight years ago, the company was then fielding about 4,000 calls a day. But Berg, Roth, and White, their eyes on the future, commissioned a system that would enable them to field 12,000 calls a day.

The Marchon distribution center is another example of the founders' long-range vision. Eight years ago, the company was

Marchon is the patent holder and exclusive distributor of Flexon frames. Made from memory metal, Flexon frames return to shape even after accidental bending and twisting.

Marchon is the largest American-owned distributor of fine eyewear and sunwear. The company has licensed collections with Fendi, Calvin Klein, and Disney, as well as successful house brands.

shipping out only 7,000 frames a day. But the system they instituted, capable of shipping up to 28,000 frames a day, works well for them today when the daily shipping estimate is between 19,000-30,000 frames.

Each of the Marchon co-presidents is extremely enthusiastic about the possibilities presented by new technologies and avidly embraces those technologies, both in planning for the company's future and in instituting enhanced levels of customer service. The company has served as a test site for both AT&T and IBM. AT&T product-tested a new caller ID system at Marchon. The result is that when a customer calls the Melville company, the Marchon operator instantly has that customer's account history up on the screen.

That call is the beginning of an order-to-fulfillment tracking system that is so comprehensive that even if the customer calls a couple of hours later to add to the order, the tracking system can immediately identify just where the order is and stop it from further processing. For these orders, which can range from a single frame for an optician's office to 2,000 or more frames for a chain, Marchon provides next-day delivery via either Federal Express or its own messenger service.

Many companies are intrigued with the marketing possibilities presented by the Internet, but Marchon has already set up its own 20-page WWW site, which is fully designed in house. In another example of Marchon's enthusiasm for technological advances, the company recently acquired the OfficeMate Software Company. By using OfficeMate practice management software, independent opticians and optometrists are assisted in maintaining a stronger position in a market that is increasingly dominated by large optical chains.

Marchon product innovation is currently best characterized by the introduction of Flexon. A Marchon exclusive, this is a frame built with a patented "memory metal" that can twist and bend, but doesn't break. The company expects that within two years, Flexon will be a $100 million segment of its business.

Much as the Marchon corporate environment stresses the fun of doing business, there's serious business at work for the company's co-presidents and their 295 team members (there are no employees at Marchon—only members of the team). Berg focuses on marketing and on general management. Roth's particular strengths are in the financial operations, but it was also Roth who spearheaded the creation of a training and support program for Marchon's 250 independent sales representatives, a sales force that like the company itself is young. White, who grew up in the optical business, is acknowledged as the company's main systems architect. He worked closely with the architects and designers of Marchon's offices and distribution center.

White stresses that Marchon's achievements—having the finest field representatives, unparalleled service, outstanding product and marketing—have been made possible because of "an environment that enables individuals to grow, to feel like an integral member of the team and to enjoy what they do for a living." •••

Marchon distributes worldwide and has state-of-the-art distribution centers in Melville, New York; Italy, and the Far East.

AMERICAN TECHNICAL CERAMICS

• • •

A MANUFACTURING SUCCESS STORY

AMERICAN TECHNICAL CERAMICS IS ONE OF LONG Island's manufacturing success stories. A leading producer of high-tech electronic components called capacitors, the company had record profits on record revenues in 1995. That result, according to Victor Insetta, president and CEO, can be attributed both to "unprecedented demand" for the company's products and to "the hard work and dedication" of the company's approximately 450 employees.

Capacitors are one of the primary building blocks of modern electronic circuits. But the ones produced by American Technical Ceramics (ATC) at its complex of four buildings in Huntington Station are made to the strictest of standards. They are used by federal agencies such as the National Aeronautics and Space Administration (NASA) and other customers in applications where reliable performance, under all kinds of conditions, is a must. Virtually all U.S. space programs have utilized ATC capacitors in their electronic circuits.

ATC's high-reliability capacitors, in fact, are used in missile systems, satellite broadcasting, high-performance aircraft radar and navigation systems, electronic counter-measure jamming systems, and a variety of other "smart weapons." Because of their high reliability and other features, they command higher prices than "commodity-type" capacitors. In fact, ATC is the leading manufacturer of multi-layer capacitors—sandwiches of ceramics and metal—for high-frequency and microwave applications.

THE REAL HERO: QUALITY

A tour of ATC's facilities shows that process and quality control are emphasized all the way through the complex production process. An emphasis on quality has fueled ATC's long-term and vigorous growth. Founded in 1964 by Victor Insetta, the company quickly gained a reputation for quality. Its focus was, and continues to be, providing passive component design solutions to meet the changing needs of engineers in a variety of applications.

ATC 100B Series Superchip® multilayer porcelain capacitors feature low ESR/ESL, low noise, ultrastable performance, and high reliability in a .110" x .110" case size.

ATC's earliest customers were in the military defense market. While this market continues to be important for ATC, approximately 14 percent of sales in fiscal 1995 was to U.S. military and aerospace contractors. About 51 percent of sales was to nonmilitary domestic customers who use them, for example, in commercial applications, such as magnetic resonance imaging systems for medical purposes, and in wireless communications systems. Meanwhile, about 35 percent of sales was to foreign customers. To facilitate foreign sales, ATC has a wholly owned subsidiary in Sussex, England.

In order to meet the increased demand for its products, ATC purchased its fourth building in Huntington Station in 1994, and upgraded its production and process equipment. It also invested in a new "thin film" facility at its plant in Jacksonville, Florida, to further diversify its product line.

Net sales for fiscal 1995 were $28,630,000, an increase of 24 percent over 1994. Net income per share climbed an impressive 89 percent. The company is listed on the American Stock Exchange.

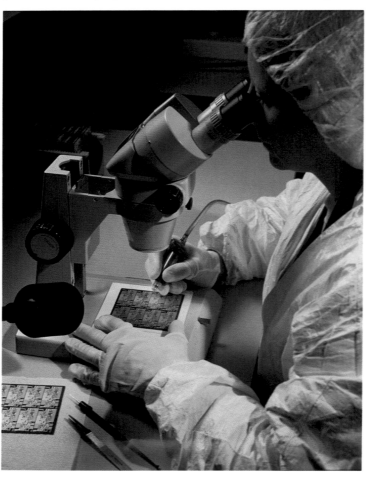

Inprocess visual inspection of gold pattern-plating on ceramic substrates.

Automated laser drilling/cutting system, with laser shown in background cutting ceramic substrate.

patterned substrates are offered to address a broad spectrum of deposition and hybrid circuit requirements. Products may include "via" holes and odd-shaped substrates in a wide choice of ceramics and dielectric materials.

JUST IN TIME

As a world leader in the manufacture of quality electronic components, ATC is dedicated to continuous improvement in customer service. From the proposal stages to order entry and follow-up, ATC is committed to serving its customer's demands for a "Just in Time" (JIT) manufacturing schedule. ATC's automated sales order-entry system is helping the company to better serve its customers with quicker computerized transactions and information tracking.

Many companies in the aerospace/wireless communications industry now prefer or require their vendors to utilize Electronic Data Interchange, or EDI, in their transactions. This technology provides for computer-to-computer communications of business transactions, e.g., purchase orders, invoices, status reports, or forecasts. Some of the benefits are: (1) eliminates rekeying of data; (2) reduces cycle time by avoiding postal systems; and, (3) eliminates errors due to rekeying of documents. The Data Processing Department at ATC has developed a system that allows the company to communicate with its customers through EDI.

Future sales automation projects will focus on worldwide computerized remote order entry. This system will encompass all time zones, enabling customers in Europe and the Far East to enter orders at their convenience.

ATC continues to expand in its quiet neighborhood in Huntington Station. A spokesperson says the company draws many of its employees from the local area and confirms that the company is "happy with the work force."

Continuous improvement in quality and customer service is a priority at ATC. And, in the words of President and CEO Victor Insetta, one way to practice this is "...to target the needs of our customers in a variety of expanding commercial applications, including wireless communications, satellite broadcasting, medical electronics, and automotive electronics, while improving our ability to serve our more traditional markets." •••

SMALLER THAN THE HEAD OF A PIN

Capacitors function within electronic circuits by storing and releasing precise amounts of electrical power. Depending on the intended application, they come in a variety of sizes, some smaller than the head of a pin. ATC's core products include it RF/microwave porcelain and ceramic multilayer capacitors. The most popular capacitors in ATC's traditional product line, its 100A, B, C, and E Series Multilayer Porcelain Superchips®, have set quality and performance standards in the RF/microwave industry for over 30 years.

Building the capacitors is done through a highly automated, many-step process using machinery designed and constructed almost entirely by ATC itself. The process includes dipping each capacitor into a silver ink so that solder will adhere and the capacitor can be put into a circuit board. All through the process, testing is done to ensure the exact performance of the capacitors. "Every single capacitor goes through every electronic test you can think of," says a manufacturing manager.

ATC's Thin Film Products and Services facility is bringing a new standard of responsiveness and quality to thin film technology. Custom metalization and

ATC 100E Series High RF Power Porcelain Superchip® capacitors, in a .380" x .380" case size.

JACO ELECTRONICS, INC.
Today Isn't Soon Enough
• • •

FOR JACO ELECTRONICS, WHICH CELEBRATED ITS 35th anniversary this year, mid-life has brought not a crisis but a period of robust growth and profits. Jaco markets and distributes passive and active electronic components to original equipment manufacturers who more than ever before want to fix their inventory costs and outsource assembly and integration of subsystems and components for their products.

Under the leadership of its founders, Joel and Charles Girsky, Jaco has adapted successfully to these needs, and used the opportunity to nearly double sales from 1992 to 1995 to $138.7 million, and increase profits six-fold to $1.9 million. Jaco has taken aggressive steps to raise capital and make acquisitions necessary to provide its customers with the value-added services they want, and to install sophisticated automation and computer systems so that Jaco can act as their source for just-in-time deliveries.

Globe Motor Modification Center.

From its start in a garage in Brooklyn, Jaco has been a Long Island success story. Now employing 150 at its Hauppauge headquarters and East Coast distribution center, the company is the 18th largest distributor, nationally, of electronic components in a field of thousands of competitors. Jeff Gash, vice president and Chief Financial Officer, says the company "is committed to Long Island for the long term," and is very proud of the longevity of the people at Jaco, many of whom have been with the company for 10 years or more. Long Island, says Gash, continues to be "a good source of the high-quality work force we require."

This year, Joel Girsky was honored by the Long Island Chapter of the American Cancer Society with its "Humanitarian of the Year" award.

THE TREND TOWARD OUTSOURCING

Jaco distributes over 60,000 stock items that are used in the assembly and manufacture of electronic equipment such as computers, data transmission and telecommunications equipment and transportation equipment. These products fall into two broad categories: passive and active components. Passive components consists primarily of capacitors, electromechanical devices, fractional-horse-power motors and resistors. Active components include semiconductors and computer subsystems that incorporate such items as disk drives, tape drives, floppy disks and controllers. Its leading suppliers are Kemet, Samsung, Mitel Semiconductor and Vishay Intertechnology, Inc.

In response to the industry trend toward outsourcing, Jaco also provides a variety of value-added services such as configuring complete computer systems, kitting the component requirements of certain customers, and furnishing contract manufacturing services.

To service the fast-growing market for computers with flat-panel displays, Jaco formed a Flat Panel Marketing Group. Jaco distributes a variety of flat panel displays (FPD's) made by, among others,

Packing orders for next-day delivery.

Computer-controlled carousel conveyors speed order picking.

DALE (plasma displays), EPSON America (graphics, LCS's) and Hyundai (LCS's). But beyond simple distribution, its Marketing Group offers value-added services for the FPD market, estimated to be worth $2.6 billion in North America alone this year. Jaco will provide kitting of FPD's, cable assemblies, touch screens and software drivers, among other solutions, and offers system integration spanning initial concept to prototype and production of PC's with flat panel displays.

Jaco's customers include several Fortune 500 companies and numerous small and mid-size OEM's. They appreciate Jaco's computerized inventory control system, which they can access themselves. It provides detailed on-line information regarding the availability of the Company's entire stock of inventory located not only in its own stocking facilities, but also at some of its major suppliers. Through Jaco's integrated real-time information system, customers' orders can readily be tracked through the entire process of entering the order, reserving products to fill the order, ordering components from suppliers, if necessary, and shipping products to customers on scheduled dates.

To increase its sales and market share, Jaco has been expanding its geographic presence by opening new sales offices and acquiring existing companies in various major metropolitan markets. Since 1993, it has opened new offices in Minnesota, Oregon Colorado, Arizona and Illinois. It also makes sales through independent sales representatives whose territories include Canada, several foreign countries, and parts of the United States where Jaco does not have its own sales offices. In addition to its 72,000 square-foot Hauppauge facility, Jaco also maintains a West Coast distribution center. The firm employs 400 at all its offices.

In March, 1994, Jaco acquired Nexus Custom Electronics, Inc., a Vermont-based turnkey contract manufacturer of printed circuit boards. According to President and CEO Joel Girsky, this acquisition gives Jaco "the ability to work with customers through the engineering and manufacturing stages and then deliver a finished, customized, populated printed circuit board.

Jaco has also expanded and diversified its product lines by obtaining new distributorships with additional suppliers. The company has become a distributor for Dale and Sprague, Inc., two subsidiaries of Vishay Intertechnology. Dale produces a premier line of resistors, as well as flat panel displays, while Sprague has a comprehensive line of capacitors.

Jaco is traded on the NASDAQ stock exchange, under the symbol JACO. In March, 1995, the company issued a 10 percent stock dividend to its shareholders. Later that year, the stock split 4-for-3, and Jaco completed a secondary public offering that raised $15.3 million in new capital. Overall, Jaco is in the strongest financial conditions it has ever been since its founding in 1961. "We are looking to expand further," said Gash, "either through opening additional sales offices or through further acquisitions or both."

Jaco's financial strength has enabled the company to build state-of-the-art, automated warehouses to make sure it keeps its promise that "Today Isn't Soon Enough." Instead of people running down warehouse aisles to retrieve stock, computer-controlled carousels brings the desired parts to Jaco's people.

Jaco's corporate warehouse and Nexus manufacturing arm have been certified as meeting ISO 9002 Quality System Standards. The ISO Program is used internationally to qualify and certify quality suppliers. For years, Jaco has also practice Total Quality Management. •••

Custom computer systems development and assembly.

DAVIDSON ALUMINUM & METAL CORP.
Succeeding Through Excellence
• • •

DAVIDSON ALUMINUM & METAL CORP. IS A multifaceted corporation with six wholly-owned subdivisions. A full-line aluminum distributor stocking more than 4,000 items, Davidson creates value for its thousands of commercial, aerospace and defense customers throughout this country and the world. Ranging from foreign and domestic governments, to major national and international defense contractors, to thousands of small, family-owned machine shops on Long Island and elsewhere throughout the country, Davidson's customers expect and receive the highest quality products and services.

Davidson Aluminum was founded in Brooklyn in 1961 by Al Davidson. Two years later he moved the company to its permanent home on Long Island. In 1965, Al was awarded a distributorship for the metropolitan area from Kaiser Aluminum; he was the youngest Kaiser distributor in the country. Currently Davidson is headed by President and Chairman Deborah Davidson and Vice President and Chief Operating Officer Jonathan Davidson. The company they lead is Alcoa and Kaiser Aluminum's number one sheet and plate distributor in the Northeast.

Just six years ago, Davidson Aluminum was a single 60-employee entity. Today, having capitalized on strategic opportunities, Davidson Aluminum employs 200 people. The company regards its employees as a team and credits team members for the fact that Davidson now ranks as a major force in the metals distribution market.

The shifts and trends of the Long Island economy have dictated Davidson Aluminum's markets and patterns of growth. In the company's early years, defense contractors such as Fairchild Republic

Deborah Davidson, president of Davidson Aluminum and Metal Corp., with son Jonathan, vice president and COO.

Aviation and Grumman Aerospace were the backbone of the local economy. Davidson Aluminum grew right along with these aerospace giants. In the face of a shrunken aerospace market and a worldwide oversupply of aluminum, Davidson aggressively reacted to these new economic realities, retaining and expanding its markets through diversification and emerging as a different company. It is Long Island's continued strengths in its technological community, manufacturing base, number of educational institutions and the resulting skilled workforce which has created the positive platform for Davidson's growth and expansion.

Davidson's new service centers were created through both expansion and acquisition. These centers specialize in plate and extruded products, sheet and coil, rod and bar, aerospace products, and blanchard and double disc grinding. Additionally, the company has increased its product line to include stainless steel and high temperature alloys.

Davidson's unique corporate structure, a program of continual investments in equipment, technology and inventory along with the placement of service centers in close proximity to customers demonstrates the privately-owned company's commitment to assisting its customers to increase profitability through reducing inventory carrying costs and receiving pre-production services.

Deborah Davidson oversees the company's charitable and philanthropic involvements. Davidson Aluminum & Metal Corp. is supportive of the relief and rescue work of UJA-Federation through its Women's Business and Professional Division. The company also supports The Rehabilitation Center in Garden City which provides services for emotionally handicapped people. Closer to home, those

Sheet and plate are among the 4,000 items in stock at Davidson Aluminum.

THE DAVIDSON ORGANIZATION OF COMPANIES

Corporate Headquarters
Davidson Aluminum & Metal Corp., Deer Park, NY

Branch Offices
King of Prussia, PA
East Hartford, CT
Farmingdale, NY
Waterbury, CT
Bohemia, NY
Hauppauge, NY
Reading, England

who drive by Deer Park High School often remark on the sculpture that highlights the school's main entrance. Within the school, there is a dedicated sculpture garden featuring the work of eight Long Island artists. The garden, along with the outdoor artwork, all donated by Davidson Aluminum & Metal Corp., signals the company's ongoing commitment to the community in which it does business and prospers—and to Long Island.

Through these community involvements, and through its continual improvements in product and services to its customers, Davidson Aluminum & Metal Corp. is committed to maintaining its key role in Long Island's manufacturing base, contributing to the region's stabilized economy and increased quality of life. •••

Headquarters of Davidson Aluminum and Metal Corp. in Deer Park.

KONICA IMAGING U.S.A., INC.
Technology to Improve Your Image
• • •

LEGEND HAS IT THAT FRANK POWERS, ONE OF the founders of the company that today is called Konica Imaging U.S.A., went to see George Eastman in the late 1920s to inquire about film for the roll-film camera he had invented. Eastman, goes the story, asked him how many of the cameras he had sold. None, was the answer. At that point, Eastman sent Powers on his way, with the advice that he should return after he had a market for the film.

Powers never went back. Instead, he and his brother decided to make film themselves. Today, their company, acquired by Konica Corp. in 1987, is a leading manufacturer and supplier of photo imaging products to the newspaper and graphic arts industries. Located in an 18-acre complex of buildings adjacent to Hempstead Harbor in Glen Cove, the 370 workers there have become so productive, in fact, that the manufacture of this specialized type of film for all Konica's international markets has been moved to Glen Cove.

The turn-around of the Powers Brothers' firm, known as Powers Chemco, Inc., has been so effective that next year world-wide responsibility for sales, marketing and distribution will also be moved to Glen Cove, resulting in the addition of an expected 75 to 100 jobs for Long Islanders. Konica U.S.A.'s President, Hideaki Iwama, has led his firm's resurgence by encouraging a blend of the best of Japanese and American work attitudes and ethics.

Konica Imaging U.S.A. is the fourth largest supplier of photo-sensitive films and papers and processing chemicals to the graphic arts industry. Sales to customers including the Gannett Newspapers, Knight-Ridder, the Tribune Company, and *The New York Post* reached about $120 million in 1995, and are expected to more than double with the expansion of their manufacturing

Konica Imaging USA maintains its headquarters and manufacturing facilities on an 18-acre site in Glen Cove.

facility and modernization of the production line during this year.

The film is produced in various widths, and in various length rolls or sheets. Because it is obviously light sensitive, the workers of necessity must labor in the near darkness, under primarily green or red light conditions.

Although the company used to manufacture industrial cameras, it now only services them, including some 50-year old models so large that they have a booth attached for the operator.

However, Konica Imaging U.S.A. recently introduced the EV-Jetcolor, a full color digital proofing system, and a product called "The Electrolyzer." "This product is a classic case of going outside the box of your industry and finding a totally different application for something," said John Orlando, Senior Vice President and Chief Financial Officer.

The Electrolyzer grew out of research into methods for reducing pollutants that are a by-product of the use of film. In testing this equipment, it was discovered that it killed bacteria, including cryptosporidium, which is dangerous to people whose immune systems have been suppressed. As a result, in addition to the expansion of its traditional business, Konica Imaging U.S.A. sees a bright future in providing the Electrolyzer to hospitals, small municipal water systems, and, ultimately, consumers, for use in the home. • • •

Preparation of emulsions is part of Konica's process of producing photo-sensitive films, papers and processing chemicals to the graphic arts industry.

PEERLESS RADIO CORPORATION
Worldwide Distribution From the Concentrated Source
• • •

AT PEERLESS EVERY TIME IS THE RIGHT TIME FOR supplying customers with any of the 35,000 electronic and electro-mechanical components and assemblies it distributes. From its 37,000 square foot headquarters facility in Lynbrook, Peerless provides customers around the world with excellent quality, first-rate technical support, and just-in-time delivery.

Founded in 1945 by Charles Shankman in Jamaica, N.Y., Peerless is still a privately-held company, and is in its third generation of management by members of the Shankman family. Charles Shankman's grandson, Steven, is company President. His son, Al, who recently celebrated his 40th anniversary with Peerless, is Senior Vice President/Finance. The company grew out of Charles Shankman's fascination with electronics and ham radio, in its infancy.

A HAM RADIO PIONEER

"My Dad lived over a bakery in Boston, and they didn't have electricity, so he would attach his wires to the bakery's electricity to power up his homemade ham gear," Al Shankman reminisced. "I don't think my Dad knew it at the time, but he was a real pioneer. His first ham radio license (call) was 1ACG."

After World War II, Shankman and a partner began Peerless as a business supplying radio and TV components to installation and repair people. Soon, the fledgling company found itself receiving calls for components from airlines, many of whom at that time had their world-wide repair facilities at LaGuardia Airport and Idlewild, the old name for today's JFK Airport. The components the airlines wanted were also needed by the military contractors and subcontractors that were clustered on Long Island, and Peerless grew steadily.

Today, Peerless has adapted to the shift away from military spending by finding new markets in the telecommunications, medical, heavy equipment, marine and other industries, while still serving it customer base in avionics and the military. The company has also widened its range of operations, by opening offices in Pompano Beach, Florida; Columbia, Maryland; and Atlanta, Georgia.

RIGOROUS QUALITY AUDITING

Peerless is an authorized distributor for manufacturers such as Texas Instruments, Eaton/Cutler-Hammer, AMP, Micro Switch, Omron, Dialight, Wieland, and Potter and Brumfield, and stocks their switches, circuit breakers, relays, connectors, indicator lights and terminal boards. Peerless is part of NADCAP (the National Aerospace and Defense Contractors Accreditation Program), and has received ISO 9002 certification, meaning that its customers have the assurance, in advance, that its operations have been quality audited to rigorous national and international standards.

Its product line is not only extremely broad but synergistic as well, so that a customer who needs switches can also get the indicator lights, relays, and circuit breakers that make the customers' products work. Peerless will also assemble the components, and legend or hot stamp them to customers' specifications.

With its advanced computer system, which is linked to its suppliers, Peerless can instantly find the inventory a customer needs. Its warehousing arrangements can afford customers the convenience of not having to invest money and commit space for inventory, and with knowing in advance that every component Peerless delivers is manufactured by a world class organization.

Peerless' employees in Lynbrook and elsewhere support the company's "commitment to customers" policies. They define Peerless' dedication to the goal of providing "unwavering quality to our Customers." Thanks to that commitment, and the foresight and adaptability of its management, Peerless heads into the 21st Century with healthy growth and strong profits. •••

(top) ONGOING TRAINING keeps Peerless' Sales and Technical Support personnel up to date with the latest technology.

CUSTOM ASSEMBLY, even in small quantities, of switches, cables, indicator lights, and terminal blocks, is accomplished by Peerless' skilled assemblers.

CHAPTER 11

· · ·

HIGH TECH

· · ·

Photo by Charles Orricho, courtesy of Frisby Aerospace.

COMPUTER ASSOCIATES

• • •

THE STATISTICS AT COMPUTER ASSOCIATES STAGGER the imagination. The company, provider of software to 95 percent of the Fortune 500, has grown from its Long Island base to become an corporation of global importance and far-reaching impact. The world's largest purveyor of business software, CA's 9,000 employees worldwide offer more than 500 products operating across mainframe, mid-range and desktop platforms which this year produced sales that topped the $3 billion mark.

Pretty impressive for a company that started out just 20 years ago with four employees and one product! The driving force behind CA's dynamic record of growth and innovation is Charles B. Wang

Computer Associates Chairman Charles B. Wang explains some of the company's newest business software applications to President George Bush.

who founded the company in 1976 with Russell M. Artzt on the seemingly simple premise that in an industry driven largely by technology, there was great opportunity for people who actually asked clients about their needs and problems. Wang now serves as chairman and chief executive officer, Artzt is executive vice president for research and development. With Sanjay Kumar, president and chief operating officer, they oversee a company that is remarkable both for its growth record and equally, for its dedication to what is widely regarded as a highly nurturing, model work environment. And Wang continues to refer to users of CA products throughout the world as clients, not customers, because, as Wang has observed, customers are people to whom you sell something to while clients are people with whom you establish an on-going relationship.

WORLDWIDE NETWORK CONTROLLED FROM ISLANDIA

A dramatic six-story atrium greets CA's many visitors to the headquarters in Islandia. This Long Island facility houses 1,600 of CA's employees. Other major business centers are maintained in 140 cities across 6 continents. What connects them is Central Control, a section of the CA Islandia building where all of the company's networks are managed along with the ability to provide thousands of client networks with technological support and necessary "fixes" transmitted electronically. This vast Central Control facility, capable of running indefinitely independent of local power, houses just about every type of new, advanced computer equipment, supplied by companies such as IBM, Hewlett-Packard, Intel, Digital, and Sun Microsystems for software testing development. Onsite also is CA's extensively-equipped Audio Visual Studio where the company produces its own 3D-animation videos and training films.

NEW SYSTEM PROVIDES INTERNET MANAGEMENT

As impressive as these facilities are, it's the CA-Unicenter/ICE (Internet Commerce Enabled) which truly dazzles with cutting-edge technological advances. A major thrust of CA's current cluster of initiatives, CA-Unicenter/ICE seeks to bring order to the Internet with nothing less than the first complete solution for securing and managing electronic commerce. Introduced late last year, CA-Unicenter/ICE aims to "bullet-proof the Net" by preventing security breaches and monitoring and managing all aspects of the Internet infrastructure. Having developed a system which manages the front-end, the back-end infrastructure and the network in between, CA Chairman Wang said: "Everyone's polishing the faucet; we're providing the plumbing." CA-Unicenter/ICE enables organizations to seemlessly manage Net-enabled applications by addressing the management needs of Web servers and Web clients with security, event management, help desk, storage management, billing and monitoring. In discussing the

Computer Associates Chairman Charles B. Wang and Microsoft Chairman Bill Gates shake hands on their historic cooperative marketing agreement.

CA employees maintain personal fitness in their company's extensive Health & Fitness Center.

implications of CA-Unicenter/ICE and the company's wide-ranging agreements with Netscape Communication Corporation and Microsoft Corp., Wang remarked "we're making the Internet ready for prime time." He noted that "If you can't manage your computing infrastructure, you can't bet your business on it." Wang vowed that the combination of CA-Unicenter/ICE and Netscape and Microsoft services would deliver "the defacto standard in Web management solutions."

EMERGING TECHNOLOGIES

And that's just the present generation of CA! The company's offerings in the latest technology include CA-Unicenter TNG—The Next Generation—range of initiatives. TNG utilizes 3-D modeling to manage complex computer environments. With the click of a mouse, a screen moves from a global computer network, to individual network locations, to the innards of a single computer—monitoring, analyzing and troubleshooting networks which range from 10 units up to hundreds of thousands of computers. Designed to meet the needs of national and multinational corporations, the system is also applicable to a more modest 100-unit network. Described as "simple to use and intuitive," the system can monitor applications running on a particular computer, can deliver software and can also be viewed through a facility known as the Business Process View, a feature of TNG which relates resources to corporate functions such as payroll, receivables or security.

CA's recent introduction of Jasmine revolutionizes Internet-based information technology. Jasmine delivers the first and only industrial strength, object-oriented database, that features a multimedia, Internet/intranet-enabled application development system. The future is here and now.

SOFTWARE GIANTS LINK STRATEGY

Charles Wang of CA and Bill Gates, founder of Microsoft, rank as the undisputed giants of their industry. Last year, in an indication of just how far enterprise computing has come in the mid-90s, the two struck a cooperative marketing agreement. An unprecedented link between the world's two largest software companies, the agreement was forged for the purpose of integrating and jointly marketing CA's Unicenter systems management software with Windows NT, Microsoft's enterprise-server operating system. Many viewed the agreement as evidence of a changing information technology industry, one in which no single entity can bring everything required to the enterprise and further, where multiple partnerships become integral to product development strategies. The companies have since extended the agreements to Internet-enable their co-branded product.

LONG ISLAND TALENTS KEY TO CA GROWTH

With CA's standing as a major multinational corporation with offices in 37 countries, one that could do business just about anywhere in the world, the question is frequently raised—Why Long Island? The answer, said Paul Lancey, a CA senior vice president, is simple: "We stay on Long Island because of its people; its pool of talent."

When CA announced that it had outgrown its Garden City headquarters, speculation was rife as to where the company would move—would it remain on Long Island or seek other pastures? Hotly wooed by many areas, the most attractive courtship was waged by Suffolk County's then-executive, Patrick Halpin, who put together an irresistible package of incentives for CA to move to the county. In 1992, the company moved into its newly-built Islandia headquarters. CA then employed 800 Long Islanders; today, the company's local roster stands at 1,600.

Attracting and retaining talent is a CA priority, one that is reflected throughout the company headquarters—an environment that is referred to at CA as Workplace 2000. Lancey remarked "we're a global business that stays on Long Island and grows on Long Island because of its people." But, he continued, "If you want to attract the best people on the globe, you have to have the facilities for them."

According to Lancey, Workplace 2000 reflects a CA commitment to "a certain type of environment, a family-friendly,

CA President and COO Sanjay Kumar (left) and Russell M. Artzt (center) greet Deng Nan, chairman of the State Science Technology Commission of China.

healthy environment which not only develops today's pool of talent but nurtures tomorrow's."

ON-SITE FITNESS FACILITIES

Worldwide, CA employees have breakfast on the company. In Islandia, many arrive early, not only for breakfast, but for morning workouts at the company's extensive fitness center which is available to employees and their spouses each day from 6:30 a.m. to 10 p.m. The fitness complex, with men's and women's locker rooms, features an aerobics room expansive enough to rival major dance studio facilities. The aerobics room is where classes are offered in such arts as yoga or jujitsu. Adjacent is a weight training room, outfitted with free weights and Nautilus equipment as well as a panoply of exercise machines such as treadmills, cycles, skiers and nordic tracks. Volleyball and racquetball courts are available, as is a full basketball court.

Outdoors, the CA property is dotted with yet other fitness facilities; tennis courts, softball and basketball courts and a running track are integrated into the landscaping.

CRIB TO COMPUTER DAY CARE

Potential CA employees are often drawn to the company because of its remarkable child development center, available only to children of employees and on a sliding scale of fees which have been described as "modest." The award-winning CA Child Development Center, designed along Montessori educational philosophy lines, has been cited by Parents Magazine as among the top five such facilities in the nation. More than 100 youngsters, all five years of age and under, spend their days in the attractively-decorated classrooms and play areas as their parents work upstairs. While parents often visit their children during the workday, tight security is maintained.

The Child Development Center, heavily subsidized by CA, has its own parking lot and entrance. Far more than a baby-watching service, the CA Child Development Center offers extensive educational activities. Lancey boasts that CA child development students are computer literate by the time they "graduate."

PROFESSIONAL GROWTH ENCOURAGED

But as much as elaborate fitness facilities and low-cost, top-quality child care act as employee magnets, what likely fuels the company's continuing attraction for new and current employees is CA's free-wheeling entrepreneurial flavor which serves to encourage professional growth. Wang, referred to throughout the company as Charles, has organized CA with no strict hierarchical lines. Eschewing cumbersome bureaucracy, Wang designed a corporate system which encour-

CA's international headquarters in Islandia.

ages an entrepreneurial spirit through such innovative techniques as the yearly "zero-based thinking" in which every aspect of the company's operations is examined and newly justified.

Deborah Coughlin, CA's senior vice president for human resources, explained that people are attracted to the company "because they look to the opportunities." While salary is certainly a consideration, what sets CA apart, said Coughlin, is that "we don't pigeonhole employees; we allow people to try many different jobs." This company tradition is exemplified by Coughlin herself. A CA employee for seven years, she started out in investor relations following a career on Wall Street. Only last year did she move into the personnel arena. According to Coughlin, what CA offers employees is "challenge, excitement and development." In turn, she added, when people move into new areas, they bring a fresh outlook or "a new view to the way we do things here."

All of these CA "differences" from standard corporate practice can be traced directly to the leadership of Charles Wang, undoubtedly the nation's most successful Chinese-American businessman. Born in Shanghai, he fled with his family at the age of eight, following the Communist revolution. The family settled in Queens. Wang attended Brooklyn Technical High School and then Queens College where he met Russell Artzt. Working appealed to him far more than academia. Company lore has it than upon college graduation, Wang scanned the help-wanted pages to discover pages of ads for computer programmers. He didn't quite know what one was but it was clear that lots of them were needed. Without any notion of how to use a computer, he wangled a job as a programmer trainee at the Electronic Research Laboratory of Columbia University. At Columbia, he mastered the art of programming. Wang and Artzt moved on together to Standard Data Corporation (SDC) where they became involved in writing and selling systems programs to enhance the usefulness of IBM mainframes for business clients. It was while traveling to service these clients that Wang and Artzt discovered the importance of actually listening to clients' problems. Said Wang of the business environment of that time, "they were not asking clients, 'What's your problem?'"

This revelation underlay their launch of Computer Association International, Inc. in 1976 and spurred the new company's success. SDC's decision to leave the software business provided their crucial opportunity. Wang and Artzt, along with two other associates, purchased SDC's software division. Wang recalls that for the first couple of years "we lived hand to mouth," but by CA's fifth year of operation revenues had grown to $17 million. The decision to take the company public in 1981 provided the springboard for a strategy of rapid expansion through acquisition and internal development.

Parallel to the acquisitions was an emphasis on product development. Today Wang says "there is no independent software house in the world that has developed more products than CA." By 1989, CA sales had risen to $1 billion, a landmark first for an independent software company. Revenues have since tripled.

Aggressive, feisty, blunt and determined are just a few of the descriptions that have been tagged to Wang. Blithely ignoring so-called common wisdom, CA's plain-speaking chairman has gone his own way, ignoring prevailing high-tech attitudes and guided instead by how to best harness technology to serve the needs of business. •••

ADEMCO

The Worldwide Leader in Security Systems

• • •

FOR OVER 65 YEARS, ADEMCO HAS BEEN SYNONYMOUS with security. The #1 protector of homes and businesses in the world, Ademco is the largest security manufacturer on Long Island, employing 1,500 people in its Syosset complex, and a total of 3,000 worldwide.

Ademco's success has been built on a commitment to quality, continuous research and development, excellent dealer support, and responsiveness to customer needs. "For a company our size, we have one of the most sophisticated manufacturing processes in the world," said Roger Fradin, Ademco's President and Chief Executive Officer. "Our investment in technology enabled us to stay on Long Island, and become a major employer of engineering, marketing and other professionals."

At the Syosset world headquarters, Ademco's product line of security systems, closed circuit TV, home automation systems, and wireless systems are designed and manufactured using the most advanced surface mount technology. Technical, sales and marketing support for Ademco's 40,000 dealers worldwide is also centered here, as well as its substantial and impressive research and development facilities. Its complex of buildings includes almost 500,000 square feet of space.

With security a major concern not only in the United States but around the world, CEO Fradin sees the outlook for Ademco as extremely positive. "The market in general is growing, and the residential market in particular is growing strongly," he said. "In addition, the international market is starting to grow faster than the U.S. market, and we are well-positioned to take advantage of that growth." An increasing portion of Ademco's sales are outside the U.S., and Ademco's products have recently been approved as meeting international ISO 9000 standards.

Every sensor product we sell is vigorously tested by one of our qualified Quality Assurance technicians. This motion detector is being tested for radio frequency (RFI) susceptibility.

The 5804 wireless key, part of our popular Vista Plus product line, lets the user arm and disarm the system with the touch of a button. There is no need to remember an alarm code!

PEACE OF MIND—AND CONVENIENCE

According to the FBI, a burglary occurs every 11 seconds in the U.S. About 1,000,000 business-related burglaries are reported to law enforcement agencies every year. Ademco's products are designed to reduce the risks, and are in use in over 15 million businesses, factories, government agencies, and homes worldwide.

A recent study shows that homes with security systems are about three times less likely to be burglarized than homes without such systems. To meet the demand of homeowners for affordable, reliable security, Ademco offers its Vista Plus family of security systems. These systems not only sound sirens or flash lights, but send a signal to a 24-hour monitoring service. They include perimeter sensors that can detect intruders when they try to break in by shattering windows or door glass, or break magnetic contacts by jimmying doors or window locks. Interior sensors, such as passive infrared detectors, report intrusion inside the house.

In addition, smoke, carbon monoxide and fire detectors can be included in the system, as well as wireless panic buttons. When the monitoring service detects a validated and verified alarm, it immediately dispatches police, fire or medical help.

But Vista Plus offers much more. Environmental sensors can be added to the system to monitor homes and protect from damage due to extremes in temperature or water leaks, for example. The system can also be used to control household appliances, making it possible to set the coffeepot to brew every morning at 7a.m. for example, or to turn on an air conditioner. Because the system can be controlled from any touch-tone

Ademco's multimillion dollar Computer-Assisted Manufacturing (CAM) Flex-Line equipment automates every production step to eliminate any possibility of human error.

telephone, users can activate appliances, or arm the system, from anywhere. Wireless electronic keys also eliminate the need to remember alarm codes, thus preventing false alarms that result from using the wrong code.

For businesses that use the Vista Plus systems, benefits can include substantial energy savings if the systems are used to automatically turn off lights and office equipment such as photo copiers. Access to valuable equipment and inventory can also be controlled with precision. For example, a delivery person can be given a remote device that will disarm the security system for only certain hours of the day.

In addition to its Vista Plus line of security systems, Ademco also offers systems made by its Fire Burglary Instruments, Inc. (FBII) division. For 25 years, FBII has been the leading supplier of value-oriented security systems. Headquartered on Long Island, its separate product line, designed and engineered to FBII's specifications, is built in Ademco's manufacturing facility.

Another Ademco division is APEX, a major supplier of home automation systems which can control lights, power, sprinkler systems, pool filters—anything electrical.

To concentrate on the design and production of the sensors that are at the heart of its security systems, Ademco recently created the Ademco Sensor Company. Ademco has been manufacturing sensors for over 40 years. The company promises a new era of sophisticated sensor design and configuration. Its motion detectors, for example, deliver false alarm immunity without compromising detection. Ademco motion detectors are available in many different models, and utilize microwaves or photoelectric beams, as appropriate, to detect intruders. Another series of detectors monitors glass breakage. All

Ademco's sensors have been engineered to make installations accurate and easy—a boon to Ademco's dealers and customers.

WIRELESS SOLUTIONS

Almost all centrally-monitored alarm systems use telephone lines to signal that a break-in or other problem has occurred, and therein lies their major vulnerability. "Telephone lines can be cut by a burglar, or a telephone pole can get hit, knocking out your line," notes CEO Fradin. "You're paying a lot of money to protect your valuable property, and then the alarm call can't get through."

Once again proving its leadership role in the security industry, Ademco has solved this problem by inventing AlarmNet, a low-cost radio service that supplements telephone notification of an alarm condition. AlarmNet is an independent radio network that Ademco has constructed in more than 20 major U.S. cities, including the New York Metropolitan area, where 22 towers send and receive the signals. These sites operate on a pair of exclusive frequencies designated by the Federal Communications Commission.

To use the system, subscribers incorporate Ademco radio transmitters into their alarm systems, which are monitored by participating independent central stations. In cities where this independent radio system has not yet been installed, customers can use Safety Net. This service, available in every population center, uses the RAM Mobile Data Network—an all-digital system that allows radio communications for monitoring building systems anywhere.

Another Ademco division, CommVentures, seeks markets for Ademco's technology outside its core business. This has resulted in a contract with Coca Cola to use Ademco's wireless radio technology to monitor vending machines. Radio signals tell Coke bottlers when the

With a Vista Interactive Phone (VIP) module, the user can call from any touch-tone phone in the world to operate the system or turn on lights and appliances.

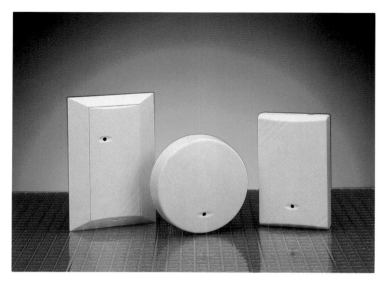

The new family of glassbreak sensors from ASC use the latest technological advancements to provide a smarter detector that performs better and reduces false alarms.

Since telephone lines can be easily cut by a burglar, AlarmNet's low cost radio service can supplement your protection to offer you superior protection.

machines need to be replenished with drinks or change, and provide other important diagnostic information.

Ademco is also the leading provider of closed circuit television monitoring systems. Its PC-based Javelin Omni Series introduced the concept of total security management using computer-based CCTV systems. The Omni can handle applications as small as 16 cameras and as large as 1,000. With the addition of Quic graphic software, the Javelin video system becomes a fully integrated security controller, capable of seamlessly linking the CCTV system to other security applications such as intrusion protection, fire alarm and access control—all from a single location.

Javelin systems are installed in over 70 countries, and at the White House, U.S. Capitol Building, the Library of Congress, and, closer to home, in the Roosevelt Field Shopping Mall.

A COMMITMENT TO QUALITY

The foundation for Ademco's success is its unwavering commitment to quality. Since 1929, Ademco has been setting industry standards that other manufacturers strive to reach. It pioneered the use of Surface Mount Devices in security equipment. These miniature electronic components are placed into circuit boards by computer-controlled robotic devices, all tied together in a Computer Integrated Manufacturing system. This multi-million dollar equipment represents the security industry's first 100 percent self-correcting technology. It can't make a mistake, ensuring that Ademco's products are the best available.

In addition, Ademco's Computer Assisted Manufacturing (CAM) gives it the flexibility to change from one product to another in a matter of minutes. This means orders can be filled without delay, and new products will be introduced more quickly. CAM also results in savings on inventory, an important factor in keeping prices down. The new

technology also made it possible to abandon soldering techniques that required cleaning solutions containing ozone-damaging CFC's.

Further guaranteeing the quality of Ademco products are the company's Quality Assurance Testing and overall Quality Assurance Program. No Ademco product is allowed to go into production until comprehensive design qualification tests assure it will stand up to the most difficult operating environments. For example, products are exposed to rapidly fluctuating cycles of extreme heat, cold and humidity in "torture chambers" where false alarms are simply not tolerated, not a single one.

Ademco products carry the Underwriters Laboratory Seal of Approval, and is a registered ISO 9001 company. This means that its manufacturing processes are constantly monitored for adherence to strict production standards. In fact, the industry's most rigorous quality control procedures are used every step of the way, from parts inventory to shipping. Assembled products have to pass a battery of diagnostic tests. For instance, the circuit board used in a Quest 2000 intruder sensor must pass over 10,000 tests as it moves through the production line.

Ademco's leadership in technology is matched by its supremacy in distribution. Ademco products are sold only through authorized dealers who are backed by the industry's largest team of technical support specialists. These technicians work side-by-side with field and technical reps to solve operating problems quickly and efficiently, with additional support provided through Ademco's 24-hour on-line information system. Dealer personnel also receive extensive training and support in marketing and technical areas.

With all these strengths in manufacturing processes, advanced technology, and distribution, Ademco will continue to harvest new opportunities, develop new products and provide customers with the benefit of their experience and expertise in the security market. ●●●

FIRST ALERT PROFESSIONAL SECURITY SYSTEMS
First in Family Safety
• • •

WHEN CONSUMERS THINK ABOUT HOME security, one name comes to mind more than any other: First Alert Professional. And with good reason. First Alert Professional Security Systems are sold only by an elite group of the finest security systems dealers in the country who see public safety as their mission. Support for that mission, as well as a wide range of other dealer support services and product innovation, comes from First Alert Professional's headquarters in Syosset.

"In each area of the country, only the top security companies have been selected as First Alert Professional dealers," say First Alert Professional Vice President of Marketing, Kenneth Weinstein. "These are the companies that have built solid reputations through superior skill, service and dependability." The 300 First Alert Professional dealers have exclusive rights within their given territories to offer security systems that provide the security and flexible control demanded by today's homeowners.

EDUCATION AND PREVENTION

But when a potential customer calls in a First Alert Professional dealer, they get a lot more than just an explanation of security technology and equipment. The dealers act as security consultants, helping the consumer understand the various perils that could threaten their property and family. They will also provide a variety of free educational materials that have been developed specifically to help people prepare for danger and protect themselves.

Thanks to the generous support of First Alert Professional, in fact, the non-profit National Crime Prevention Council has been able to print helpful booklets such as "How to Make a Habit of Personal Safety." First Alert Professional is also a leading supporter of the "Take A Bite Out of Crime" program, which features McGruff, the Crime Dog. A complimentary "McGruff Safe Kids Identification Kit" gives parents step-by-step instructions—and

even the necessary ink—to fingerprint their children, and to create a permanent personal identification record for each child. The national award-winning, non-profit, educational safety program, "Playing It Safe," for children ages three to seven is also sponsored by First Alert Professional, which has underwritten the printing of a booklet of "Safety Tips To Help Protect Our Children."

First Alert Professional also supports a special Crime Stoppers program designed to help school administrators control crime in their schools, and has co-sponsored a booklet called, "Your Fire Escape Plan" with the International Association of Fire Chiefs. Dealers can also provide a variety of other educational booklets, such as "Away From Home—A Primer on Travel Safety," and "Poison—Help Protect Your Family From the Dangers of Poison."

ELITE TRAINING FOR ELITE DEALERS

Chosen at the outset because of their reputations and competence, First Alert Professional dealers increase their expertise and skills at the First Alert Professional University during classes held throughout the country. The dealers receive help with management, marketing and sales, including TV and radio commercials to use in their local media. They are also intensively schooled in the technical and design aspects of Enhanced Security technology, and how to help their customers use this advanced technology to improve their life style, as well as remain safe. It offers superior security plus the ability to operate lights and appliances. By using a wireless key, a homeowner can open a garage door, disarm the system and turn on an interior light. All this can be accomplished with the press of a button.

People who wish to obtain any First Alert Professional safety publication can contact their local dealer, or request it via the World Wide Web at http://www.first alert.com/firstalert. • • •

(top) First Alert Professional Security Systems employ the most sophisticated technology, yet they are so simple to operate even a child can use the system.

By continuing to educate themselves through classes at First Alert Professional University, our authorized dealers remain at the top of their field.

FESTO USA

Innovative Design Solutions for Low Cost Automation

• • •

INSIDE THE MANUFACTURING plants that make the products that we use in our daily lives are complex machines that lift and push, clamp and sort, rotate and feed... all operations that are part of an automated production process. In applications where moderate force, high speed and low cost are required, this automation may well be driven by pneumatic cylinders, valves and systems from Festo USA.

Festo USA is a subsidiary of Festo K.G., a privately-held, 70-year old German company that does business in 176 countries. Founded on Long Island in 1978, Festo USA began manufacturing in 1983, and by 1985 had built a 100,000 square foot facility in Hauppauge.

Currently growing at a rate of about 25 percent a year, Festo has just added another 17,000 square feet of manufacturing capacity, and is building a new, expanded warehouse.

Festo USA President Horst Saalbach said he expects sales to reach almost $60 million this year. Expansion on Long Island was made possible by incentives arranged with the help of Suffolk County Executive Bob Gaffney, and the county's Economic Development organization. Festo USA employs 110 Long Islanders, and another 120 people nationwide at 12 regional centers.

THE POWER OF AIR

Pneumatic means air or gas, and "pneumatics" uses compressed air as the power source to provide linear and rotary motion for industrial automation. Compared with the alternative control technologies—hydraulics, electronics or mechanical systems—pneumatics is fast, clean, low-cost, and provides long-life, dependable operation in a wide variety of industrial applications,

Horst Saalbach, president, discusses pneumatic cylinder production at Festo.

including hazardous environments.

Festo began in 1924 as a woodworking machinery company. After World War II, Dr. Kurt Stoll, who had learned about pneumatics in the United States, saw a huge opportunity for pneumatics as a solution to help rebuild Europe's factories. Automation control technology in the U.S. was focusing more on electronic systems, but in Europe the enormous cost of rebuilding made pneumatics a more attractive option. Festo rode this wave of opportunity.

In 1978, Horst Saalbach started Festo USA with $500,000 and 5 employees. At first, the operation involved only warehousing of products imported from Germany. But in 1983, Festo USA began manufacturing pneumatic cylinders on Long Island, and by 1985 had built a 100,000 square foot facility in Hauppauge.

Today, still under the leadership of Dr. Kurt Stoll and his brother, Dr. Wilfried Stoll, Festo manufactures about 5,000 standard products made up of 10,000 different components. These devices are used in every industry. Festo USA counts among its customers 75 percent of the Fortune 500 companies, including the big three automotive manufacturers. Festo's cylinders have also been applied in the European space program.

These customers are supplied from Festo USA's Logistics Center, a computerized, robotic warehouse that uses Festo's own pneumatic technology.

STRENGTH THROUGH INNOVATION

To maintain its position and grow in a highly-competitive market, Festo relies first on producing a comprehensive

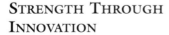

Festo combines pneumatic and electronic expertise for complete control system solutions.

Our automated warehouse provides fast retrieval and accurate inventory control.

range of valves and cylinders that function reliably and with precision. But it is engineering innovation, as well as a constant emphasis on learning and training, that sets Festo apart.

In 1981, Festo invented a unique magnetically coupled "DGO" rodless cylinder. This virtually leak-proof pneumatic actuator uses magnets to move a yoke from one end to the other, eliminating the need for a piston rod. The benefits of this patented device include savings of up to 50 percent on space, extra-long stroke lengths, and the ability to operate under water or in splash conditions.

In 1991, Festo made another important breakthrough: it eliminated the wiring headaches of connecting the pneumatic devices with their controllers by inventing a Field Bus Valve Manifold Now in its third generation of development, Festo's new plug-in, modular Fieldbus Valve/Sensor Manifolds eliminate hardwiring completely with true plug-and-play capability. In addition, smart electronic controls are now embedded in the manifold itself, completely eliminating the need for a separate control cabinet.

Thanks to these unique innovations, Festo can provide a single source solution to its customers, combining drives, sensors, controllers, software, and hardware in carefully coordinated system solutions. And, when a customer's requirements are so specific that standard series components can only partially fulfill them, Festo develops products of special design.

A LEARNING COMPANY: FESTO DIDACTIC

But training and teaching are also cornerstones of Festo's success. Festo's Hauppauge headquarters includes a permanent classroom equipped with modular training systems. It is used to provide generic training in all kinds of manufacturing control technology, with an emphasis on pneumatics. Engineers, personnel and students from manufacturing organizations, come to Hauppauge to learn to apply, hands-on, the theoretical

knowledge they acquired in universities. Festo provides the missing link between theory and practice.

Around the world, in fact, every year Festo conducts over 1,600 seminars in 28 languages in 100 countries, for trainees in industry, skilled workers, technicians, engineers and instructors.

On Long Island, the State University at Farmingdale has benefited from Festo's contribution of training systems for teaching students about manufacturing automation. "I chose Farmingdale 15 years ago to make my contribution as a business leader and to say "Thank You" for what this country has offered me," said Saalbach, who is a member and past president of the Farmingdale Foundation. In addition to providing equipment, Saalbach has helped raise money and has attracted scholars to the campus to share the latest information on automation technology.

Festo's Didactic Division sells its patented modular production system to universities and technical training schools. Schools can also make use of Festo's complete Learnline 2000 curriculum, which includes courses, workbooks—everything needed to teach factory automation.

Festo USA also uses its classrooms and training equipment for its own employees, spending about 2 percent of its gross profit each year on this effort. Festo operates, in fact, as a "learning company," according to Saalbach. This means, he says, that "I want to empower every employee to be the entrepreneur of their business, and to run it like their own." Because of Festo's vast range of products, and constant innovation, learning must take place constantly.

"Every employee, regardless of position, is as important as the president himself," says Saalbach. "Everyone needs to be empowered to make decisions without being afraid. Nobody at Festo ever lost a job for making a wrong decision—as long as they don't make the same mistake twice or three times. We offer the opportunity for every employee to prosper and grow at their own speed." •••

Festo Didactic offers educational courses and hardware for automation control technology.

THE NATIONAL AVIATION & TRANSPORTATION CENTER®

Transportation's "Solutions Integrator" ™

• • •

A BOLD INITIATIVE, THE National Aviation and Transportation (NAT) Center, is the first academic complex in the United States that is completely dedicated to the study of transportation—an industry that is expected to employ fully one in ten workers by the year 2005. The NAT Center stresses that what it defines as "intermodal transportation," in which separate transport modes of land, sea, air and space are seen as a whole, is the paradigm for the transportation industry's advances into the 21st century. Underlying The NAT Center's intermodal approach is the belief that transportation systems of the future, in order to interact with one another successfully, will need to seamlessly connect across continents, cultures and languages.

Groundbreaking for The NAT Center, a projected $70 million facility on a 105-acre campus adjacent to Brookhaven Calabro Airport, was in 1993. Astronaut Neil Armstrong, the first man to walk on the moon, was keynote speaker and guest of honor at the ceremony. He told those assembled: "Today we mark the initiation of a center for transportation education and research—with sincere belief that it can and will make a difference, by equipping tomorrow's leaders with the transportation skills that will enable them to meet tomorrow's challenges."

The NAT Center opened in the fall of 1994. At the ribbon cutting, Mercury, Gemini and Apollo astronaut Wally Schirra noted that "all you need is an environment that is conducive to exploration,

Upon completion in the year 2005, The NAT Center will be comprised of seven interrelated learning centers and a residential village.

innovation, the questioning of 'established truths' and the ability to push our imaginations further than we ever thought possible." Now a three-building complex, the NAT Center is projected to expand within the decade to seven education buildings accommodating an on-site student enrollment of 3,000 with residential space for 2,200.

At the heart of The NAT Center is Dowling College's School of Aviation and Transportation, which has built a reputation for innovation and leadership over more than 30 years. Other components housed at The NAT Center currently are the Suffolk Aviation Academy of Eastern Suffolk BOCES (Board of Cooperative Educational Services) and the Mid-Island Air Service, a fixed based operator that provides flight training for 100 individuals as well as providing other aviation services. Plans for The NAT Center call for the additional components of a Learning Resource Center, Contextual Learning Center, Conference and Continuing Education Center, Simulation Center, Research Incubator, and a Cultural and Language Center.

With its opening, The NAT Center became the world's leading research and teaching facility for the preparation of tomorrow's transportation leaders and the source for solutions for problems in transportation. This far-reaching status was achieved with the support of extensive government funding, corporate and research support, and national and international partnerships. Committed to research and resource sharing, The NAT Center expects to be disseminating information worldwide on the safe, timely, and cost-effective movement of people, products, and information.

Before breaking ground for this ambitious undertaking, critical relationships and partnerships were forged with local and federal

The National Aviation and Transportation Center is the first facility of its kind dedicated to fulfilling the promise of intermodal transportation planning, education, research and training.

Leading edge technologies in the Meteorology Laboratory at The NAT Center enable students to simulate real-life weather emergencies and related learning modules.

governments, corporations and academic institutions around the world that would enable the new facility to not only provide undergraduate training in its School of Aviation and Transportation but to become a resource for public elementary and high-school education, a source for post-graduate professional opportunities, and an international incubator for new ideas and technologies.

Toward these ends, The NAT Center holds technology and student/faculty exchange agreements with top aerospace and aviation universities in Russia, China and France, as well as other countries. Additionally, The NAT Center participates in many international aviation and transportation organizations. The NAT Center's global impact is further recognized by its status as the United States headquarters for Specialized Training in Transportation-Aeronautics and Research (ST²AR), a consortium of more than 200 corporations and educational institutions, based primarily in Europe.

The wide range of educational programs currently offered at The NAT Center or planned for the near future are run either by Dowling College or in partnership with other educational, business and governmental institutions and organizations. These programs have as their goal a full educational continuum providing

• Expansion of articulation linkages regionally and nationally with community colleges, secondary schools, and four-year colleges and universities supported by distance learning capability.

• Adding value to American public education through K-12 programs that focus on science, technology and goal setting.

• Education of students toward the view of the transportation system as a whole, based on risk-free simulation training.

• Education of teachers who will prepare and inspire young people to pursue careers in aviation/transportation, mathematics, technology and science.

• Improvement of teacher preparation through the innovative use of simulation, multimedia presentations and information technology.

• An educational resource center of excellence that will house FAA, NASA, DOT and related aviation/transportation materials.

• An enhancement of applied research and training through faculty and student involvement in partnerships with government, business and Dowling College to develop commercially relevant applications.

• Retraining and continuing educational opportunities to the transportation workforce.

The NAT Center will clearly have a major impact on the international transportation industry. Its impact on the Long Island and wider regional economy has been and will continue to be no less profound. Dr. Victor P. Meskill, Chief Executive Officer of The NAT Center, pointed out that with 860 jobs having been created through the construction of just its first facility, The NAT Center "will have an enormous impact regionally, both in terms of revenue generation and jobs." It is estimated that the 11-year construction cycle will cumulatively increase regional income by $123.1 million and generate 1,355 jobs. With its 1994 opening, The NAT Center began to add $26.2 million to regional income and 458 full-time jobs each year, augmenting federal, state and local tax collections by $ 7.5 million. By full implementation, during 2004/5, The NAT Center will annually be generating $128.3 million in income and 1,620 jobs, resulting in additional tax revenues of $37.3 million.

The NAT Center will additionally benefit the region and the industry by addressing the continuing education and retraining needs of the more than 4,000 regional companies engaged in transportation. In combination with the Long Island Association, Suffolk County and the NYS Department of Transportation, The NAT Center is also likely to be pivotal in finding solutions to Long Island's transportation problems, resulting again in direct economic benefits to the region.

The NAT Center is envisioned by its founders as a "think tank" that will play a critical role in finding commercial uses for defense products, implementing the theoretical, and assisting in the transportation planning of the future. As Vice President Albert Gore, Jr., noted at the Center's ribbon cutting ceremony: "The NAT Center represents the pioneering spirit of America, one willing to use its imagination, its technology and the best resource we have always enjoyed in order to create the future for all of us." •••

The NAT Center's Stan and Pat Henry Aviation Complex houses the Dowling College School of Aviation and Transportation, Mid-Island Air Services, Inc., and Eastern Suffolk BOCES Air Academy hangars; helicopter and fixed-wing flight simulators; human factors and meteorology labs; an instruction resources center; and administrative offices.

AIL SYSTEMS INC.

Nation's Partner in Defense... Creative Products for Peacetime

• • •

WHENEVER AMERICANS have been called to armed conflict—from the days of World War II, to Vietnam, Panama, Libya, the Persian Gulf, and the former Yugoslavia—AIL's sophisticated electronic systems have played a pivotal role, defending our nation's interests and safeguarding the lives of U.S. armed forces personnel.

When German submarines were devastating allied shipping during World War II, the federal government commissioned a group of scientists from Columbia University, Massachusetts Institute of Technology and Harvard University to develop a system for detecting U-boats. The group met this challenge with a breakthrough system called the Magnetic Airborne Detector (MAD). The system went into production in 1942 and helped to turn the tide of the battle of the North Atlantic. The World War II organization that accomplished this was called Airborne Instruments Laboratory; it was the predecessor of AIL Systems, and MAD was AIL's first product.

Just like people, companies have cultures that establish a unique identity. Rapid response in times of national need has always been a very proud part of AIL's culture. In 1944, the Germans had brought into action two types of radio-guided missiles, and there was ample evidence that they were working on other weapons of this type. In mid-April of that year, the U.S. Navy placed an order with AIL for a high-power jammer to counter these missiles. A prototype of the new system was delivered to the Navy in just over two weeks. It is believed this is an all time record for the design and production of a major countermeasure system.

In late 1990, shortly before the onset of Desert Storm, the U.S. Navy requested that AIL provide a new jamming capability for its EA-6B Prowler aircraft. The job of the Prowler is to protect other

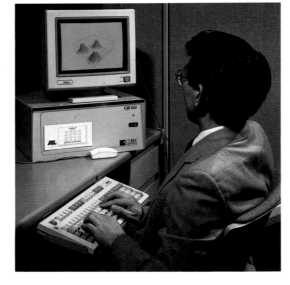

A massively parallel processor is used at AIL to develop advanced processing algorithms, which have application for the next generation of collision avoidance radar, air pollution monitoring equipment, mobile communications, and navigation systems.

strike aircraft from enemy radars. Starting one week before Christmas, the AIL team worked through Christmas and New Year's Day and the new jamming equipment was successfully flight tested by the Navy on January 10, 1991, 24 days after start. Several days later, the equipment, including major spare parts, was shipped to the Persian Gulf.

Diversity and creativity are essential to any description of AIL's culture. Following World War II, AIL moved rapidly into scientific areas that were able to draw on the company's storehouse of defense technology. The new areas included medical instrumentation and satellite payloads. In the late 1950s, AIL developed the cytoanalyzer, used to analyze PAP test samples for the presence of uterine cancer. The phonocardiotachometer, another AIL medical device, recorded fetal cardiograms and analyzed them 100 times faster than previous methods. AIL payloads for making atmospheric and earth measurements were aboard the NASA *Topside Sounder* and *Skylab* satellites in the 1960s and 1970s, and AIL's water vapor radiometer system will be aboard the U.S. Navy's *Geosat* satellite in 1996, as part of a system to precisely measure subtle differences in sea surface height.

On the morning of October 21, 1993, President Clinton announced that AIL was among the first companies to receive federal government grants to assist in transitioning defense technology into the commercial marketplace. AIL President James M. Smith was invited to the White House to attend President Clinton's press conference announcing the awards. The award to AIL was for a unique gamma ray imaging product that would be employed to detect nuclear leaks. Six weeks later AIL was informed that it had received a second grant under the same program, for a remote molecular monitoring product that represented a major breakthrough in the rapid

A key assembly in one of AIL's most recent defense electronic systems incorporates double-sided surface mount technology and state-of-the-art Application-Specific Integrated Circuits (ASICs).

The U.S. Navy's EA-6B Prowler aircraft, with AIL's AN/ALQ-99 Tactical Jamming System, protects friendly aircraft from hostile radars in air combat situations.

examination and mapping of the air quality surrounding urban and industrial areas. AIL's creativity and skill for diversity had once again been demonstrated.

AIL adheres strictly to the principle that diversification must build on technology developed over the years for its defense systems, which continue to be the mainstay of the company's business. AIL has a rich heritage of past and present systems developed and produced for the armed forces. These include the Army's standard portable ground surveillance radar system, 1,500 of which were produced; the electronic intelligence system that flew 3,500 missions aboard the Air Force's SR-71 Blackbird aircraft, providing ultra-high-sensitivity information throughout the cold-war years; the defensive avionics system on board the Air Force's B-1B bomber, the largest and most complex electronic warfare system ever devised; and the tactical jamming systems on board the Navy's EA-6B Prowler and the Air Force's EF-111A Raven aircraft, which have become absolutely essential to any air combat missions undertaken by the United States and its allies. Ravens equipped with AIL's tactical jamming system were the first American aircraft to penetrate Iraqi airspace during Desert Storm.

It is said that change is the only constant, and AIL is no stranger to change. Beginning with its founding by Dr. Hector R. Skifter in September of 1945 as a private corporation, AIL was acquired by Cutler Hammer in 1958, and the company became a part of Eaton Corporation when Eaton acquired Cutler Hammer in 1979. In 1988, Eaton restructured AIL as a subsidiary with its own board of directors, chaired by Neil A. Armstrong.

Along the way the company was housed in many locations, but always on Long Island. The facilities journey started in Mineola in 1945 and led to the current fully modernized facility in Deer Park where all of the company's New York operations are now located. AIL also has a Technical Services Operation in Lancaster, California, and a wholly-owned subsidiary, American Nucleonics Corporation, in Westlake Village, California.

The final critical element in AIL's culture is its people; entrepreneurial, creative, self-starting Long Islanders who take pride in getting the job done, and done right. In 1989, the company launched AIL 2000, which is AIL's way to implement TQM, Total Quality Management. AIL

2000 emphasizes continuous improvement of all processes, delighting customers both inside and outside the company, and empowerment of every employee to seek maximum responsibility and have a bias for action. The banner of AIL 2000 is "Excellence… Through People." New York State acknowledged this excellence in 1994, when AIL became a recipient of the New York State Governor's Excelsior Award—the highest recognition the State can grant for overall corporate excellence.

With over 50 years as a Long Island company, AIL has a special place in the community. A strong sense of social purpose begins with the company's leadership and extends throughout the work force. AIL senior managers have served as chairman of the Long Island Association and as board members of WLIW/Channel 21, United Way of Long Island, and Dowling College. For many years, the company has supported local hospitals, colleges, and universities, along with other community organizations and activities too numerous to list.

A very special activity is undertaken each year by the employees of AIL, who lead and participate in "Have a Heart," a program that helps needy Long Island families through individual employee contributions of toys, clothing, and food.

AIL takes pride in being one of Long Island's anchor companies, helping to lead the community into a high technology 21st-century future. •••

AIL's completely modernized 700,000-square-foot facility, located on 103 acres in Deer Park, New York, includes extensive manufacturing, cleanroom, test and assembly areas, as well as office space and a conference center-auditorium complex.

BROOKHAVEN NATIONAL LABORATORY
• • •

SINCE IT OPENED IN 1947 ON THE SITE OF A FORMER Army camp, Brookhaven National Laboratory has been changing the world—and been a vital part of Long Island's economy. If you thought that someone in Japan must have invented the

first video game, you thought wrong. Scientists working at Brookhaven Laboratory not only invented the first video game, but also developed the use of L-Dopa for treatment of Parkinson's disease, invented magnetically levitated trains, developed the radioactive isotope used in over 85 percent of the world's nuclear medicine procedures, and made other pioneering discoveries, four of which led to Nobel Prizes.

These discoveries and inventions are all part of Brookhaven's mission to use the "big machines" that now populate its 5,300-acre campus in mid-Suffolk County to perform basic and applied research in physics, biology, chemistry, medicine, and other fields.

Scanning probe microscopy techniques are employed to examine surface films that make alloys such as stainless steels resistant to corrosion. The work is aimed at improving these films so that alloys can be used in more aggressive industrial environments.

ONE OF NINE NATIONAL LABS

Located amid a pine forest full of deer and other wildlife, Brookhaven's campus is complete with living quarters for visiting scientists and students, a firehouse, and even a gas station. Unlike the ivy-covered buildings of a college, however, the buildings here range from barracks left over from Army days to a massive dome, modern laboratories, and miles of earth-covered tunnels.

Brookhaven is one of nine multiprogram national laboratories owned by the U.S. Department of Energy. Although federally funded, Brookhaven is operated by Associated Universities, Inc. (AUI), a

nonprofit educational corporation that was formed specifically to manage the lab. The arrangement grew out of the World War II partnership between the federal government and scientists recruited from universities. In the new era of peacetime research, planners understood that "the federal government should accept new responsibilities for promoting the creation of new scientific knowledge and the development of new scientific talent in our youth," according to a 1945 federal report.

Today, AUI manages Brookhaven's annual budget of about $400 million and is the employer for its staff of 3,300. A June 1995 report by the Suffolk County Planning Commission described Brookhaven as "a crucial and irreplaceable asset to the Long Island economy…" The report found that over a 10-year period, Brookhaven was worth $6.83 billion to the Long Island economy. In addition, through cooperative research and development agreements with local industry, the lab is playing a critical role in helping to transform Long Island's economy from defense-dependent to a high-technology basis.

In addition to its own 3,300 employees, another 4,000 guest scientists and students come to the lab each year to use the unique and awesome "big machines" for which Brookhaven is famous.

THE "BIG MACHINES"

Their names do not easily roll off the tongues of nonscientists. The National Synchrotron Light Source; the Alternating Gradient

Cost-effective and environmentally acceptable biotechnologies have been developed for energy production. For example, microbes can enhance oil recovery from wells or clean up geothermal brines.

A Brookhaven-invented medical kit is widely used in diagnostic nuclear medicine procedures for imaging body organs.

Synchrotron; the High Flux Beam Reactor; the Scanning Transmission Electron Microscope: These are the machines that scientists travel thousands of miles for the privilege of using. While their workings may mystify the uninitiated, the results achieved with them have made—and will continue to make—a big difference in people's everyday lives.

For example, clinical trials are now in progress at Brookhaven on a treatment for an especially deadly form of brain cancer, glioblastoma multiforme. The still-experimental technique uses low-energy neutrons to irradiate malignant tumor tissue that has already absorbed a special boron compound. Clinical trials are being conducted in collaboration with a local hospital, and so far the results look very promising, say researchers in Brookhaven's Medical Department.

Other projects include testing of a method that uses citric acid to clean up material dredged from harbors; a test for early diagnosis of Lyme disease; a system for detecting air leaks from hospital isolation wards;

and a technique for encapsulating nuclear wastes in polyethylene.

Brookhaven's newest "big machine" is under construction, with completion expected by the end of the 1990s. Known for short as "RHIC," the Relativistic Heavy Ion Collider will "recreate conditions that existed in the universe at the earliest moments of its creation," according to Nicholas Samios, director of the lab. This $500 million machine will send two beams of heavy ions whirling in opposite directions around a 2.5-mile underground tunnel.

BUILDING BRIDGES

Meanwhile, Brookhaven is still following its mission of developing new scientific talent. Its educational programs involve about 30,000 people a year, from local Long Island schoolchildren to postgraduate students doing a year's worth of research with a professor.

Local high-school kids participate in the annual bridge-building contest. They submit hundreds of small, wood bridges, all constructed according to exact specifications, to Brookhaven judges who test them to find the strongest design.

It's all part of Brookhaven's determination to make the public's investment in science worthwhile. "As always," reflects Samios, "Brookhaven is doing its very best to ensure that the United States sees a high rate of return on its investment" in Brookhaven National Laboratory. •••

Inside the giant tunnel for Brookhaven's next world-class machine—the Relativistic Heavy Ion Collider—over 1,700 superconducting magnets will help RHIC unlock the secrets of the early universe.

UNDERWRITERS LABORATORIES INC.
UL Makes a World of Difference
• • •

MOST PEOPLE TAKE FOR GRANTED THAT THE appliances and equipment they use at home won't start a fire, give them a deadly shock, or leak gas or other harmful substances. But, for the 815 people who work at Underwriters Laboratories' Melville facility, the safety of commonplace objects is part of the very mission they pursue every day.

Opened in 1963, the 294,147-square-foot complex is the second largest of the five laboratories operated by Underwriters Laboratories, the recognized leader in the United States and North America in product safety certification. (The largest is the Northbrook, Illinois, Corporate Headquarters.) UL's distinctive mark is the most trusted safety certification mark in the United States, one that most consumers look for on the products they buy all over the world, each year.

A UL listing, in fact, means that representative samples of the product have been tested and evaluated to UL's recognized safety standards with regard to fire, electric shock, and related safety hazards. Only if products pass or exceed the tests and requirements, and their manufacturers agree to ongoing audits, may the products be labeled with the coveted UL mark, recognized by government jurisdictions in the United States as proof of compliance with UL's standards requirements, national fire, and other codes. Last year, more than 9 billion products displayed the UL mark.

THE PALACE OF ELECTRICITY

When the organization began in 1894, no one could have predicted that the idea of one man, William Henry Merrill, would be realized on such an immense scale. Merrill was one of the first electrical experts, and he was hired by the Chicago Board of Fire Underwriters because they were concerned that the spectacular new Palace of Electricity was instead a lethal fire trap. Merrill's investigations showed him that a vital new need had been created, and he began UL with two helpers.

Run today as he envisioned—independent, impartial, and not-for-profit—UL helps its more than 40,000 clients to engineer their products for safety. UL has written 648 safety standards,

Engineer Marie Pustorino investigates a surveillance camera.

26 of which were introduced in 1994. Although best known for evaluating household appliances and electronics, UL tests a broad range of other products as well, including building materials, fire and burglar alarms, and commercial food service equipment, to name only a

Underwriters Laboratories Inc. — Melville, New York

Ed Bochan, Engineer Technician, tests the transient voltage surge supressors (TVSS), which are intended to limit the maximum amplitude of transient voltage surges on power lines to specified values.

few of the more than 16,500 product types it tests.

Today, UL's reach has extended beyond our borders, and its vision is of the global acceptance of products it tests. UL's tests of U.S. products to Japanese, Canadian, and British standards are now accepted by those governments and the European Common Market. Thanks to the North American Free Trade Agreement (NAFTA), in fact, UL now offers access to certification for all of North America. UL also works directly with Japanese testing and quality assurance organizations to help manufacturers receive authorization to display the Japanese S-mark.

ONE OF LONG ISLAND'S LARGEST EMPLOYERS

These new global opportunities, plus heightened concern about product liability in general, have made it possible for UL to double the number of Long Islanders employed at the Melville lab over the past 10 years, making it one of the Island's largest employers. The Melville lab serves not only the Northeast United States, but also the Far East and Western Europe.

Though born in the Midwest, UL's East Coast presence dates to 1911 when an old Edison building in New York City was converted to a UL electrical testing facility. After numerous expansions in Manhattan, the lab moved to Melville. It is still known best for its testing of electrical products such as telephones, computers, TVs, cable, appliances, and medical equipment. All this activity has made the Melville facility one of the 10 largest users of electrical power on the Island. The basement houses a power transformer large enough to remind one of a Long Island Lighting Company station.

UL Melville's capabilities go beyond electrical products, however. New facilities have been added recently to test gas-fired products, such as household and commercial ovens, deep-fryers, steam tables, and other food-service products. The Melville

facility also has a new testing lab for electromagnetic emissions. New standards for these emissions have been put into effect by the European Union this year.

TORTURE TESTING A HAIR DRYER

A typical test in progress inside the Melville plant not long ago involved a hand-held hair dryer. A senior laboratory technician wrapped the dryer in white toweling, covering the air intake vents to deliberately obstruct the cooling flow of air into the unit.

Periodically, the dryer was automatically turned on and allowed to run until it overheated enough to shut itself down automatically. The dryer would be tested in this manner for seven hours, and then other tests of its safety features would be completed.

UL's corporate mission statement reflects its dual concern with safety and service to the manufacturers whose products are tested at their own expense. As stated recently by Bill O'Grady, general manager of the Melville lab, that mission is "an unwavering commitment to public safety and societal well-being, while providing the highest possible level of conformity assessment services to our global clients."

Given that mission, it is not surprising that staff members act quickly when they see a product on the market that is misusing the UL mark and may pose a hazard to the public. For example, a few weeks before last Christmas, some Melville employees were suspicious about a so-called "Christmas Tree Alarm," a gold ball that looked like an ordinary ornament but was supposed to sound an alarm if the Christmas tree started to burn.

After further testing, UL found that the plastic housing had been tested, but that the internal components had not. UL issued a public notice warning consumers that the product had not been submitted to UL for testing and, therefore, any references to UL are not authorized. Mission accomplished. •••

Senior Lab Tech, Terrence Walker, oversees the Circuit Breaker Overload Test.

GENERAL INSTRUMENT-POWER SEMICONDUCTOR DIVISION

. . .

THE POWER SEMICONDUCTOR DIVISION (PSD) of General Instrument Corporation is the world's leading supplier of quality power rectifiers and transient voltage suppressors (TVS) devices. It has reached and sustained this position because of its passion for customer satisfaction and its commitment to excellence. The division is the market share leader in North America, Southeast Asia and Europe, in the design, manufacture, and sale of low-to-medium power rectifiers and transient voltage suppressors in axial, bridge, surface mount, and array packages, producing more than 15 million of these devices every day. PSD is also the largest non-Japanese supplier of axial, surface mount and bridge rectifiers to the Japanese market. The rectifiers are used in virtually everything that is electric from televisions to automobiles, to convert AC power to DC. The transient voltage suppressors provide protection to sensitive electronic circuits.

PSD's commitment to excellence led directly to the decision that Long Island is the best place to maintain its global headquarters. "Long Island is critical to our success because our infrastructure is here, we have the right team of excellence," says division President Ron Ostertag. "We could not replicate what we have without a significant loss. This is, and will remain, division headquarters."

In Melville, a staff of over 100 employees manage the sales and marketing, operations, technology, finance, information systems, and human resource functions for North America and the worldwide organization. Production facilities are in Westbury, Long Island; Macroom, Ireland; Taipei, Taiwan; and its newest venture, Tianjin, China. Sophisticated information systems and video/tele-conferencing enable direction of these global operations from Long Island, where PSD began 32 years ago.

COMMITTED TO EXCELLENCE

In 1995, PSD exceeded both its revenue and operating income targets, achieving a phenomenal $414 million in sales (a 31 percent growth over 1994), with 73% of its sales generated outside North America. PSD's ever-expanding global customer base includes, among others, Sony, Samsung, Ford Motor Company, AT&T and Siemens. To satisfy such customers, PSD has compiled an impressive record of meeting the toughest Just-In-Time schedules at a part-per billion defect level.

PSD's Westbury plant, which employs over 50 technicians, researchers and managers, has been certified to the ISO9001 Quality Standard. This 13,000 square foot plant uses state-of- the-art Gemini Epitaxial Reactors to produce silicon epitaxial wafers at a rate of 1,800 wafers per day, at extremely competitive costs. This output satisfies the wafer requirements of the entire division.

General Instrument's production facilities in Ireland and Taiwan have not only met ISO9000 standards, but have also satisfied quality standards developed by the major American auto manufacturers for power rectifiers and transient voltage suppressors. In fact, both the Ireland and Taiwan facilities were certified to the QS9000 standard two years ahead of the auto industry's deadline.

The walls of the waiting area in PSD's headquarters are lined with plaques and certificates awarded to the division for its excellence. "We're really proud of our quality achievements," says Ron Ostertag.

PHENOMENAL GROWTH

The Power Semiconductor Division is one of four divisions of General Instrument Corporation, which had sales in 1995 of more than $2.4 billion. PSD was founded in Hicksville 32 years ago, and made products primarily for military use. The division has been completely out of the military market for about 5 years, evolving to fill the needs of rapidly-growing industries such as telecommunications, automotive, consumer electronics and computers.

Employed by General Instrument since 1978, Ron Ostertag became president in 1990, and moved headquarters to Melville in 1994. A resident of Northport, he added staff in a variety of areas including finance, information systems and marketing.

"PSD's strengths are the quality of

Ron Ostertag

its products, its strong worldwide sales and distribution channels, its employees, and the value-added manufacturing of its worldwide operations," says Ron Ostertag. "These strengths enable PSD to effectively compete globally in all major end markets."

Under Ron Ostertag's leadership, PSD has increased its market share from 15.5% in 1991 to 23% in 1995, and more than doubled its sales, representing a compound growth rate of 20.2%. Future plans call for expansion of its manufacturing facilities in Ireland and Taiwan, further automation, new product development, and strategic acquisitions. Its new 100,000 square-foot complex in Tianjin, China, is viewed as critical to the future support of worldwide customer demand and the growth of the Chinese economy. In explaining the Division's success, Ron Ostertag points to the people who make up the enterprise, all of whom, he says, are "firmly committed to Total Customer Satisfaction."

THE EMPLOYEES AT GI

The atmosphere and culture within the division is one of openness to challenge, risk-taking and creativity. Our mission statement proclaims that "respect for, responsiveness to and empowerment of our employees" is fundamentally necessary for success. Backing up this statement is the goal, as part of Total Quality Management, of providing each employee with 40 hours of training each year.

This training covers a

Mr. Tian Guiming, Vice Chairman Economic-Technological Development Area Administrative Commission, presents official business license to Ron Ostertag, during visit to Melville, L.I.

broad range that is responsive to organizational and individual needs, and includes: computer programs, job safety, an immersion program in Mandarin Chinese, and English-as-a-second-language instruction for foreign-born employees. In cooperation with BOCES, the division received a Workplace Literacy Grant in 1994, one of only 54 in the country, to develop skills in business writing, math and English, as needed. Farmingdale University provides a wide array of computer training programs for PSD's employees, and is conveniently located only 2 miles away.

In addition, the division encourages employees to advance their formal education through tuition reimbursement and on-site classes in the Melville office. C.W. Post offers classes on site in undergraduate, graduate, and management courses. Eight employees completed their MBA through CW Post's program, and twelve others are working toward their Bachelor's Degree in Business.

The Power Semiconductor Division is also generous to the Long Island community, supporting the Huntington Breast Cancer Action Coalition, United Way, and the American Heart Association.

In recognition of these activities, and its importance to Long Island in general, The New Long Island Partnership awarded the division a Certificate of Commendation in 1995. It commends General Instrument for "your commitment to Long Island and your leadership and contribution toward the economic growth of the region." •••

SYMBOL TECHNOLOGIES
Linking Information Systems to the Physical World
• • •

HOW IS IT POSSIBLE FOR THE UNITED PARCEL Service (UPS) to track the millions of packages it ships each year? How did officials a t the 1996 Olympics in Atlanta ensure security for thousands of athletes and spectators without inconvenience for everyone concerned? How have lengthy waiting lines been eliminated at the Arizona Department of Motor Vehicles? The answer to all these questions is data transaction systems from Symbol Technologies, with headquarters in Holtsville.

Data are the building blocks of today's knowledge-based enterprise, and data transaction systems from Symbol Technologies serve as the vital link that connects information technology to the physical world of raw materials, manufactured goods, retail merchandise, packages, paper and people.

Symbol Technologies is the world leader in data transaction systems based on wireless local area networks, hand-held computers and bar code laser scanning, with more than 3.5 million scanners and hand-held computers installed world-wide. The company designs, manufactures and markets bar code reading equipment, hand-held computers, and wireless data communications systems. These make it possible to provide up-to-the-minute access to critical information such as the whereabouts of packages or the verification of ticket holders entering an Olympic stadium.

Such applications of data-management technology, essential to industries that have embraced the business management practices of Just-In-Time Manufacturing, Quick Response, and Efficient Consumer Response, have made Symbol a high-technology powerhouse. Revenue for 1995 was $555 million, up from $465 million in 1994, and net income was $46.4 million compared to $34.9 million in 1994. Traded on the New York Stock Exchange under SBL, Symbol has undergone spectacular growth, doubling its revenue since 1990 and employing 2,600 people, 1,500 of them on Long Island.

WORLD HEADQUARTERS

The company's headquarters is situated in a 174,000-square-foot building fronting the Long Island Expressway in Holtsville that formerly housed Grumman Data Systems.

"Long Island speculates on whether high tech can replace defense-related jobs in this

region," says Dr. Jerome Swartz, Symbol's chairman and chief executive officer. "Symbol's replacing Northrup Grumman on this site is a tangible event, representing an important step in the right direction."

Symbol's manufacturing and distribution facilities total 210,000 square feet of space at Islip's Airport Industrial Park. The company sells products through more than 150 sales, service and support locations, including subsidiaries in Austria, Belgium, Denmark, France, Italy, South Africa, Spain, the U.K. and Germany, and sales offices situated in Australia, Beijing, Canada and Singapore. In today's worldwide market, 40 percent of Symbol's sales now come from outside the United States.

Symbol was co-founded in 1973 by Dr. Swartz, who continues to serve as the company's chief scientist. At the time, bar codes, in the form of universal product codes, were being scanned in supermarkets with oversize devices that were built into the checkout countertops. Dr. Swartz saw the need for portable hand-held scanners, and in 1980 Symbol introduced Lasercheck, the first hand-held lightweight device ergonomically designed for the "aim-and-shoot" bar code scanning that is a retail standard today. Further miniaturization and the integration of scanning and computing into a single product have extended the application of the technology throughout retailing and introduced data management systems to new markets like logistics and transportation, warehouse management and manufacturing.

TWO-DIMENSIONAL BAR CODING

Building on Symbol's history of technology innovation is Symbol's two-dimensional bar code symbology, which stores more than a kilobyte of data in a symbol the size of a postage stamp. Known as PDF417, the portable data file stores data both horizontally — as in traditional bar codes — and vertically. A one-dimensional bar code must be read and then given meaning by a central computer database, but a two-dimensional bar code is the database. It can contain an entire bill of lading for a shipment, for instance, or the identity and medical history of a blood donor, or information about a driver such as birth date, driving history and so on.

Applications such as these are developed by Symbol in close concert with customers

Symbol Technologies Chairman and CEO, Dr. Jerome Swartz, (L), and Tomo Razmilovic, President and COO.

Portable laser ring scanners developed by Symbol enable warehouse personnel to scan items while leaving both hands free for other tasks.

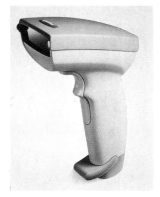

The LS4000 scanner series brings a new level of performance, comfort and value to retail commercial bar code scanning.

that include Kmart, Wal-Mart, JCPenney, Home Depot, Volvo, Ford Motor Company, the United States Postal Service, AT&T, MetPath New England, the U.S. Department of Defense, Coors Brewing Company, Waldenbooks and UPS, which has a 12-year relationship with Symbol.

"JERRY-GRAMS"

Symbol Technologies is organized as two business divisions: the Scanner Products Division for linear and 2D scanner product lines, and the Mobile and Wireless Systems Division for systems based on Symbol hand-held computers and wireless networks. The appointment of Tomo Razmilovic, who previously led international operations as well as worldwide sales and service, to president and chief operating officer emphasizes the focus throughout the Symbol organization on satisfying the needs of its customers.

Dr. Swartz continues as a driving force at Symbol Technologies. Staff members report that during meetings, as a new idea is introduced or an exciting concept is presented, Dr. Swartz is known to suddenly pull a 3 x 5 inch file card from his pocket to make a quick note. These "Jerry-grams" then find their way to staffers throughout the organization. Dr. Swartz is credited with 73 technical publications and U.S. patents, and he invented two-dimensional bar codes in conjunction with Theo Pavlidis, a Stony Brook University Professor of Opto-Electronics, and Ynjiun Wang, who was then a CUNY graduate student. Overall, Symbol has obtained more than 200 patents on new technology, 34 of them in 1995 alone.

While technology innovation is Symbol's core strategy, the company's products function in the mainstream of business. This means its products integrate easily with established software and hardware, and the products are designed to set the standard within industry. For example, Symbol's two-dimensional symbology has been selected as the standard

by the U.S. Department of Defense, American Association of Motor Vehicle Administrators and the ANSI accreditation committee, as well as other bodies.

Symbol continues to evolve beyond its position as the leader in bar code laser scanning into a company that supplies total systems solutions to help its customers capture and transact information vital to the management of their business. The benefits of these solutions are greater productivity, increased accuracy, higher efficiency and enhanced effectiveness. Symbol systems are based on the unique strengths of application-specific hand-held computers, wireless local area networks and, of course, expertise in bar code laser scanning technology.

The Spectrum One local area network, Symbol's first wireless product, has 14,000 installations already in use connecting portable and fixed-station data collection devices. Symbol created the next generation of this network, Spectrum24, to comply with an emerging wireless LAN interoperability standard that allows users to integrate wireless LANs with existing wire-based networks.

POINT & SCAN

One of Symbols newest products is a wearable "ring" scanner that allows the user to simply point a finger to scan a bar code, leaving both hands free for tasks such as sorting and loading packages. UPS has signed a multi-million dollar contract with Symbol to use the scanners for parcel sorting in the 250 UPS regional distribution hubs in North America.

In the future, Symbol's portable scanners may revolutionize grocery shopping by drastically reducing checkout time. Ohio-based Finast Supermarkets, as well as Dutch and British chains, are the first supermarkets to provide customers a better way to shop by letting them scan their own groceries as they put them in their baskets.

The user friendly SpeedCheck Express system provides the shopper with a personal scanner. By placing Symbol's advanced scanning and mobile computing devices directly in the hands of consumers, Symbol is changing the economics of its retailing business, and perhaps retailing itself. Consumers of the future may well be using a Symbol scanner to better utilize shopping time.

These products, along with others under development at Symbol Technologies, promise to change the way we live and work. They are not far-off pipedreams but real-world solutions, in preparation today to meet the needs of customers and consumers in the years ahead. •••

Symbol Technologies' new 174,000-square-foot corporate headquarters in Holtsville.

CANON U.S.A., INC.
The Power of Imaging

• • •

IF IT CAN BE IMAGED, CANON LIKELY PRODUCES IT. Imaging technology is the science, some say art, of creating a visual reproduction. Canon U.S.A., Inc., a leader in the field of imaging, is a multibillion dollar company which develops, designs, produces, markets and distributes imaging products that influence the personal and business lives of millions of people throughout North America. Just some of those products are cameras, copiers, color copiers, facsimile machines, printers, semiconductors, typewriters, video camcorders, word processors, computers and many other specialty products used in the fields of optics, electronics, chemicals and precision engineering.

Haruo Murase, the president and CEO of Canon U.S.A., explained that whatever the business objective, "Canon U.S.A. is a company committed to getting there first." According to Murase, this "drive for excellence" is a common thread that runs throughout the corporation. Speaking of the company's recent accomplishments, Canon's president noted an expansion of the camera division's product lines, a revitalization of the photographic market in every category, and progress in Canon's semiconductor manufacturing operation. He further remarked on the "challenging opportunity" that is presented for Canon by the increasing use of computing networks throughout the business sector.

Underlying Canon U.S.A.'s product development initiatives is the belief that the ability to manipulate images will define the 21st century. For Canon, what was once a fairly passive act of seeing a picture or reading a page has become an active capability of saving, shaping, and sharing an image to meet one's needs and imagination. So the company gears its resources toward the development of products that will increase the ability of businesses and individuals to bring visions and expressions to life.

Historically, Canon has been driven by market imperatives. Product and technology developments are based on demonstrated customer needs and are the result of research and development in areas where the company has

particular skills. Numerous Canon-developed technologies, among them bubble jet printing, laser beam printing, plain paper copying, plain paper faxing and color laser copying, are regarded as among the most important technologies in office equipment today.

Office equipment constitutes 88 percent of Canon U.S.A.'s business today. While only eight percent of Canon's revenue is currently related to its camera business, here too Canon is in the forefront of research and development. The autofocus system of Canon EOS 35 mm cameras has completely revolutionized the process of taking quality photographs. This autofocus process has been even further refined by another Canon invention, Eye Controlled Auto Focus.

The diverse international corporate giant that is now Canon had its beginnings in 1933 with the founding in Tokyo of a predecessor company, Precision Optical Instruments Laboratory. By the mid-1930s, the company had introduced the Hansa Canon, a 35mm focal-plan-shutter camera. The same year, the company registered Canon as its trademark. In 1947, the company assumed a new identity—Canon Camera Co. Camera technology advances for the consumer market and fledgling television industry continued to be Canon's major strengths through the 1950s and 1960s. But at the same time, Canon planned for its entry into the business machine market. Early achievements in this sphere were the 1964 introduction of the world's first 10-key electronic calculator and the 1965 introduction of Canofax 1000, Canon's first photocopier.

Canon U.S.A. was established in 1955. The company's business machine market exploded through the 1970s and 1980s with technological innovations such as plain paper copying, laser beam printing, electronic typewriters, facsimile machines, color bubble jet and laser printing, high speed as well as personal copiers, office computers and color laser copying. Parallel to these landmark achievements for

Canon U.S.A., Inc., is headquartered in Lake Success, New York. More than 800 employees are located at the facility to oversee the operations of the 7.1 billion dollar company. Canon U.S.A. has more than 9,000 employees throughout North America at 30 facilities.

(right) Canon began as a camera company in 1937. It is the world leader in camera sales, featuring such models as the EOS Elan II E.

(below) Canon Camcorders are feature rich with such models as the ES5000 with eye control and a color LCD view finder.

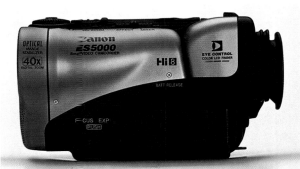

the office business market were Canon's many advances in optical equipment for the medical, broadcast, and semiconductor production industries.

Canon U.S.A.'s view is the long view. Over the past five years, Canon has doubled in size and in revenue. It fully anticipates that the next five years will witness yet another doubling. To assure that happening, the company has adopted a multifaceted strategic plan that is expected to bring about even greater force for Canon in all of its markets. Aspects of the Canon strategy for the next five years include further establishing a clear and concise corporate and brand identity; integrating Canon's office equipment product line into a cohesive unit to further integration of the digital office; bringing the efficiencies and power of high-end imaging tools to more affordable machines produced for the small business and home office markets; advancing technologies for products critical to the information age, particularly semiconductors, application software and personal computers; and to firmly establish its proprietary technologies and market viability through strategic alliances and original equipment manufacturer agreements.

For the burgeoning consumer market, Canon is creating even easier-to-use cameras, bringing new levels of fun and creativity to the use of cameras and video camcorders, thus demonstrating that taking pictures can be as entertaining as looking at them. For its core business, office equipment, Canon looks toward "the office of tomorrow" for which it is linking imaging functions and introducing connectivity to its equipment so that products work as a cohesive unit.

Canon has demonstrated an almost unprecedented commitment to corporate social responsibility; this commitment has been particularly expressed through the bold environmental initiatives of the company's Clean Earth Campaign. The goal of

this campaign, which began with a system for collecting and recycling Canon-manufactured toner cartridges, is "to conduct and support activities that make a measurable difference to the environment." The campaign has ventured into several areas of environmental concern, including promoting recycling and conservation in the workplace, conserving environmental resources, conducting scientific research and environmental education, and encouraging outdoors experiences and appreciation. Canon is the underwriter of the Public Broadcasting System's "Nature" series and also provides funds to support the National Office Paper Recycling Project, a program which is viewed by the Environmental Protection Agency as having national importance.

Canon has established its reputation for environmental activism by reaching out to and forming collaborative partnerships with well-respected and business-compatible environmental organizations. Currently, the company is associated with the National Park Foundation, the official non-profit partner of the National Park Service; The Nature Conservancy; and the National Wildlife Federation. For the National Park Foundation, Canon supports a species inventory in national parks, a project which will ultimately contribute to the health of each park. Canon supports The Nature Conservancy ongoing research on the status of plants, animals and insects throughout the country and also sponsors the Conservancy's site on America Online. Through the National Wildlife Federation, Canon underwrites programs that provide outdoor experiences for inner-city families.

Canon regards its products as tools for the imagination of its customers. As partners in their customers' visions, Canon gives users the power to create and share ideas, intelligence and other expressions of uniqueness.   •••

Canon is the industry leader in copier placements. Its line of copiers includes a full range of black and white and color copiers such as the CLC800.

CORAL GRAPHIC SERVICES, INC.
Digitally Integrated Printing into the 21st Century
• • •

CORAL GRAPHIC SERVICES IS AT THE FOREFRONT of high quality, innovative printing. Headed by President Frank Cappo, Coral has a reputation for innovation, personalized, expert service, and a willingness to not only try, but successfully execute the most difficult projects. Coral prints annual reports, advertising, posters, "shelf talkers" for cosmetics clients, and other commercial work. In addition, when book publishers want jackets for their books that are so gorgeous and eye-catching that readers can't resist them, the publishers generally turn to Coral for printing.

Coral, in fact, is the second largest printer of book components in the United States, with work in progress on hundreds of titles, six days a week, at its Hicksville plant.

Coral was the first printer to perfect the techniques necessary to produce jackets with both matte and gloss finishes. Thanks to Coral, a glossy picture of Martha Stewart, for example, shines out from the book jacket for her cookbook, surrounded by the softer matte finish of the rest of the cover.

Coral's customers include all the major book publishers, giants such as Random House, Simon & Schuster, Penguin USA, Bantam, Doubleday, Dell, Harcourt Brace, and Book-of-the-Month Club. Its general commercial customers include Lorillard, Computer Associates, and Cosmair, for whom Coral helped launch the Ralph Lauren Safari line of products. Coral's performance consistently wins praise not only from satisfied customers but also from the Association of the Graphic Arts, whose Certificates of Special Merit line the corridors of Coral's offices.

Coral's 60,000' refurbished building, a showplace for state-of-the-art imaging and high quality multi-color printing.

STATE-OF-THE-ART PRINTING

Coral was incorporated in 1982, and functioned in the beginning as part of a larger commercial printing plant. Two years later, the company moved to its own 18,000 square-foot building in Plainview. There were 12 employees, 2 presses, and 1 laminator.

In 1994, after several expansions in Plainview could no longer contain its growth, Coral bought a 60,000 square foot building previously occupied by the Grumman Corporation. Where pilots used to simulate flying, seven presses now run 24 hours a day, six days a week, producing millions of book jackets a year. Growing at a rate of about 10 percent a year, Coral employs 180 people, and also operates a satellite printing plant in Tennessee.

According to Cappo, he worked with Kim Lazarovich, Vice President for Production and Administration, and Bill Curran, Vice President for Manufacturing, to take advantage of their move to the new space by designing it for the most efficient work flow. Jobs move through the plant in a neat "U", starting with the Scheduling Office, where a jobs-in-process board tracks progress. It is one of the few areas of the plant where computers were found to be inferior to a color-coding system that reveals at a glance the status of each job.

Disks provided by the publishers are "ripped" in the pre-press department, where experts can work magic on the images through the use of three Scitex Superstations and work stations. Dolev 800 and 400 Imagesetters output film in two sizes, 19-by 25-inches, and 32-by 44-inches. In the spotlessly

The "Systems Room", part of Coral's digitally integrated prepress department.

clean printing area, Heidelberg and Komori presses, two of them 40-inch, and five of them 28-inch, print in from two to six colors, with some waterless.

Coral prints not only on traditional types of paper but also on see-through vinyl or plastics. Its four 30-inch Billhoeffer Film Laminators, and one 30-inch D&K Film Laminator can do gloss and matte mylar and polypropylene laminations, as well as post embossing with linen weave finish.

Two 30-inch U.V. blanket coaters do both gloss and matte U.V. A 40-inch Sakurai silk screen press is capable of producing inks, overall gloss and matte U.V., and spot gloss and matte coatings within critical tolerances.

These days, copies of book covers can be stored on tape, ready to be re-printed as needed. Films of older book covers, such as the Diary of Anne Franke, however, are stored in a special vault.

BOOM IN THE BOOK BUSINESS

A few years ago, book publishers were predicting a down-turn, and Coral prepared for it by successfully shifting resources to winning commercial work such as annual reports for Chyron and Seaman Furniture Company. But the down-turn never materialized. "The publishing industry went crazy," says Lazarovich. "There were more titles, larger quantities and tighter schedules." Coral printed 100,000 copies a week, week after week, of "In the Kitchen with Rosie," for example, Knopf's best-selling book ever.

"Everyone wants to read about the latest sensation, people's educational level is rising, and the publishers do a great marketing job," added Cappo. In this fast-paced market, book covers are critical because buyers make up their minds on whether to purchase a

book based on a seven-second inspection of its cover, according to the industry.

Despite the continued strength of book publishing, Coral has continued to expand its general commercial printing. Its leading edge technology can produce the highest quality sales materials, corporate communications, counter displays, and other print media.

SEMINARS FOR PUBLISHERS

Coral maintains long term, close working relationships with its vendors, and constantly strives to update its processes based on the latest technological advances and new manufacturing trends. It also maintains long-term, close working relationships with its customers, using its location in Hicksville, only 45 minutes from Manhattan, to advantage.

Publishers want to see their book jackets on the press before giving final approval for printing. Coral makes this easy by sending cars to Manhattan to bring publishers' representatives to the plant. Coral also runs seminars for their customers in which they explain the latest innovations and techniques in the printing industry.

These frequent visitors have learned to ask whether the day they visit happens to be a "theme day," when Coral's employees all get into a food theme such as Mexican, comfort food or barbecue, and bring in dishes to share. An ample indoor kitchen and eating area, as well as a lovely, landscaped patio, make these occasions most pleasant.

When Frank Cappo began Coral, he had the typical entrepreneur's belief in himself and the future, but reality has gone beyond his expectations. Now that Coral is the second largest printer of book components, he has set his sights higher still. "It is our intention to become first," he says, "and we are striving for that goal." •••

The finishing department — final step in the high quality manufacturing process.

HIGH TECH • 303

AMERICAN REF-FUEL

Setting the Standard for Waste-to-Energy Conversion

• • •

IF NOT FOR AMERICAN REF-FUEL, NEARLY 914,000 tons a year of solid waste generated by Long Island residents would have to be trucked off the Island. The trucks would add to the regions traffic and air pollution, and the owners of distant landfills would end up with millions of Long Island tax dollars.

To solve its escalating waste disposal problems, the Town of Hempstead, Long Island's most populous township, contracted with American Ref-Fuel Company in 1985 to build and operate a plant that would solve its waste disposal problem.

That plant, located in Westbury, is projected to save over $500 million in disposal costs over the next 20 years, and the equivalent of 53 million gallons of imported oil. It transforms not only Hempstead's waste, but much of Brookhaven Town's as well, into inert ash and electrical energy.

What's more, American Ref-Fuel achieves all these benefits in an environmentally sound way, and with care and concern for the community around it.

"We operate this plant with the billboard philosophy, said Plant Manager William Wareham. "That means, 'don't ever do anything you couldn't put out on a billboard.'"

If American Ref-Fuel were actually to erect a billboard, it would herald its 1994 Waste-To-Energy Systems Excellence Award, from the Solid Waste Association of North America. It would also include designation as a participant in the Volunteer Protection Program of the federal Occupational Safety & Health Administration, in which the company partners itself with OSHA on worker safety issues.

Safety and concern for the environment, in fact, take top priority for American Ref-Fuel. Printed notices, signed by all the company's officers, reinforce this commitment and are posted everywhere in the plant. American Ref-Fuel's attention to details has been obvious as the Hempstead facility has set the standard in all areas for waste-to-energy plants throughout the country.

Formed in 1983, American Ref-Fuel is a joint undertaking of Browning Ferris Industries, Inc. of Houston, Texas, and Air Products and Chemicals of Allentown, Pennsylvania. Under contract with the Town of Hempstead, it owns and has been operating the Westbury plant since 1989. The company also operates three other waste-to-energy plants, all in the Northeastern United States.

Before American Ref-Fuel began operation, Hempstead faced a major problem. State law prohibited burying untreated garbage in landfills (a measure passed out of concern for underground water supplies), forcing Hempstead to ship its waste 97 miles away. By contrast, American Ref-Fuel processes post-recycled household and commercial waste locally, greatly reducing shipping costs.

Located just off the Meadowbrook Parkway, the Westbury plant has a $14 million operating budget and employs about 75 people, as well as numerous contractors for on-going maintenance and repairs of its three boilers and the turbine generator. Because the plant maintains a slight draft within the tipping hall and refuse bunker, a visitor to the plant notices no odor, despite the continual arrival of over 300 garbage-laden trucks a day. The trucks tip their loads into a huge, enclosed bunker. An overhead crane mixes the waste and drops it into hoppers that lead to a roller-grate system that tumbles and distributes the waste so that it can be thoroughly burned.

The heat generated by burning produces steam in waterwall boilers powering

American Ref-Fuel's Hempstead Resource Recovery Facility located in Westbury, Long Island.

From American Ref-Fuel's computerized control room, the waste-to-energy process is managed by highly-trained operators.

American Ref-Fuel processes almost 914,000 tons of Long Island's post-recycled municipal solid waste each year.

turbines that produce electricity both to run the plant itself, and for transmission to LILCO. The ash that remains—about one-tenth the volume of the original waste—is sent to Brookhaven for disposal in a state-of-the-art, lined landfill.

The entire waste-to-energy process is managed from a computerized control room. American Ref-Fuel is particularly proud of the reliability of its operation. No processable waste has ever been turned away, and since commercial operation began in 1989, the Hempstead refuse-fired boilers have operated at over 95 percent availability, one of the highest on-line percentages in the industry.

The facility's environmental record is also a matter of pride for the company. Thanks to constant monitoring of the emissions by American Ref-Fuel's technicians, highly-efficient flue gas scrubbers, and sophisticated "bag-house filters," the New York State Department of Environmental Conservation has consistently found the Hempstead Resource Recovery Facility to exceed all standards.

American Ref-Fuel's facility and the Town of Hempstead's recycling program are living proof that waste-to-energy conversion and recycling work together. Hempstead Town's waste stream is now recycled through a curbside collection program, and the recycling rate has gone from near zero before the Hempstead Resource Recovery facility opened, to 35 percent. In addition, American Ref-Fuel has supported the town's Stop Throwing Out Pollutants (STOP) Program, which provides for the proper disposal of house-

hold chemical waste.

In 1993, American Ref-Fuel donated $100,000 to Hempstead Town to help initiate this important environmental program.

From day one, American Ref-Fuel Company has strived to be a good neighbor and an active member of the community. That commitment has extended beyond the highly-efficient, and clean operation of the facility, to support of numerous charities and local activities.

American Ref-Fuel sponsors a local youth soccer tournament that includes 200 teams and 5,000 kids. It runs a recycling poster contest in local elementary schools, with over 1,500 children participating each year. 3,000 visitors tour the facility annually as part of an on-going educational program. It participates in over 50 different charities, including the Girl Scouts of Nassau County, Long Island Coalition for Child Abuse & Neglect, and food drives for a local pantry. Employees are also enthusiastic supporters of Long Island United Way, achieving leadership status for the past three years.

Asked what the company sees ahead, Wareham notes that the Westbury plant could provide service to more communities on Long Island. An affiliate of American Ref-Fuel, TransRiver Marketing, was formed in 1985. TransRiver's goal is to ensure the plant continues to operate at capacity, and looks to maximize American Ref-Fuel's position in the growing Long Island waste disposal market, as well as throughout the Northeastern United States. •••

As active members of the community, American Ref-Fuel and its employees regularly support numerous local charities such as this local food pantry.

CENTRAL SEMICONDUCTOR CORP.
Manufacturer of World Class Discrete Semiconductors

• • •

CELL PHONES, PAGERS, FAX/MODEMS, PALM TOP computers and other hand-held, portable wonders still to be built, all require ever-smaller, ever-lighter and constantly more efficient semiconductors. One of the leading manufacturers of these devices is Central Semiconductor Corp., whose dedication to quality and customer satisfaction has led to spectacular growth.

Central's 30,000 square foot Hauppauge headquarters is the center for all of the company's engineering, design, testing, quality control and other functions, as well as the control point for worldwide manufacturing operations. President and CEO Jack Radgowski defines quality for Central as "100% customer satisfaction, consisting not only of failure-free product, but also, on-time delivery, competent service and cost-effective pricing."

Thanks to its dedication to these goals, Central's sales have more than doubled since 1993, reaching $16 million in 1995. Seventy percent of sales are made in the United States and Canada. Growth this year will be controlled at about 25 percent, in order to maintain Central's standards.

Central's corporate headquarters and state of the art manufacturing center.

LEADING EDGE & TRAILING EDGE

Central was founded in 1974 by Jack and his wife, Dot, to manufacture semiconductors made of germanium. Major chip manufacturers such as Motorola, Delco and Texas Instruments were phasing out germanium semiconductors, leaving many of their customers, who had used the devices in their products, with a major problem. They would either have to find another source for germanium chips, or be forced into crash redesign programs at great cost.

This was the beginning of Central's commitment to "trailing edge" technology and the manufacture of semiconductors that have a long life span. As other manufacturers moved on, Central would supply their former customers' needs. It was not until 1984, in fact, that Central finally phased out its manufacture of germanium semiconductors.

While Central was still using germanium, it began, in 1975, to work with silicon. In the years that followed, it built an increasingly wide array of transistors, rectifiers and diodes in a variety of categories including Schottky, general purpose, ultrafast, fast recovery, Zener, and others. Simultaneously, it was expanding its marketing efforts to Europe, first on a private label basis, and, in 1980, under its own name. In 1987, Central developed its first Surface Mount Devices (SMD), semiconductors that took up less space and weighed less, making them suitable for the early generations of portable electronic and computerized devices. SMD became Central's leading edge niche, and the company now offers the widest range of technologies of surface mount devices in 14 case styles. Its SUPER™mini SMD Technology allows for truly efficient use of board space and maximum circuit density. In comparison to industry standard devices, the SUPER™mini's save anywhere from 29 to 65 percent of board space with from 35 to 70 percent less weight.

In addition, Central is an excellent choice for any customer interested in lowering their costs for standard catalog semiconductors. On the other hand, Central also will build to order selected, special and custom devices for

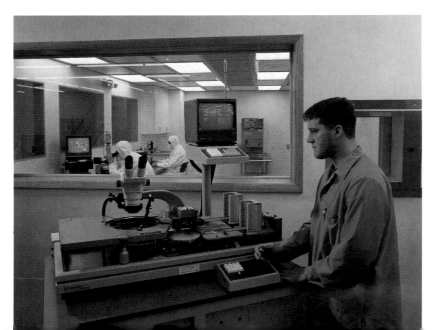

Fully automatic Electroglas Wafer Probe System and Class 1,000 Clean Room.

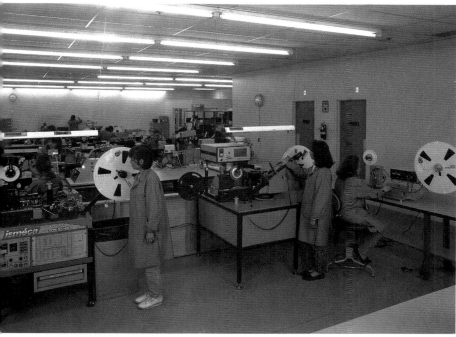

Fully automatic production line for manufacturing Surface Mount Devices (SMD).

applications that require improved or tightened electrical parameters or other unique needs. Central's 1996 Product Guide, in fact, now offers 3,500 different device types.

PERFECTION - THREE TIMES OVER

Central's Mission Statement calls for it to provide "perfect service, perfect delivery and perfect quality to our customers at a cost effective price." Proof of Central's success in fulfilling that mission is a customer list that includes AT&T, IBM, Intel, Symbol Technologies, Standard Microsystems, General Motors Delco Division, TDK, GE, Honeywell, and Rockwell. In 1995, Central shipped 117 million semiconductors.

Customers like Intel and IBM do not tolerate imperfection. To achieve delivery of defect-free semiconductors, Central has invested heavily in equipment, facilities and training of its people. Every Central semiconductor is subjected to rigorous and numerous test procedures. One test system, designed to make sure the semiconductors function perfectly in climates from Alaska to Miami, first subjects them to 15 minutes at -65 degrees Centigrade, and then, within three seconds, conveys them to an oven with temperatures of 150 degrees Centigrade.

Other equipment X-rays the chips; another, a wafer-probe system, inspects each of the 30,000 to 40,000 devices on a single four-inch in diameter wafer and puts a dot of ink on any that are defective. The wafers themselves are handled in a Class 1,000 clean room, where the air is changed more than 50 times a minute. The fully-inspected chips are prepared for shipment by inserting them into tape, which is wound on to reels formerly used for movie film.

Central is committed to meeting ISO 9001 standards.

TRADE SHOW SAMPLES

One of Central's major marketing techniques is to take part in trade shows. At these shows, the marketing staff gives out engineering samples of its semiconductors. In an effort to be a caring corporate citizen, Central has these sample kits made at United Cerebral Palsy's nearby workshop. Central is also a supporter of the Long Island Philharmonic, Children's House and Cancer Care. It is also a member of the American Electronics Association, the Hauppauge Industrial Association, and the Long Island Forum for Technology.

Besides its marketing activities, Central focuses many of its resources on research and development. According to Steven Radgowski, Vice President Marketing, Central constantly strives to make its semiconductors "smaller, faster, lighter, and more efficient." Central's products do not compete with chips that carry integrated circuits capable of performing complex tasks, such as processing for a Personal Computer. Instead, Central's chips are used around the processor, in applications that require handling of power for a computer mouse or a video screen, for example.

As wireless technology spreads widely over the next several years, demand will grow exponentially for smaller, lighter and faster portable devices for communication of voice, data and images. Central seems certain to play a key role in this strongly expanding market. "We are most interested in joining with our customers and vendors, utilizing effective communication, to build long term relationships and muturally beneficial partnerships," concludes President Radgowski.

• • •

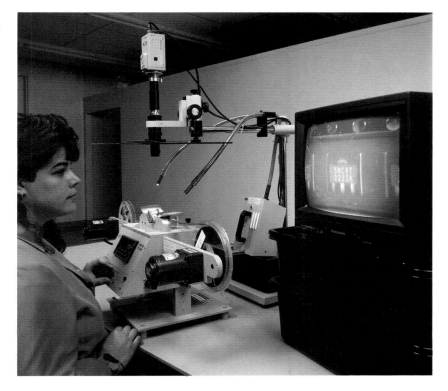

Visual Inspection of Surface Mount Devices (SMD) using a Panasonic video camera and Bausch and Lomb zoom technology.

APPLIED VISIONS, INC.
Systems and Software Engineers
• • •

FROM THE WINDOWS OF HIS OFFICE SUITE, ON THE picturesque corner of Bayview Avenue in Northport, Frank Zinghini, Jr. can see the sights he grew up with. The beautiful world of the village dock and Northport Bay, moored sailboats, and working lobster and clam boats, contrasts sharply with the virtual world that he and his staff deal with every day.

Zinghini is the president of Applied Visions, Inc., a consulting and contract software development company he founded in 1987. Applied Visions takes on a variety of complex software projects, including client/server business systems, simulation and training systems, and a number of Windows products. A common thread throughout AVI's work is its expertise in the development of graphical user interfaces: the objects that computer users click their "mice" on to make programs work. Applied Visions also developed and markets a software product called ObjectGraphics, a toolkit that is used by other programmers to add graphical features to their Windows programs.

AVI's early commitment to graphical user interfaces (they "were doing Windows when Windows wasn't cool," says Zinghini) proved to be wise, thanks to the spectacular success of Microsoft's Windows95. "Windows95 cemented the concept of the graphical user interface," says Zinghini. "Now, everything is based on manipulating objects that appear on the computer screen, just as everyday life is filled with objects you work on."

Craig Miller was the first employee to join Applied Visions. Twenty more had joined by the end of 1995 to handle new and repeat business from AVI's satisfied customers. Major clients include Merrill Lynch, for whom the company designs client/server-based international trading systems, and Nielsen Consumer Information Services (part of A.C. Nielsen, the well-known TV ratings gatherer). Nielsen uses a system developed with AVI to analyze its database of consumer purchases.

For each client, Applied Visions assembles a development team and "almost fuses it" with the client's own development group, according to Zinghini. If a special need arises, such as printing in a Windows environment, then a specialist in that area is added for that part of the job.

AVI's retail product, ObjectGraphics, is used by other developers to create their own products. However, having experienced the quality of ObjectGraphics, some users have turned to AVI as a partner in development of their applications. These include a computer-aided-design (CAD) tool and a financial investment analysis application. In fact, of the first 24 programs officially stamped by Microsoft as "Compatible with Microsoft Office," two were developed by Applied Visions.

One of Zinghini's major challenges, he says, is finding programmers skilled in graphical user interface design to join his company. "One of the keys to our growth is to help the local schools put out people who do what we do here," he says. Several of his staff started as interns from the State University of New York at Stony Brook, Zinghini's alma mater.

Zinghini plans to continue to grow his company right in Northport. "It's a great place to be because the work is intellectually very demanding, but you can let loose, go outside, have lunch in the park, and just watch the sailboats go by." • • •

The management team of AVI. (L to R): Craig Miller, Frank Zinghini, Jr., Ebbe Reker, and Ken Doris.

AVI's staff on the historic Northport Dock.

CHEYENNE SOFTWARE, INC.
World Leader in Network Storage Management
• • •

IF THERE'S A FIRE IN THE OFFICE COMPUTER CENTER, or a storm disrupts electrical power to the network, or a piece of software suddenly starts corrupting data, computer network managers probably won't panic. That's because they've probably backed up their data with software created by Cheyenne Software, Inc.

Founded in 1983, and publicly held since 1985, Cheyenne Software is the world leader in network storage management, with over 68 percent of the market. Under the leadership of its President, CEO, and Chairman of the Board, ReiJane Huai, Cheyenne developed ARCserve for NetWare, the first method for backing up Novell networks at the servers containing the programs and data storage.

This flagship product, plus an expanding line of similar products designed to work on UNIX, Microsoft® Windows NT™, and other platforms, has resulted in fast-track growth for Cheyenne. From revenues of $8.2 million in 1991, Cheyenne closed its 1995 fiscal year with $127.9 million in sales.

That achievement resulted in Cheyenne's receiving the number one Top Revenue Growth Award for 1995 from the L.I. Investment Forum at Hofstra University.

Cheyenne employs 500 people at its two offices on Long Island—its Roslyn Heights headquarters and a Lake Success location, which houses a state-of-the-art customer center for making presentations on the company and its products. The company also has wholly owned subsidiaries and sales and technical support offices around the world, from England to Australia, and Beijing, with an Asia regional headquarters in Singapore.

Cheyenne's young and dedicated staff regularly work late into the night

on further developing Cheyenne's local area network solutions. This concentration on LAN technology and partnership with companies such as Novell have resulted in unparalleled technological and professional expertise within the company, and given Cheyenne a strong competitive advantage in the industry. Among its other well-known products are InocuLAN® antivirus software and FAXserve®, which allows for the monitoring, queuing, sending, and receiving of faxes on the file server.

A major engine of Cheyenne's growth has been its partnerships with major computer industry companies. In 1995, for instance, Novell gave Cheyenne its first Most Valuable Partner Award in recognition of its record of "bringing the highest quality of Novell-certified products to a broad market," according to Bill Mason, director of partner marketing for Novell's NetWare Products Division.

Compaq Computer Corporation ships Cheyenne's ARCserve software on its SmartStart CDs for both Novell NetWare and Windows NT applications. Companies such as Fujitsu, Ltd., Hewlett-Packard, Mitsubishi Electric Corporation, Santa Cruz Operation, Inc., and NEC Corporation also partner with Cheyenne. Computer Associates markets Cheyenne's high-performance, image-based backup and RAID fault tolerance technology as options to UNIX and Windows NT versions of CA-Unicenter.

According to President ReiJane Huai, "A key factor in Cheyenne's past and future success is its ability to form and strengthen business alliances that showcase our technology and endorse our leadership position in the storage management arena." •••

(above) Cheyenne's flagship product, ARCserve® for Netware, permits backup of Novell local area networks at the server.

(left) ReiJane Huai, President, has led Cheyenne to its position as world leader in network storage management.

GULL ELECTRONIC SYSTEMS
PARKER BERTEA AEROSPACE • PARKER HANNIFIN CORPORATION
Avionic Supplier of Choice
• • •

WHEN GULL AIRBORNE INSTRUMENTS WAS formed in 1966, it had a dozen employees and made aircraft instruments for two big customers, McDonnell Douglas and the Navy. Today, Gull is a division of the global Parker Hannifin Corporation, employs 500 people, and supplies products used in a virtual "Who's Who" of military, commercial and business aircraft.

As part of the Parker Bertea Aerospace Group, it designs, manufactures, tests and repairs digital fuel systems, flight deck displays and systems, flight inspection systems, electronic controllers and other aviation products. Business is divided evenly between commercial and military programs.

This was not always the case. In the past, Gull's business was largely military. In 1995, less than half its business was commercial, but by the turn of the century, the company expects commercial business to account for nearly three-quarters of its sales.

A VISION OF EXCELLENCE

Gull's vision statement is carried by its employees on wallet-size, laminated cards. It reads: "Our vision is to be the supplier of choice for innovative avionic components, systems and support to aircraft manufacturers and users worldwide."

Gull's quality policy, printed on the reverse of the card, is to be "the industry leader in customer satisfaction by being the best value supplier of superior products and premier customer service."

These words are supported by constant measurement of customer satisfaction objectives including on-time delivery, product quality, repair turnaround time, and field performance, among many other factors. These high standards are noticed outside Gull. The company is certified by the Federal Aviation Administration (FAA) for repair of its own equip-

ment. Gull is a McDonnell Douglas Silver Certificate Supplier, is a Blue Ribbon Contractor with Kelly and Tinker Air Force bases; and has top performer status with several other customers.

In 1995, Gull was one of the first companies on Long Island to receive ISO 9001 certification, which brought with it certification by the Standards Council of Canada and the Dutch Council for Certification.

WINNING TWO OUT OF THREE

Gull's customer-service performance and global competitiveness have lead to much success in the marketplace. Gull wins an average of two out of three jobs on which it bids, and 70 per cent of its wins in the past two years have been international contracts.

Gull is a major supplier to McDonnell Douglas, providing products for all Douglas commercial aircraft, including the new Douglas MD-95 aircraft. Gull provides products to Bombardier, Boeing, Cessna, Dassault, Gulfstream, Westland, and others, as well as engine manufacturers Pratt & Whitney, Rolls Royce and others.

Although Gull's business is shifting toward the commercial sector, the company has been successful on current defense-related programs. Gull is a major subcontractor on the C-17 Globemaster III, one of the largest defense programs in recent history.

In 1988, Gull was acquired by Parker Hannifin, a Fortune 500 company based in Cleveland, Ohio, that is a worldwide producer of motion control products for the industrial and aerospace markets. Being part of Parker Hannifin gives Gull both global marketing and customer support.

Gull and its employees contribute annually to many organizations such as local chapters of the United Way and March of Dimes, the Smithhaven Ministries and Long Island Cares.   • • •

Parker-Gull's products are used in most of the major commercial, business/general aviation, commuter and military aircraft produced globally today.

Parker-Gull's modern, 150,000 square foot main facility is augmented by a 50,000 square foot satellite facility, which was its original home in Suffolk County. Both are located near each other in Smithtown/Hauppauge.

MILL-MAX MANUFACTURING CORPORATION
The Name You Connect with Trust
• • •

AT MILL-MAX MANUFACTURING CORPORATION, total control of the manufacturing process, from raw materials to finished product, has made the company North America's leading manufacturer of precision-machined interconnect components.

These components are utilized in a wide range of applications, including computers and peripherals, cable TV, telecommunications, industrial controls, instrumentation and medical electronics. In addition, Mill-Max interconnects are used in hearing aids, heart pacemakers, automobiles and cellular phones.

The interconnects are produced by Mill-Max at its 140,000 square foot facility in Oyster Bay. Each week, the company turns out between 80 and 100 million interconnects—about 5 billion a year.

Mill-Max's modern manufacturing plant is located on Pine Hollow Road in Oyster Bay.

VERTICAL INTEGRATION

Mill-Max was established in Port Washington in 1971 by Roger Bahnik, company President and Chief Executive Officer. In its early years, the company utilized its machining expertise to make components for timing mechanisms which were used in products such as pressure gauges and parking meters. As the electronic industry started to grow, the company began focusing on producing pin receptacles, printed circuit pins and solder terminals, primarily for circuit boards.

In 1987, Mill-Max decided to expand its product line to include IC sockets and connectors. By 1990, the company needed more space, and added 70,000 square feet to its existing 70,000 square-foot plant. No longer just a maker of individual pins, the company's product line now includes SIP, DIP and PGA sockets, board-to-board interconnects, pin headers, surface mount and custom products. Engineering, tooling, primary and secondary machining, stamping, plating, injection molding and assembly, are performed by a work force of 210 people.

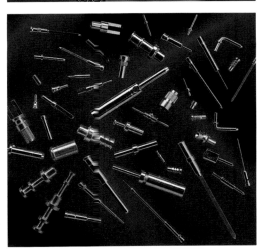

SPECIALIZED HIGH SPEED TURNING

What particularly distinguishes Mill-Max is its use of proprietary high speed turning machines. On Mill-Max's factory floor, hundreds of automated machines turn copper alloy rod and wire at high speed as cutting tools shape each pin. This method means that Mill-Max's products can hold tolerances to +/- .0005 inches. High-speed turning machines also offer the flexibility to be easily and quickly reconfigured to make pins in different sizes and shapes. This makes the task of producing custom products simple.

The company's design guide catalog shows the numerous sizes and varieties of its family of interconnect components, including full technical specifications and graphs. In addition, Mill-Max specializes in making custom sockets as well as surface mount adaptors with insulators injection-molded or machined from epoxy laminate.

TOTAL CUSTOMER SATISFACTION

Mill-Max's customers have access to the largest inventory of machined interconnect components in North America. Through its sales representative organizations, Mill-Max products are sold directly as well as through a network of over 40 distributors in more than 135 locations. From order entry to shipping product, Mill-Max focuses on the total satisfaction of its customers. • • •

(above) Wide range of IC sockets and connectors.

(left) Precision machined pins, receptacles and terminals.

CEDAR GRAPHICS
Success Through High Technology and High Levels of Service
• • •

WHEN THE AUTHORS OF THE LONG ISLAND Association's *Project Long Island* identified graphics as one of the key areas that will fuel the region's future growth, they may well have been thinking of the success of Cedar Graphics and the increasingly important role played by the company on Long Island and in New York City.

Twenty years ago, Cedar Graphics opened its doors as the smallest of small start ups. Today the company operates out of two large showcase plants and employs almost 200 workers. Despite the ups and downs of the economy, Cedar Graphics has posted gains of 100 percent or more every two years since its 1976 inception.

Robert and Joanne Herman inaugurated Cedar Graphics as a service to print brokers. The company's first home was a rented 1,000 square foot Hampton Bays basement. From the outset, Joanne, who serves as Cedar's president, handled the front office responsibilities while Bob did the actual production work. They didn't get an overwhelming amount of work the first year—merely a few assignments to produce film and plates for other printers—but on the assignments they did get, the Hermans demonstrated their commitment to providing quality work, fair price and always meeting their clients' deadlines. This commitment was to be the Herman's recipe for the success which followed.

The fledgling company, which had expanded its services within its first year to include color separations and laser scanning, soon outgrew its rented basement quarters. In 1981, Cedar purchased a 10,000 square foot building in Riverhead and installed its first four-color printing press. By 1987, with Cedar's having added additional high-tech printing equipment and also having established a widespread reputation as a supplier to the printing industry, the Riverhead plant was perking along 24 hours a day, seven days a week. Another expansion seemed imminent. Actually, the Hermans commenced on two expansions: they brought in Michael Clark as a partner and they opened Cedar West in downtown New York.

With sales continuing to boom, the Riverhead plant fell short of the growing company's needs, and so another business expansion was explored. With the help of the Town of Islip which provided tax incentives and connected Cedar with capital for expansion through the town's Industrial Development Agency, Cedar Graphics moved into its new 40,000 square foot headquarters in Ronkonkoma in 1995; within a year Cedar began construction of almost 50,000 square feet of additional space.

As one of Long Island's fastest growing companies, Cedar Graphics prides itself on being at the cutting edge of printing technology. What that has meant in recent years is the company's leap into high resolution screening and waterless printing. Waterless printing, which now constitutes more than 70 percent of Cedar's overall output, is described by Joanne Herman as a superior process that provides better contrast, more uniform dot, and allows for the printing of photo realistic images.

The commitments which spurred Cedar Graphics original growth continue to underlay its operation today. Joanne Herman remarked that Cedar's business plan for the future is "to continue printing so economically, and with such high quality and speed that we will never lack customers." • • •

As seen in the Ronkonkoma pressroom, Cedar Graphics' depth in equipment is the key to the company's continued growth.

Cedar Graphics' professional production staff oversee planning and scheduling of work through each step of the manufacturing process.

FONAR CORPORATION
Medical Pioneer & Industry Leader in Magnetic Resonance Imaging
• • •

HE CALLED IT "INDOMITABLE." IT WAS THE FIRST magnetic resonance scanner capable of looking inside the human body, and its construction was a testament to the unyielding belief of Dr. Raymond Damadian that it could be used to find cancers.

Built in 1977, Indomitable is now in the collection of the Smithsonian Institution. Today, FONAR Corporation, the company that Dr. Damadian created to bring his revolutionary invention to the public, has manufactured, installed, and services 200 magnetic resonance imaging systems all over the world. Located in Melville, and employing 235 Long Islanders, FONAR and Dr. Damadian continue not only to lead their industry, but also the fight to strengthen patent enforcement for the benefit of all inventors and American workers.

The latest model MRI's developed by FONAR and manufactured on Long Island offer the most open design of all the so-called "open" MRI's. The QUAD™ 12000 is the first high field open MRI, and, at .6 Tesla, is extremely powerful, producing exquisite pictures of all organs of the body. The QUAD™ 7000, rated at .35 Tesla, incorporates the same open architecture. They are priced at $895,000 and $695,000 respectively, which represents a deliberate effort on Dr. Damadian's part to make the systems more affordable and therefore more available to patients.

THE FATHER OF MRI

Dr. Damadian has been called "The Father of MRI," and has been honored for his achievement by induction into the National Inventors Hall of Fame, and by his receipt of the National Medal of Technology from President Reagan. But in 1970, when he would explain to people that he was working on a way to hunt down cancer by scanning human organs with radio signals and magnets, he remembers they would react with a skeptical, "Yeah, sure."

After writing a seminal paper in Science Magazine in 1971, showing that the nuclear magnetic resonance signal could detect cancer, he received the first patent for MRI in 1972. He formed FONAR in 1978, and took it public in 1981(Symbol: FONR, traded on the NASDAQ).

No other company enjoys a longer list of "firsts" than FONAR. First to win FDA approval

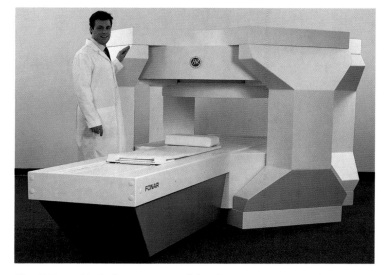

The QUAD 12000 is the most powerful and most open MRI on the market, a boon to both patients and physicians.

for a mobile MR scanner; first to achieve oblique imaging of the human body; first to create scanners without loud noises and claustrophia-inducing tunnels. Through a continuing series of patented innovations, FONAR continues its technological dominance of the industry.

FIGHTING FOR PATENT ENFORCEMENT & JOBS

The cars of employees parked outside FONAR's facility all wear a bumper sticker that says:. "Restore Long Island Jobs— Enforce U.S. Patents." In speeches and articles, Dr. Damadian has crusaded for his belief that America's prosperity is founded on revolutionary inventions and the protections given their inventors by patent rights written into the U.S. Constitution.

"The American people have been denied the new business and new employment that would have been created by inventors since the end of World War II," says Dr. Damadian, by the failure of American courts to enforce patents. Dr. Damadian has successfully and aggressively defended FONAR's patents, and promises to continue his fight for patent protection for all Americans. • • •

Raymond V. Damadian
Founder, President and Chairman

LOCKHEED MARTIN FAIRCHILD SYSTEMS CORP.

• • •

LOCKHEED MARTIN Fairchild Systems is a leading manufacturer of airborne tactical and reconnaissance video and photographic systems for military use. Founded in 1920 by Sherman M. Fairchild, who called it Fairchild Aerial Camera, the Syosset-based company today is a major developer of electro-optical and infrared sensors and systems.

These systems are used by the U.S. Navy and Air Force in jet fighters and reconnaissance aircraft for navigation, missile guidance and cockpit television. Lockheed Martin Fairchild has been a business unit of the Lockheed Martin Corp. since April, 1996, when it acquired the business from the Loral Corporation. Led by its President, James Dunn, the company employs 500 Long Islanders at its headquarters just north of the Long Island Expressway.

This facility contains tools for the design, development, fabrication and testing of complex optics, including equipment suitable for testing of visible optics up to 120 inches in focal length and 18 inches in diameter. Called a "collimator," this equipment is housed in an environmentally-controlled area and mounted on a 40-ton vibration-isolated slab. The manufacturing area is fully compliant to military quality control and environmental standards. It includes a class 10,000 clean room and a state-of-the-art circuit card assembly facility.

The F/A-18 took this photo from 10,000 feet in the air, while flying at 530 knots, using the ATARS medium altitude electro-optic sensor. Pictured is the Vienna, Maryland Power Plant, a simulated target. Objects as small as truck tires can be made visible by enlarging the image.

McDonnell Douglas as the prime contractor, Lockheed Martin Fairchild supplies electro-optical and infrared scanners as part of the Advanced Tactical Airborne Reconnaissance System for the F/A-18 aircraft These permit the crew to obtain high resolution images from three to five miles away, without direct over-flight, in any weather, day or night.

The Division has also produced over 16,000 cockpit television cameras for 23 different military fighter/attack aircraft. It currently produces the Color Cockpit TV Sensor for in-flight video recording for both Head-Up and Head-Down Displays. Other systems provide day and night images from aircraft more than 40 nautical miles from their targets.

"GLASS-EYED SPIES"

Lockheed Martin Fairchild's history parallels the development of American aviation, and, in particular, military aviation. Sherman Fairchild's original product was a single type of aerial camera "of an entirely new and radical design," according to a 1939 Fairchild publication. This original camera was elaborated on to meet the needs of the U.S. Government, which in that era paid as much as $14,500—an astronomical sum—for a five-lens mapping camera.

In its early decades, Fairchild

RECONNAISSANCE FROM A DISTANCE—IN ANY WEATHER

In today's era of trying to help restore peace to regions torn by conflict, the U.S. military requires sophisticated reconnaissance that can be performed while keeping American pilots safe. Lockheed Martin Fairchild provides solutions to these needs. For example, with

not only produced cameras but also performed aerial photography and mapping. Once, it aerial photographed all of the five boroughs of New York City. During World War II, its cameras, known as "glass-eyed spies," took photos from which the military made relief maps of enemy territory. Historical photos from the era show troops intently studying the maps before going into battle.

Now, as part of the $30 billion Lockheed Martin Corp., the company founded by Sherman Fairchild seems certain to continue as an important part of aviation's future. •••

CHAPTER 12

BUSINESS & FINANCE

Photo by Deborah Ross.

LONG ISLAND ASSOCIATION
Fueling Long Island's Economy
· · ·

THE SMALL GROUP OF BUSINESS LEADERS WHO formed the Long Island Chamber of Commerce in 1926 probably wouldn't recognize either its present-day successor organization, the Long Island Association (LIA), or the diverse, sophisticated business community the organization now serves 70 years later. When that original Chamber was formed, Long Island—a designation that then included Brooklyn and Queens—was a network of small towns and villages; the years of booming suburban expansion were far in the future.

But today, Long Island is no longer a bedroom community. The bi-county region has long stood as an independent economic market with its special business and corporate needs. Those needs are met by an association that has expanded right along with the region it serves. To the media and to political officials at the county, state, and federal levels, the LIA stands as the voice of Long Island's business and civic communities. Consensus on issues ranging from world trade to transportation, education, energy, health services, environment, small business, and tax policy is arrived at by the membership at the committee level, then communicated to legislators for action that will nourish and propel Long Island's economic health.

Speaking of how the organization has positioned itself to respond to evolving needs, LIA President Matthew T. Crosson observed that "Long Island is at a critical turning point; our economy is changing significantly." Long Island's efforts to "forge our economic future by identifying industry clusters that will attract high-paying, quality jobs" have been boosted by the LIA's formation of Project Long Island. Crosson described the project's mission as "identifying high-tech manufacturing industry clusters and developing an action agenda to strengthen those clusters."

Among the industry clusters already identified by Project Long Island as key to the area's future growth are graphic communications, medical imaging and health care information systems, emerging electronics, biotechnology/bioengineering, and computer software.

With a plan to actively support these industry clusters, LIA estimates more than 28,000 jobs will be created by the year 2000.

According to Crosson, although the LIA spearheaded the establishment of this regional economic initiative, "it is publicly and privately funded and has its own steering committee." The goal for participants, which include a cross section of the area's major banks, utilities, universities, and industry leaders, was simply stated by Crosson as "to bring more high-quality jobs to Long Island."

At the LIA-sponsored Long Island Summit, more than 250 action items to improve the local business climate were identified and presented to the public. Called the Long Island Action Plan, these items were the result of a series of open town forums held across the Island, as well as a community-wide review of various recent studies and reports.

The Long Island Partnership, created under the leadership of the LIA to bring together business, government, utility, and private sector economic development professionals, already has helped almost 300 local companies representing some 30,000 workers in efforts to relocate, expand, or remain on Long Island. Looking toward the increasingly global economy, the Partnership also has sponsored and promoted Long Island companies in overseas trade shows.

While Long Island's business community has undergone some changes in recent years, what has remained absolutely the same throughout the LIA's history is the importance to the region of small businesses. Crosson called small businesses—those with 100 employees or less—the backbone of the business community. "We're very entrepreneurial here; a fertile ground for small businesses," explained Crosson.

The LIA's Small Business Council (SBC) was established to specifically meet the interests, concerns, and expansion needs of Long Island's small businesses. SBC, through monthly meetings and Business After Hours, a periodic business networking show, provides small business owners with the timely opportunities they need to place their products or services before the

**Long Island
Association president
Matthew T. Crosson**

Business networking opportunities abound at the LIA's popular Business After Hours.

Matt Crosson joins News Anchor Drew Scott in questioning NYS Governor George Pataki on Focus 55.

public. Members may exhibit their own products and services at Business After Hours, but just as important is the opportunity to survey what fellow members have to offer. Among the other SBC services are frequent seminars led by specialists in growing and maintaining small businesses. Additionally, SBC members have the opportunity to speak directly with legislators about issues that affect small businesses through an LIA-sponsored annual bus trip to Albany.

Smaller businesses have been able to turn to the LIA for the past three years to resolve an issue that beleaguers businesses of all sizes: health insurance. The LIA Health Alliance, New York State's first private health care purchasing cooperative, offers low cost and a wide choice of health insurance to Nassau and Suffolk county businesses employing from 3 to 50 people. LIA officials along with many in the business community regard the Health Alliance as among the organization's major, and most important, initiatives of recent years.

Launched at about the same time as the Health Alliance was the LIA's Buy Long Island campaign, a crusade to encourage Long Islanders to solicit local companies for all of their business and personal needs. This major media push was spurred by the LIA in order to promote regional business. In the true spirit of volunteerism, all aspects of Buy Long Island are donated. Ads are prepared by a participating agency on a pro bono basis; space and air time to run the ads are donated by print and broadcast media.

Last year, the LIA also added a full-time staff economist. General economic information is generated for the benefit of all members, and the economist also makes available

reports specific to individual members' markets permitting companies to do far more informed forward planning.

Looking toward the changing world and the increasing importance of markets far from home, the LIA has brought its members into cyberspace via the Association's World Wide Web site. All LIA members are now listed on the Web; those wishing more in-depth Web coverage may purchase their own pages through the LIA at rates lower than they could obtain on their own Through "hyperlinking," these member pages can be tied to LIA pages, thus offering greater exposure. The LIA site also is linked to many other sites with information about Long Island.

The LIA's outreach to the business community, like its many services, is multifaceted. *Long Island*, a four-color glossy monthly magazine, is likely the LIA's most well-known vehicle for communicating news of the Association as well as information vital to those doing business on Long Island. Various television shows regularly hosted by LIA President Crosson also offer a platform to discuss issues that directly affect business people in the bi-county region.

Finally, it's the LIA that provides the podium for major policymakers to address the Long Island business community. Speakers at LIA breakfast and luncheon sessions—events which typically draw 1,000 attendees—have included every governor of New York State in the past 20 years, the state's two U.S. senators, both county executives, and other political and national figures important to the region, including U.S. General Colin L. Powell (ret.), U.S. Senator Lloyd Benson, and U.S. Senator Al Gore.　　•••

The Nassau and Suffolk county flags join the Stars and Bars outside the LIA's headquarters in Commack.

HQ BUSINESS CENTERS

• • •

AMERICAN MOVIE CLASSICS (AMC) HAD A problem. The company's building had been declared "sick" and had to be vacated while potential pollutants were investigated. They might have been out of business for the duration, but instead AMC turned to a unique Long Island company, HQ Business Centers. Within 24 hours, AMC and its staff of 60 were up and running in one of the region's premier office buildings, complete with phone and fax service and full backup support systems.

The AMC situation, said HQ Business Centers owner Robert Arcoro, was unusual both for its size and speed of implementation. But getting companies, and even individual business people, into an instant, professional, fully serviced office environment is what HQ Business Centers is all about. Although prime space is an important part of the company's menu of offerings, Arcoro stressed: "We're not in the real estate business; we're in the business of service."

Arcoro's company is part of a larger worldwide HQ Business Centers network. He estimated that there are some 150 centers throughout the globe in 14 countries. In the United States, there are about 125 locations. Arcoro is the owner of HQ Business Centers facilities at EAB Plaza on Long Island, eight in New York City, and in three California locations: San Francisco, San Mateo, and Century City. In New York City, HQ Business Centers offices are available on Park Avenue, Fifth Avenue, Avenue of the Americas, Seventh Avenue and Wall Street.

HQ Business Centers numbers amongst its clients many of the Fortune 500, high-tech companies, start-up businesses, sole practitioners, and professional practices. In fact, just about any type of business is a potential HQ client. Arcoro explained that the current trend toward downsizing is one of the factors that fuels the growth of his business: "Companies want to be on a flexible type of basis where they're not maintaining permanent locations throughout the country." AT&T, for instance, is one of the major national companies that utilizes HQ Business Centers for its locations in various U.S. cities.

Some HQ Business Centers clients use a facility for as short a period as 3-6 months; others have been with the company for 10 years or more. An average stay, said Arcoro, is 18 months. While there are other temporary office companies available to the business community, Arcoro noted that HQ Business Centers is distinguished as "the most service-oriented company of its kind."

Another HQ Business Centers hallmark is the type of office building it offers. The company operates under "very strict standards" regarding building selection. Arcoro said that the HQ Business Centers facility in any given city would be "the premier building in the premier location."

EAB Plaza, the "Rockefeller Center of Long Island," is home to HQ Business Centers' Long Island operations.

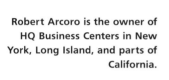

Offices equipped by HQ Business Centers feature complete electronic and personnel support systems.

Robert Arcoro is the owner of HQ Business Centers in New York, Long Island, and parts of California.

HQ Business Centers clients have fully equipped conference facilities at their avail for long or short-term use.

Most HQ Business Centers clients avail themselves of HQ staff as well as its office space. Available staff includes receptionists as well as secretarial and word processing personnel. While some clients do bring staff with them, Arcoro said that one of the company's attractions for clients is "our ability to provide instant, trained staff."

That "instant, trained staff" can be just about anywhere in the world. HQ Business Centers clients have access to facilities worldwide. So a business person who is a Long Island client can be provided with instant office space in Los Angeles, or even London, through the HQ network. For its clients only, HQ Business Centers offers eight-hour complimentary usage per month—perfect for the business traveler who must host a quick conference for out-of-town clients.

Arcoro is a lifelong East Meadow resident. He came to HQ Business Centers via a somewhat unusual route. As a young "business doctor," he had been retained by United Technologies (UT) to liquidate HQ Business Centers, one of UT's troubled subsidiaries. But Arcoro became intrigued by the HQ concept. Instead of liquidating the company, he bought it! He recalls a company losing money because of "too much staff and too much overhead." Arcoro streamlined HQ Business Centers and "nursed it back to health." He expanded the company and sold the franchised businesses back to the franchisers—one of whom is Arcoro himself, the

franchisee for New York, Long Island, and parts of California. Arcoro's "cure" for the company has obviously had a positive impact: when he purchased HQ Business Centers in 1985, the various locations generated $6 million in sales; last year Arcoro's locations generated $21 million.

HQ Business Centers' entrance to the Long Island market was fairly recent, but the move was pondered for many years. As a Long Islander himself, Arcoro knew he wanted to be in what he has called "one of the top markets in the country." So, over a seven-year period, Arcoro studied Long Island, seeking the perfect opportunity. That opportunity came with EAB Plaza, a facility that Arcoro regards as "the Rockefeller Center of Long Island." He felt that the mirror-like towers of EAB, a landmark for all of central Nassau County, offered his clients the same level of prestige and professionalism as his Manhattan locations already did. EAB Plaza also allows HQ Business Centers to be poised at the cutting-edge of technology, with such services as videoconferencing available to clients.

Through HQ Business Centers, a small company or even a single-practitioner business, with space requirements well under the minimums of such prestigious locations as EAB Plaza, can still conduct their businesses from an EAB-type Class A building. According to Arcoro, the company that needs only 1,000 square feet couldn't think of renting at EAB Plaza. But that small user could contract for just one office from HQ Business Centers, gaining in the process top location, numerous building amenities, and access to the full range of services that are the hallmarks of HQ Business Centers. Not surprisingly, Arcoro is seeking a second Long Island location—only top-quality buildings need apply. •••

BETHPAGE FEDERAL CREDIT UNION

Providing Comprehensive Financial Services for Member-owners

• • •

BETHPAGE FEDERAL CREDIT UNION (BFCU), Long Island's largest credit union, provides low-cost financial services to over 75,000 member-owners. Established in 1941 to serve the employees of Grumman Corporation, BFCU now brings its exceptional blend of products and services to employees of more than 50 premier Long Island-based companies. Headquartered in Bethpage, with assets of over $750 million, BFCU ranks among the top 1 percent of all federal credit unions.

THE CREDIT UNION DIFFERENCE

The essential difference between credit unions and other financial institutions is their member-owned, not-for-profit status. While other financial institutions must return a profit to their stockholders in the form of dividends, credit unions return "profits" to member-owners in the form of favorable rates. Describing the difference between credit unions and banks, President and CEO Peter J. Seitz explained "we're only in business to serve our member-owners."

Seitz added that because of this orientation, "credit unions can offer savings rates that give members an earning advantage and loan rates that lower their borrowing costs." This unique philosophy may explain why nearly 70 million people nationwide, or about 30 percent of the population, opt to manage their finances at credit unions.

Individuals typically become member-owners of BFCU through their employers, who regard credit union services as an enhancement to their company benefit programs. Companies participate by agreeing to provide direct deposit of paychecks at BFCU for employees who request the service. Employees can, in turn, pass the benefits of BFCU membership along to their family members. Computer Associates International Inc., Cablevision Systems Corp., Avis Rent A Car Systems, Inc. and Symbol Technologies, are just a sampling of the many companies providing BFCU services for their employees.

Bethpage Federal Credit Union Headquarters
South Oyster Bay Road, Bethpage, Long Island

A FULL SPECTRUM OF PRODUCTS & SERVICES

With just a $5 deposit to activate membership, BFCU members can enjoy a wide range of financial services, including basic savings, checking, vacation and holiday accounts, money market accounts, certificate accounts with flexible maturities, and a high yield IRA; loans of all types, including vehicle and personal loans, mortgages and home equity loans; VISA cards; and investment services through a wholly-owned subsidiary located in their main office.

Seitz remarked that many new members, especially those who are unfamiliar with credit unions, begin their association with BFCU with just a checking account. "Since the checking account is basically free," said Seitz, "members realize a substantial savings right away. As they become comfortable with us, they're likely to use BFCU for their other financial needs as well."

ANYTIME... ANYWHERE ACCESS

You don't have to live near one of their branch offices to "bank" with BFCU. In fact, noted Seitz, many members organize their entire financial lives without ever visiting a branch. That's because BFCU offers state-of-the art delivery systems that provide access anytime, anywhere members live or work. With the use of electronic services, members can elect direct deposit of their paycheck, perform transactions with ART (BFCU's telephone banking system), apply for a loan with their automated loan service and access cash at thousands of network ATMs worldwide. Through participation in a credit union shared branch network, members can also transact business at hundreds of shared branch locations nationwide. And, wonder of wonders in today's banking environment, it's possible to speak with a real person, day or evening, toll-free, at BFCU's Telephone Service Center.

EMPHASIS ON MEMBER SERVICE

"Our most important service," remarked Seitz, "is quality member service. Although we continue to stay on the leading edge of technology," he explained, "we understand that computers cannot replace personal service." BFCU continues to invest resources in technology and employee training and development programs required to provide outstanding member service. The credit union's annual meeting, along with on-going member surveys, provide a forum for member input. Results consistently show an extraordinarily high level of member satisfaction, and identify member needs that form the basis for future program development.

MOVING INTO THE FUTURE

Continuing its tradition of growth established over 5 decades ago, BFCU looks forward to another 50-plus years of success. Although it is already the largest credit union on Long Island, BFCU will continue its strategy of adding sponsor organizations to give the credit union the strongest and most diverse member base possible. Membership efforts will be aided by plans for the expansion of the credit union's product lines, as well as the development of innovative delivery systems to improve access and convenience for members. From this solid financial and technological foundation, BFCU moves into the future confident that it can effectively fulfill the need of its current and future members.   •••

The Loans & Member Services Department provides one-stop financial shopping in a conference-style setting.

LONG ISLAND COMMERCIAL BANK
An Independent Bank that Stresses Service

• • •

I N THE FACE OF MEGA MERGERS WHICH HAVE produced giant banking institutions, Long Island Commercial Bank seems almost an anomaly. The hometown ambience at this bank, headquartered in Islandia, evokes an earlier age; a time when people actually knew their bankers personally and when decision making on urgent financial matters wasn't delayed by unwieldy layers of bureaucracy.

Long Island Commercial Bank, Long Island's youngest financial institution, was chartered by the state of New York in November of 1989 and opened its doors in January of 1990. Despite a recession which initially slowed the bank's growth, by 1995 Long Island Commercial's assets had grown to $102 million.

The bank's founding chairman is Perry B. Duryea, Jr., the well-respected former speaker of the New York State Assembly and minority leader. Known throughout the state, Duryea's reputation and widespread contacts served as a springboard for the new institution's success. Among the other 14 founding directors were professionals and entrepreneurs with expertise in the diverse arenas of insurance, real estate development, law, medicine, retail and several other private sector fields.

The deep roots in the banking industry of Long Island Commercial's founding president and chief executive officer, Douglas Manditch, also served to position the organization solidly within the business community. Manditch started his banking career at Security National Bank, now a part of Chase, moving on to community banking

institutions thereafter. His reasons for leaving Security back in 1973 were much the same as his motivation to head the new Long Island Commercial: "I didn't want to work for a big bureaucratic company. I prefer to work where I can see the results of my efforts."

The mega mergers that had come to characterize the banking industry were the impetus behind the formation of Long Island Commercial Bank. Manditch explained "we decided that a new bank was needed in Western Suffolk because of the many consolidations that left very few independent banks on Long Island." The corporate mission for Long Island Commercial Bank from the outset has been to provide service excellence to the niche market that the new independent bank set out to serve—Long Island's broad community of small businesses and professional practices. The bank has also become well known as a source of construction lending.

In the same way that a small vessel may swiftly change course where a large ocean liner will need miles before it can turn, Long Island Commercial Bank prides itself on its ability to swiftly meet its customers'

Doug Manditch (right), president and CEO of Long Island Commercial Bank, visits the offices of bank customer William H. Munch (left) of Donaudy Munch Marketing Communications.

The headquarters of Long Island Commercial Bank are in Islandia.

Perry B. Duryea, Jr. (right), chairman of the board of Long Island Commercial Bank and Douglas C. Manditch, president and CEO.

individualized needs in a way that larger banks cannot. Manditch offered the example of an insurance company client that is responsible for paying out firefighter pension benefits in several states. Long Island Commercial customized a system for this client which allows for payment of benefits in different ways according to the laws and statutes of the state in which the benefits are being paid. According to Manditch, "this would be difficult for a bigger bank to accommodate." He explained that because of the bank's small size, "we can customize products for small companies where larger banks may only be able to offer them products 'off the shelf.'" Small companies also look to Long Island Commercial Bank for lock box and currency services that their size denies them at larger banking institutions. Among the other traditional commercial lending services available to Long Island Commercial customers are lines of credit, revolving credit, term loans, commercial mortgages, construction loans and letters of credit.

Long Island Commercial Bank's lean, unbureaucratic system allows for what Manditch calls "a sense of urgency" in responding to customers. He said that the bank's mission is to respond, and to respond swiftly. Manditch personally believes that a quick no may be almost as valuable to a businessperson as a yes. With rapid response an established company byword, Manditch said "we're probably best known for our ability to provide quick answers."

Where Long Island Commercial Bank does not provide a particular service, Manditch and his staff will guide the customer to a network of other service providers. "By helping them find the service they need, we are servicing our customer," said Manditch.

He also states that the bank "will do everything we can to make a loan possible." At Long Island Commercial Bank, what this means is that loan evaluation encompasses many factors, collateral being just one among them. The bank's officers also assess cash flow and the history and character of the individual requesting the loan. Visits to the customer's business site are a typical part of the review process because the bank "seeks to build relationships, not do single transactions."

Long Island Commercial Bank has responded to the region's shifting housing patterns by becoming more active in home construction loans. But today, in contrast to earlier years, developers are not building homes in the hope of attracting buyers. In fact, Manditch has noted among the dozen or so builders the bank regularly works with that "nobody's building houses that they don't have buyers for." Move-up housing is the briskest sector of the new housing market today, according to Manditch.

Currently Long Island's smallest bank, Long Island Commercial looks toward a future of independence and controlled growth. Growth patterns will be tempered by the bank's continued initiatives in completely automated back office services and operations. In 1995, the bank inaugurated its first branch office. The full-service Babylon branch of Long Island Commercial Bank is expected to be joined by one new branch office a year.

While exploring physical expansion and broadening its customer base, Long Island Commercial Bank has also shared its resources with institutions that serve the Long Island community. Among the organizations for which the bank has provided direct financial support or financial services are YMCA, Child Care Council, Transitional Services of New York for Long Island, Long Island Women's Coalition, Inc., and Boy and Girl Scouts. •••

Long Island Commercial Bank has moved into the forefront of home construction loans. Shown at a Southampton construction site are Doug Manditch (left), Mel Vizzini (center), senior vice president and senior lending officer of Long Island Commercial Bank; and Bernard Karwick (right), the president of Bridgehampton Homes Inc.

PEOPLE'S ALLIANCE FEDERAL CREDIT UNION

Helping People to a Better Quality of Life

• • •

IF YOU WANT TO DO YOUR BANKING AT A PLACE where even the smallest saver is treated like a VIP, then there's no better place than People's Alliance Federal Credit Union (PAFCU), whose headquarters is on Wireless Boulevard in the middle of the Hauppauge Industrial Park.

Founded in 1940 as the Pan American World Airways credit union, PAFCU today serves 32,000 employees of 300 different companies, many of them all over the United States, but most of them Long Islanders. At People's Alliance, there are no customers—everyone is a member and owner of the credit union, and receives friendly, respectful service from a staff and senior management that have many years with the organization.

President Nicholas Lacetera, for example, has been with PAFCU for over 30 years. "We are non-profit, and that means the money we make goes back to our owners as higher dividends and lower interest rates on loans," says Lacetera. "The people who come here know that this is their financial institution."

PAFCU senior management. Seated, left to right: Kenneth C. Hess, Chairman, Board of Directors; Nicholas M. Lacetera, President/CEO. Standing, left to right: Walter M. O'Connell, VP Internal Controls; Patricia A. O'Connell, VP Human Resources; John A. Romanchek, Executive Vice President; Carol A. Allen, VP Finance; William O'Connell, Sr. VP, Operations. Not pictured: Joanne Steigerwald, VP Operations.

BETTER THAN A BANK

A credit union is a cooperative financial institution organized to serve people who have a common bond of association, such as employment with a company or membership in an organization. People's Alliance is a Federally-chartered credit union whose operations are supervised by a U.S. government agency, the National Credit Union Administration (NCUA), which also insures deposits up to $100,000.

Because it is a non-profit cooperative, PAFCU can offer a complete package of very consumer-friendly services at very favorable rates. For example, checking accounts are free, and even the checks themselves are free if the member's

paycheck is automatically deposited in their account on payday. Loan rates are generally lower than at for-profit institutions, and dividends on savings accounts are higher. Members can purchase $500 Share Certificates to earn even higher rates.

Thanks to a wide array of electronic and phone services, members have easy and convenient access to their accounts and all of PAFCU's services. Fees for using NYCE and Cirrus automated tellers are low—only $1 a transaction.

"WE DON'T LIKE TO SAY NO"

People's Alliance has $111 million in assets, and capital reserves of 10 percent. The NCUA has not only given People's Alliance a top rating for its financial performance, but has also granted PAFCU blanket approval to immediately enroll any company located within the Hauppauge Industrial Park.

Among PAFCU's member companies are Waldbaum's, 1-800 Flowers, TNT Trucking, Parker-Hannifin Gull, Microwave Power Devices, and the Rugby Group, covering the entire spectrum of industries. These companies have recognized that credit union membership is a valued employee benefit that at the same time can make being an employer easier as well.

"Sometimes, companies loan money to their employees or provide cash advances when necessary, but once they join PAFCU they can refer the employees straight to us," says Lacetera. "We don't like to say no. We will work with each and every member as a unique individual. We'll do everything we can to help members consolidate their debts and have more disposable income to make their lives easier. That's what we're all about—service. And it's this kind of service that has enabled People's Alliance to grow and prosper on Long Island." • • •

People's Alliance FCU headquarters in the Hauppauge Industrial Park.

MARINE MIDLAND BANK
Banking for the Real World
• • •

FOUNDED NEARLY 150 YEARS AGO TO FINANCE trade along the Great Lakes, Marine Midland entered the Long Island marketplace in 1970 through the acquisition of the Community Bank of Lynbrook and Tinker National Bank. Today, Marine has 34 branches and more than 350 employees in Nassau and Suffolk counties, and is ranked as the #2 Small Business Administration lender on Long Island. Besides being a major force in banking, Marine is one of the leading sponsors of cultural and charitable programs on the Island.

At Marine Midland, efforts to provide customers with quality products and services are guided by a series of core principles. First and foremost among these is "looking at every action from the customer's perspective." The 8:30 AM to 4:30 PM banking hours at every Long Island branch is just one simple example of this principle being put into daily practice.

Thanks to its focus on understanding and responding to customers' needs, Marine was rated the "best bank in New York State" last year by *Money* magazine. Marine was singled out for this honor because of products such as Marinextra, a relationship banking package that was redesigned to include the suggestions of 9,000 customers, and is now enjoyed by more than 2,000 Long Islanders.

According to Carol Kennedy, Senior Vice President in charge of the Long Island District for Marine, Marinextra "rewards our customers for banking with us." It entitles customers to no-fee and discounted services, reduced loan rates, and premium savings rates. These benefits, she said, are based on combined balances "not just in savings or checking accounts, but under consumer facilities and mortgages that consumers have with us."

Another product that rewards customers for their loyalty is MarineAdvantage. This program gives credit card customers points for every dollar of purchases, cash advances and finance charges on their cards, and offers them a wide selection of awards including travel discounts and new car rebates.

"We believe in building long-term relationships with our customers," Ms. Kennedy said. "We want to serve them from their college days through their retirement." That's why Marine offers special

Leading Marine: Carol A. Kennedy, Long Island District Executive, and Patrick Doulin, Queens/Long Island Commercial Executive.

student banking services such as savings and checking accounts, ATM access and a student credit card, as well as a wide range of estate and retirement planning programs.

For Long Island's businesses, Marine's relationship with HSBC Holdings plc, headquartered in London, England, gives access to an array of services that are invaluable when conducting business internationally. Marine is part of the HSBC Group of commercial and investment banking businesses, which has more than 3,300 offices in 72 countries, making it one of the largest such organizations in the world.

Because of its HSBC Group connections, Marine offers bilingual retail and commercial banking services to Chinese and Indian customers, who benefit from special divisions established expressly to meet their needs.

"Along with traditional banking products, we can assist our commercial customers with letters of credit, foreign exchange services, and cash management," says Kennedy.

Customers utilize Hexagon™, an electronic banking system, to access their accounts 24 hours a day, make payments and wire transfers, open letters of credit, and check outstanding trade facilities.

Businesses of all sizes take advantage of these commercial banking services, and small businesses benefit from a variety of programs set up to meet their special needs. Marine is an active participant in numerous Small Business Administration programs, including the Export Working Capital Program. In addition, Ms. Kennedy said, "We have restructured our application and credit approval process so that loans under $100,000 are submitted electronically and typically processed within a day."

Marine takes pride in its activism as a corporate member of the Long Island community. Through the volunteer efforts of employees, event sponsorships, and contributions to non-profit organizations, Marine demonstrates an abundance of community spirit. Committed to building a better future for all on Long Island, Marine recently established a Long Island Advisory Board, comprised of local business people, to provide valuable insight and offer recommendations on how Marine can best serve the community. •••

THE NEW CHASE

• • •

CHEMICAL BANK AND CHASE MANHATTAN HAVE completed an historic merger, creating one of the strongest banks in the nation, with a tradition of service to New York area businesses that dates from the late 1700s. The combined institution has nearly $300 billion in assets and $20 billion in shareholder's equity, with 75,000 employees in 52 countries and 39 states. The bank is number one in the New York area in branch banking, consumer deposits, and banking for small and mid-sized companies.

"The new Chase" is the leading bank for business on Long Island. With more than 90 branches across the Island, and the largest team in the banking industry of experienced Relationship Managers dedicated to serving Long Island companies, Chase provides a full range of services:

- financing of all kinds, from commercial mortgages to working capital to leasing
- cash management services to enhance cash flow
- investment products and advice
- operating accounts for every purpose
- 401(k) retirement savings plans for employees
- discounted banking packages for employees
- access to lower-cost health care insurance for employees
- services for family-owned or -operated businesses
- merger and acquisition finance and advice
- international trade services, including letters of credit, foreign exchange, bankers acceptances
- private banking for the company's principals
- seminars and programs on financial topics

TOP-RANKED BY LONG ISLAND BUSINESSES

According to Kenneth J. Daley, Senior Vice President and head of business banking on Long Island, "Long Island's mid-sized companies rank the bank number one in many categories, including the quality of our relationship managers, international expertise, and aggressiveness."

Daley added, "Our first market surveys were carried out in 1982. In every annual survey since, we have ranked as the leading bank for small and mid-sized companies—a record we work hard to maintain."

This strength is the result of a concerted effort to focus on growing companies. The new Chase was the first bank to realize the potential and importance of the "middle market," and the first to create a fully-dedicated organization charged with addressing the needs of this market—Middle Market Banking.

Kenneth J. Daley, Senior Vice President and head of the new Chase's business banking on Long Island.

CORPORATE FOCUS ON BUSINESS BANKING

Middle Market Banking is one of the major functional units of the bank, headed by an Executive Vice President, and staffed with a cadre of credit-trained relationship managers. The average banking experience of relationship managers is 13 years; the average banking experience of senior managers exceeds 20 years. Many relationship managers and senior managers have dedicated their entire careers to middle market banking.

In addition to credit officers, the bank has specialist groups to handle technically complex banking needs. For example, the bank's international unit provides an assigned specialist to each customer with international needs to help with strategy and execution, and the Structured Finance Group provides guidance in structuring complex financings as well as expertise in asset-based financings.

DEDICATION TO THE COMMUNITIES OF LONG ISLAND

"The great majority of Chase employees who work on Long Island live here, too," said Daley, a Glenn Head resident who has been with the bank for more than 40 years. "You'll find our people working in hundreds of ways to help, from hospitals, local government and schools to coaching baseball, the Girl Scouts, and religious groups." The bank actively supports this work and provides financial support to hundreds of charitable organizations on Long Island.

In addition, Chase is a sponsor of the New York Islanders and the Corporate Challenge footrace, and hosts major sports events for customers throughout the year.

A COMMITMENT TO SMALL & MID-SIZED BUSINESSES

The new Chase believes that small and mid-sized businesses are one of the most important sectors of the American economy. Small and mid-sized businesses create more jobs than large corporations and are frequently on the leading edge of innovation in American industry. The bank is committed to serving this major, growing sector of our economy. • • •

CHAPTER 13

PROFESSIONS

Photo by James McIsaac.

BRENNER/LENNON PHOTO PRODUCTIONS, INC.

Expert Photographic Services for the Corporate Community

• • •

THE UNINITIATED MIGHT THINK THAT JAY BRENNER and Jim Lennon are just taking pictures. But the principles of Brenner/Lennon Photo Productions, Inc. understand that the real goal of their work is to create and enhance corporate and advertising images.

This executive meeting was photographed at the Olympus facility in Woodbury L.I. for an Olympus Pearlcorder package.

Brenner/Lennon Photo Productions of Plainview has established itself as the premiere photography resource on Long Island. They combine four full time photographers, a full production staff, plus digital and darkroom technicians to offer one of the most comprehensive photo "think tanks" available. Ideas come to life in an environment that plays host to a wide assortment of Long Island's leading corporations through over 750 projects every year.

Both Brenner and Lennon are exiles from New York City. Despite the success each had achieved in the highly competitive New York photographic market, they decided that Long Island would be a more pleasant place to establish their future business. Given the ease

of travel today and the immediacy of electronic communications, they found that they can be across the country on a photo shoot as readily from Plainview as from Soho, and that clients across the country can be serviced via fax and modem as readily as clients down the road. A Manhattan address turned out to be a less crucial determinant as it once was in landing high-profile clients and assignments. Said Brenner, "I took the attitude that if I could be successful in Manhattan, I could be successful out here." He was right. Within two years of the 1987 move to Long Island, Brenner and Lennon were billing as much as they ever did in Manhattan. With the original staff of three having since been expanded to more than a dozen, Brenner/Lennon's work has been recognized with awards from the Association of the Graphic Arts, The One Show of the NYC Art Directors Club, Art Direction Magazine, the Long Island Advertising Club and Graphic Design Magazine. They have also been honored with cover stories and cover photos on photographic industry magazines such as *Studio Photography*, *Industrial Photography*, *The Photo District News* and *Popular Photography*.

The company's lengthy roster of prestigious local clients include Acclaim Entertainment, Computer Associates, King Kullen, CMP Publications, Publishers Clearing House, Olympus America, 800-Flowers, Northfork Bancorp, Suffolk Bancorp, Citibank, EAB, Nikon, Natures Bounty, Winthrop University Hospital, News 12, Cablevision, Marchon Eyewear, Bennett X-Ray, Henry Schein, Weight Watchers, Sbarro's, Geraghty & Miller, Pall Corporation, and Tilles Center for the Performing Arts. Many of the Island's leading advertising agencies and graphics services depend on the company's photographic expertise in servicing their own clients. The Brenner/Lennon portfolio includes photographs used in national ad campaigns, business-to-business promotions, consumer brochures,

This photograph was produced for an NEC Publication called "In Touch." The studio had the swirled steel pedestals built to hold the computer equipment and NEC telephone.

This photograph for Haagen Daas ice cream required a staff of nine people to execute the complicated task of capturing the actual ice cream product at its best without any additives or artificial ingredients.

editorial assignments, display and trade show material, product catalogues, and, of course, annual reports. Particular areas of specialty for Brenner/Lennon are still life and food photography, executive portraiture, location photography, and product and aerial photography for large industrial, corporate and advertising agency accounts.

Brenner/Lennon describes what they offer their clients as "the most diverse selection of photo services possible under one roof." Working within stated budgets and deadlines, the company delivers creative support and technical excellence. Brenner stated: "We attack all of our projects with energy, originality and optimism, and we are truly ready for anything." The result is that they often find that their clients are amazed to find out what their resources have to offer.

Brenner/Lennon has added state-of-the-art digital photography to the many capabilities it has to place at the avail of its corporate and advertising clients. According to Brenner, digital photography, a process that he said is revolutionizing the photographic industry, allows for sophisticated, filmless photo production and also for editing and archiving of superior quality. The tools Brenner and Lennon have selected to deliver this new process are Leaf Digital Camera Backs and MacIntosh PowerPC work stations. Through digital photography, which is both Mac and PC compatible, images are instantly reproduced on the computer screen right on the photo set. These images are immediately available for image enhancement and manipulation. By eliminating scans and retouchers, digital images have the advantage of placing creative and editing options right at the designer's fingertips. In addition to far greater creative control, digital images do not suffer degradation through duplication. For clients, Brenner/Lennon's use of digital

photography translates into savings of both time and money.

The studio's four photographers work very close with each other and constantly advise, assist and share their knowledge and information on projects and photo shoots. "It's quite exciting" says Mr. Lennon "to see the work of so many different photographers on the lightbox every day. The clients like seeing the results of other projects also." The studio is a very busy environment transforming itself daily to accommodate anything from full scale set production to a large volume catalogue projects. Smaller projects are handled with incredible efficiency due to the availability of all the resources on hand for larger projects. With all the photographers simultaneously working on different projects, the production staff constantly arranges, co-ordinates, schedules and communicates with clients on a daily basis. All of this allows them to maintain an impressively smooth and efficient pace.

Location photography has its own unique problems that require well planned solutions. Indoors or outdoors, day or night, you've got to be prepared for it all. Location assignments have taken Brenner/Lennon throughout the United States as well as out of the country. A uniquely designed combination of travel equipment enables them to efficiently get in and out of places with fantastic results and a minimal amount of disruption.

The final statement of quality control is reflected in the processing and finishing of the film or files of the captured images. Brenner/Lennon owns and operates its own professionally staffed black & white and color photo processing lab that adheres to the strict standards of the Kodak Q-Lab Processing System. Their-state-of-the-art Digital Services Division teams up some of the most advanced computer technology available with an experienced staff of Scitex-trained professionals. On staff design and multi-media capability carries the high quality photography into the future with their home-page and interactive CD presentations and productions. All things considered, its no wonder that Brenner/Lennon has surfaced as Long Island's premiere photography resource. This organization is considered to be a forerunner in the digital marketplace, providing expert photographic services for the corporate community. •••

This image for California Microwave is made up of 10 conventional studio photographs and two photographs provided by NASA. All the photos were combined using state-of-the-art computer imaging equipment to produce the final image of the darts heading towards their target.

SCULLY, SCOTT, MURPHY & PRESSER, P.C.
Bridging the Gap Between Technology & Law

• • •

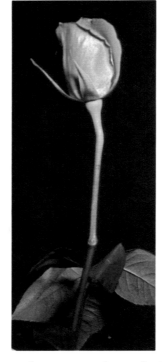

NO ONE HAS YET PRODUCED A BLUE ROSE, BUT biologists in Australia have learned to manipulate the biochemistry of flowers so that their colors can be changed. Eventually, they hope to grow roses that are blue. In the meantime, they need to protect their discovery.

Four companies have applied for the same patent for batteries having a built-in gauge showing how much power remains. Two of those companies, Duracell and Eveready, are both marketing batteries with the gauge although only one of them probably has the legal right to do so. They need to sort out their dispute.

While most people enjoyed the computer-animated movie, "Toy Story," it did not make the executives of a major defense industry contractor smile. They believe the 3D graphics technology used in the movie, and which is now quickly moving into the consumer PC world, infringes their patent on graphics developed for flight simulators used to train pilots for Desert Storm. They want their patent enforced.

Some companies have discovered that trademarked names for their products have been registered to others for use as domain names on the Internet. They think their trademarks have been infringed, and want to get back the Internet use of those names.

In all these cases, companies have turned to Scully, Scott, Murphy & Presser, Long Island's largest intellectual property law firm. Based in Garden City, Scully, Scott, Murphy & Presser conducts a national and international practice that specializes in patents, trademarks, copyrights, trade secrets, unfair competition and related trade regulation matters.

The firm is comprised of 23 lawyers, all of whom also have scientific expertise in the fields of biotechnology, genetics, micro-biology, computer science, electronics, chemistry, metallurgy, physics or mechanics. Two have Ph.D's, and six have Masters Degrees in scientific disciplines. This combination of legal and scientific expertise enables Scully, Scott, Murphy & Presser to effectively represent companies whose intellectual property is at the core of their enterprises. The firm represents both Fortune 100 companies and start-up businesses.

"We're dealing with matters in which the patent is a monster business tool," says partner Frank S. DiGiglio. "We handle major cases that demand that the power of the patent be used to not only obtain a substantial monetary award for infringement, but also to shut someone down who is infringing."

PATENT LAW INTERNSHIP

Scully, Scott, Murphy & Presser was formed in 1973 to specialize in intellectual property. One of the founding attorneys, John F. Scully, held a Ph.D. in organic chemistry. He taught patent law at Hofstra University, and organic chemistry at Queens College. Early on, he recognized that education in technology as well as law would be essential to the protection of intellectual property.

Scully, Scott, Murphy & Presser was among the first law firms to employ Ph.D. scientists to work on their cases. Several of these scientists went on to law school themselves. Furthering this principle, the firm has developed and established the first patent law internship for graduate students in the life sciences with the Center for Biotechnology at the State University of New York at Stony Brook. This program provides each student with insight into the intellectual property field that will be both an asset to that individual's career, and will also foster

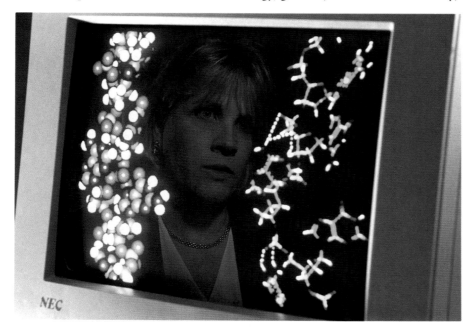

SSM&P combines legal and scientific expertise to provide a wide range of services for the effective representation of its clients. Here, Ann R. Pokalsky, an attorney specializing in plant genetics, contemplates recent developments in the law protecting new ideas in molecular biology.

A litigation team, formed to help a major defense contractor enforce a patent covering a flight simulator, employs networked computer litigation support systems, on-line searching of technical databases, and the Internet to provide effective legal services.

the growth of high technology on Long Island.

Partners Kenneth L. King and Stephen D. Murphy also work pro bono with the Long Island Research Institute to review the patentability of technology that has been developed at various non-profit Long Island research facilities. This technology may be appropriate for an incubator project.

"Patents will play a big part in the successful transition of Long Island from dependence on the defense industry to new ventures in biotechnology and computer science," says Paul J. Esatto, Jr, also a partner.

PROTECTION OF INTELLECTUAL PROPERTY WORLD-WIDE

Scully, Scott, Murphy & Presser provides a full range of intellectual property services that are tailored to help clients achieve their business objectives. The firm advises clients on the patentability of new concepts as well as the validity and infringement of issued patents. The firm's experts in licensing provide clients with invaluable assistance in commercializing their inventions.

The firm prepares and prosecutes patent and trademark applications in the United States and abroad. The firm's extensive international practice, developed by founding partner Anthony C. Scott, uses the Patent Cooperation Treaty, the European Patent Office, and direct filings to obtain patents in almost every foreign jurisdiction.

Although Scully, Scott, Murphy & Presser recognizes that its clients want to conduct business, and not litigation, "litigation is sometimes a business tool," notes Murphy. The firm is vigorous in enforcing patents and trademarks, and has protected multi million

dollar licensing programs, including that for the prostate specific antigen (PSA) diagnostic test. The firm also litigated the first patent case in which fraud was found and which involved an asserted violation of the RICO statute.

The firm offers experience in all aspects of trademark and unfair competition litigation, including trade dress infringement, counterfeiting, false advertising, "gray market" actions and trade disparagement.

INSTANT ACCESS TO PATENT, SCIENTIFIC LITERATURE

For effective representation in complex matters, Scully, Scott, Murphy & Presser organizes its professional staff into teams of two to four attorneys, who are assisted by a support staff of 35. On-line computers provide instant access to patent and scientific literature world-wide, including records in the United States Patent and Trademark Office, the registers of various states, and thousands of brand name directories, telephone books, and news and information sources. These electronic capabilities, however, may be supplemented by a search of the hard copies of patents maintained at the patent office in Washington, D.C.

Scully, Scott, Murphy & Presser has been able to secure patents and trademark protection for intellectual property as diverse as a patent on computer software for Symbol Technologies' bar code reader, and the trademark for Long Island's "First Family of Fireworks," the Grucci's. It was this descriptive phrase of the Grucci's, in fact, which the firm preserved in an action against a competitor just before the U.S. Bicentennial.　•••

Law firm conferences are called on a regular basis to review major matters entrusted to the firm. Through imaginative initiatives and full consideration of the business issues, SSM&P avoids unnecessary legal expense and controversy in the representation of its clients.

RAINS & POGREBIN, P.C.

Representing Management in Labor & Employment Law & School Law

• • •

RAINS & POGREBIN IS A SMALL TOWN FIRM WITH a large city practice. From its main office in the same landmark building in Mineola for 50 years, the firm has developed a national practice in labor and employment law as management representatives. It is among the largest labor law firms in the New York Metropolitan area, and has one of the largest public sector

The Rains Building in Mineola, a well-known landmark and home to Rains & Pogrebin for 50 years.

practices in New York State. In recent years, the firm, which also has an office in Manhattan, has expanded its practice to include representing school districts as general counsel.

Clients of the firm include IBM, Coca Cola, Avis, PolyGram, Hudson General, Global Computer Supplies, Cybex, Dairy Barn Stores, Henry Schein, State Farm, Steris Labs, the Village Voice, Joyce Theater, about 25 school districts, including the New York City Board of Education, and many municipalities, including Suffolk County.

The firm is particularly proud of its inclusion in the National Law Journal's *Directory of the Legal Profession*. The Directory includes smaller, specialty firms only when "considered prominent by (their) peers," and Rains & Pogrebin was one of only three specialty firms in the country included that engage in labor and

employment law representing management.

Thirteen partners and eight associates serve the firm's clients. When Harry Rains hung out his shingle in Mineola in 1947, the practice of labor law on behalf of employers had everything to do with unions. Strikes, negotiations, arbitrations, grievances, and union organizing drives: these were the every day practice that Rains pursued, always from the point of view of management.

While union matters still occupy the attorneys, the focus of the practice now includes labor and employment consequences of business restructuring, equal employment opportunity and discrimination law, wage and hour regulation, employment agreements and restrictive covenants, employee discharges, occupational safety and health law, and litigation of employment-related issues. "There has been an explosion of legislation that affects everything that takes place in the work place," said partner Bruce Millman."

A FAST & EXCITING PACE

Bert Pogrebin was fresh out of Harvard Law School when he came out to what he imagined would be a somewhat sleepy, small law practice. When he arrived for his appointment with Rains, instead of sitting down for a quiet chat, Rains grabbed him and took him with him to Roosevelt Raceway, where he was involved in a union negotiation. The horses were trotting, the atmosphere was colorful and charged with energy. Pogrebin was hooked: he joined the firm. It was 1959.

The atmosphere and pace inside the historic old courthouse on the corner of Old Country Road and Mineola Boulevard that houses

**The partners of
Rains & Pogrebin.**

The legal staff of Rains & Pogrebin, outside their headquarters on Old Country Road.

Rains & Pogrebin is still fast and exciting. "In this practice, you need to be able to respond quickly to clients' needs," said partner Fred Braid. "Clients call and need immediate answers to very practical problems that increasingly have legal consequences."

An employee accuses a supervisor of harassment, and the manager needs to know what to do that same day. Or, an owner drives into work to find a picket line in front of his business that is blocking all deliveries. Still another employer asks for help with an employee who doesn't show up for work or even call in for three days, only to arrive with a note from his doctor claiming a debilitating job injury. The employer needs to know whether the employee can be fired for violating company rules of conduct, or if he is entitled to leave under federal law or company policy, or perhaps to some accommodation to enable him to do his job.

"Age discrimination, sex discrimination, disability and handicap laws—almost everyone is in at least one protected class," said partner Bruce Millman. "And in the public sector, we often face issues of constitutional dimension—issues of due process, equal protection, freedom of speech, establishment of religion, privacy issues," added partner Terry O'Neil.

Other situations that demand immediate attention have to do with downsizing or selling businesses. An owner may have a potential buyer for the company, but the buyer does not want to deal with an existing labor union. Another company has to lay off workers, and wants to avoid backing into an age discrimination claim, or triggering the WARN Act, or falling into a score of other possible legal pitfalls.

"With most of our clients we develop a relationship where we are like in-house staff," said Millman. "We counsel them on how to keep out of trouble, and out of litigation, or, if there might be litigation, how to take steps to assure that the outcome will be favorable."

JUNIOR OR SENIORS

The Rains & Pogrebin practice transcends the boundaries of typical law school "Labor Law" courses. There are no "seniors" or "juniors." The firm trains its new lawyers in the practical aspects of labor and employment law by involving them in all facets of the practice from the inception of their careers at the firm. Partners and associates not only counsel clients, but prepare witnesses, participate in litigation, write briefs, and argue orally before federal and state courts and an alphabet soup of agencies. All participate in collective bargaining, contract administration, mediation and fact finding.

From the clients' point of view, this means that one attorney is made responsible for them. Cases are not transferred to different attorneys or departments as they reach different stages. Legal research is done by the attorneys involved in the case, not by randomly-assigned associates who might not understand the larger picture.

The partners are very active in teaching, writing, and professional organizations. For example, Pogrebin has been Adjunct Professor of Labor Law at New York and Hofstra University Law Schools, and has been visiting lecturer at Yale Law School. David Wirtz is an Adjunct Professor at Cardozo Law School. Mona Glanzer is past chair of the Labor & Employment Law Section of the New York State Bar Association, and former President of the Nassau/Suffolk Women's Bar Association. Terry O'Neil is an Editor of a widely-used treatise on Public Sector Labor Law. Fred Braid is one of the authors of a treatise on occupational health and safety laws. Millman is President of the Long Island Chapter of the Industrial Relations Research Association, and Chair-Elect of the State Bar's Labor and Employment Law Section. •••

The senior partners of Rains & Pogrebin. Standing (l to r): Terry O'Neil, Mona Glanzer, Fred Braid. Seated (l to r) Bert Pogrebin, Bruce Milman.

KPMG PEAT MARWICK LLP
A Guiding Force in Long Island's Corporate & Civic Communities
• • •

THE SUCCESS OF LONG ISLAND IN THE 1970S hinged on the prowess of defense manufacturers and suppliers. In the 1980s, the area's business landscape was marked by financial and insurance back-office operations, along with a boom in residential and commercial development. Today, high technology, health care and quality business management are the watchwords of the region's corporate community.

One constant in the continued success experienced by this vibrant, challenging environment over the past three decades has been KPMG Peat Marwick LLP, the largest professional services firm on Long Island and the component of KPMG, The Global Leader among professional service firms. Based in Jericho, New York, KPMG has since 1966 played a dominant role in the development of the local business and civic communities.

"At KPMG, we are committed to helping Long Island, its residents and its businesses make the most of the opportunities that are available to them," said Lawrence J. Waldman, managing partner of KPMG's Long Island office. "Because of our pro-active management services and position as a leader in the Long Island community, KPMG is recognized by executives here as the professional service firm best-suited to helping businesses establish Long Island roots and build upon them for a successful, profitable future."

Comprised of 190 tax and audit professionals, KPMG provides the finest and broadest array of accounting, audit and management consulting services. The firm's local client roster currently includes many of Long Island's leading retailers, manufacturers, financial services organizations, software companies, biotechnology firms, health-care providers, higher education and governmental bodies and information/communications enterprises.

Central to all of the professional services provided by KPMG is a commitment to meet and exceed the demands of its clients. "Our main goal in every relationship," said Waldman, "is to provide high-quality services that help improve the position and profitability of our clients."

A particular strength of KPMG on Long Island is its ability to provide management consulting and accounting services for businesses operating in virtually every industry category. KPMG's Long Island office is divided into five specific practice areas: financial services; manufacturing, retailing and distribution; health care and life sciences; information, communications and entertainment; and public services.

Each practice area provides the firm's clients with a team of professionals focused solely on that client's industry. KPMG professionals know first-hand the problems industries have experienced in the past, the issues facing them today and the trends being discussed for the future. More importantly, they put that knowledge to work by developing the right strategies to maximize revenue, profitability and productivity for each of the firm's clients.

Of course, KPMG's services are not only limited to dealings on Long Island. For clients with national or international operations, the

Led by 14 partners, KPMG is Long Island's largest professional services firm with nearly 200 professionals dedicated to providing complete management consulting and accounting services for local businesses.

Lawrence J. Waldman, managing partner, KPMG's Long Island office.

To better serve clients in a broad spectrum of industries, KPMG's Long Island office is divided into five specialized practice areas comprised of teams of professionals well versed in the specific needs and issues affecting their clients.

Long Island office regularly works closely with other members of the KPMG worldwide network, which comprises 1,100 offices in 134 countries.

Among the world's preeminent professional service firms, KPMG maintains a staff of more than 76,000 professionals who provide high-quality service to more than 180,000 clients around the world.

"Being able to make business decisions based on Long Island concerns is important," said Waldman. "However, as the globalization of business continues, more and more companies need to make decisions that will succeed in the international community as well. Whether it involves a simple tax filing in New York or the acquisition of a company abroad, KPMG is uniquely qualified to meet the needs of every Long Island business."

Beyond being the dominant provider of accounting services to local businesses, KPMG Peat Marwick LLP also serves as an advocate of Long Island itself—playing an active role in developing and implementing economic, governmental and social programs geared to advance and improve the community.

Perhaps the best example of KPMG's effort in this area is the firm's role as founder and sponsor of "The Entrepreneurial Spirit Awards." Begun in 1986,

the awards program annually recognizes both the Top 50 and 25 Fastest-Growing privately held companies on Long Island and showcases them as examples of the business and employment growth that is possible in the region. Furthering this commitment to Long Island businesses, KPMG began sponsoring in 1996 the Long Island Investment Forum to spotlight the region's top public companies.

KPMG clients also benefit from the firm's connection to local business leaders through its membership and activism in such organizations as the Long Island Association and the new Long Island Partnership. What's more, partners in the firm hold memberships in such business organizations as the New York Software Industry Association, the Long Island Coalition for Fair Broadcasting and the Nassau County Sports Commission.

However, the firm's efforts extend beyond the Long Island business community. In an effort to better the "neighborhood" that is its home, KPMG actively supports an array of not-for-profit institutions dedicated to improving the quality of life for local residents.

The United Way of Long Island, the Sid Jacobson Jewish Community Center, the Long Island Philharmonic, the Boy Scouts and the American Cancer Society are just some of the charitable and arts organizations that have benefited recently from KPMG's financial and personal support. Several Long Island-based educational and research institutions have also received significant attention from the firm, including Hofstra University and The Cold Spring Harbor Laboratory.

"Long Island truly offers the best of both worlds," said KPMG Peat Marwick's Waldman. "For businesses, there is a wealth of resources and a highly educated workforce. For the people who own and manage those businesses, there is an array of exciting and interesting attractions and activities to enjoy. At KPMG Peat Marwick, we're proud of the role we play in helping both 'worlds' grow and prosper." •••

KPMG founded and annually sponsors the Long Island "Entrepreneurial Spirit Awards" program to honor the success of local businesses. Here, U.S. Senator Alfonse D'Amato (second from left) is thanked by KPMG's Lawrence J. Waldman, Hofstra University President Dr. James M. Shuart and Hofstra Provost Dr. Herman A. Berliner for serving as keynote speaker at a recent "Salute to Long Island's Entrepreneurial Spirit" awards luncheon.

FARRELL, FRITZ, CAEMMERER, CLEARY, BARNOSKY & ARMENTANO, PC

Full-Service Legal Representation for Long Island's Public & Private Sectors

• • •

WIDELY KNOWN AS FARRELL, FRITZ, THE FIRM of Farrell, Fritz, Caemmerer, Cleary, Barnosky & Armentano ranks as one of the largest law firms on Long Island. A full-service, general practice firm representing businesses, financial institutions, governments, trade and professional associations, as well as individuals, Farrell, Fritz partners and associates provide clients with expertise on just about every type of legal matter. Some of the firm's broadly comprehensive range of practice areas include: banking law; appellate practice; business and corporate law; commercial law; criminal law; employee benefits and compensation; health care; estate litigation; municipal law; litigation; tax law; and wills, trusts, and estate planning.

The firm represents many of Long Island's municipalities and serves as special counsel for a number of towns and the County of Nassau. Long Island's banks and other banks doing business on Long Island often turn to Farrell, Fritz for transactional work involving loans and litigated matters.

Farrell, Fritz is perhaps best known, and most highly regarded, for its work in complicated litigated matters. As partner John J. Barnosky put it: "We're a lawyers' law firm. Firms come to us for matters concerning their clients that are beyond their ken."

Despite the renown of its litigation practice, it's a stated Farrell, Fritz goal to save its clients the time and cost of protracted litigation by settling cases through other, negotiated means.

According to Barnosky, Farrell, Fritz is "an efficient, more economical alternative to the big New York City firms." Barnosky pointed to the fact that Farrell, Fritz's partners are involved in all the firm's cases as one of the means by which clients receive higher levels of service than they might at a large New York City-based firm. Farrell, Fritz's periodic newsletters and frequent updates are yet other

Jack Barnosky (2nd from right), Managing Partner of the firm and head of the Trusts & Estates Department, meets with members of his department to discuss a complicated Estates litigation matter. Left to right: Eric Kramer, Sally Donahue, Jack Barnosky and John Morken.

means of providing clients with a high level of service. Through these communications, the firm advises clients of important legal changes and developments that might affect their businesses. This outreach also assists clients in complying with applicable laws and rules, often helping them to avoid legal problems before they arise.

The Farrell, Fritz client roster includes many Long Island businesses, as well as national and international corporations based in the New York metropolitan region seeking representation in Long Island matters requiring expertise in litigation, acquisitions, and environmental law. Barnosky's wide-ranging practice, for instance, includes estate planning and administration as well as extensive estate litigation. It was Barnosky's particular expertise in estates and wills that recently involved the firm in two widely publicized matters: the complex, highly-litigated estates of artist Andy Warhol and heiress Doris Duke.

Partner Andrew J. Simons, who has earned a broad reputation for his handling of environmental law cases, involved the firm in yet

Charlie Strain (standing, right), partner in charge of the Real Estate Department and Tom Killeen (standing, left), head of the Corporate Department, review a deal with Real Estate partner Bob Guido (seated, left) and associate Nora Link (seated, right) which involves both departments.

Research by partners and associates. Front to back: John Cleary, Jim Wicks, Chris Daly and Mike Healy.

another well-known issue. The Federal Superfund litigation over a Glenwood Landing site, a priority on the national toxic waste site roster, involved almost 400 parties. Simons' client, one of approximately 100 third-party defendants, didn't own or contaminate the site. Instead, the company was named in the suit because it had sent its toxic waste to this state-approved site. What was at issue was the extent to which each of the parties to the suit would be held responsible for contamination and further the extent to which they would have to contribute financially to the clean-up. Seeking to reduce his client's liability, Simons was instrumental in involving 200 additional companies as defendants in this litigation. According to Simons, by the time of its resolution, this case had come before five federal judges and every federal magistrate in the Long Island district of New York State. The ultimate settlement, which resulted in the state's assuming a portion of the responsibility, was described by Simons as "an immense accomplishment."

The firm of Farrell, Fritz arose from a partnership founded by John Caemmerer and George Pratt in the early 1960s. In 1976, Caemmerer and Pratt merged the firm with the practice of George J. Farrell, Jr. In 1971, Farrell, Fritz was a four-lawyer firm. Today, over 50 lawyers are partners or associates in the firm. Barnosky stated that this growth has made Farrell, Fritz one of the three largest firms on Long Island but stressed that this has been "controlled growth." He explained that growth has been important for the firm because "a larger base enables us to do more for our clients."

Caemmerer, now deceased, was at one time a New York State legislator, and Pratt went on to appointment as a federal appellate judge. This was the start of a distinguished Farrell, Fritz tradition of public service that continues to the present day. A number of the firm's current members are past or present state senators, assemblymen or judges. Many have taught or lectured at Long Island's colleges, universities, and law schools; have widely written on topics relating to their areas of practice for various legal publications; have served as trustees for their hometown municipal governments and on the boards of philanthropic, cultural, business, and professional organizations that serve the legal field and the region.

Among the many Long Island institutions that currently or in the past have had the benefit of participation by members of the Farrell, Fritz firm are Cold Spring Harbor Laboratory, Molloy College, the Long Island Association, Winthrop-University Hospital, the Long Island Coalition for Fair Broadcasting, the Salvation Army, the Fire Island Lighthouse Preservation Society, Tilles Center for the Performing Arts, the Leukemia Society of America, the Family Service Association of Nassau County, Island Harvest (a food bank), New Beginnings (an international adoption agency), and Nassau County's Legal Aid Society.

Thus, through their professional and private commitments, the lawyers comprising the firm of Farrell, Fritz have woven themselves throughout the fabric of the legal profession and of the public and private sectors of Long Island. • • •

Dolores Fredrich (seated, left), head of the Commercial Litigation Department, and John Armentano (standing, center), head of the Municipal Litigation Department, discuss a case with associates from both departments. Standing left to right: Jon Ward, John Armentano and Kathleen Tomlinson. Seated left to right: Dolores Fredrich and Judith Hepworth. (All photos by Brian Ballweg.)

BLUMLEIN ASSOCIATES, INC.

• • •

ENVIRONMENTAL DESIGN FOR CORPORATE Clientele—From massive theme park environments for a major multi-national corporate client to design continuity for a Long Island museum exhibition, Blumlein Associates, Inc. has earned a reputation as one of the nation's premier industrial design organizations. The company specializes in exhibition design, corporate conference centers, and retail- and entertainment-related design. Although they may not know the company name, millions and millions of Americans have seen and enjoyed Blumlein design products at EPCOT Center, Universal Studios in Florida and California, The Museum of Modern Art, the Massachusetts Institute of Technology, Lincoln Center, and Cirque du Soleil, one of the world's most highly-regarded circus troupes. Here on Long Island, Blumlein design commissions have been for various historic societies, the Nassau County Museum, the Vanderbilt Museum and The Museums at Stony Brook for which the company created the design of a definitive exhibition on Robert Moses.

Fred Blumlein, president of the Greenvale firm, explained "we basically design unique spaces and environmental graphics." He said that his company is a major supplier of design concepts for Sony and AT&T, among others.

Operating out of a red barn-like structure nestled just off of busy Northern Boulevard, the small staff of Blumlein Associates, Inc. easily communicates with its national clientele through advances in computer and telecommunications technology.

Oddly, the company seems better known in the national high-tech arena than it is to Long Island's own technological community.

A life-long Long Islander and a faculty member of the graduate division of Pratt Institute's Industrial Design Department, Fred Blumlein acknowledges that, given the national nature of his company's commissions, he really could run the business just about anywhere in the country. But he continues to be attracted to the Island's history, environmental beauty, and strong community spirit. Another lure for Blumlein is the local availability of high-quality technical support. So Fred Blumlein and his staff remain on Long Island—but he does ponder the irony of the company's national reputation in the face of its low-profile, almost "well-kept secret" status, here at home. • • •

Some of the environments created by Blumlein Associates, Inc. for AT&T (clockwise from top) include the VIP Center in Spaceship Earth at EPCOT Center, Orlando, FL (photo credit: Eric Dusenberg); the Innoventions Exhibition, also at EPCOT (photo credit: Presentations South, Inc.); and the AT&T Learning Center at Basking Ridge, NJ (photo credit: William Arbizu).

Blumlein-designed environments include (left to right) the AT&T Consumer Products Gallery in Parsippany, NJ (photo credit: Fabian Diaz); and the Sony Open House Traveling Exhibition (photo credit: Joe Orlando, Inc.).

BERKMAN, HENOCH, PETERSON & PEDDY, P.C.

A Law Firm That Puts Service First

• • •

WHEN THE LONG ISLAND LAW FIRM OF BERKMAN, Henoch, Peterson & Peddy, P.C. was planning to open a Westchester office, managing partner Steven Peddy made a telephone call. He told the supervisor of the Westchester Division of a major banking client that the firm would soon be available to perform closings and other services in their market.

"Let me tell you about our firm," Peddy began. The supervisor stopped him immediately. "You don't have to tell me anything," he said. "I also run our Lynbrook office, and I know you. No other firm gives us the kind of service you do."

Some law firms may make their reputation because of a spectacular case, or a flamboyant partner. But this banker's unsolicited testimonial showed that Berkman Henoch has made its reputation the hard way: through consistently excellent service to a roster of demanding clients.

Founded in 1982, Berkman, Henoch, Peterson & Peddy, P.C. is not only solid and well-established, but young, aggressive and growth-oriented. Since its founding, it has been best known for service to the banking and real estate industries, but its practice has expanded to estate planning and administration, commercial litigation and a sophisticated corporate practice. Today, the firm consists of 38 attorneys (including 14 partners), 57 paralegals and more than 70 support personnel working in the headquarters office in Garden City, as well as six other offices throughout the Metro New York area.

Among the firms banking clients are: Citibank, N.A., Fleet Bank, Marine Midland Bank, Dime Savings Bank of New York, Roosevelt Savings Bank, Chase Manhattan Bank, Reliance Federal Savings Bank, The Bank of New York, Republic National Bank, European American Bank, Emigrant Savings Bank and National Bank of New York City.

The firm also maintains litigation, school law, foreclosure, bankruptcy, trusts and estates, municipal, zoning and corporate practice

The firm's senior partners bring a potent combination of legal talent and prominent community leadership. (Clockwise L-R): Kenneth S. Berkman, Gregory P. Peterson (Hempstead Town Supervisor), Steven J. Peddy, and Gilbert Henoch.

groups. Other major clients include: McDonald's Corporation, Crest Hollow Country club, Mid-Island Hospital, Corporate Property Investors, J.D. Posillico Inc., the Federal Deposit Insurance Corporation, the Towns of Huntington and Babylon and the Villages of Hempstead and Freeport.

Partner Gil Henoch attributes the firm's growth to a recognition by Long Island companies that they need not jump to Manhattan for excellent legal representation. "The talent here is just as good," contends Henoch, "and we know Long Island—the politics, the players, where to tread softly."

Peddy noted that every client, including municipalities and other government entities, are looking at costs, and asking for budgets. "Big companies have turned to us because our fees are more reasonable, and because everyone in this firm, not just the lawyers, but the secretaries, paralegals and clerks, understand that we're in a service business, and we deliver service," said Peddy. "It's a combination of accuracy, reliability, attention to detail, responsiveness and attitude."

The members of the firm hold many prominent elected, professional and philanthropic positions. Partner Gregory Peterson is Hempstead Town Supervisor; while partner Gilbert Henoch is a member of the Planning Board of Lloyd Harbor and a Past President of the New York Association of School Attorneys. Partner Peter Peterson is a member of Hempstead's Town Zoning Board and Planning Commission. Partner Steven Peddy oversees the firm's diverse legal team and lectures frequently on real estate law. He is a founding member of the Board of Trustees of the Long Island Children's Museum. Several of the partners are currently serving as local magistrates. • • •

Headquartered in prestigious Garden City, Berkman, Henoch, Peterson & Peddy has 38 attorneys. The firm also has offices in the 110 Corridor in Melville, Suffolk County.

MARKS SHRON & COMPANY, LLP
CERTIFIED PUBLIC ACCOUNTANTS
• • •

SUCCESSFUL BUSINESS PEOPLE KNOW THAT ONE OF the keys to their achievement is the advice and services of an expert accountant, one who knows not only how to prepare a thorough financial statement, but also understands their individual business. "We partner with our clients," said Arnold Gruber, managing partner of Marks Shron & Company, LLP, "providing the advantages of business guidance plus the financial services they need to achieve their goals."

The firm was founded in 1946 by George Marks, who was joined soon after by William Shron. Today, Marks Shron, headquartered in Great Neck, has a Manhattan office as well. The firm has 14 partners, more than 100 professional staff, and ranks as one of the largest accounting firms on Long Island.

Through the years, Marks Shron has earned a reputation for quality services and a commitment to helping clients build their companies. "You could give a column of

Arnold Gruber, managing partner of Marks Shron

The partners of Marks Shron

numbers to 100 CPAs, and hopefully they would all get the same result," explained partner Barry Seidel. "What sets us apart from the other 99 is our personal approach."

Both Gruber and Seidel say the process requires that each partner be able to take on a variety of roles, including chief financial officer, mentor, and sometimes, psychologist. "Estate and succession planning are particularly sensitive areas," said partner William Jennings. "Very often, conflicting interests get to such a point that family members stop talking to each other. We are there to prevent the shattering of these relationships and to help families come

together for everyone's benefit."

Marks Shron clients range from small start-up companies to large corporations planning for an acquisition or public offering. "Our clients, no matter the size, enjoy a continuity of service that I believe is unmatched by other firms," noted Gruber. "In fact, working together so closely, we find that the professional relationship very often becomes a personal one as well."

According to partner Rochelle Barnett, "Marks Shron clients also have the advantage of working with a firm in which every partner can provide them with broad-based knowledge. That's very different from a 'Big 6' firm where each partner specializes in only one area."

Although Marks Shron's roots are in the real estate and home building industries, the firm has expanded its areas of expertise to include mortgage banking, expatriate tax work, the oil heat industry, low-income housing, nonprofits, the alarm industry, and printing and publishing. The firm also offers automation support to its clients, advising on both hardware and software applications.

The firm's professional expertise goes hand in hand with its commitment to professional education and community activities. "Our partners make a point of 'giving back,'" noted Seidel, who has lectured extensively and serves on the council of the 320,000-member American Institute of CPAs. Gruber, for example, writes on tax and real estate issues for the professional and general press, and is a director of the Association for a Better Long Island. Jennings serves on the Board of the North Amityville Taxpayers Association, which is setting up a program to develop low-income housing.

Barnett is the chair of the "Committee of 100" of the National Association of Women Business Owners and chairs the Committee on Bankers and Other Credit Grantors of the Nassau County Chapter of the New York State Society of CPAs.

The firm continues to grow, and recently both the Great Neck and Manhattan offices have expanded. Notes Gruber, "As we approach a new century, we will continue to provide our clients with the sound financial and business advice they have come to expect from Marks Shron professionals." •••

BUILDING

Photo by Bruce Bennett.

RECKSON ASSOCIATES
Pioneers in People-Oriented Office Building Environments
• • •

A S LONG ISLAND WENT THROUGH ECONOMIC AND demographic transformations, Reckson Associates, the largest owner and manager of Class A office and industrial properties, also transformed to meet the needs of the Island. A family-run business since 1959, the company has grown to be one of the tri-state's most prominent developers of office buildings, high-tech facilities and industrial space. Reckson is a full-service, integrated organization providing in-house expertise in leasing, development, construction, property and asset management, architectural services and financial planning. In late May of 1995, Reckson Associates underwent another historic transformation by becoming a publicly traded company on the New York Stock Exchange. Innovative design and a bold willingness to redefine what it means to be a real estate company has enabled Reckson Associates to adapt to changing real estate cycles and earned Reckson its prestigious reputation.

"Early in the company's history, we decided that the key to our success was going to be flexibility and a willingness to change with the times," explained President and Chief Executive Officer, Donald Rechler.

Reckson's innovative design and marketing can be traced back to 1959 when William Rechler and his partner, Walter Gross, developed the first park of planned, grouped industrial buildings. In 1962, with great foresight, they purchased 800 acres of ITT's Voice of America site in Hauppauge bringing the industrial frontier to Suffolk County. Today, with over 54,000 people employed, it is the heart of the second largest industrial park in the country.

In 1968, the second-generation, Donald and Roger Rechler, embarked on an ambitious venture on 200 acres across from MacArthur Airport in Bohemia. Airport International Plaza (AIP), the first planned high-technology park, was designed for Long Island embryonic research and development industry. AIP earned Reckson Associates numerous awards for design, landscaping and economic development.

The next project was the one million square foot County Line Industrial Center in Melville, another research and development park built for Long Island's fast-growing, high-tech business community. Today, with over 900 high-tech companies, Long Island is the third largest high-tech economic region in the country.

In the 1970s, Long Island's increasingly affluent community brought about the emergence of a service economy. Reckson responded by developing office sites. Vice Chairman Roger Rechler explains: "Some of the larger corporate firms came out to the Island to do studies and found that it has the best white collar workforce in the nation, partly due to their high level of education."

The company's goal of adapting to market conditions was fully realized in 1978 with the North Shore Atrium (NSA). The 120,000 square foot Grumman building had been the facility where the Lunar Module was designed. Reckson converted the space into a 310,000 square foot, Class A, amenity-laden office environment.

Reckson Associates' award-winning North Shore Atrium features the first health club facilities, restaurant and teleconferencing center in a Northeast suburban office building.

The 575,000 square foot Omni at Nassau West Corporate Center, the flagship in Reckson's portfolio, offers the finest amenity package in the Northeast.

The 495 Expressway Plaza is part of Reckson's Huntington Melville corporate complex.

The North Shore Atrium featured the first health club, racquet and tennis courts, tele-conferencing center, sundecks and restaurant in a suburban office building. Reckson secured a foothold in the early years of the office market with NSA and earned its first Archi Award from the American Institute of Architecture.

It was at NSA that Reckson's trademark "people places" were first incorporated into the design. Reckson's work environments are people-oriented and include spacious lobbies, sculptures and paintings, food service and other features to make employees feel at home while at work.

Reckson followed this success with the ambitious five-building Huntington-Melville Corporate Center, called the first "smart" buildings in the region because of their totally controlled environment that enables tenants to have the optimum in energy-efficient management.

In the late 1980s, Long Island faced the difficult transformation from a defense-based economy to a service and high-tech economy. While the market's economy suffered, Reckson held its course, maintaining its reputation by managing its quality portfolio. By the mid-1990s, Long Island's had almost all of its vacant space absorbed by the growing high-tech and service firms.

Reckson was poised to provide Class A working environments for service firms at prestigious office buildings, including the Omni. The flagship in the Reckson portfolio, the 550,000 square foot Omni offers the finest amenity package in the Northeast. The ten-story building, part of Reckson's Nassau West Corporate Center, is designed to address every business and quality-of-life need of a tenant.

Today, Reckson Associates spans three generations. While family leadership has been central to the company's success, the company generally benefits from staff stability demonstrated by 12 of Reckson's senior staff having served more than 15 years.

In 1995, in order to unify its business structure, enhance the competitive edge, and to allow greater access to capital, Reckson Associates took a transformative step, becoming a publicly traded company. As a Real Estate Investment Trust, Reckson has maintained its philosophy on expansion: "Reckson has always grown only when it has been opportunistic to do so," explained Donald Rechler. "Our acquisitions are always a response to opportunities we see in the marketplace and trends we see in the economy."

Since becoming a public company, Reckson Associates Realty Corporation has acquired over $140 million dollars of property in the tri-state area. While some substantial acquisitions have taken place on Long Island, the most significant purchase for Reckson is the $86 million Halpern Enterprises deal comprised of eight suburban office buildings for a total of 935,000 square feet representing Reckson's introduction into the Westchester market.

"What attracted us to the Westchester market is its similarity to the Long Island market," said Chief Operating Officer, Scott Rechler. "It is an in-fill market with a highly educated, white collar workforce. We see great potential in this market."

Reckson Associates has always been very supportive of the arts and of various causes on Long Island. This year, Tilles Center will honor the company's commitment to the arts with a series named Reckson Jazz at Tilles. Reckson also lends support to Friends of the Arts, Long Island Jewish Medical Center, Huntington Breast Cancer Coalition, Island Harvest Food Bank program, and Long Island Children's Museum.

A diversity in properties and the vision to grow with changes in the economy, has earned Reckson its reputation. The company's devotion to Long Island's quality of life has been the main theme underlying its philosophy and its success.   •••

The Expressway Corporate Center in Melville typifies Reckson Associate's people-oriented approach to office building.

BRESLIN REALTY DEVELOPMENT CORP.
Developing for Tomorrow
• • •

FROM THE SALE OF A SINGLE HOME TO THE development of a major retail, residential and commercial complex, Breslin Realty Development Corp. plays a dynamic leadership role in Long Island's real estate community. Offering a comprehensive range of services, including commercial and residential brokerage, consulting, management, appraisal, financing and development, Breslin Realty has been guided by its corporate philosophy that "real estate development is the art of building today for the needs of tomorrow."

Breslin Realty was founded by Wilbur F. Breslin more than 40 years ago, a time when Long Island was experiencing the post-war housing boom that brought so many city dwellers to the region's expanding suburban communities. Started as a small residential brokerage business in West Hempstead and East Meadow, Breslin Reality matured right along with the communities it served.

Although the company has long since extended its markets well beyond the residential sector it initially served, Breslin Realty remains active as a builder of homes. In participating in the development of residential communities such as Fisherman's Wharf in Babylon, the Woodlands and Woodland Pond in Woodbury, Willow Wood in Wantagh, Northern Woods in East Hills, Lexington Village in Bay Shore, Oceancrest in Oceanside and Westwood Village in Westbury, Breslin realizes that nothing is as close to the American heart as the dream of having a home of one's own. Committed to making that dream come true, Breslin Realty's goal is to create housing that enhances the lives of its occupants. Having already developed more than 5,000 residential units, Breslin Realty continues its ongoing quest to create the kind of lively, livable communities that make a residence into a home by closely monitoring the demographic, economic, and employment fluctuations that impact on Long Island's residential neighborhoods.

As Breslin's—and Long Island's—residential communities grew, so did the region's need for more sophisticated shopping, office, and industrial facilities. Moving into these new markets, Breslin Realty's projects served to spur Long Island's growth from a chain of suburban communities dependent on New York City to an independent market providing opportunity for employment, shopping, and recreational and cultural activities close to home for its growing population.

Over the years, Breslin Realty has demonstrated its ability to create working environments that are geared for growth. Drawing on its depth of experience in all aspects of commercial development, Breslin Realty creates a blend of customized services that gives each project a substantial head start toward achieving a long and healthy growth curve. For projects such as Willow Wood Shoppes in Wantagh, Smithhaven Plaza in Lake Grove, Woodbury Plaza in Plainview, Kmart Plaza in Sayville, Clearmeadow Mall in East Meadow, Huntington Square Mall in Huntington and its own corporate headquarters in Garden City, Breslin Realty considered every aspect of the project's development—from inception, to site selection, to building design, to establishing a retail tenant mix—with an eye towards producing the optimal experience for its tenants and visitors. In creating shopping centers, Breslin's extensive knowledge of the retail market, along with ongoing market research, produces results that increase consumer traffic.

Similarly, Breslin Realty's well-located shopping centers are built on a firm foundation of development fundamentals: applying proven rules of accessibility, versatility and tenant comfort, and then combining them with Breslin's profound familiarity with building codes, markets, trends and financial institutions. The result is that Breslin's commercial developments have become characterized by a uniquely-integrated, unusually growth-oriented business environment. Being part of such a favorable business environment is seen by Breslin Realty as critical to the establishment of a good business. Breslin Realty has extended its markets to Louisiana, Mississippi, Nebraska, New Jersey, Pennsylvania and upstate New York.

It's Breslin Realty's view that just about any builder can alter an

Huntington Square Mall, a Breslin Realty project, provides an optimal experience for both tenants and visitors.

Willow Wood Shoppes in Wantagh exemplifies Breslin Realty's commitment to creating well-located shopping centers on a firm foundation of development fundamentals.

Olney Square in Philadelphia are among Breslin Realty s significant property redevelopment projects.

Through its land planning activities, Breslin Realty has placed itself at the forefront of envisioning Long Island's future: a guiding principle of the company is that "we don't develop land, we develop for the future." The most ambitious of Breslin's visionary projects to date is North Shore Properties in Yaphank, a 2,150-acre proposal that will encompass 5,000 residential units, a 1,600,000 square foot regional shopping mall, a 300,000 square foot community shopping center, and 3,000,000 square feet of office space and research and development facilities. Breslin's bold initiative will serve to turn a raw tract of land in central Suffolk County into a thriving, mixed-use community. In creating this planned community, Breslin has taken into account a myriad of environmental and commercial land planning concerns including affordable housing, amenities, road and traffic patterns, water and waste systems, organization of retail locations, and preservation of the area's natural beauty. In bringing North Shore Properties toward fruition, Breslin has brought to bear its long years of planning and building expertise, along with its intimate knowledge of financing, zoning, and property sales and management. Breslin Realty played an important role in the creation of the Core Preservation Law and was one of the prime negotiators in the Land Use Plan that was jointly supported by environmentalists, developers and builders and ultimately endorsed by Governor Pataki.

existing structure. But in Breslin's redevelopment projects, the company's goal is no less than to alter existing perceptions. Breslin officials regard conversions and rehabilitations as one of the most challenging areas in the realm of real estate development. They maintain that since the developer s vision must be tempered by structural and stylistic limitations as well as the public perception of the building's former use, the challenge for the developer is to reach beyond these limitations with creativity and skill. Further, the developer must bring extensive knowledge of unusual structures, construction techniques, and interactive architecture to the table. Over more than a quarter century, Breslin Realty has wielded these skills and knowledge to

The company founded by Wilbur F. Breslin more than 40 years ago is a leader in Long Island's real estate community.

create some of the Northeast's most respected conversion and rehabilitation projects. Woodbury Plaza in Plainview, Kmart Plaza in Middle Island, Levittown, Babylon and Sayville, Bay Harbor Mall in Lawrence, TJ Maxx Plaza in East Northport, White Plaza and One &

Representing important local, national and even international corporations in their Long Island building projects, in undertakings as diverse as brokering a lease for commercial space, fashioning creative financing packages, or planning what will be no less than a brand new city at the edge of Long Island s suburban frontier, Breslin Realty has placed itself squarely at the center of the region's maturation into a flourishing economic and residential community. •••

Woodbury Plaza in Plainview is among Breslin Realty's many significant property redevelopment projects.

KLEIN & EVERSOLL, INC.
Building Quality Homes for Long Islanders Since 1976
• • •

WHEN HOMEOWNERS IN A KLEIN & EVERSOLL community put their homes on the market, they advertise that it's a "Timber Ridge" home. That's because Klein & Eversoll's Timber Ridge communities have become the standard for outstanding value and uncompromising craftsmanship in home building.

Peter Klein, Donald Eversoll, and Donald Cowdell, the three principals of Klein & Eversoll, Inc., are now marking the company's 20th year as one of Long Island's largest development organizations. In addition to the approximately 1,800 Long Island Timber Ridge homes they've built, Klein & Eversoll build and manage a variety of commercial properties. Best known for their work in the residential sector, Klein & Eversoll have constructed homes ranging from affordable housing, in conjunction with the town of Riverhead, to luxury homes in Nassau and Suffolk. Commack, Coram, Holbrook, Holtsville, Huntington, Kings Park, Smithtown, Stony Brook, and Westbury are just a few of Timber Ridge's outstanding locations.

In recent years, with the graying of Long Island's population, Klein & Eversoll have turned their attention to planned adult communities. Klein noted a general trend: "People don't want to leave their families and friends behind, so 94 percent retire within 50 miles of where they last lived. And," continued Peter Klein, "because Long Island beaches, parks, and golf courses offer a high quality of life, many Long Islanders opt to retire close to home."

Timber Ridge at Leisure Glen in Ridge is a 650-unit

Klein & Eversoll's Timber Ridge homes are known throughout Long Island for quality and value.

Homeowners at Leisure Glen have the distinction of living in the region's premier adult community.

adult community that Donald Eversoll calls "the premier retirement community on Long Island." He cited a large clubhouse with a theatrical stage; hobby areas such as ceramics, sewing, and woodworking facilities; a library; complete health, fitness, and recreation facilities; a 24-hour attended entry gate; and transportation to local shopping and houses of worship as just some of the amenities.

Strong believers in the resilience of the Long Island economy, the principals of Klein & Eversoll are committed to doing business on Long Island and to contributing to the continuing economic health of the region. Peter Klein is a past president and chairman of the Long Island Builders Institute, a founding member of the Long Island Housing Partnership, and a director of the National Association of Home Builders; he also serves as an officer of the Long Island Association and is chairman of its Economic Development Committee. Donald Eversoll has served as president of both the Long Island Builders Institute and the New York State Builders Association. He is a life director of the National Association of Home Builders and chairman of the Suffolk County Planning Commission. A staunch supporter of environmental issues, Eversoll is also a trustee of the Long Island chapter of the Nature Conservancy and has served as vice chairman of the Suffolk County Pine Barrens Review Commission. Donald Cowdell, Klein & Eversoll's newest principal, is similarly involved. He is a member of the Long Island Builders Institute and has served on the institute's Liaison Committee with the Long Island Lighting Company. • • •

CHAPTER 15

· · ·

EDUCATION

· · ·

Photo by Deborah Ross.

LONG ISLAND UNIVERSITY
Access to the American Dream
• • •

CAMPUSES OF LONG ISLAND UNIVERSITY RANGE from one tip of Long Island to the other—from the bustling urban streets of Brooklyn, to a fabled Gold Coast estate, to Suffolk County's bucolic East End. But this comprehensive private university, one of the largest in the nation, extends its geographical reach well beyond the 120-mile stretch of Long Island. With the acquisition several years ago of the eight international cen-

ters of the Friends World Program, Long Island University has a presence throughout the world, prompting University President Dr. David J. Steinberg to observe: "The sun never sets on Long Island University."

Dr. David J. Steinberg, president of Long Island University.

Describing the multicampus University's mission, Steinberg said: "We educate 23,540 students— one at a time." In service to a University-wide student population that typically represents the first generation of a family to attend college, Long Island University nurtures and creates for its thousands

of students "access to the American dream."

The Harvard-educated Steinberg recently marked his 10th year as president of Long Island University. Among his many initiatives have been the establishment of a central administration governing all campuses and the 1988 implementation of the LIU Plan, a cooperative education program that stresses experiential learning and intensive counseling of students.

The various components of the LIU Plan, which aims to produce a "well-rounded, well-educated individual," include college and career goal assessments, paid experience for students in chosen professional careers, and opportunities for networking and resume building. Underlying the LIU Plan is one-to-one academic and career counseling from advisors who help students decide upon a career and coursework that best suits their professional and lifestyle goals. Through the University's cooperative education job bank, students obtain paid employment related to their career goals. The work yields academic credit as well. Some LIU Plan students work part time; others alternate semesters of study with semesters of full-time work. All students opting for the LIU plan participate in a freshman year small-group course providing students with the tools and support needed to maximize their college experience.

The magnificent C.W. Post Campus is the former Gold Coast estate of heiress Marjorie Merriweather Post.

The ethnically-diverse and culturally-rich Brooklyn Campus is just 10 minutes from Manhattan.

On Long Island, the University has three residential campuses: Brooklyn, C.W. Post, and Southampton; each offers the LIU Plan option. Additionally, Long Island University's non-residential campuses are in Brentwood and in Rockland and Westchester counties.

EDUCATING A DIVERSE POPULATION

Brooklyn, founded in 1926, is the oldest of Long Island University's campuses. This campus boasts the University's newest facility: The William Zeckendorf Health Sciences Center. The six-story building, which opened last fall, provides state-of-the-art facilities for the Arnold & Marie Schwartz College of Pharmacy and Health Sciences, a highly-selective program which has produced nearly one of every four pharmacists in the New York area. The Zeckendorf Health Sciences Center also provides classrooms and labs for programs in physical therapy, sports medicine and nursing. Gale Steven Haynes, provost of the Brooklyn Campus and a Long Island University graduate herself, remarked that in the face of a national shortage of pharmacists, nurses, physician assistants and other health professionals, "students educated in the health professionals are certain to find employment and the University can fulfill a vital society need."

Special programs available to students at Long Island University's Brooklyn Campus include an award-winning University Honors Program in which students develop their own coursework and proceed at their own pace; the United Nations Seminar, a 16-credit semester allowing students to participate in United Nations activities; the Higher Education Opportunity Program offering tutoring, counseling and financial assistance to academically and economically disadvantage students; Clark Leadership Fellows, a program that recruits and retains talented Hispanic students; and Minority Access to Research Careers, providing a broad-based education in the sciences to accomplished minority students.

The landmark Brooklyn Paramount Theater has been renovated for use as a student center, housing the student government, newspaper, student union and a cafe. Generations of Brooklynites will be gratified to find that the theater's historic Wurlitzer organ is still in place, now a focal point in the building's gymnasium. The rich campus cultural environment at Brooklyn includes a Jazz Plus Program featuring prominent artists such as Tito Puente, Lionel Hampton and Billy Taylor; the Triangle Theater holds dance, music, poetry and theatrical events; art exhibitions at four campus galleries; the American Literature lecture series and the Spike Lee Film Workshop, "Forty Acres and a Mule." But cultural opportunities for Brooklyn students are not limited to the Campus; nearby are the Brooklyn Museum, Brooklyn Academy of Music and the Brooklyn Botanical Gardens. Just across the Brooklyn Bridge is Manhattan, the world's biggest cultural emporium.

Long Island University's Brooklyn Campus is notable in its service to older, non-traditional students, many of whom are single mothers. Reflecting the diversity of the region it serves, the student population of Long Island University's Brooklyn Campus is 42.6 percent African-American, 15.3 percent Hispanic and 11.8 percent Asian or Pacific. In recent years, the Campus has seen an influx of Eastern European students, drawn especially by the School of Pharmacy.

CAMPUS RISES FROM GOLD COAST ESTATE

Long Island University's magnificent C.W. Post Campus has been described as "something out of an F. Scott Fitzgerald novel." Distinguished by rolling green lawns and formal gardens, the Campus, founded in 1954, was once the estate of Post Cereal heiress Marjorie Merriweather Post. Her Tudor mansion, called Hillwood, is regarded as among the finest examples of Gold Coast architecture. The mansion continues to be the centerpiece of the Campus and its Great Hall is often the site for important

Students earn credit and hands-on marine experience through the nine-week SEAmester aboard the 125-foot "Spirit of Massachusetts."

At all of Long Island University's campuses, students are taught by expert, award-winning faculty.

University events. The C.W. Post Campus now has almost 50 buildings and more than 300 acres. The many sculptures gracing the Campus comprise the largest outdoor public art program in the metropolitan area.

A strong liberal arts college, C.W. Post maintains the School of Education, certifying more teachers, administrators and counselors than any other university in New York State. The C.W. Post Campus is also the home of The Palmer School of Library and Information Sciences, the area's only library school. Palmer students pursuing graduate education in library or information sciences earn a M.S. degree that is accredited by the American Library Association. Unique to the C.W. Post Campus is the School of Professional Accountancy. Now marking its 20th anniversary, the school's graduate tax program is ranked among the highest in the nation.

The many degree program at Post's School of Visual and Performing Arts include ceramics, fine arts, computer graphics, photography, music, public relations, theater, broadcasting and journalism. Especially notable are the state-of-the-art computer graphic design facilities and a new television studio which affords students the opportunity to master animation and television production. Broadcasting students garner on-the-job career training at the Campus's radio station, WCWP.

Nestled within Hillwood Commons, the student center, is the Hillwood Art Museum. One of only 10 percent of museums nationwide that is accredited by the American Museums Association, Hillwood's diverse exhibitions are curated by C.W. Post's visual arts faculty. The exhibitions range from lively explorations of contemporary and Pre-Columbian art to showcases for the work of graduate students and faculty, many of whom are among the region's best-known artists. The Museum manages a permanent collection of 3,000 artworks and 50 outdoor sculpture works and also sponsors performances and lectures.

LONG ISLANDS WORLD-CLASS ARTS CENTER

Adjacent to Hillwood Commons is the jewel of the C.W. Post Campus: Tilles Center for the Performing Arts, the premier concert hall for the 2.8 million people of Nassau and Suffolk counties. Tilles Center was founded in 1981 as the C.W. Post Concert Theater. A 2,200-seat world-class facility built at the cost of $4.4 million, it was immediately regarded as an acoustical success. In 1986, following the generosity of a $1.2 million gift from Long Island developer and philanthropist Gilbert Tilles, the Center was renamed for him and his wife, Rose.

The Center presents its own seasons of classical and popular entertainment for adults and children and is also the theatrical home for many of Long Island's leading arts organizations, including the Long Island Philharmonic, Friends of the Arts, Eglevsky Ballet, and the Sea Cliff Chamber Players.

The world's most honored orchestras and soloists have performed at Tilles Center, as have popular artists of Broadway and Hollywood and leading dance companies from the United States and around the globe. Tilles Center boasts regular appearances by the New York Philharmonic and Invitation to the Dance, which features such internationally-renowned dance ensembles as the Martha Graham Dance Company and the Paul Taylor Company. Through public programs and school outreach activities, the Center introduces young Long Island audiences to live performances by highly acclaimed artists from the worlds of dance, music and theater.

SMALL COLLEGE PRODUCES TOP SCHOLARS

A record of 18 Fulbright Scholars in 20 years would be a remarkable achievement for any institution of higher learning, but it's nothing

Southampton College is a campus where the student comes first, where the individual matters and where a sense of community exists.

Tilles Center for the Performing Arts is Long Islands premier concert hall.

less than extraordinary for a college of 1,500 students at the graduate and undergraduate levels. Southampton College, founded in 1963, is a small, intimate school where classes generally don't exceed 18 students. The Campus features what The New York Times called "the perfect mix of mental, social and environmental stimuli." Overlooking Shinnecock Bay, the 110-acre Southampton campus has as its focal point a 260-year-old windmill. Minutes away from the historic village of Southampton, the College reflects the artistic and literary prominence of the East End community. Each spring, the East End social season has its "official" kick-off with an art gallery benefit for Southampton College's John Steinbeck Reading Room. Kurt Vonnegut and E. L. Doctorow are among the world-renowned East End writers who regularly participate in Southampton College programs.

But despite this strong artistic and literary bent, Southampton College is probably best-known for its highly-regarded programs in marine and environmental science. Working within the area's natural, untouched beauty and the school's proximity to bays, the ocean, salt ponds, tidal creeks, dunes and salt marshes, students in these programs have access to a fleet of boats which includes a 44 foot ocean-going research vessel. As part of SEAmester, Southampton marine science students sail for nine weeks aboard the 125 foot schooner "Spirit of Massachusetts" along the Eastern Coast of the United States to the Caribbean, gaining first-hand field experience in topics such as coastal ecology and ichthyology. Marine science students also have the option of study at Australia's Great Barrier Reef and other South Pacific locations.

INTERNATIONAL EDUCATION

Globetrotting by Southampton students is not confined to the marine sciences program. The Campus is home to the Friends World Program, a non-traditional college experience in which students devise their own study plan with an advisor. Freshman year for all Friends World students is at Southampton, the Program's North American Center. Students then go on to at least two of Friends World's eight worldwide centers. The goal at each Center is to achieve total linguistic and cultural immersion in that country. Typical study fields have included the origins of Chinese Buddhism, African wildlife, Malaysia's flora and fauna, and Japanese ceramics. Field study goals and objectives are formulated with advisors and all students are expected to maintain detailed diaries which are graded.

Long Island University's Southampton campus is home to Long Island's only National Public Radio station. In 1994, WPBX upped its power from 1,000 to 25,000 watts, vastly boosting the listening range for devotees of programming offered by NPR and Public Radio International. The station's format includes a blend of jazz, classical and progressive music. As on the C.W. Post Campus, the presence of a campus radio station affords Southampton's broadcasting students valuable professional experience.

Southampton College of Long Island University is undergoing a comprehensive restructuring of physical plant and academic offerings. Southampton's new master plan will emphasize four major areas of study: marine science, environmental sciences, fine arts, and writing.

ADULT LEARNERS ARE FAST TRACKED

Long Island University's non-residential Campus in Brentwood serves Suffolk County's transfer and graduate students. At the undergraduate level, programs are offered in fields such as accounting, business administration, management, marketing and finance, criminal justice and elementary education. Primarily a graduate facility, Brentwood's Fast-Track program enables students to earn an M.S. or M.B.A. degree in only 16-24 months. Long Island University's Westchester Campus is strictly a graduate institution, offering 36 programs in the arts and sciences, business administration, education and the health professions that are tailored to the needs of working people. Similarly, the University's Rockland Campus stresses programs for working graduate or continuing education students. •••

Through cooperative education, the cornerstone of the LIU Plan, students gain paid professional experience in the chosen careers.

DOWLING COLLEGE

The Personal College with a Global Reach

• • •

OWLING COLLEGE IN OAKDALE IS AN INDEPENDENT, coeducational institution that combines the advantages of a small personal education environment with a far-reaching global approach. Dowling brings together scholars from around the world to focus on understanding the world as an interrelated whole.

At the undergraduate level, Dowling offers its students 22 majors leading toward a Bachelor of Arts degree, 4 majors toward a Bachelor of Business Administration and 15 majors toward a Bachelor of Science degree. Some of the Bachelor of Science majors—among them, various aeronautics programs, and others in travel, tourism and transportation—form a special niche area for Dowling and have proved to be a magnet for students regionally, nationally, and internationally.

In its graduate division, Dowling offers certificate programs in computer information systems, international finance, intermodal transportation, environmental quality in transportation, transportation planning and management and transportation safety. Those pursuing an M.B.A. in aviation management, banking and finance, general management, public management or total quality management also find a home at Dowling, as do those seeking a Master of Science degree in Education. Post-Master's professional diploma programs include computers in education, school district administrator and school administrator and supervisor. Post-Master's certificates are offered in aviation management, banking and finance, public management and total quality management.

Fully accredited by the Middle States Association of Colleges and Schools, Dowling College maintains memberships in 153 national and international associations in a broad variety of academic, civic and professional disciplines. Its degree programs are registered by the New York State Department of Education and its aviation programs are further certified by the Federal Aviation Administration.

The College's 52-acre campus in Oakdale, along the banks of the Connetquot River on Suffolk County's South Shore, is the former Idle Hour estate of William K. Vanderbilt. Dowling's innovative National Aviation and Transportation Center®, founded in the fall of 1994 to prepare and train future generations of leaders of the transportation industry, is located at a 105-acre site at Brookhaven Calabro Airport. Satellite programs are offered in Manhattan and Queens in New York City, on Long Island at Riverhead, and at various corporate locations throughout the region. The Dowling Institute fosters educational growth by forging partnerships between the College and business, government and community organizations. Among Dowling's Institute partners are The World Trade Institute, the College of Aeronautics at LaGuardia Airport, Telephonics and the Long Island Rail Road. Dowling's international educational partnerships involve institutions of higher learning in France, Russia and China.

First established in 1955 as an extension of Adelphi University and Suffolk's first four-year college, Dowling became independent in 1968, a move that allowed the young educational institution to become more

No matter what their major, students at Dowling receive a well-rounded education with required courses from across the curriculum, including the arts, sciences and humanities.

The Kramer Science Center offers Dowling students a learning environment conducive to grasping scientific concepts, formulating new theories, and exploring the exciting world of science.

While Dowling is one of the fastest growing colleges in the region, it has maintained its Personal College philosophy by keeping classes small—none ever exceeds 40 students—and promoting an environment that maximizes the individual's learning potential.

Dowling's Oakdale campus offers students the latest in information technology through its Academic Computing Lab.

approach in which not one class exceeds 40 students; an educational environment that recognizes and encourages the development of each individual's potential; flexible programming designed to meet individual student needs; the caliber of the faculty; and the depth of curriculum and visionary outlook.

Dowling College is governed according to a philosophy that encompasses the following seven goals and objectives:

• To be a personal college where students feel comfortable, important and involved and where they develop a more positive self-image. Toward this end, the school provides extensive support through counseling and tutoring, maintains low teacher/student ratios in a positive atmosphere for learning, makes constructive academic and intellectual demands, and affords its students the opportunity to participate in the decision-making process.

• To liberate students from the constraints of provincial and prejudicial thinking through free and open discussion, and through courses of study based on the liberal arts tradition of understanding of and respect for different perspectives.

• To promote the excitement of life-long learning by providing its students with opportunities to improve their abilities to understand, critically analyze and communicate complex issues.

• To provide its students with opportunities enabling them to advance in their economic and professional lives with an education that develops many skills, and with assistance in identifying and exploring career potential.

• To recruit and retain students from diverse populations by offering diverse educational programs of high educational quality, and by assisting students in securing financial support.

• To assure that its graduates have mastered fundamental skills of analysis and communication, and have achieved competence in their major field of study. To achieve this goal, Dowling regularly assesses the effectiveness of its curriculum, quality of instruction, and procedures for assessing student competence.

• To serve as a resource to its communities by sharing cultural and physical programs, and by providing consultation and informational services relevant to regional needs.

Lofty and comprehensive goals, indeed. But, said Dr. Meskill, it is because of the school's strict adherence to these stated commitments that "Dowling is the college where everyone grows." •••

responsive to Suffolk's needs. The school was named after its benefactor, Robert W. Dowling, a financier, aviator and patron of the arts.

Of Dowling College's diverse student population of almost 6,000, 63 percent are undergraduates, and 37 percent are enrolled in graduate programs. The average age of the school's undergraduates is 26, and of graduate students, 32. While the student population is drawn primarily from Long Island, Dowling College President Victor P. Meskill, Ph.D. said that the College's foreign students are drawn from 31 countries. Increasingly, noted Dr. Meskill, Dowling's recruitment efforts have become national and international in scope. In the past decade, Dowling's dramatic growth of 150 percent has been the largest of any college on Long Island. Dr. Meskill credited several factors including the school's commitment to its personal college

STONY BROOK
STATE UNIVERSITY OF NEW YORK
A Great Research University which also Emphasizes the Undergraduate Experience
• • •

A NOBEL PRIZE FOR PHYSICS, A PULITZER FOR poetry, an Obie for playwriting, four MacArthur Fellowships, many Guggenheim fellowships and grants from the National Science Foundation are just some of the awards bestowed upon faculty members at the State University of New York at Stony Brook. The Stony Brook faculty, almost 95 percent of whom hold Ph.Ds, have built a record of academic and scientific scholarship that any university might envy, but one all the more extraordinary for an institution founded less than 40 years ago.

A center for both teaching and learning, Stony Brook is a source of new ideas and knowledge that fuel economic growth and business development, advance science and technology, improve health care, and strengthen government. The campus is part of a small national constellation of major institutions of higher learning known as Research I universities. Long Island's sole such entity, Stony Brook is the leading research university campus of the State University of New York.

According to Shirley Strum Kenny, president of SUNY-Stony Brook, the university's role in the economic redevelopment of Long Island has become a core value for the institution. She explained that Stony Brook's "research mission is essential not just nationally but locally if Long Island - and therefore New York State—is to flourish." Stony Brook's connections with the business, educational, cultural and governmental communities are seen by President Kenny as "the lifeblood of the University." Speaking of these connections, Kenny said "we are making our home base strong economically, intellectually, culturally, medically, and technologically."

"To be a great national university," said Kenny, "you must be a great local university." Therefore, she views as one of Stony Brook's most important roles "creating, supporting, and staffing the Long Island industries of the future."

Mindful of the powerful economic role Stony Brook plays in the region, Kenny cited statistics developed by Lee Koppelman, executive director of the Long Island Regional Planning Board, which demonstrate that Stony Brook's $175 million in New York State funding is the basis for generating about $2.5 billion into the regional economy.

Stony Brook has been singularly successful in pursuing its scientific mission. During 1995, funding for the university's many research programs passed the $100 million mark. Currently, Stony Brook's 1,800 research-supported employees are engaged in 1,300 sponsored projects. Since the university's inception, it has given rise to 398 invention disclosures, 114 licenses and options and 110 patents. Among the most noteworthy of Stony Brook's recent scientific landmarks are Professor Paul Grannis' co-chairing of the team that established the existence of the Top Quark; the National Medal of Technology won by Material Sciences Professor Richard Gambino; and the discovery by Dr. Barry Coller of ReoPro, a drug that alleviates various problems arising during cardiovascular surgery.

A central concern of every strong research university is how well it is able to integrate its vast academic and scientific resources into the education of its undergraduates. Last year, President Kenny assumed a leadership role in finding ways to achieve this integration when she inaugurated the National Commission on Educating Undergraduates in the Research University. Funded by the Carnegie Foundation for the Advancement of Teaching, the Commission, said Kenny, will seek to establish a blueprint for a "symbiotic, mutually supportive relationship

(top) Light floods into the dramatic lobby of Stony Brook's Frank Melville, Jr. Memorial Library.

(left) Nearly 5,000 students receive their degrees each year at commencement ceremonies held in Stony Brook's Sports Complex.

The Fine Arts Plaza and Staller Center are the sites for numerous performances of music, dance, theater and film.

world-class scholars and researchers. For instance, faculty member C.N. Yang, a Nobel Prize winner in physics and the director of the Institute of Theoretical Physics, is also the instructor of Stony Brook's introductory physics course.

Professor Yang's section is one of more than 1,700 offered to Stony Brook's undergraduates and graduates. Undergraduates select from among 50 majors and 50 minors. Stony Brook offers 39 doctoral programs, 31 masters programs, medical and dental degrees and 21 advanced certificate programs. Courses are offered by the College of Arts and Sciences, the College of Engineering and Applied Sciences including the Harriman School for Management and Policy, Schools of Nursing, Social Welfare, and Health Technology and Management, the Marine Sciences Research Center, the School for Professional Development and Continuing Studies, the School of Medicine and the School of Dental Medicine.

While Stony Brook's 11,500 undergraduates are primarily from New York State, the undergraduate/graduate student community of nearly 18,000 hails from 42 states and 78 countries. Stony Brook's 1,100-acre campus is in one of the North Shore's most attractive areas and is convenient to rail, air and highway links. Students have access to a two million volume library system and cultural opportunities within the campus' Staller Center for the Performing Arts. Staller Center's 1,100-seat theater is the site for faculty concerts as well as music, dance and theatrical presentations by artists of national and international renown. The performing arts center also houses an art gallery that mounts an eclectic schedule of rotating exhibitions.

between the three major components of a university: research, graduate education and undergraduate education," providing "an undergraduate experience that is enriched and enlivened by the excitement of participation in research at the frontiers of learning."

One of the vehicles used by Stony Brook to bring its undergraduates into the excitement of research is the URECA program in which students participate with faculty members on research and creative projects. In another initiative to enhance the undergraduate experience, Stony Brook established Living/Learning Centers. Students in any one of six academic areas (arts, science and engineering, human sexual and gender development, international studies, wellness, or environmental studies) may opt to live in residence halls devoted to that study area so that they live and work with others in the same major and also participate in out-of-classroom activities related to their areas of study. Students selected for Stony Brook's Honors College can also choose to reside in a special Living/Learning Center that provides on-site, multi-discipline enrichment programs.

At Stony Brook, undergraduates and graduate students have an opportunity to study with

Making Stony Brook "the place to come" is among President Kenny's highest goals. Toward that end, she has focused new energy on the quality of undergraduate life and education.

Rehabilitation of residence halls and development of streamlined registration and bill paying systems are just some of the initiatives instituted as part of Stony Brook's on-going quest to enhance the student experience and diversity of campus life by building community on and off campus. •••

Stony Brook is set in one of the loveliest areas of Long Island's North Shore.

TOURO LAW CENTER
Legal Education for a Changing World
• • •

TOURO LAW CENTER, ONE OF THE NATION'S youngest law schools, has already built a proud record of educating its students for a legal environment that is increasingly global. Touro was the first American law school to have a summer program in India. Another summer program is maintained in Moscow. Touro students also have access to internship opportunities throughout Europe and the Middle East. Explaining the reasons behind the school's international education initiatives, Touro's Dean Howard Glickstein predicted that "soon all aspects of law will have international implications." He added that these programs are "preparing lawyers to pioneer the new global legal systems of the 21st century."

Touro Law Center was established as a division of Touro College in 1980; two years later the school moved from Manhattan into its Huntington campus. Touro is fully accredited by the American Bar Association and is a member of the Association of American Law Schools. Governed by a Board of Visitors that includes many of the area's major businesspeople, lawyers, and judges, Touro seeks to exemplify the ideals of the Touro family, the 19th-century philanthropists who founded the famed Touro Synagogue in Newport, Rhode Island. These ideals, which underlie the philosophy of Touro Law Center, encompass a commitment to academic excellence, the ethical and moral principles associated with the Jewish heritage, and the values of social justice and community service.

Director of International Programs Harold Abramson discusses Touro's international programs. Students interested in international law will find a wealth of opportunities and choices at the Law Center.

Touro annually graduates a class of approximately 250 students, 25 percent of whom are minority and 40 percent of whom are women. About two-thirds of the class are in a full-time, three-year program; about one-third attends a part-time, four-year program, which is the only part-time law program in Nassau or Suffolk. This part-time program has been a magnet for many working professionals, including many governmental leaders. Numbers of Long Island's state senators, assemblymen, county legislators, and town council members have earned their legal degrees in Touro's part-time program. The Law Center also offers several graduate programs. Among them are a master of law program designed to meet the needs of foreign lawyers who already have law degrees from another country, an M.B.A. program run in conjunction with Dowling College, and a master's in taxation, run jointly with Long Island University.

Touro students learn in what Glickstein described as a highly student-centered environment. The intimate size of each class and the universal availability of teaching assistants promote this favorable environment for learning. According to Glickstein, Touro is one of the few law schools nationwide where all students are eligible to work with teaching assistants. Speaking of this program, a Touro student remarked: "The teaching assistants were a great asset during my first year of law school. They helped to put the law in common everyday language, and they offered me a pipeline of advice and friendship."

The distinguished Touro faculty is comprised of 40 full-time professors and 12-15 adjunct members who are specialists in areas such as trial practice, patent law, and admiralty law. This faculty is widely noted among students for its accessibility. This availability has likely accounted for the school's high ranking in the *National Jurist Magazine*—Touro was ranked first in satisfaction with faculty and third overall satisfaction out of 13 New York area law schools.

Law students at Touro also profit from the school's close

Students receive valuable assistance with reference and legal research queries from a skilled staff of professional librarians. Further strengthening research capabilities is the availability of the LEXIS/NEXIS, WEST-LAW, DIALOG, Dow Jones News Retrieval, and AUTO-CITE computerized legal research systems for online use by all students.

Touro's Alumni Courtyard provides a quiet, restful place for study or the interesting exchange of ideas.

This concern for social action is a thread that runs throughout Touro Law Center and its programs. According to Glickstein, the school's sense of social responsibility is "deeply rooted in the moral and ethical traditions of Judaism." He added that Touro's commitment is to bring these traditional values to the practice of law.

relationship with the regional legal community which regards Touro and its 350,000 volume and document library as a valuable resource. When it comes time for internships, Touro students often look no further than the many local firms that work with the school's internship program. In fact, a glance through the list of patrons for a recent Touro benefit dinner reveals that Touro supporters include just about every major law firm in New York City and Long Island, and many smaller ones as well.

Other "real world" experience for Touro students results from the clinical program. The many clinics help students to "bridge the gap" between theory and practice while performing a true community service at the same time. Touro is one of very few law schools in the country to have a *pro bono* requirement for graduation. Touro students work under faculty supervision and provide *pro bono* representation for many public interest organizations, among them Nassau/Suffolk Legal Services, the Coalition Against Domestic Violence, and the Legal Aid Society.

The "changing world" that Touro educates its students for refers to far more than providing the tools for effectively practicing international law. Some of the many national concerns addressed in Touro's classrooms and clinics include domestic violence, elder law, family law, employment discrimination, environmental law, civil and criminal housing rights, and human rights.

Among the vehicles to transmit these values is Touro's Institute of Jewish Law, one of the goals of which is to make the Jewish legal tradition an active force in legal scholarship. Other special Touro programs include the Institute of Local and Suburban Law; the Distinguished Lecture programs; the Distinguished Jurist in Residence program, which recently featured Supreme Court Justice Antonin Scalia; and the Distinguished Public Interest Lawyer in Residence program.

Each year, Touro Law Center presents the Bruce K. Gould Book Award to recognize outstanding authorship of a work related to the law or the legal profession. Authors so honored traditionally deliver a public address and then join faculty and students for a reception. New York's Senior Senator, Daniel Patrick Moynihan, was a guest at Touro following the honoring of his book, *On the Law of Nations.* Notable graduation speakers have included former New York City Mayor David Dinkens and Sol Linowitz, the former ambassador and chairman of Xerox Corporation.

As is typical at contemporary schools of law, Touro students have access to the incomparable online research services offered by such systems as LEXIS/NEXIS, WEST-LAW, DIALOG, Dow Jones News Retrieval, and AUTO-CITE. And now Touro is on the World-Wide Web itself. Through the Internet, said Glickstein, "the latest regulations in zoning and ordinances soon will be available, as well as up-to-date information on intellectual property issues." Touro is one of only two law schools nationwide to provide daily decisions by the United States Court of Appeals for the Second Circuit at its Web Site.   •••

Touro's law library, headed by Professor Daniel Jordan, is designed to encourage and support teaching, studying and scholarly research.

St. Joseph's College
More Than a Degree... an Education
• • •

FROM ITS BEGINNINGS AS A WOMEN'S COLLEGE IN the early part of the century, St. Joseph's College has evolved into a comprehensive coeducational facility which currently serves the educational needs of 3,700 students at its two campuses located in Brooklyn and in Suffolk County. Throughout its long history of burgeoning growth, SJC has adhered to a time-honored standard of personal, student-centered education at the most modest tuition fees possible.

SJC was founded in the historic Clinton Hill section of Brooklyn in 1916. The school's first graduates set a pattern of success that continues today. Of the 12 women comprising the original graduating class, several went on to obtain legal, medical or doctoral degrees. In 1934, SJC added a child study program that was to become central to the school's future academic growth patterns. In 1971, the school inaugurated a Suffolk branch campus in Brentwood. In 1979, SJC acquired the Seton Hall property in Patchogue which then became the Suffolk campus. The first Patchogue class had 325 students; today more than 2,400 students are enrolled in the Suffolk campus' College of Arts and Sciences and Division of General Studies. Explaining this dramatic growth spiral, an SJC official observed: "We had the programs people wanted... academically solid programs."

SJC's liberal arts and pre-professional programs include bachelor degree programs in child study and special education, business administration, accounting, social sciences, mathematics and computer science, nursing, community health, human services, health administration, and management of human resources. SJC grants the region's only four-year degree in therapeutic recreation, a program which enables students to prepare for careers as administrators in parks and other recreational facilities, nursing homes and homes for the disabled.

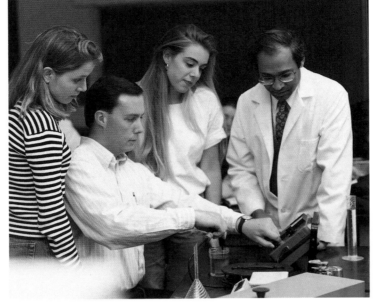

Associate Professor of Biology Dr. Mohammad Rana guides students in environmental science studies.

At the graduate level, SJC offers Long Island's only Master of Arts degree in Infant/Toddler Therapeutic Education. An innovative program geared for teachers and others working with babies and young children, it was developed in response to a growing need for trained professionals able to address the needs of babies born drug-addicted, HIV/AIDS infected, or otherwise developmentally challenged. Also at the graduate level, SJC participates in two cooperative

St. Joseph's College's Callahan Library, built in 1991, is a resource for students, faculty and the surrounding community.

The new state-of-the-art Athletic Center at St. Joseph's College exemplifies the school's commitment to the ideal of the scholar/athlete.

programs: Long Island University's M.B.A. program and New York College of Podiatric Medicine's D.P.M. program.

Since SJC is strictly a commuter school, special emphasis is placed on establishing values related to social responsibility, peer communication, cultural development and strong faculty/student relationships. Freshmen participate in an orientation course which integrates them into the college and the community and sets the tone for their careers at SJC. The school stresses extracurricular activities such as visiting a museum, attending a play or serving a charitable organization. These social and cultural activities combine with academic studies to create the well-rounded education that is SJC's goal.

Faculty accessibility is a hallmark of the SJC environment. Through attendance at campus clubs and faculty/student committees, SJC students are able to provide input to the campus decision-making process and also to have their concerns heard and addressed swiftly. The academic staff has been described as a strong, accessible teaching faculty who are highly concerned and creative. One of the means by which SJC cultivates this unusual spirit is the informal, voluntary faculty retreat held once a year where teaching staff share concerns and techniques. Keeping fresh and up to date is an important part of the agenda for these off-campus get togethers.

With SJC students very much a part of the surrounding community, the school has experienced none of the "town/gown" disputes that often mark college communities, particularly colleges which have had to expand as much as SJC has to meet growth needs. To the contrary, school officials report that the community has been tremendously supportive. The local chamber of commerce, and local Rotary, Kiwanis and Lions club chapters have all sponsored athletic and other events on campus. In turn, the extensive Callahan Library, built in 1991 and now holding more than 75,000 volumes and 500 periodical titles, is open for use by community members. Campus-sponsored cultural and informational events are also open to the community, often at no charge. Senior citizens are invited to audit SJC classes free of charge on a space-available basis. The presence of senior auditors has proved stimulating—for students and auditors alike. The most popular classes selected by seniors have been in the arts, history, literature, the humanities and philosophy.

SJC's Clare Rose Playhouse is another campus entity that serves the surrounding community. Sister Grace Edna Rowland, the Playhouse director, runs the SJC theater program and also sponsors many outreach programs with nursing homes, orphanages and facilities for the handicapped. Local theater groups often use the Playhouse as their theatrical home. Additional community outreach is demonstrated by the several student clubs that center their activities around clothing, food, and blood drives for Suffolk County residents.

As a strong liberal arts institution, SJC embraces the ideal of a sound mind in a sound body. Exemplifying that commitment to physical as well as intellectual well being, the school recently unveiled Phase II of its master plan: the new Athletic Center. The facility encompasses a six-lane 25-yard swimming pool, an elevated jogging track, a competition basketball court, facilities for aerobics, dance, fitness and weight training, and bleacher seating for 1,500 spectators. SJC, a school which does not award athletic scholarships, competes in Division III of the NCAA. Under the leadership of Don Lizak, SJC's athletic director, the school fields 10 teams with four more planned for the near future. All students who join a team have the opportunity to play because at SJC, playing on a team is regarded as an important learning experience, one in which winning is not the only agenda.

The philosophy which underlies the governance of SJC is perhaps best described by a graduate who went on to advanced study and now holds an executive position in the financial services field. Speaking of his years at SJC he said: "I experienced learning in a positive, realistic manner… a traditional approach, focusing on each student as an individual (and) a faculty devoted to excellence and strong personal and professional relationships." •••

St. Joseph's College students involved in student government review several campus publications.

MOLLOY COLLEGE
A Classic Education
• • •

MOLLOY COLLEGE, FOUNDED IN 1955 IN THE Catholic and Dominican tradition by the Sisters of St. Dominic of Amityville, is an independent, 4-year coed college of over 2,300 students in Rockville Centre, NY. The College is proud of its strong liberal arts curriculum which combines career and professional preparation, assuring every Molloy graduate of a classic, comprehensive education.

Despite more than 40 years of growth and change, Molloy is still true to its original goals and mission. Molloy students learn to seek the truth, to promote human dignity and to alleviate social ills. While pursuing any of more than 30 courses of study, they are also required to complete credits in philosophy, theology, English, modern or classical languages, mathematics, history, the natural sciences, fine arts and the social sciences.

"Molloy's heritage combines a strong liberal arts curriculum with career and professional preparation," says Dr. Patricia A. Morris, Vice President for Academic Affairs. "This comprehensive education is achieved in the framework of an academic community which upholds the exercise of freedom, the spirit of inquiry, and the dignity of each person."

A WIDE CHOICE OF MAJORS

A commuter college located on a 25-acre campus on Long Island's South Shore, about a 35 minute drive to New York City, Molloy gives its students a wide choice of majors and degrees in many up-and-coming and hard-to-find programs. This includes the Bachelor's degree in cardio-respiratory sciences and Associate's degrees in health information technology, nuclear medicine technology and respiratory care. Some other available majors are accounting, art, business management, communications, computer science, music therapy, nursing, philosophy, political science and social work.

Molloy also offers New

York State approved teacher certification programs in elementary, secondary and special education. Its music therapy program leads to approved certification by the American Association of Music Therapy. For students whose goal is medicine, dentistry, veterinary or law, the College offers pre-professional programs as well.

The College is accredited by: the Board of Regents of the University of the State of New York; the Middle States Association of Colleges and Schools; the National League for Nursing; the Commission on Accreditation of Allied Health Education Programs; the American Health Information Management Association; the Joint Review Committee on Educational Programs in Nuclear Medicine Technology; the Joint Review Committee for Respiratory Therapy Education; and the Council on Social Work Education.

Molloy's nursing program is the largest in New York State, and includes a Nurse Practitioner Program at the Master's degree level, as well as a Post-Master's Nurse Practitioner certification program. Molloy was the first college in Nassau County to offer a Master's track in this exciting new field of nursing.

"It's a whole new world out there, and the nurse practitioner may eventually prove to be the general practitioner of the future," says Professor Lorraine E. Magnani, R.N., Ph.D., director of the nursing department's graduate program.

GETTING READY FOR REAL LIFE

Molloy's internship programs act as a bridge from the academic world to the real world of employment. Internship programs with supervision, and for credit, are available in many fields of study. Among these are retailing, criminal justice, sociology, international peace and justice, business management and gerontology.

Attending Molloy is an intimate, nurturing experience centered around small classes. The student-faculty ratio is 10 to 1 and faculty members

(top) Molloy's Music Therapy Program leads to recognized certification.

(left) Students learn modern communications and production techniques in Molloy's television studio and media center.

Molloy's Wilbur Arts Center displays student and professional productions.

develop close relationships with the students. A broad range of support programs are available for students who need them, including a peer tutor program in which approximately 100 students help other students to gain the skills they need to excel.

Molloy expands on the "Writing Across the Curriculum" programs available at many colleges. Its "Communicating Across Curriculum" program helps students express themselves logically and coherently when writing or speaking, and "has the special advantage of being implemented in a school noted for its low student-faculty ratio," commented Jane Gilroy, coordinator of the program "Our students can exercise their skills in a seminar-type atmosphere, even on the undergraduate level, which is an ideal setting in which to develop not only communication skills, but also the confidence to use them in the work-a-day world."

Molloy's comprehensive education is also available to students who can not attend full-time during the work week. Evening students enjoy the same superior instruction and personal attention as day students. Courses are scheduled for maximum convenience and evening students may attend full or part-time. Evening students can obtain Bachelor's degrees in accounting, business management, computer science, English, gerontology, nursing, psychology, and social work.

Molloy's faculty is known for its professionalism and personal caring. Expertise in their respective fields is demonstrated not only by their academic accomplishments, but by their scholarship beyond the classroom as well. Molloy College faculty are actively involved in publishing, research projects, work exhibitions, performances, clinical practices, and lectures. They remain at the forefront of developments in their fields through professional memberships, conferences and organizations. In fact, many have received special honors and recognitions, both in the United States and abroad.

LUSH & GREEN

The campus is composed of attractive buildings set in the lush greenery of manicured lawns and mature trees. The James Edward Tobin Library is augmented by on-line connection to libraries around the world and to the nearly infinite resources of the Internet and World Wide Web.

A television studio and media center encourage students to learn modern communications and production techniques, hands on. Molloy's plush Hays Theater displays the students' creative productions, as well as offering professional theater.

Athletics also play a central role in student life. The College is part of the NCAA, ECAC and NYCAC, as well as the Intercollegiate Horse Show Association. Men's teams include baseball, basketball, cross-country and golf. The women's softball team won the ECAC Championship in 1995. Women also participate in intercollegiate basketball, cross-country, equestrian, soccer, tennis and volleyball.

Rounding out the campus facilities are language labs, modern computer labs, a glass-enclosed weight and training room and even an ice cream parlor, appropriately called "Scoops."

Most Molloy graduates stay on Long Island to live and work. For them, Molloy remains a focal point, a place to which they can return for renewal and continued growth. Attending Molloy is an experience that "will work for you for the rest of your life." ●●●

Lush greenery surrounds Molloy's Kellenberg Building.

HOFSTRA UNIVERSITY
Nationally Recognized for Academic Excellence
• • •

IN 1970, WITH AN ENROLLMENT OF APPROXIMATELY 12,000 students and resources that were considered to be excellent at the time, Hofstra University was widely recognized as an outstanding example of a successful American university. Today, with an enrollment that matched that of a quarter century ago, Hofstra has doubled the resources it offers to students as the University continues to be a model of excellence for other institutions.

In 1996, Hofstra's 12,000 full-time and part-time students benefit from an academic tradition of excellence that includes the national recognition of respected accrediting agencies and honor societies such as Phi Beta Kappa, the American Assembly of Education, the American Psychological Association, the Accreditation Board for Engineering and Technology, and the American Bar Association. With small classes, a strong advisement program, the current student/faculty ratio of 16:1 offers Hofstra students the opportunity to study in a small college environment on a campus that can boast a level of resources equal to or greater than any large university might offer.

Hofstra students of the 90s study, relax, and reside in a total university environment that has truly doubled in resources over the past 25 years. There are now 112 buildings located on Hofstra University's 238-acre campus, including classroom buildings, computer laboratories, residence halls, recreation facilities,

Hofstra University's journalism students study electronic broadcasting with state-of-the-art equipment at George G. Dempster Hall.

an indoor olympic-size swimming pool, and a newly expanded stadium. In 1970, the 49 buildings then located at Hofstra were used mostly by students who commuted daily to the university. Although the current enrollment at Hofstra is about the same as it was in 1970, life on campus has changed dramatically.

Today, approximately 4,000 of Hofstra's 7,000 full-time undergraduates live on campus in an exciting variety of modern, comfortable and secure residence facilities situated throughout the north campus. Whether a student sleeps in a Hofstra residence hall or commutes daily to campus, all students have access to acres of athletic fields used for baseball, softball, tennis, and soccer. These fields are surrounded by the award-winning landscaping of the Hofstra Arboretum.

The north campus also houses two sports complexes. One of these, the University's Physical Fitness Center, includes an arena for NCAA Division 1 Athletics along with Hofstra's olympic-size swimming pool. Another athletic facility, the Recreation Center, includes an indoor track, weight room, playing courts and exercise rooms available seven days a week to members of the University community.

Evenings throughout the year, Hofstra USA, the student night club, is host to capacity crowds who enjoy an extensive schedule of concerts, parties and other student oriented activities. An adjacent deli and dining area have made the Hofstra USA complex into a full-service dining and entertainment complex.

The Hofstra Student Center joins Hofstra's north and south campus. The Student Center includes the largest of Hofstra's eight dining facilities. While in the Student Center, students can enjoy a full course meal, hold student organization meetings, grab a slice of pizza, visit the multi-level Hofstra bookstore, watch a first run movie, or just relax.

Walking through the Hofstra Unispan, an enclosed climate-controlled walkway crossing over

The lush landscaping of the Hofstra Arboretum has been recognized with awards.

Hofstra University's notable outdoor sculpture gallery includes this piece by Henry Moore.

Hempstead Turnpike, the student of the 1990s prepares to enter the academic community of the University. The 1.4 million volume Joan and Donald E. Axinn Library, located at the south end of the Unispan, is one of the largest and most utilized libraries in the nation. The open stacks of the fully-automated Hofstra Library are supplemented by the latest in computer resources, allowing students full access to all of the library's volumes and services.

The south campus includes a number of classroom and laboratory buildings. Some of those buildings were present on campus twenty-five years ago and have since grown significantly in resources. Today, every Hofstra facility is fully accessible to people with disabilities. With easy access to classrooms, laboratories and rest room facilities, Hofstra continues to demonstrate a commitment to offer every interested student access to all Hofstra has to offer.

Academic highlights include George G. Dempster Hall, a remarkable state-of-the-art broadcast and teaching facility that is home for Hofstra's new School of Communications and the studios of its expanded WRHU-FM radio station. Dempster Hall includes three well-equipped television studios, a computer laboratory, control rooms, editing suites and other equipment that places this facility among the largest and most up-to-date such facilities in the east.

Breslin Hall, Hofstra's newest classroom building, offers several classroom atmospheres providing students with the latest in educational technology. Computer laboratories are another addition to the Hofstra campus. Located throughout the campus in over a half dozen

convenient locations, Hofstra's computer labs offer students access to the latest computer technology seven days and nights a week.

Another recent addition to Hofstra's south campus is the Student Administrative Complex. Featuring a one-stop shopping system of registration, financial aid, tuition, residence and food service payment, this service has converted a time consuming, complicated system into a convenient task and so has been replicated by other institutions throughout the nation.

Some of the changes at Hofstra over the years are obvious, such as the new addition to the Hofstra School of Law which includes a law library that is second to none. But others are not so obvious. For instance, Hofstra's theaters, the John Cranford Adams Playhouse and the Emily and Jerry Spiegel Theater (formerly the Little Theater) outwardly appear the same as ever. Inside, however, the two theaters have been enhanced through renovations and the addition of up-to-date equipment.

Hofstra's students enjoy the many benefits of small classes, due in large measure to the fact that the University's faculty has doubled in size since the 1970s. Despite this major personnel expansion, Hofstra's support of its professors has not been compromised. Each professor has an individual computer-equipped office, aiding his or her ability to work with students and do meaningful research.

Many across the nation who may not be familiar with Hofstra's academic programs know about the University because of its Presidential Conference Series which began in 1982. The series, which has won international recognition, has featured scholarly seminars on the administrations of most of the nation's presidents since Franklin D. Roosevelt.

An in-person visit is a must for those haven't yet met the Hofstra of the 1990s. From the student athlete competing in the newly-renovated Hofstra Stadium or exercising at the Joseph M. Margiotta Hall Field House, to a Fine Arts class exploring the galleries of the nationally-accredited Hofstra Museum, from the lectern of a Hofstra professor inspiring her class in Breslin Hall, to an aspiring journalist learning the basics of electronic journalism in Dempster Hall, to the freshman spending a day among the stacks of the Axinn Library... Hofstra University is an example of the best that American higher education has to offer today. •••

Enthusiastic Hofstra cheerleaders rehearse a routine in front of Hofstra Hall.

CHAPTER 16

• • •

HEALTH CARE

• • •

Photo by Bruce Bennett.

THE UNIVERSITY HOSPITAL & MEDICAL CENTER AT STONY BROOK

Bringing Research to Life

• • •

A CENTER FOR SCIENTIFIC DISCOVERY. AN institution of higher learning. A hallmark of outstanding medical care, and a beacon for broad-reaching community service programs. University Hospital and Medical Center at Stony Brook shares daily in shaping the vision of a Long Island health care system—a network designed to provide all Long Island residents with easy access to the services they need.

University Hospital and Medical Center is recognized as an outstanding health care and education resource for the entire Long Island community. Through innovative partnerships with health professionals, managed care companies and other hospitals, Stony Brook offers compassionate and highly specialized medical services to all who seek them.

Situated within a complex that includes a Health Sciences Center and a basic science facility, the twin towers of University Hospital offer a faculty and staff sharply focused on delivering excellent health care in a demanding and challenging health care environment.

HEALTH SCIENCES CENTER

Established in 1972 to addresses the shortage of health care professionals and improve access to the most sophisticated types of medical care for residents of Nassau and Suffolk counties, the

(above) University Hospital and Medical Center is an outstanding health care and education resource for the entire Long Island community.

Stony Brook's School of Medicine is the flagship biomedical research institution for the State University of New York.

Health Sciences Center at Stony Brook functions as Long Island's only comprehensive academic health center, pursuing a mission of excellence in education, patient care, research and community service.

The center's five school's (Dental Medicine, Health Technology and Management, Medicine, Nursing, and Social Welfare) offer degree-granting programs to approximately 2,000 students, and the School of Medicine's 45 approved specialty programs serve more than 400 residents each year. The schools are directly linked to University Hospital, which serves as the chief clinical resource for students and residents. The Health Sciences Center and its schools hold affiliations with many institutions and agencies. Among the major resources for the schools' educational, research and clinical programs are Brookhaven National Laboratory Clinical Research Center, Medical Department; the Nassau County Medical Center; the Veterans Affairs Medical Center at Northport; and Winthrop-University Hospital.

THE SCHOOL OF MEDICINE—PACESETTER FOR ACADEMIC RESEARCH INSTITUTIONS

The School of Medicine at Stony Brook is the flagship biomedical research institution of the State University of New York system and a pacesetter for academic research institutions across the globe.

The curriculum provides training through seven basic science and 18 clinical departments. The school's strong thematic research programs offer students the experience of working with world class researchers on the cutting edge of scientific discovery, while Stony Brook's ultramodern University Hospital provides them with exposure to the broad range of clinical care and management issues that physicians encounter in their practice.

Basic science instruction at Stony Brook equals that of the most excellent medical programs in the nation. Mentored by faculty engaged in uncovering the newest biomedical information, Stony Brook students learn to understand medicine as a scientific discipline. Faculty help students grasp the complexities of modern clinical methods, which require an understanding of science at the molecular level. The

Stony Brook's Institute for Medicine in Contemporary Society links medicine to other dimensions of contemporary culture.

academic program centers on a systems approach that presents all aspects of a study area on a continuum from the cellular level to clinical therapy. Stony Brook also promotes excellent exposure to a variety of exciting clinical rotations, enabling students to develop skills for practicing in the full range of medical settings, from tertiary to primary care. Stony Brook is strongly committed to primary medicine. The Primary Care Education Project—a new interdisciplinary initiative—allows students to work closely with family physicians in academic settings, public health centers, private practices, HMO's and other sites.

Stony Brook houses a large number of centers, laboratories and institutes, many of which are externally funded. The Institute for Medicine in Contemporary Society was established in 1990 at the School of Medicine to develop interdisciplinary programs that explore the relationship of medicine to other dimensions of contemporary culture. Encouraging understanding of the complex experiences of being ill and caring for the ill, the Institute serves as a catalyst for discussion, educational experiment and research in the multi-cultural environment of Stony Brook. Coursework challenges students to think, talk and wrestle with a number of relevant medical issues ranging from codes of ethics to national health care systems to HIV infection.

Stony Brook's young and vigorous programs encourage medical students to seek and find their useful place in society. The school's orientation to teaching small groups enables students to develop personal relationships with many faculty members. And a commitment to diversity training promotes understanding of multiple viewpoints, and development of the sensitivity and skills needed for successful interaction with a variety of ethnic and traditionally underserved groups.

STONY BROOK—TRANSLATING RESEARCH TO PATIENT CARE

The School of Medicine's Strategic Plan for Research stresses the collaborative and interdisciplinary approaches that have become the

hallmark of biomedical research. The School's strong thematic research programs emphasize interdepartmental, interdisciplinary, and interinstitutional collaborations. They build on existing strengths by filling crucial gaps in the science base, providing an infrastructure and core facilities that will facilitate biomedical research, and strengthening translational research programs that apply advances in basic science to clinical problems.

School of Medicine faculty engaged in biomedical research represent a major asset to the University and contribute significantly to its outstanding productivity. The School takes advantage of the exceptional regional concentration of biomedical research institutions on Long Island, including Cold Spring Harbor, Brookhaven National Laboratory, Plum Island Laboratory, and the Picower Institute.

During the School's early years, the basic science departments led the way in establishing high-quality research and graduate training programs. Today, according to data provided by the American Association of Medical Colleges, the basic science faculty rank in the top 10 percent of medical schools in research funding per individual investigator.

Stony Brook investigators pursue clinical research, new diagnostic methods and patient therapies, as well as basic research into the causes and mechanisms of disease at the cellular and molecular levels. The School of Medicine is developing major research programs in human genetics and structural biology.

Stony Brook faculty members contributed significantly to the development of Magnetic Resonance Imaging (MRI) technology, anticlotting factors to halt coronary blockages, and what is now the standard protocol for colon cancer treatment. Stony Brook researchers helped identify the bacterium that causes Lyme disease

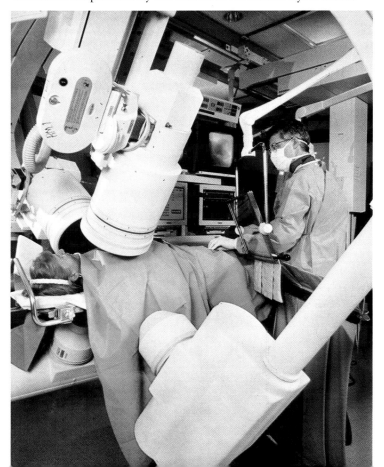

Stony Brook's advanced Bi-plane Swing Cardiac Catheterization Laboratory is one of the many outstanding facilities available to Stony Brook's School of Medicine through University Hospital.

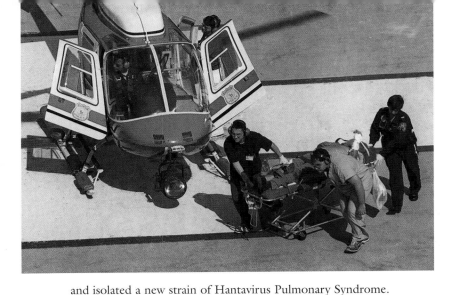

and isolated a new strain of Hantavirus Pulmonary Syndrome.

Many of Stony Brook's clinical researchers serve as principal investigators for nationwide research studies and Stony Brook is the regional center for numerous clinical trials in cancer and other areas. Recently, the medical center was one of 24 centers nationwide designated by the National Institutes of Health to conduct the Women's Health Initiative. This series of clinical studies seeks to determine the influence of environmental, genetic, and lifestyle factors on health and disease in women.

UNIVERSITY HOSPITAL AND MEDICAL CENTER

Conceived 20 years ago as an academic medical center that could provide the highest level of tertiary health care to Suffolk County's 1.3 million residents, Stony Brook's University Hospital and Medical Center has since exploded into a diverse, forward look-ing institution that succeeds at delivering a broad range of tertiary, urgent and primary care services to its diverse patient base.

Now serving the varied needs of young, old, rich, poor, critical and healthy patients, the University Hospital is a frontrunner in delivering a wide array of excellent preventive, diagnostic and treatment services to residents across all of Long Island. Committed to ensuring accessible health care to a wide range of patients, the medical center has developed a network of community-based outpatient and primary care centers.

When the University Hospital admitted its first patients in the fall of 1980, it sought to provide Long Island with a regional center for advanced patient care, education, research and community ser-vice. Today, University Hospital cares for more than 25,000 inpa-tients and treats more than 46,000 people in its emergency depart-ment each year. Close to 3,200 babies are born here each year, and nearly 510,000 patients visit the medical center for physician care, and ambulatory diagnostic and treatment services. With extensive laboratory services including diagnostic radiology imaging, magnetic resonance imaging, stereotactic core breast biopsy, special proce-dures, interventional radiology and nuclear medicine, as well as sophisticated instrumentation and computerized physiological mon-itoring systems, Stony Brook offers the most highly specialized

diagnostic and treatment programs available.

Helicopter and ground transports deliver Suffolk County's most seriously injured and ill patients to University Hospital, the region's designated Level One Trauma Center and the county referral center for all psychiatric emergencies. The emergency department's seven-bed shock trauma room is specifically designed to handle the most critical patients with problems ranging from multiple trauma to cardiogenic shock.

With 504 beds, the hospital operates nine intensive care units dedicated to anesthesia, burn, cardiovascular, coronary, pediatric, medical, neonatal, surgical and transplant patients. Through coordinated services that guarantee our patients the specialized attention they need, highly skilled teams of physicians, nurses, nutritionists, physical therapists, laboratory technicians, social workers, and chaplains care for adults and children with a variety of chronic conditions, such as diabetes, cystic fibrosis, Lyme disease, and multiple sclerosis.

The University Heart Center's comprehensive cardiovascular service offers the most advanced detection and treatment equipment available. With its bi-plane swing cardiac catheterization laboratory and its sophisticated cardiovascular intensive care unit, Stony Brook is positioned on the leading edge when moments count and expertise makes the critical difference. Stony Brook cardiologists pioneered enhanced external counterpulsation—a truly innovative, noninvasive, and remarkably successful treatment for patients suffering from coronary artery disease. Whether patients need high-risk open heart surgery or preventive care, the University Heart Center is available as a resource for all Long Island residents.

Stony Brook's neonatal intensive care unit provides the only tertiary care for premature and newborn infants in Suffolk County—babies who require careful observation and monitoring. Stony Brook's neonatologists and specially trained nurses work closely with

A wide variety of interdisciplinary care assures Stony Brook patients the specialized attention they need.

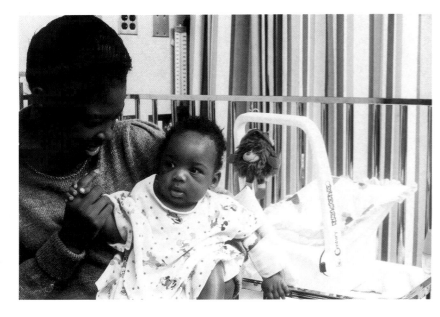

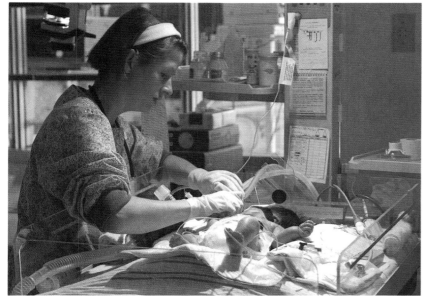

cardiologists, surgeons, and other specialists to guide these and other seriously ill babies along the path to a speedy and full recovery.

A LEADER IN CANCER RESEARCH AND TREATMENT

With the resources of a major academic medical center, University Hospital's physicians and researchers provide great leadership in the field of cancer research and clinical care and play a prominent role in evaluating and developing the treatment methods that eventually become standard protocols for treating patients with cancer. Stony Brook researchers led the world in developing biochemical modulation, a technique that uses drug combinations to enhance the effectiveness of chemotherapy. Stony Brook's medical oncologists are presently testing the next generation of biochemical modulation therapies while frontline research initiatives push forward in gene therapy, tumor control and immunotherapy.

Stony Brook was selected as a site for an international trial of monoclonal antibodies, also known as *magic bullets*, for breast and colon carcinomas. One of the few locations in the world offering intracarotid chemotherapy for brain tumors, surgeons conducting bone marrow transplantation, and researchers actively studying cancer language (the mechanisms of cell growth), Stony Brook continues its tradition of excellence in cancer treatment and prevention.

Advancing women's medicine, Stony Brook opened a comprehensive Breast Care Center with diagnostic and treatment facilities, a full range of surgical services, complete counseling and referral services, and a strong research component—all in a community-based setting located at the Stony Brook Technology Center in East Setauket. The breast center's interdisciplinary focus allows patients to consult with oncology and reconstructive surgeons, medical oncologists and counselors all in the same day.

LONG ISLAND'S RESOURCE FOR COMMUNITY SERVICE

Stony Brook's Health Initiative for Underserved Communities plays a key role in improving access to medical and dental care in localities that have been underserved by health professionals. And Stony Brook's community service mission brings health education programs, as well as breast cancer, prostate cancer, cholesterol, blood pressure and other screening programs to communities throughout Suffolk County.

The Department of Preventive Medicine's Division of Occupational and Environmental Medicine provides an innovative community health service for Long Island. The division's highly specialized staff serves individual workers, unions, and industries throughout Long Island. The division has achieved national recognition and provides expert consultation throughout the country. The service is the most comprehensive in the region, providing clinical and diagnostic occupational and environmental medicine, referral, and treatment services, as well as industrial hygiene and safety training, and education to those in the public and private sectors.

The medical center's outreach program includes the region's first Cancer Helpline staffed by professional oncology nurses. Stony Brook's Healthcare Teleservices system provides community physicians and prospective patients with a direct link to physicians and medical services at Stony Brook. Callers wishing information about medical services, physician referrals, or appointment scheduling may call HealthCalls, our consumer helpline.　　　•••

THE ST. FRANCIS-MERCY CORPORATION

• • •

IN MARCH OF 1996, THE MOST REV. JOHN R. MCGANN, D.D., Bishop of the Roman Catholic Diocese of Rockville Centre, announced that St. Francis Hospital, The Heart Center, in Roslyn and Mercy Medical Center in Rockville Centre had merged parent corporations and will operate under unified governance and management. The two institutions, both *accredited with commendation* by the Joint Commission on Accreditation of Healthcare Organizations, operate under the common sponsorship of the Diocese of Rockville Centre. The new entity, now known as The St. Francis-Mercy Corporation, operates under the authority of the new Corporation.

The union of these two institutions was undertaken to achieve economies of scale and a strengthened market position to meet the challenges and demands presented by the expanded managed care marketplace. The St. Francis-Mercy Corporation is a new whole which has thus become greater than the sum of its two parts: as a cardiac specialty center, St. Francis Hospital meets its need for diversification within the new Corporation; Mercy Medical Center, as a community institution, now benefits from the unique programs and resources offered by St. Francis Hospital.

The St. Francis-Mercy Corporation represents a shared strategic vision for an enhanced health care delivery system that serves the needs of the regional community with high quality, high compassion, low cost primary and specialty services. This union is particularly distinguished by breadth, diversification and a shared Catholic

Mission which supports the health care ministry of the Diocese of Rockville Centre.

The subsidiaries which comprise the new St. Francis-Mercy Corporation are St. Francis Hospital, The St. Francis Research & Education Corporation, The St. Francis Hospital Foundation, Mercy Medical Center and Mercy Hospice. "It is the shared vision of the Boards of both institutions to form the nucleus of a delivery system that will meet the needs of the communities served by St. Francis Hospital and Mercy Medical Center with high-quality, high-compassion, cost effective health care," said Robert F. Vizza, Ph.D, president and chief executive officer, The St. Francis-Mercy Corporation. "By combining the strengths of both institutions, this objective will be achieved and the capabilities of both institutions will be enhanced."

ST. FRANCIS HOSPITAL
THE HEART CENTER

The only designated Heart Center in New York State, St. Francis Hospital ranks second nationwide in the number of open heart surgeries it performs. A voluntary, not-for-profit cardiac specialty hospital, St. Francis Hospital was founded in 1922 and has long established a reputation as an innovator in delivering superior cardiac services within a cost-efficient, caring environment. As New York State's number one provider of open heart surgeries, St. Francis Hospital has the Northeast's highest cardiac caseload and also has the state's highest survival rate for cardiac surgery. It is the state's lowest cost provider for 6 of the 10 most common cardiac procedures.

According to a *Modern Healthcare* survey by the international accounting firm KPMG Peat Marwick, St. Francis Hospital is among the 30 best-managed hospitals in the United States. The hospital is a teaching affiliate of the Columbia University, College of Physicians and Surgeons and

St. Francis Hospital, The Heart Center, performs the largest cardiac caseload in the region and the second largest in the United States.

The Cardiac Fitness Program at St. Francis Hospital provides a medically supervised program and an individualized exercise prescription for people who have had heart attacks, open heart surgery, or are at risk for cardiac illness.

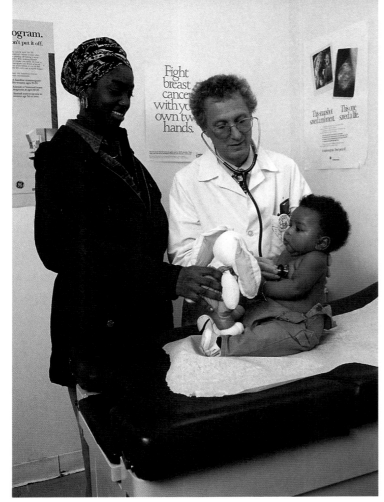

St. Francis Hospital pediatric cardiologists provide cardiac screening to hundreds of local children each year at the Pediatric Cardiology Outreach Program in Freeport, which is the only free clinic of its kind on Long Island.

The Presbyterian Hospital in the City of New York.

St. Francis Hospital's leadership role as an innovator in health care has resulted in many advances in cardiac care treatment, among them non-invasive imaging technologies such as 3-D echocardiography and ultrafast CT scanning; new pacemaker and defibrillator technology; access to investigational medications; and clinical research in preventive cardiology, ischemic heart disease, heart failure and arrhythmia.

As the region's premier Heart Center, St. Francis Hospital leads the way in the community-based application of emerging cardiac technologies.

The professional staff at St. Francis Hospital is committed to the belief that heart disease, the nation's leading killer, is a preventable disorder. In 1992, the Hospital founded The DeMatteis Center for Cardiac Research and Education which is dedicated to reducing the incidence of heart disease through community-based programs in risk reduction and health education. The DeMatteis Center also conducts comprehensive research programs into cardiac disease detection and prevention at its 51-acre campus in Old Brookville.

The DeMatteis Center encompasses a state-of-the-art fitness facility, a complete community health education curriculum, ongoing research protocols and continuing medical education programs for

health care professionals. Through these and other programs, The DeMatteis Center meets its twofold mission: to assist patients recovering from heart attack and open heart surgery in developing an active, healthy lifestyle, and to lead the community at large toward awareness of heart healthy living.

The Cardiac Fitness Program at The DeMatteis Center was one of the first programs nationwide predicated on the theory that high-risk cardiac patients can successfully achieve and maintain a healthy level of physical activity. A model for programs now instituted across the country, St. Francis' Cardiac Fitness Program establishes individualized, medically supervised exercise therapy for people recovering from heart disease or those identified as being at high risk for coronary artery disease.

The DeMatteis Center also presents community health programs which comprise an important component of St. Francis' mission as a Heart Center. These programs, including nutrition counseling, weight loss, smoking cessation and stress management workshops, cardiac disease prevention lectures and emergency medical training, provide members of the community with up-to-date information on cardiac health and disease prevention and also help to promote healthy lifestyles. A wide range of cardiac screening programs to detect the presence of heart disease, or risk factors leading to heart disease, are offered by St. Francis Hospital at The DeMatteis Center so that individuals have the opportunity to avert cardiac problems by altering lifestyles that are likely to result in heart disease.

In keeping with its Catholic Mission, St. Francis Hospital reaches out to the Long Island community and even to the wider world with programs to reduce health risks and to provide critical cardiac care to those in need. A part of the Gift of Life Program, St. Francis arranges for children from around the world to be transported to the Hospital for lifesaving cardiac surgery. Through this program, which

St. Francis Hospital, located in Roslyn, Long Island, is the only specialty designated heart center in New York State.

Mercy Medical Center in Rockville Centre offers advanced technology with compassion.

is sponsored by Rotary International, St. Francis Hospital has provided open heart surgery to more than 500 children from more than 37 countries, donating its services and facilities in each case.

Responding to the medical care needs of Long Island's low-income residents and the region's rapidly growing immigrant population, St. Francis provides a mobile cardiac outreach team which travels throughout Nassau County and parts of Suffolk County to conduct free cardiac screening for those who cannot pay for these services. The St. Francis team, consisting of a cardiologist, registered nurse and bilingual secretary, sets up temporary clinics at various churches and schools in low-income communities. They conduct cardiac evaluations through medical histories, blood pressure screening and EKG testing and also provide follow-up diagnostics and care at the Hospital when needed.

This nationally-recognized cardiac center additionally reaches out to meet community needs through its collaboration with Nassau County's Handicapped Children's Program at the Nassau County Department of Health Clinic in Freeport. This program accepts children referred through health clinics across the county and arranges for youngsters to be examined by a St. Francis Hospital pediatric cardiologist right at the Freeport clinic, the only free clinic of its kind on Long Island.

Patrick J. Scollard, president and chief executive officer of St. Francis Hospital, remarked that the hospital operates these programs as a service to the community and as an extension of the Hospital's dedication to early detection of heart disease. Speaking of St. Francis' status as the nation's second largest provider of cardiac care, he said: "This level of proficiency, along with our Mission as a Catholic hospital, compels us to share our services with the medically and financially needy. It is very important that we reach out to this segment of our population."

MERCY MEDICAL CENTER
ADVANCED TECHNOLOGY IN AN ATMOSPHERE OF COMPASSION

Founded in 1913 by The Congregation of the Infant Jesus, Mercy Medical Center is a 387-bed community medical center and Level II Trauma Center which offers a wide range of inpatient and outpatient services to people throughout Long Island and beyond. With the opening of The Long Island Cancer Institute in 1995, and the addition to the Institute in early 1996 of The Bishop McGann

Center for Oncology and Imaging, Mercy Medical Center has placed itself in the forefront of the diagnosis and treatment of cancer.

The advanced technological equipment available at The Bishop McGann Center includes a linear accelerator which allows for pin-point treatment of tumors, and the latest computerized tomography, ultrasound, and magnetic resonance imaging equipment available anywhere in the nation. Included in the cancer services Mercy offers is a program for the treatment of prostate cancer with radioactive seed implants. Mercy's Prostate Cancer Seed Implant Program has become one of the leaders in the Northeast in performing this proceedure.

Other specialty areas which have recently been initiated or expanded by Mercy Medical Center include maternity care, physical medicine and rehabilitation, pediatric special care, radiology, hemodialysis, mental health, and pain management. Mercy is also an area leader for its services in obstetrics and gynecology, pediatrics, eye and ear surgery, endoscopy and orthopedic surgery.

A major landmark for Mercy came in 1996 with its *accreditation with commendation* by the Joint Commission on Accreditation of Healthcare Organizations, the oldest and largest accrediting body in the health care field. Mercy's score of 99 out of a possible 100 is evidence of the Center's commitment to high quality care.

Mercy Medical Center prides itself on delivering state-of-the-art technology in an atmosphere of compassion. This commitment is demonstrated by services as diverse as the advanced technological

A linear accelerator is just one of the many leading edge technologies available for the diagnosis and treatment of cancer at The Bishop McGann Center of Mercy Medical Center.

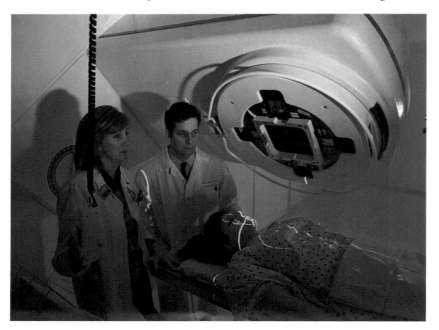

With a history of more than 145,000 births, Mercy Medical Center has become a Long Island leader in maternal care.

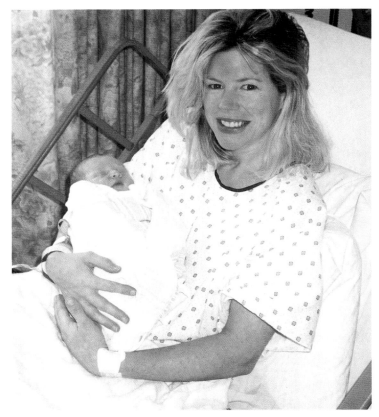

facilities for the diagnosis and treatment of cancer and other serious illness, and Mercy's planned new Maternity Center which will feature an LDRP program in which labor, delivery, recovery and postpartum care take place all in one homelike, family-oriented setting. Mercy's history of more than 145,000 births makes it a Long Island leader in maternal care.

Mercy follows up its extensive OB-GYN program with a Neonatal Intensive Care Unit for the treatment of babies born with serious illnesses or defects. To serve the needs of critically ill or injured children, Mercy opened a four-bed Pediatric Special Care Unit providing comfortable quarters for parents to stay close to their children overnight.

In addition to its well known strengths in cancer diagnosis and treatment and maternal and child care, Mercy excels in a number of other medical and surgical specialties. Mercy's Endoscopy Suite performs thousands of diagnostic and treatment procedures each year. More corneal transplants are performed at Mercy than at all other Long Island hospitals combined. The Rockville Centre hospital is Long Island's only provider of Cochlear ear implants, a procedure which restores hearing to the profoundly deaf. In collaboration with St. Francis Hospital, Mercy has opened an Electrophysiology Laboratory to diagnose electrical abnormalities in the heart. Mercy's Vascular Laboratory is the state's sole training site for teaching the use of imaging systems that are a vital diagnostic tool in carotid endarterectomy

surgery for stroke patients. Patients with orthopedic injuries are treated at Mercy with laser arthroscopic surgery or laparoscopic surgical techniques. Mercy's 25-bed Physical Medicine and Rehabilitation Unit, dedicated in 1994, speeds the recovery of patients who have experienced strokes, traumatic injuries or other neurologic or orthopedic problems.

Nassau County's largest provider of mental health services, Mercy administers a wide range of inpatient and outpatient mental health programs. To meet the needs of terminally ill patients and their families, Mercy established a home-care program, Mercy Hospice. Other Mercy initiatives to fill unmet medical needs in the community include a Sleep Disorders Center, a Pain Management Service, and a Multiple Sclerosis Center.

On an outpatient basis, Mercy offers parents-to-be programs for expectant mothers, fathers, siblings and even grandparents; wellness programs, cardiac rehabilitation; physical therapy; educational and treatment programs for alcoholism and chemical dependencies; and various community service screenings, support groups and educational lectures and workshops.

Mercy Medical Center has honored its commitment to compassionate patient care as it has moved forward with the latest high-tech innovations. Mercy maintains its place at the forefront of modern medicine while adhering to its Catholic Mission of providing quality, compassionate health care services that respond to both technological advances and community needs. •••

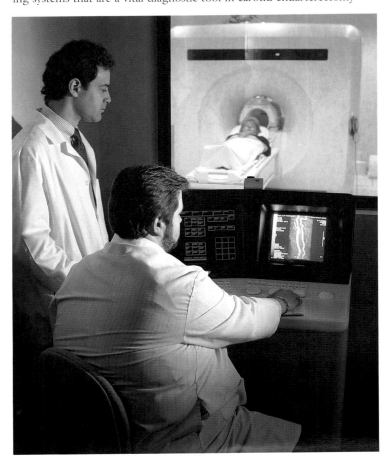

Mercy Medical Center staff members monitor a patient undergoing magnetic resonance imaging.

LONG ISLAND JEWISH MEDICAL CENTER
A Leader in Long Island Health Care
• • •

STRATEGICALLY LOCATED ON THE BORDER OF Queens and Nassau counties, Long Island Jewish Medical Center (LIJ) is a magnet hospital for the population from metropolitan New York to rural eastern Long Island. In an area that can boast many fine community and acute care hospitals, LIJ is recognized as a leading medical resource with an outstanding staff of specialists whose work is enhanced by the latest technology. The Medical Center has one of the largest graduate teaching programs in New York State and the high caliber of its clinical and basic research attracts prestigious government and philanthropic grants.

The 829-bed Medical Center, on a 48-acre campus, encompasses three distinct divisions: Long Island Jewish Hospital for all aspects of adult health care; Schneider Children's Hospital, the only metropolitan area hospital built specifically for children; and Hillside Hospital, a pioneer in modern psychiatry.

When its doors opened in 1954, LIJ set an ambitious pace by becoming the first community hospital in the country to appoint full-time physicians as department heads. Today, the Hospital is a highly respected regional resource with 16 departments and a staff that spans all specialties. An emphasis on teaching and learning means being part of the rapidly expanding universe of medical discoveries and scientific progress. This is further reflected in its 48 approved residency programs with almost 600 Residents and Fellows, in extensive continuing education for health professionals and in LIJ's role as the Long Island Campus for the Albert Einstein College of Medicine.

LONG ISLAND JEWISH HOSPITAL

As the adult care division of the Medical Center, the 452-bed Long Island Jewish Hospital draws patients from throughout Long Island as well as elsewhere in the country and abroad. They come for advanced treatment protocols in the Institute of Oncology, Heart Institute, Vascular Institute, Stroke Center, Pain and Headache Treatment Center, the Urology Department's Stone Center, Sleep Disorders Program, Bone Marrow Transplantation Unit, Hearing and Speech Center and many other programs noted for their excellence.

More than 5,000

babies are born annually in the Labor/Delivery/Recovery Suites, one of the area's first facilities with a private, home-like setting for giving birth. Recently, LIJ opened the Women's Comprehensive Health Center in its Manhasset Ambulatory Pavilion. Designed as a "one-stop" source for women's total health requirements, it covers the spectrum from adolescence through reproductive years and after.

One of the earliest hospitals in the area to utilize high powered Magnetic Resonance Imaging, LIJ has just completed expansion of its Radiology and Radiation Oncology facilities including the latest generation MRI and linear accelerator. This, and emphasis on broadening the scope of already extensive outpatient programs, exemplify LIJ's mission of progress and quality in medical care.

SCHNEIDER CHILDREN'S HOSPITAL

The first time children and their parents come to Schneider Children's Hospital (SCH), they are often surprised. With its bright and cheerful lobby, imaginative artwork, toys and colorful furnishings, it hardly seems like a hospital. The 154-bed facility was built with the understanding that to a sick child, hospital walls contain a small universe. At SCH, this universe was planned with insight and compassion. The caring staff adds to an environment that is both reassuring and supportive to patients and their families.

SCH is the only hospital in the New York metropolitan area built especially for children, serving all their medical, surgical, psychiatric and dental needs. Board certified pediatric specialists treat all ages, from premature infants to adolescents.

"The Flying Squad," an intensive care transport, brings seriously ill children to SCH from community hospitals. A Neonatal Intensive Care Unit is connected by a corridor to the Medical Center's obstetrics suite.

A resource for Long Island and the metropolitan area since its opening in 1983, SCH is known for specialized care, including cancer, heart disease, digestive disorders, neurological problems and surgery.

The Long Island Jewish Medical Center campus is the site of three distinct hospitals: Long Island Jewish Hospital, dedicated to comprehensive adult care; Schneider Children's Hospital for pediatrics; and Hillside Hospital for the full range of mental health services.

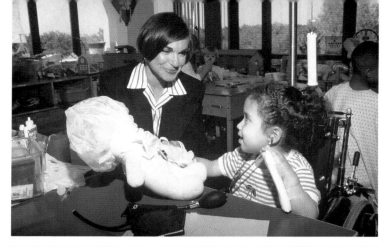

Hillside Hospital's greenhouse and programs such as Supported Employment enable patients to meet their personal living and work goals through a variety of rehabilitation and therapy approaches.

In keeping with the supportive environment of Schneider Children's Hospital, Child Life Playrooms on each unit use play therapy to ease the stress of hospitalization for young patients.

Psychiatric services, including a 17-bed inpatient unit, a Hearing and Speech Center, special services for deaf patients, the Bone Marrow Transplantation Unit, Eating Disorders Center and extensive Adolescent Medicine programs, attract patients from all over the region. A Ronald McDonald House on hospital grounds provides a home-away-from-home for families of children undergoing treatment.

Medical services at SCH are complemented by a large network of support services. Specially-trained social workers, psychologists, Child Life specialists, even clowns from the Big Apple Circus, are all sensitive to the needs of young patients and help alleviate the stress of hospitalization.

With an eye toward bringing specialized health care services to many more communities on Long Island, the Children's Hospital has opened satellite offices in Hauppauge and Hewlett and is expanding into other areas as well.

HILLSIDE HOSPITAL

Since 1927, Hillside Hospital, the psychiatric division of Long Island Jewish Medical Center (LIJ), has been working to unravel the mysteries of the mind and its illnesses. A pioneer in mental health, Hillside is internationally known for seminal research as well as its high level of patient care and clinical education. It is one of only four sites in the U.S. designated by the National Institute of Mental Health as a clinical research center to study the causes and treatment of schizophrenia, the most devastating and costly of mental illnesses.

Hillside provides patients of all ages with a progressive model of care in a compassionate environment and broad range of treatment programs. Patients are encouraged to actively participate in the structuring of their treatment with an emphasis on returning to productive lives within their communities. Family involvement is strongly encouraged. Comprehensive treatment teams comprise psychiatrists and clinicians from psychology, nursing, psychiatric rehabilitation, social work, and where appropriate, substance abuse services. The person in crisis or in need of immediate hospitalization is accepted any time, 24 hours a day, seven days a week.

The 223-bed Hospital, which serves residents of Queens, Nassau and Suffolk counties, merged with LIJ in 1978. Facilities include athletic fields, a playground, a greenhouse, gymnasium, library, rehabilitation and occupational workshops and a commissary. Patients have the benefit of the full medical services of LIJ.

Hillside offers patients of all ages a comprehensive continuum of care featuring many modalities of treatment. These include inpatient and ambulatory care, day treatment, partial hospitalization, and community-based programs with an array of specialty clinics and services such as vocational rehabilitation, geriatric psychiatry, phobia and obsessive-compulsive disorder clinics, and drug and alcohol abuse services.

Millions of dollars are awarded annually to Hillside's research programs in grants from federal and other agencies. Over the years, internationally respected clinical studies have produced effective treatments for anxiety disorders, depression, and, most notably, schizophrenia.

As part of LIJ, Hillside provides the psychiatric component of medical students' clinical curriculum for the Albert Einstein College of Medicine. It offers extensive postgraduate training and clinical experience for psychiatrists and psychiatric residents and fellowships for highly advanced training in subspecialties. Training and clinical experience is also provided to psychology, nursing, social work and psychiatric rehabilitation students. •••

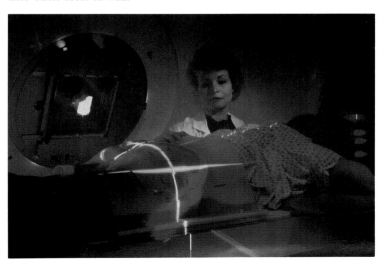

The powerful linear accelerator in the Radiation Oncology Department is an integral component of conformal 3-D treatment of cancer. It permits greater accuracy in delivery of high radiation doses than possible with standard techniques.

WINTHROP-UNIVERSITY HOSPITAL
A Century of Excellence... Cornerstone for the Future
• • •

WINTHROP-UNIVERSITY HOSPITAL IS ROOTED in a 100-year tradition of fulfilling the health care needs of Long Islanders. Founded in 1896 as Long Island's first voluntary hospital, Winthrop opened with 19 beds as the only health care facility between Queens and Montauk. During its first year, the Hospital admitted 91 patients, performed 27 operations and recorded 2 births.

The Winthrop of today is a premier regional health care resource with nearly 600 beds, a full complement of comprehensive inpatient and outpatient services, and a deep commitment to medical education and research. In a typical year, care is provided for more than 25,000 adult and pediatric inpatients, over 5,000 births are chronicled and the emergency department logs nearly 40,000 visits. In addition, over 16,000 surgical procedures are performed, including nearly 1,000 open heart operations. The Winthrop medical staff of approximately 1000, including more than 150 full-time faculty members and Ph.D. medical researchers, and a nursing staff that numbers about 700 offers the broadest possible range of services for a lifetime of health care.

WOMEN'S HEALTH SERVICES

Winthrop addresses every stage of a woman's life with respect, trust and dignity. From obstetricians, maternal-fetal medicine specialists, midwives and other professionals who focus on routine and high-risk pregnancies, as well as treatment of fertility and reproductive disorders, to gynecologists offering treatment for complex problems of the reproductive system, exercise and counseling for women in menopause, and programs for early detection and treatment of ovarian cancer... Winthrop has always been a special place for women.

CARE FOR CHILDREN

Winthrop is a regional resource for the treatment of premature babies and newborns with serious health problems. The expertly trained Neonatal Intensive Care Unit (NICU) staff treats complex problems that arise in babies born at Winthrop and transferred from other hospitals with the most sophisticated technology available today.

For babies, children, and adolescents,

Winthrop's pediatricians provide comprehensive primary and critical care, as well as subspecialty services that address problems such as growth disorders, cardiac and pulmonary conditions, cancer, developmental and behavioral difficulties, hereditary diseases, and neurological disorders.

At every level, the emotional well-being of every patient and family is deemed as vital as their medical care.

TREATING THE ELDERLY

Care for the aging at Winthrop is based upon the assumption that the process of growing older can occur gracefully with independence and dignity. Geratricians, geriatric nurses and social workers team with other specialists to provide a continuum of care that promotes health, prevents disease, and treats illness through personalized, progressive and supportive care for older individuals.

THE LUNG CENTER

Patients with serious lung conditions such as emphysema, asthma, and other chronic obstructive pulmonary diseases turn to Winthrop for treatment by its nationally recognized pulmonary and critical care medicine specialists. Known for providing the broadest scope of pulmonary services in the region, and for operating one of the few critical care programs in New York State fully accredited by the American Board of Internal Medicine, Winthrop's pulmonary and critical care medicine experts oversee care in the medical, respiratory and surgical intensive care units, providing advanced life support management for severely ill patients. Outpatient care is also a priority. The Hospital's distinguished Pulmonary Rehabilitation Program and Sleep Disorders Center treat hundreds of patients annually.

THE HEART INSTITUTE

A comprehensive resource for cardiac health, the Heart Institute utilizes the most current diagnostic technologies and disease prevention programs supervised by an experienced team of cardiologists, cardiovascular surgeons, cardiac nurses, physician assistants and technologists. They assess and correct circulatory and coronary problems through the full range of advanced cardiovascular care techniques, including angioplasty, valvuloplasty, angiometry, and other Doppler

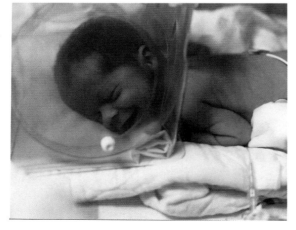

Babies in the Neonatal Intensive Care Unit are attended by exceptionally skilled newborn medicine specialists. In addition to caring for Winthrop babies, the NICU staff provides services for many babies transported here from other hospitals for intensive newborn care.

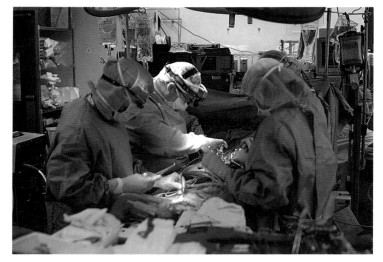

Winthrop's open heart surgery program has been rated as one of the best in New York State. It is the only hospital in the State to have achieved this outstanding rating for three consecutive years.

(below left) Nuclear medicine technology is part of the broad spectrum of advanced diagnostics used at Winthrop.

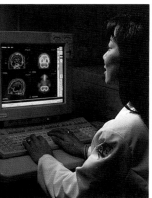

technology, as well as a Heart Surgery Program repeatedly recognized by the New York State Department of Health as one of the state's best.

SURGICAL SERVICES

A full spectrum of surgical specialists work in coordinated, multidisciplinary teams, operating at Winthrop in the inpatient Operating Room Suite, as well as in the ultra-modern Ambulatory Surgery Center. Winthrop surgeons pioneered the use of videolaparoscopy in abdominal surgery, and were the first on Long Island to use this minimally invasive technique to remove gall bladders. They have also set the pace for its use in colon surgery, appendectomies and hernia repair, resulting in reduced postoperative discomfort, shorter hospital stays and more rapid recoveries. Also at the cutting edge are Winthrop neurosurgeons and orthopaedic surgeons, who work in teams to perform complex spinal surgery on patients with serious disk and spinal curvature problems.

TRAUMA SERVICES

As a Level I Regional Trauma Center, Winthrop has a "round-the-clock" dedicated trauma team and a full range of surgical subspecialists to perform even the most complex procedures in emergency situations. Many of Nassau County's most seriously injured trauma patients are rushed to Winthrop via helicopter by the Nassau Aviation Bureau.

CENTERS FOR SPECIAL CARE

Winthrop's Special Care centers include the Long Island Regional Poison Control Center, the Dialysis Center, the Diabetes Education Center, the Osteoporosis Diagnostic and Treatment Center and the Lyme Disease Center.

COMMUNITY HEALTH NEEDS

To underscore its deep commitment to maintaining the health of the community, Winthrop offers a wide variety of

Hands-on nursing remains a top priority in this regional health care resource, which, despite its sophistication, continues to practice people-to-people medicine and provide those who turn to Winthrop for their health care—from newborns to the elderly —with a lifetime of care.

free health services for the public among them health screenings for cancers, vascular conditions and cholesterol; flu immunizations for senior citizens; health information/education programs; and a wide range of support groups related to many health-related issues.

TRAINING TOMORROW'S PHYSICIANS

As a Major Teaching Affiliate of the SUNY-Stony Brook School of Medicine, Winthrop has made a serious commitment to providing physicians with a stimulating learning environment. Post-graduate training is offered through 21 approved Residencies and Fellowships in a wide range of disciplines, including cardiology, critical care medicine, endocrinology/metabolism, gastroenterology, infectious disease, internal medicine, obstetrics/gynecology, pediatrics, pulmonary medicine and surgery.

RESEARCH INITIATIVES

Winthrop, has committed significant resources for basic and clinical research, which is supported by the Hospital, as well as by government grants and grants from individuals, foundations and corporations. Current investigations by Winthrop researchers include nationally recognized studies of women and heart disease, breathing problems in premature babies, osteoporosis and the use of antibiotics in critical care.

MEETING THE FUTURE

To better meet the challenges of the future, Winthrop has established relationships with other Long Island health care facilities. The Hospital is an equal partner with South Nassau Communities Hospital, operating under a parent corporation—Winthrop-South Nassau University Health System, Inc. Winthrop is also affiliated with Massapequa General Hospital, Mid-Island Hospital and United Presbyterian Residence.

The indomitable spirit and vision that fueled the birth of Winthrop-University Hospital a century ago continues to kindle its progress. Simultaneously large and small, regional as well as local, Winthrop successfully blends the progressive philosophy, sophistication and advancements of a widely respected teaching and research institution with a very personal approach to care. As a result, Winthrop provides the highest quality care without compromise.   •••

EPISCOPAL HEALTH SERVICES
Championing the Underserved with Quality Health Care
• • •

FOUNDED IN 1851 AS THE CHURCH CHARITY Foundation, Episcopal Health Services Inc. is now the sixth largest health care network in New York State. In Brooklyn and in Queens, Nassau and Suffolk counties, Episcopal Health Services provides a continuum of care which includes primary, acute, emergency, ambulatory, long-term and residential living.

Episcopal Health Services' network, which is accredited by the Joint Commission on the Accreditation of Healthcare Organizations, the oldest, largest and most prestigious such body in the health care field, is guided by the teachings and traditions of the Episcopal Church. It meets its Episcopalian Mission by offering quality medical care, health education programs, pastoral care and outreach services to all without regard to religious creed, race, ethnicity, or economic status.

The extensive Episcopal network includes St. John's Episcopal Hospital in Far Rockaway, a 314-bed community teaching facility; St. John's Episcopal Hospital, Smithtown, a 366-bed acute care facility; St. John's Ambulatory Surgery Center, also in Smithtown; the Bishop Jonathan G. Sherman Episcopal Nursing Home, a 240-bed facility on the St. John's campus in Smithtown; the Bishop Charles Waldo MacLean Episcopal Nursing Home, a 163-bed long-term care facility in Far Rockaway; the St. John's Episcopal Homes for the Aged and Blind, a 97-bed long-term care facility in Brooklyn; and The Village of St. John, a residential care facility of 298 one bedroom apartments located on the Smithtown campus. Additionally, MedPort primary medical service centers are maintained in one Nassau County and three Suffolk County communities.

The hospitals of Episcopal Health Services provide medical care, human services and educational outreach to the communities they serve and they provide a source of acute care backup for the long-term nursing home facilities maintained by the network.

St. John's Episcopal Hospital, South Shore serves the densely populated, culturally and economically diverse and medically underserved communities of Far Rockaway and the Five Towns. Affiliated with the State University of New York, Health Science Center in Brooklyn and The Mount Sinai Medical Center in New York City, St. John's South Shore is widely regarded as having one of the finest graduate medical education programs in the metropolitan area. Among the hospital's more notable programs are the only 24-hour obstetrics/gynecological service on the Rockaway Peninsula; a certified midwifery service; cardiac diagnostic, monitoring and treatment services; and enhanced medical and surgical offerings in otolaryngology and facial plastic and reconstructive surgery, radiology and nuclear medicine.

St. John's Episcopal Hospital and Ambulatory Surgery Center in Smithtown, a graduate medical education center, is affiliated with the State University of New York, Health Science Center in Stony Brook, and The Mount Sinai Health System. The Smithtown hospital's greatest strengths are regarded as cancer care/oncology, tertiary spinal surgery, reimplantation surgery, orthopedic implants, hemodialysis, and cardiopulmonary rehabilitation. As a Level I Area Trauma Center for Suffolk, the Smithtown facility includes a fully-equipped acute care room for trauma, cardiac and respiratory patients. An Emergency Unit Fast Track Center was opened in 1995 within the emergency services department. The new Center features such advances as a modular wall unit that allows equipment that is normally unmovable to become mobile to fit certain circumstances.

Responding to the challenges and demands of a shifting health care environment, Episcopal Health Services moved forward under the strong new administrative leadership of Chief Executive Officer, Dr. Jack N. Farrington. Dr. Farrington sharpened the organization's marketing focus and elevated its mission to champion the underserved with expanded health care and human services. Many initiatives were

St. John's Episcopal Hospital, Smithtown is a 366-bed acute care facility.

The Bishop Jonathan G. Sherman Episcopal Nursing Home is a 240-bed facility located on the St. John's campus in Smithtown.

launched, among them the forging of new health care partnerships, and the beginning of construction of an important new nursing home in central Brooklyn. To be called the Bishop Henry B. Hucles Episcopal Nursing Home, the 240-bed facility for the community's frail elderly and chronically ill residents is expected to open during 1997.

By joining The Mount Sinai Health System, Episcopal Health Services gained increased advantages for its patients and physicians while remaining financially and administratively independent. Dr. Farrington summed up the challenges, transitions and progress of the past year by noting that while the network's traditional services were enhanced with new health care delivery systems and human services, "our accomplishments and plans also express our commitment to managed care and primary care."

Under its MedPort program, Episcopal Health Services has established primary care centers in Medford, Islip, Northport and Hempstead. The MedPort community sites provide complete primary family medical services, including preventive, routine and diagnostic

testing services. Through MedPort, Episcopal Health Services finds it is able to continue to bring high-quality care to medically underserved communities. Utilizing the resources of the broad Episcopal network, Suffolk County MedPorts are linked to St. John's Episcopal Hospital in Smithtown while the Hempstead MedPort is linked to St. John's Episcopal Hospital in Far Rockaway.

Episcopal Health Services assumed a prominent role in the managed care arena when it became an equity partner in the FirstChoice Network, a consortium of health care providers. It is the philosophy of Episcopal Health Services that managed care, appropriately administered, will result in high-quality care, cost savings and benefits to physicians and patients alike. Episcopal Health Services has addressed the increasing importance of managed care with the formation of a new managed care division which will be responsible for the establishment of a management services organization, and will oversee all quality assurance, utilization review, claims administration, network development, and marketing functions for primary and acute managed care patients. Through these, and other developments and partnerships, Episcopal Health Services has poised itself to be at the forefront of change and to better serve the health needs of the growing population of managed care Medicare and Medicaid recipients. •••

The 314-bed St. John's Episcopal Hospital, South Shore serves the densely populated, culturally and economically diverse communities of Far Rockaway and the Five Towns.

The Bishop Charles Waldo MacLean Nursing Home is a 163-bed long-term care facility in Far Rockaway.

THE NORTH SHORE HEALTH SYSTEM
Evolving to Meet Today's Health Care Needs

• • •

QUALITY AND COMPASSION ARE THE CORNER-stone ingredients upon which a successful health care system must be built. For more than four decades, the North Shore University Hospital in Manhasset has made quality and compassion its hallmarks. The hospital has cared for tens of thousands of men, women, and children, all the while expanding its medical base, its scope, and its facilities. In so doing, North Shore has built a legacy of which it is justifiably proud.

In recent years, however, it became evident that the hospital could not rest upon its accomplishments. Because of rapidly changing trends all across this country in the way health care is delivered, it has been necessary for North Shore to heed the word of a public clamoring for universal care at much reduced rates. At the beginning of this decade, the decision was made at North Shore to provide what the public has been calling for, but to do it in such a way that neither the quality of medical care nor the level of human compassion would be sacrificed. The people of Long Island have come to expect no less from the name North Shore.

The answer seemed to lie in the creation of the North Shore Health System, a network that would include hospitals capable of providing everything from tertiary to primary care; nursing homes; physician practices, including internists, surgeons, specialists, and subspecialists; research centers; ambulatory facilities; home-care services; laboratories; preventive medicine education; and much more as the need arises.

All of this had to be based upon the commitment the hospital has always maintained, and will continue to maintain, which decrees that no one in need of medical care, regardless of race, color, creed, or ability to pay, will ever be turned away.

Today, the North Shore Health System has grown to encompass a regional network that includes seven hospitals: North Shore University Hospital at Manhasset, North Shore University Hospital at Glen Cove, Huntington Hospital, North Shore University Hospital at Plainview, Franklin Hospital Medical Center, North Shore University Hospital at Syosset, and North Shore University Hospital at Forest Hills. Additionally, there are two nursing homes, a research center, and ambulatory programs and services at more than 20 other sites in a five-county area. There are also affiliations with several other hospitals for purposes of sharing programs and services, and to allow for far more efficient, cost-effective, bulk purchasing of supplies and equipment.

North Shore University Hospital at Manhasset dramatically accentuates the landscape.

A North Shore Health System surgical team at work in an operating room.

A linear accelerator is employed by the North Shore Health System in providing state-of-the-art stereotactic radiosurgery.

York University School of Medicine, which carries out programs of accredited undergraduate and graduate medical education. North Shore is, therefore, among the nation's academic medical centers that adhere to criteria established by the Association of American Medical Colleges and in which NYU Medical Center has been a long-standing member. These institutions are considered the major educational and clinical institutions in the country.

The other hospitals that comprise the North Shore Health System are smaller, community facilities, which provide superb primary and secondary care in their individual geographic regions.

For more specialized forms of treatment, these community hospitals refer patients to North Shore at Manhasset. the tertiary-care facility within the system. Such a network allows the patient to remain in one health system for life, forming a close relationship with a single primary physician who can then follow that patient through any needed medical treatments from birth to death.

Although the building of the North Shore Health System is still under way, its foundations are strong thus far. The system strictly and unceasingly monitors its own activities to ensure access for all, to control costs, and to maintain quality. There is constant strategic planning, dependent upon regional medical needs, along with establishment of further goals in an effort to meet the challenge to create true and meaningful health care delivery. The North Shore Health System is now—and intends to remain—in the forefront of that challenge. •••

The system includes 2,400 hospital beds, or nearly 25 percent of all hospital beds in the Nassau/Suffolk region. It has a roster of more than 4,300 affiliated physicians and an annual budget of roughly $1.2 billion. The North Shore Health System is also one of the region's largest employers.

North Shore University Hospital in Manhasset remains the core of this broad system. It is a tertiary-care facility, capable of providing the most sophisticated, state-of-the-art care available in all medical disciplines. The hospital has a full academic partnership with the New

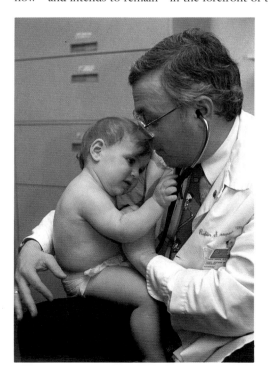

The needs of a very young patient are seen to by one of the 4,300 physicians affiliated with the North Shore Health System.

HIP And The Queens-Long Island Medical Group, P.C.

Caring for the Long Island Community

• • •

FORTY-FIVE YEARS AGO, THE HEALTH INSURANCE Plan of Great New York (HIP) broke ground in Hicksville to build the first state-of-the-art, multi-specialty medical center on Long Island. "It was an auspicious beginning to HIP's vision of providing residents with innovative health care," noted Richard Mayer, executive administrator for the HIP-affiliated Queens-Long Island Medical Group, P.C. The center would unite high quality care with the convenience of having experienced physicians and specialists, a variety of medical services, cutting-edge technology and a comfortable setting, all under one roof.

That vision has burgeoned into 20 full-service HIP medical centers staffed by the Queens-Long Island Medical Group, a network of affiliated physicians in private offices and two fully-staffed HIP mental health centers. Now serving more than 300,000 HIP members throughout Nassau, Suffolk and Queens, the medical group employs more than 300 primary care physicians and specialists and is affiliated with the prestigious hospitals of the North Shore Health System.

Each medical center offers a full range

Providers from the Queens-Long Island Medical Group, P.C., offer HIP members personalized, quality care.

of primary and specialty care, and is staffed by many board certified physicians and well-trained support staff. Medical specialties run the gamut from Allergy & Immunology... to Cardiology... to OB/GYN care. And many centers have an on-site pharmacy and laboratory. So members don't need to trek all over town to have lab work done, see a specialist or fill a prescription.

Coordinated care is a benefit too. Each member's files are consolidated in one medical record, which is kept up to date by doctors and staff. And, as Mayer noted, "the immediacy allows a specialist to discuss a case with the patient's primary care physician in person, to ensure proper treatment."

Many centers keep their doors open after hours for urgent care visits, and HIP's Emergency Service Program guides members to medical resources any time of the day or night.

When a patient's condition requires specialized care not available within the medical group, HIP offers the services of consulting specialists considered tops of their fields and affiliated with some of the finest institutions in New York.

The Queens-Long Island Medical Group also advocates prevention as the best form of medicine, and offers an array of health-related activities, programs and literature. HIP members, for instance, can learn how to reduce stress, stop smoking or keep asthma in check. The medical group also hosts community health fairs, as well as free cholesterol, prostate and mammography screenings for area residents at HIP medical centers. "Long Island has one of the highest breast cancer rates in the country," cited Mayer, "which is why we've found an especially pressing need to screen and educate the female population."

And so, throughout four and a half decades of providing high quality, personalized health care to residents, HIP and its affiliated Queens-Long Island Medical Group, P.C., have become part of the intricate mosaic of Long Island. • • •

HIP members visiting HIP's Babylon Medical Center in North Babylon, L.I., enjoy the convenience of having physicians, specialists and state-of-the-art services all under one roof.

GOOD SAMARITAN HEALTH SYSTEM
Serving the Community's Health Care Needs
• • •

FROM ITS BEGINNINGS MORE THAN 35 YEARS AGO AS a not-for-profit community hospital serving southwestern Suffolk County, Good Samaritan Hospital, the core facility of the Health System, has emerged with a greatly expanded size and mission. The evolutionary growth is exemplified by the institution's name change to Good Samaritan Hospital Medical Center and by its growing Institutes of Excellence.

The Institutes of Excellence concept was developed as the umbrella for what the hospital considers its specialties. These include prevention and wellness programs; cardiac diagnostic care; cancer care, especially radiation oncology; women's healthcare and vascular services.

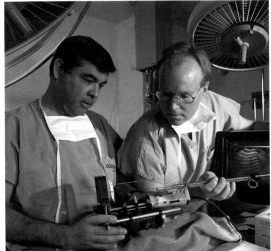

Good Samaritan Hospital Medical Center offers one of Long Island's few programs that treat prostate cancer with high-technology brachytherapy seed implantation.

The Breast Health Center at Good Samaritan was created in response to the community's need for a comprehensive patient-focused program of early detection and diagnosis, counseling and support, and effective treatment that utilizes the latest state-of-the-art equipment in the battle against breast cancer. Previously, area patients had to travel to New York City hospitals for this level of comprehensive care and support. With the establishment of Long Island's first complete Breast Health Center, Good Samaritan made it possible for women to receive compassionate and sophisticated treatment close to home.

Home health care of mothers and newborns is carried out by Good Samaritan Hospital Medical Center's maternity unit nursing staff.

Up-to-date technologies and techniques are the hallmarks of Good Samaritan's radiation oncology services. Hospital facilities include a linear accelerator and one of Long Island's few brachytherapy (seed implantation) programs for the treatment of prostate cancer.

The hospital's vascular care program is a very progressive one that has emerged to deal with circulatory problems. Good Samaritan's vascular patients, as exemplified by those having symptoms of difficulty in walking, are treated with minimally invasive procedures to alleviate the condition and restore normal function.

Another element of the Good Samaritan Health System is the Home Health Care Agency, an alternative that has become particularly critical for the community in the face of managed care-mandated shorter hospital stays. For example, with maternity stays now shorter than ever, Good Sam follows up with a home visit by a member of the maternity unit nursing staff within 48 hours of discharge. Called the "Mom and Me Care Program," this innovation enables the hospital to continue to monitor both the new mother and her baby.

The Good Samaritan Health System also includes the Good Samaritan Chronic Dialysis Center, the Good Samaritan Nursing Home and the Good Samaritan Hospice Program. The nursing home, a 100-bed facility in Sayville, emphasizes an interdisciplinary approach that begins with the patient's whole family during the admission process. For those with "a limited life expectancy," Good Samaritan's hospice program provides pain management, counseling services, dietary consultation, medical supplies, equipment, and other supportive care services.

Most of this dramatic growth in state-of-the-art community health services at Good Samaritan developed during the tenure of Daniel P. Walsh, the hospital's president and CEO for more than 13 years. Sylvia Guarino, Good Samaritan's Vice President of Marketing, Communications and Development, said that "Good Samaritan's jump into high technology, its designation as a cancer care program by the American College of Surgeons, and the entire movement toward Good Sam becoming a regional center for health care have taken place under Walsh's leadership with the support of a committed board of trustees, medical staff, volunteers and employees." • • •

HOSPICE CARE NETWORK

• • •

NO ONE WANTS TO DIE ALONE AND IN PAIN, IN an unfamiliar place, with only strangers around. Family members do not want their loved ones to die that way either, but modern medical technology often seems to lead inexorably to that end. Hospice Care Network offers an alternative that more and more people are choosing.

Hospice Care Network provides terminally ill patients with pain and symptom control and gives their families the emotional, spiritual and practical support they need to provide this care in their own homes. Each day, in Nassau, Suffolk, and Queens counties, patients live their last days with the help of the services of Hospice Care Network, surrounded by their relatives, their books, their music, and their friends, rather than the sights and sounds of an institution. For those unable to remain at home, hospice care is provided in hospitals and in nursing homes.

"If people know they can be pain free and that their symptoms can be managed, they prefer to be in their own familiar surroundings," noted a hospice administrator.

The services are fully paid by most insurance carriers and will be provided regardless of an individual's ability to pay. "Thanks to the active involvement of its Board of Directors and hundreds of volunteers, many of whom were previously helped by hospice, fundraising efforts allow hospice to provide care to people with limited resources," noted a spokesperson for the agency.

Hospice patients are primarily cared for in the home, surrounded by loved ones and caring professionals. "Accompanying the dying is a very intimate and painful time," noted a family member. "Hospice helped us ease the pain and live each moment like a special gift."

Hospice Care Network is the new name for an organization born from the 1996 merger of the first two hospices on Long Island: Hospice Care of Long Island, serving residents of Nassau and Queens counties, and Hospice of the South Shore, serving residents of Suffolk county.

"At times a patient's symptoms cannot be managed at home," it was noted. "Hospice Care Network has contracts with many of the major hospital centers on Long Island where patients can go for short term care to control pain and to provide respite for the caregivers. In addition, we place many patients in nursing homes, where hospice and nursing home staff members work side-by-side to bring good care for the dying."

"A new Supportive Care Program was established in February 1996 to provide counseling to patients and families not ready for hospice or for those whose diseases may have gone into remission."

Death does not end the services. Bereavement counselors work with families, and groups are offered for up to 13 months after the death. These sessions include special ones for children as young as 4 and are open to any child who has lost a loved one.

Long term plans call for establishment of a free-standing hospice residence for patients who cannot be cared for in a home.

The experience of people who give care to their terminally ill loved ones with hospice help can be both positive and painful. "There was a case where the son was the caregiver to his father, an end-stage Alzheimer's patient," recalled a hospice social worker. "One night they were watching the Gene Kelly movie, *Singing in the Rain*, and his father started humming the song. Even though his father could no longer speak any words, the two held hands, hummed the song, and connected through the music. 'It was very moving,' the son had noted."

"It was the Hospice program that allowed us to be at home, rather than in an institutional setting, and to share this special moment together," the son had told us.   • • •

Bob Nystrom (rear), of the New York Islanders, greeted youngsters at Hospice Care Network's first Children's Bereavement Reunion and made it a special occasion for the many young people coping with loss. The program, called CHILDREN GRIEVE, TOO, is free to any child living in Nassau, Suffolk, and Queens and receives its support from grants and private donations.

SOUTHSIDE HOSPITAL

• • •

A DISTINGUISHED COMMUNITY HOSPITAL

FOUNDED IN 1913, SOUTHSIDE HOSPITAL IS THE oldest and largest community hospital on Long Island. Located in Bay Shore, the not-for-profit hospital fulfills its mission by rendering quality health care to anyone in need through a continued commitment to providing the finest diagnostic, treatment, and rehabilitative services.

From its beginnings as a 21-bed hospital in an old house in Babylon Village, Southside today is a proud institution with 451 beds, 461 affiliated physicians, and a dedicated force of over 500 volunteers who devote countless hours to supporting the hospital and its patients.

Southside's special services include the region's first Brain Injury and Coma Recovery Unit for adults, and a Physical Medicine and Comprehensive Rehabilitation Center that includes all the necessary services at one center, eliminating the need for patients to be transported throughout the facility.

COMPREHENSIVE IN-PATIENT REHABILITATION CENTER

Southside Hospital's Comprehensive In-Patient Rehabilitation Center is distinguished by its wide breadth of quality services under the medical direction of board-certified physiatrists. The program encompasses the full complement of physical, occupational, and recreational therapies, as well as speech pathology, psychology, and neuropsychology, performed by a team of therapeutic and rehabilitation specialists. The center serves as a special Physiatry Residency Program teaching site in conjunction with Long Island Jewish

Medical Center. The hospital also offers the oldest and most comprehensive Family Practice Residency Program on Long Island, making Southside a vital resource for quality medical education.

"Family involvement is a vitally important link in the Southside Hospital Rehabilitation Center," explained Theodore A. Jospe, Southside Hospital's president and CEO. "Family members are considered part of the rehabilitation team and are involved in the patient's care from admission all the way through to their continuance as outpatients."

REGIONAL CENTER FOR BRAIN INJURY AND COMA RECOVERY

The Southside Hospital Brain Injury and Coma Recovery Unit provides a unique and specialized setting for adults who have suffered a brain injury. The unit is specially staffed and equipped with the latest technology available to assess and treat these patients.

"One of the things that sets us apart from other brain injury programs in the country is that we have full-time medical and neuropsychologic physicians on staff to complement our full team of therapists," said Mr. Jospe. "The full-time presence of these physicians ensures a higher level of patient care. And thanks to our repatriation program, Long Island's brain-injured population is returning home again after having had to seek care out of state because this type of facility did not exist here."

Recently, due to its reputation for providing excellent emergency care, Southside Hospital also won another distinction by being named, in conjunction with a neighboring facility, a "New York State Designated Area Trauma Center." The hospital's Emergency Department is one of the busiest on Long Island, caring for approximately 40,000 patients a year.

Overall, the hospital's strong community spirit and outreach efforts have earned it a special place in the hearts of the many Long Islanders who have come to rely on its many community services and programs.   • • •

Southside Hospital is a recognized leader in physical therapy and rehabilitation. The hospital's facilities incorporate the latest in state-of-the-art equipment with the finest trained professionals to provide superior patient care.

The Southside Hospital's spirit of caring is also shown through the good works and dedication of our many volunteers. Here, a youngster delights in delicious home-baked goodies available for purchase at the volunteer's annual "Great South Bay Country Fair."

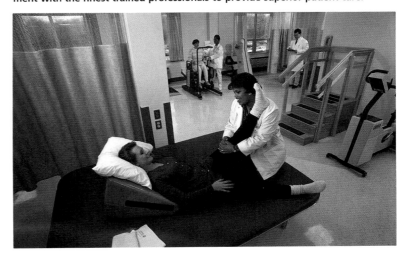

SOUTH NASSAU COMMUNITIES HOSPITAL
Setting a Standard of Excellence in Health Care
• • •

INCORPORATED IN 1928, SOUTH NASSAU COMMUNITIES Hospital is an acute care, not-for-profit, voluntary teaching hospital located in Oceanside. This 429-bed hospital provides inpatient, ambulatory, home health, restorative, preventative and emergency medical care to residents of Nassau County and surrounding communities. In addition, *Modern Healthcare* magazine recognized South Nassau Communities Hospital as 1 of the top 50 hospitals in managing costs in the United States.

With a staff of more than 500 physicians, South Nassau offers a broad range of services for adults and children on an in- and outpatient basis. The Hospital excels in cancer and cardiac care, and offers comprehensive diagnosis, treatment, rehabilitation and support services. Since a patient's comfort is of significant concern, a Pain Management Program was created to address this priority.

South Nassau has one of the most used trauma-receiving emergency rooms in the region. A special "Qwik Care" facility expedites the treatment of minor injuries.

South Nassau's Department of Surgery has been a leader in clinical trials for the past 19 years in adjuvant, hormonal/chemotherapy in the surgical treatment of breast cancer. It has successfully introduced breast preservation to its armory of breast cancer options. One hundred ninety women treated at South Nassau voluntarily entered into clinical trials, which proved that breast preservation and adjuvant/hormonal therapy significantly improve the treatment of breast cancer.

The Hospital's specialized breast service links essential diagnostic, treatment, and preventive education services together, facilitating breast health by offering women a convenient resource within their own community. State-of-the-art equipment such as Mammography's stereotactic biopsy table bring the most advanced technology to patient care.

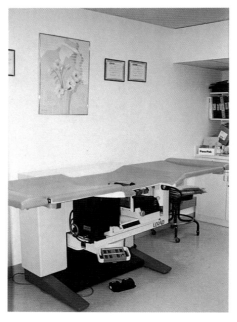

South Nassau's accredited mammography program features an upright mammography unit and a "prone position" stereotactic biopsy table.

The addition of advanced brachytherapy equipment, a second linear accelerator and modernized laser equipment significantly enhances the treatment of prostate, head and neck, cervical, uterine, gastrointestinal and lung cancers. New operating room equipment now makes commonplace advanced medical care such as laparoscopic and thoracostomy procedures.

Genetic counseling services, programs in CPR training, breast self-examination, weight control, smoking withdrawal, PATH (People Activated Toward Health, a medical self-help course geared toward seniors), and children's Teddy Bear clinics are all part of South Nassau's comprehensive services. Screening programs and health lectures are also offered to businesses and community groups.

For newborns who require extra care, South Nassau's neonatal services have been expanded with additional staff and equipment, and are bolstered through a working relationship with Winthrop-University Hospital. The Maternity Unit also provides parenting classes, which reinforce the philosophy of family-centered care.

Integral to a comprehensive approach to a person's treatment is care of the psyche as the patient adjusts and/or copes with illness. More than a dozen support and counseling services are offered to patients and their families. Meetings are free, most feature a guest speaker, and all are open to the public.

South Nassau's Mental Health Counseling Center, in existence since 1969, offers a wide range of outpatient programs and services, including a Center for Family Therapy and a six-week, outpatient program providing more intensive therapy. The Counseling Center also offers support groups for breast cancer survivors and for caregivers.

South Nassau continues to adapt to the needs of the communities it serves. Newly opened in 1996 is the Carlos R. Galeon, M.D. Stem Cell Unit at South Nassau, which provides advanced oncology services. •••

South Nassau has one of the most used trauma-receiving emergency rooms in the region. The special "Qwik Care" facility expedites treatment of minor injuries.

LONG BEACH MEDICAL CENTER
A Unique Environment for Healing
• • •

DEFINING LONG BEACH MEDICAL CENTER IS LIKE painting a picture of the ideal community hospital—and then adding the world-class resources of Mount Sinai Medical Center at your fingertips.

"We are seeking the perfect balance of care and efficiency. Everything, from our affiliation with Mount Sinai to examining and reexamining our internal procedures, points toward that goal," explained Martin F. Nester, Jr., CEO of Long Beach Medical Center. "This is a dynamic, exciting time at a special place."

As the hospital that patients rated highest among the 105 that were measured in the Metro New York area, Long Beach Medical Center is admired in its local area and among its professional peers as a premier health care facility.

With comprehensive state-of-the-art technology and expertise in more than 50 medical specialties and sub-specialties, Long Beach offers a unique environment for healing. Its staff, from world-renowned doctors to storied nursing staff, are largely responsible for its 92% approval rating among patients. But its true strength emanates from a considered philosophy that emphasizes the confidence and comfort of patients during an age when the human side of caring often is obscured by the business concerns of medicine.

A FEW—OF MANY—COMMUNITY FEATURES

Long Beach Medical Center is a community within the communities it serves… a network of health care associates and programs that coordinates broad outpatient and outreach services and administers care through its waterfront facility.

Health Styles Culinary Hearts Kitchen, a program promoting easy-cooking, heart-healthy, delicious foods, has been applauded by participants.

A magnificent waterfront setting is part of the healing process at Long Beach Medical Center.

Other groups provide needed support and information.

Rehabilitation programs at Long Beach Medical Center range from an inpatient unit to an outpatient practice that numbers more than 500 patients.

With more than 1,000 patients in its general psychiatric, substance abuse and alcohol programs, outpatient counseling services at Long Beach Medical Center are among the largest of its kind on Long Island.

INSIGHTFUL FACILITIES

A key component of the area's community health programming is The Family Care Center at Long Beach Medical Center. A combination doctor's office and comprehensive care program, The Family Care Center promotes preventive care measures through a team of staff members whose goal is the total health of the child and the well-being of the entire family.

"Preventive care for children promises the best returns of any health care investment," said Angela Menghraj of Long Beach Medical Center's Family Care Center. "Not only will children enjoy their health throughout their lives, but the health care system and the community will reap the rewards of a healthy society."

While the quality of care provided is the central issue for any hospital, Long Beach encourages recuperation with some compelling human elements.

"Secure patients get better faster—and the familial, familiar atmosphere at Long Beach Instills confidence," says Myles Gombert, Medical Director of Long Beach. "The staff Tenure here is among the longest in our profession. Ingrained in our teamwork ethic is a system-wide understanding of how to create a productive relationship with our patients. This elevates our profession and the excellent care we offer as an every-day commitment." • • •

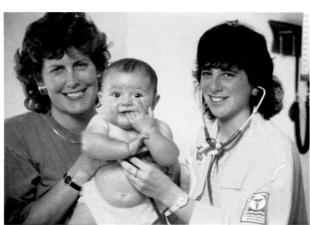

The goal of Long Beach Medical Center's The Family Care Center is the total health of the child.

SUNRISE MEDICAL LABORATORIES
Combining the Most Advanced Technologies with Decades of Dedication
• • •

BY DAY, SUNRISE MEDICAL LABORATORIES MAIN facility in Hauppauge is busy but quiet. By night, however, uniformed couriers arrive steadily with insulated boxes containing specimens gathered from patients all over the New York Metropolitan area. The centrifuges spin, the biomedical analyzers and computers run, and the staff of professionals work steadily to complete most tests in time to be reported to doctors by the next morning.

This is the heart of the service offered by Sunrise Medical Laboratories, the largest, privately-held, regional testing laboratory in the New York Metro area. Headed by CEO Larry Siedlick and President Pat Lanza, Sunrise has 150 employees and a growing client base of health care providers, including physicians, hospitals and dialysis centers. Sunrise was recognized in 1995 as the 10th fastest-growing private firm on Long Island, and also received a Business Achievement Award from the Hauppauge Industrial Association last year.

"Computerization, high tech equipment and breakthrough testing methods have played a key role in our success," says Lanza, "but it is our steadfast commitment to the patient that is our most valuable asset."

FULL-SERVICE MEDICAL TESTING

Sunrise provides its physician clients with a broad range of routine and specialized tests utilizing advanced instrumentation and technically proven methodologies. The complex array of laboratory testing offered by Sunrise makes it one of the region's premier diagnostic lab centers. Its expertise in laboratory medicine, including pathology, immunology, endocrinology and virology enables Sunrise to act as a reference laboratory, or a "lab's lab" for other laboratories who may perform only standard tests.

Detailed reports of test results are delivered to doctors' offices via printers or a SunData™ direct computer link. "Physicians who have the SunData™ system in their offices have instant access to test results as well as test trending that enables the physician to provide patients with a higher level of care, 24 hours-a-day," said Siedlick. Sunrise operates 24 hours-a-day, 7 days-a-week, to meet patient needs.

A COMMITMENT TO EDUCATION & QUALITY

Sunrise began as a community-based laboratory in Valley Stream with three employees and 25 clients. Today, Sunrise is a regional testing center performing over 1,000,000 tests a year. In addition to its Hauppauge headquarters, the company has 12 community-based Patient Service Centers where samples and specimens are collected. Its professional staff includes board certified medical doctors, Ph.D. and Master's level scientists, and medical technologists who have the minimum of a Bachelor's degree.

In addition to traditional quality control methods, Sunrise further ensures the quality and accuracy of patient testing by participating in external proficiency testing programs, and by providing its professional staff with a continuing education program. In addition, Sunrise's management and technical staffs keep abreast of developments in laboratory technology and their industry through membership in 16 different professional and trade associations.

As part of its commitment to the Long Island community and to education, Sunrise annually awards scholarships to students to help them continue their education in medical laboratory technology. Sunrise is also an approved intern training site for State University of NY medical laboratory technology students. • • •

Computerization, high-tech equipment and breakthrough testing methods are used by Sunrise's professional staff to perform a complex array of laboratory testing.

Sunrise Medical Laboratories regional testing center in Hauppauge performs over 1 million medical tests each year.

VYTRA™ HEALTHCARE
Creating Partnerships in Health Care
• • •

VYTRA, THE FIRST, LARGEST, AND FASTEST-GROWING Managed Health Organization headquartered on Long Island, views its members as the focal point of an intimate, lifelong relationship with three strands: physician, member, and plan. This dynamic relationship-centered philosophy has guided the organization since its 1985 founding. Eleven years ago, Vytra was at the cutting-edge of the managed care revolution. Today, with its emphasis on the three-part physician/member/plan partnership, Vytra continues to set the pace, defining newer, more effective means of placing members at the center of their own health care by empowering them as full partners.

Vytra provides its network of physicians access to nationally known experts, as part of their continuing education.

Fostering positive relationships between patients and physicians is a primary goal of Vytra Healthcare.

Vytra's home is Long Island. What that means for the company's more than 200,000 members in Nassau, Suffolk, and Queens counties is that help is only a local call away — and that help comes from a neighbor, not from an 800 number in a distant city.

The Vytra physician network is comprised of about 3,000 Queens and Long Island professionals, each of whom is subject to intense credentialing, including board certification. This physician network is one of the largest offered by an HMO in the Long Island market

and includes relationships with virtually every hospital on Long Island and about 98% of the pharmacies.

Vytra's regional focus on the Long Island area is based on the belief that the best health care plan has the flexibility and responsiveness that a regional plan provides. By focusing solely on Queens and Long Island, Vytra is working hard to change the way health care is delivered by organizing groups of doctors to deliver patient-centered, population-based medicine.   •••

Vytra Healthcare representatives are an important part of establishing a successful relationship with members.

WEST SUFFOLK SURGICAL GROUP, P.C.

Specializing in General & Vascular Surgery Since 1962

• • •

WHEN THE WEST SUFFOLK SURGICAL GROUP opened in 1962, no one could have imagined today's managed health care system. The three physicians who set up the practice were not only medical entrepreneurs but also "old-fashioned doctors" who considered it their responsibility to be available to their patients 24 hours-a-day, 7 days-a-week.

Today, all physicians must contend with the managed care systems that have developed, and West Suffolk Surgical Group is no exception. But Dr. Frank Pindyck, who did his surgical training at the Mount Sinai Medical Center in New York and is presently the lead practitioner in the group, retains the attitudes of his predecessors. "I've been available seven days-a-week for 22 years," he says, "since there are no short cuts to maintaining quality of care for surgical patients."

West Suffolk is one of the oldest surgical groups in Suffolk County. Dr. Pindyck, and his colleague, Dr. Joseph Patane, who completed his surgical training at the St. Vincent's Medical Center in New York, maintain their offices on a residential street near Huntington's downtown shopping district and within easy reach of Huntington Hospital. They perform general surgery, which includes GI, biliary, breast, pacemakers, laparoscopic procedures and vascular surgical procedures such as arterial bypasses, aortic aneurysm resection and carotid endarterectomies.

Dr. Frank Pindyck, lead practitioner of the West Suffolk Surgical Group.

Although Dr. Pindyck describes himself as an "old-time" surgeon, he and Dr. Patane are very much up with the latest trends in the practice of general and vascular surgery. Dr. Pindyck is Chief of Surgery at Huntington Hospital, and Clinical Associate Professor of Surgery at New York Medical College and supervises a surgical residency that is an affiliate of St. Vincent's Hospital in New York City.

Huntington Hospital itself is part of the North Shore Regional Health System, an alliance of facilities including seven hospitals,

giving Drs. Pindyck and Patane the benefit of greater contact with other physicians and medical developments. For example, recent federal legislation mandated a study of whether environmental contaminants increase the risk of breast cancer among women on Long Island. This collaborative effort includes Huntington Hospital, with Dr. Pindyck designated as the hospital's principal investigator.

Dr. Pindyck points out that having a surgical residency program at Huntington Hospital sets it apart from other community hospitals. "A hospital-based surgical residency program means there is a surgical resident on-site 24-hours-a-day to respond to the needs of surgical patients." he says. The residents are physicians who are undergoing five years of post-graduate training.

Dr. Pindyck operates with the residents each day, and says, "It's a big thrill to teach the next generation of surgeons and watch them develop into skilled practitioners." Dr. Pindyck was chosen as "Outstanding Teacher" in 1988 by the residents from Stony Brook University Hospital.

West Suffolk Surgical Group continues to provide the quality of surgical care for which they have become known, and is an active participant in many of the comprehensive plans that are being offered throughout Long Island.   • • •

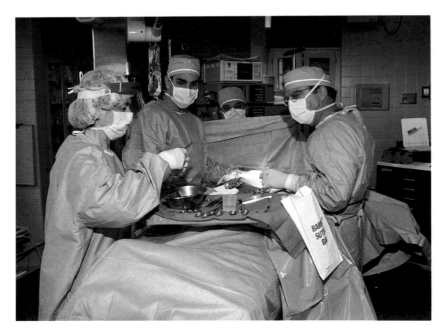

Dr. Pindyck performing breast surgery at Huntington Hospital. The group's practice also includes GI, biliary, pacemakers, laparoscopic procedures and vascular surgical procedures such as arterial bypasses, aortic aneurysm resection and carotid endarterectomies.

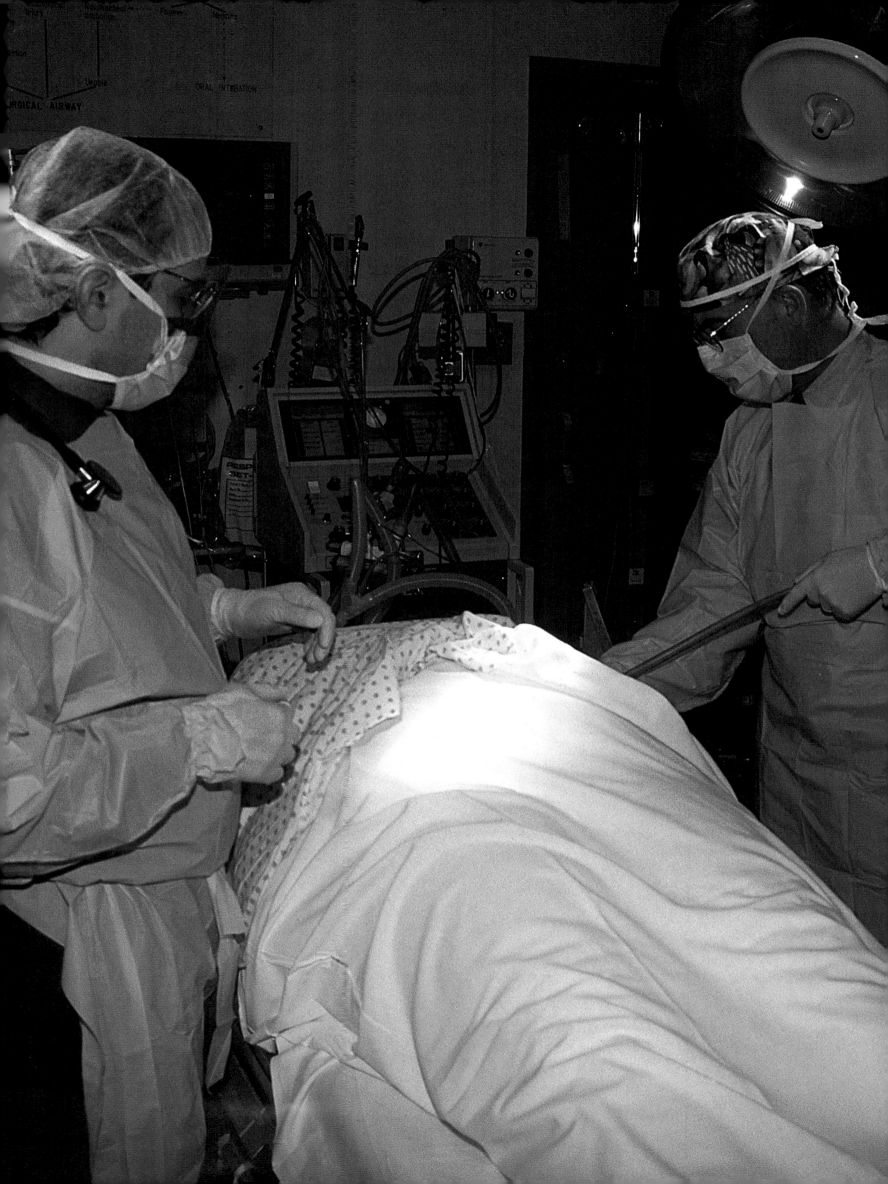

CHAPTER 17

• • •

MARKETPLACE

• • •

Photo by Deborah Ross.

SHERATON LONG ISLAND
A New Look for the 1990s
• • •

WHEN THE SHERATON LONG ISLAND DECIDED to show off its sparkling newly renovated facilities last year, it did so in the style Long Islanders have come to expect of this full-service hotel—it threw a big, splashy, lavish, and delightfully imaginative party.

The renovation project, begun in 1993, a year after the hotel came under the management of HEI Hotels, completely changed the face of what had been Long Island's first first-class luxury hotel when it opened in 1981. The unveiling of the new Sheraton Long Island came in January of 1995. Ernest J. Catanzaro, the Sheraton's director of sales and marketing, described the reintroduction party as "a client appreciation gala with an international theme." Guests were given passports as they arrived; these passports included visas for "countries" such as guest rooms, the executive health club, the restaurant, the bi-level luxury suites, the lobby, and meeting and conference rooms. Once every country was visited and every visa stamped, guests could then enter the ballroom where they were greeted with numerous dazzling buffets representing the cuisines of many countries of the world; service was by waiters garbed in various national costumes. "For days following the event," said Catanzaro, "the Sheraton's phones were ringing off the hook with kudos from delighted guests, many of whom said 'they'd never seen such a party.'"

ONE-STOP MEETING PLANNING

It's no wonder that the Sheraton staff had the know-how to put together such a memorable event. They organize hundreds of private, corporate, and charitable parties each year along with about 2,500 meetings and trade shows. In fact, according to the Sheraton's general manager, Edward Giamette, the demand for meeting/conference rooms has spiraled to the point that the hotel has added two new executive meeting managers who offer conference planners "one-stop shopping." Now one Sheraton staffer is responsible for every aspect of the meeting, including food and beverage service, guest rooms, audiovisual requirements, transportation needs, concierge services, and entertainment and recreational needs of all participants. Explaining the increased calls for conference facilities and the Sheraton's comprehensive response to the demand, Giamette credits a stronger Long Island economy. He said that "when business is stronger, more meetings are needed." Giamette observed that as businesses grow they need to train new as well as current employees and must hold increased numbers of off-site sales and training meetings. The hotel's general manager has noted a parallel jump in room

The earth-toned brick and glass exterior of the Sheraton Long Island is visible from the nearby Long Island Expressway.

Sheraton Long Island's top floor Executive Club Level offers business travelers the ultimate in convenience and service.

A circular staircase distinguishes the bi-level suite adjoining the heated indoor swimming pool.

occupancy rates. Calling the rise "dramatic," Giamette said that this too reflects "what we see as a resurgence of Long Island's economy."

The Sheraton's Seminar Room is specifically geared to the needs of these training sessions. Capable of accommodating up to 80 participants, the room has built-in, classroom-style tables that are raked front to back so even those seated at the very last row have a clear field of sight to the front. The Seminar Room, of course, boasts a state-of-the-art sound system, a built-in screen that pulls down from the ceiling, and a video projector.

NEWLY VIBRANT BALLROOM

Adjacent to the Seminar Room is the particular price of the Sheraton Long Island: the Grand Ballroom. "Completely redone, the ballroom has been brought into the 1990s," said Giamette, "with vibrantly bright decor." Through a series of movable walls, the ballroom is flexible enough to be used for groups as small as 30—or as large as 800. For elegant sit-down dinners, the Sheraton's ballroom has a capacity for 600 guests.

Once a tropical paradise, the Sheraton's glamorous atrium lobby now welcomes visitors with a lush garden environment. The focal point of the multilevel, skylighted lobby is a 35-foot ficus tree. Perched at the highest level is the intimate Treehouse Piano Bar.

Another bar is just steps up from the main level. The relaxing, soothing sounds of running water emanate from two ponds. The garden theme is carried out with whimsical picnic settings, a faux vegetable garden, picket fences, and a brick porch complete with picnic table and rocking chair. Throughout, handsome post lighting and lanterns dot the landscape.

The Seminar Room is the site for training sessions of up to 80 people.

Off the lobby is the Garden Cafe that, in keeping with the 1990's decor trend toward cozy, comfortable surroundings, is now adorned with homey florals and plaids. The Garden Cafe, open for breakfast, lunch and dinner, offers a moderately priced American continental menu. Breakfast is served buffet style. From 5-7 p.m. each day, there's a value-packed "Prime Time to Dine" early-bird full-dinner menu. Among the specialty dinner choices are grilled swordfish steak with avocado, cilantro, and lime, and veal, beef, fish, and chicken dishes in an imaginative variety of preparations. With today's health consciousness in mind, each menu also has a selection of low-calorie, low-fat selections.

THE SPORTING LIFE

Fans of the old Whispers, take note! This favorite among Long Island's watering holes also has a new image for the 1990s. It's now an Edwardian social pub so inviting that Bertie himself would have made it a "home away from home." Wooden floors below, tin ceilings above and handsome wainscoting across the walls set the design theme. Comfortable sofas beckon visitors to join in conversation. But the conversation may be cut short by the latest games from around the world, which can be viewed on the many television sets set about the pub; 12 are regular sized, and one is a giant 40-incher. Weekends, a dance floor and deejay are added to complete the party atmosphere.

ROOMS SERVE BUSINESS TRAVELERS

The first phase of Sheraton Long Island's major renovation was the 209 guest rooms. Catanzaro said that every room was completely redone with the needs of travelers,

The Grand Ballroom is festooned with balloons for a gala New Year's Eve dinner for 600 guests.

Christmas decor highlights the Sheraton Long Island's spectacular atrium lobby area.

especially business travelers, in mind. Each of the rooms now has a working desk with two telephone lines and a data port to plug in laptop computers. Coffee machines, hair dryers, irons, and ironing boards are standard, as is morning delivery of *U.S.A. Today*. Nonsmoking rooms and rooms designed to meet the needs of handicapped people are available on request.

On the new Executive Club Level, the amenities are even more posh. Guests have access to a club lounge offering an extensive continental breakfast in the morning, cocktails and hors d'oeuvres at the end of the business day, and even milk and cookies at bedtime. The club concierge is on tap to assist in changing flights, and arrange for car rentals and show tickets. Each room on the Executive Club Level offers a welcoming terry cloth robe and turn-down bed service. Summing up the elegant level of attention guests receive on the Executive Club Level, Edward Giamette said: "We created the Club Level to provide the business traveler with an environment that is as home-like and service-oriented as possible."

Adjacent to the Sheraton's indoor pool are three bi-level suites. Guests in these luxurious accommodations can journey out of their suite through a sliding glass door and enjoy their morning coffee poolside.

All Sheraton guests, whether in standard or Executive Club Level rooms, are afforded express check in and checkout, and free shuttle service to and from Islip MacArthur Airport and nearby railroad stations. They also earn frequent-flyer mileage points through Sheraton Club International. All guests have access to the Sheraton's refurbished health and fitness center, a brightly lit, mirrored facility located right off the pool area, which encompasses a sauna, a steamroom, and jacuzzi.

SERVING ADJACENT INDUSTRIAL PARK

Catanzaro discussed some of the many community organizations that call the Sheraton home for their business and social events. The hotel is home base for the Hauppauge Industrial Association (HIA), a group that represents the approximately 1,000 businesses and 30,000 workers in the surrounding 1,400-acre Hauppauge Industrial Park, one of the region's major business hubs. In fact, Giamette remarked that serving the business and social needs of the Hauppauge Industrial Park was the spur for the development of the Sheraton 15 years ago. HIA's trade shows, seminars, and monthly luncheon meetings featuring talks by important sports figures and business leaders are typically held at the Sheraton. Catanzaro noted that for the HIA's annual trade show, the Sheraton constructs a huge outdoor tent setting complete with phone lines, lighting, and carpeting. Advancement for Business and Industry (ACI) is another major business networking organization that frequently has its large monthly luncheon meetings at the Sheraton.

GIVING BACK TO THE COMMUNITY

Deeply involved in the nonprofit charitable organizations that serve the health, social, educational, and cultural needs of Long Islanders, the Sheraton is host hotel for the annual March of Dimes

Sheraton Long Island's refurbished Health and Fitness Center offers guests an attractive setting for exercise and health needs.

The homelike comforts
of Sheraton Long
Island's Presidential
Suite include a parlor
fireplace.

Cooperative Education Services (BOCES), the Sheraton Long Island provides employment and teaches job skills to organizations' clients. With Long Island Cares, the Sheraton is involved in a training program that serves battered and abused women. Through BOCES, the hotel works with young teens who gain experience in simple work tasks and enjoy a Sheraton lunch as well.

Walkathon. Every spring, more than 4,000 marchers meet at the Sheraton for a fund-raising walk through the industrial park; the walk's finishing point is also at the hotel. The event's organizers use the hotel for the Walkathon kick off and for sleeping accommodations. The Sheraton's close association with the March of Dimes stems from Catanzaro's own commitment—he's a board member of the organization's Long Island branch.

A Sheraton staffer also serves on the board of Apple a drug rehabilitation facility with several locations on Long Island. "Live from the Sheraton" is how WBAB radio personality Bob Buchman runs his annual Charity Begins at Home telethon. For the full week between Christmas and New Year's Day, Buchman broadcasts live from the Sheraton 24 hours a day. With space, food, and sleeping rooms for staffers all donated by the Sheraton, the telethon raises $30-40,000. Another telethon that's at home at the Sheraton Long Island is Jerry Lewis' annual muscular dystrophy event. The Sheraton serves as the event's Suffolk headquarters. As with Charity Begins at Home, the hotel donates rooms, telephone lines, food, and space for all workers.

But the Sheraton doesn't limit its community service to major public events like telethons and walkathons. Working with public and private organizations, such as Long Island Cares and the Board of

Where Catanzaro devotes much of his time to the March of Dimes, he is an enthusiastic supporter of Promote Long Island, an organization that seeks to promote the Long Island address and the benefits of life on Long Island. The five-year-old group has its meetings and plans its fund-raisers at the Sheraton. It was Catanzaro's involvement with Promote Long Island as a board member that led the hotel to change its name last year from the Sheraton Smithtown to the Sheraton Long Island.

As a result of the hotel's many hosting activities, greeting famous and prominent visitors is "business as usual" for the Sheraton. Catanzaro said that as host hotel for the Hamlet Cup, a major tennis tournament, the Sheraton has welcomed such guests as Stephan Edberg and Ron Laver. NBC sportscasters moved into the Sheraton for last year's Centennial U.S. Open Gold Tournament at Shinnecock Hills. The Sheraton has hosted numerous celebrities from the worlds of film, stage, and television. Bob Denver, Bobby Brown, Ann Jillian, Bobby Rydell, Danny Aiello, and Harrison Ford have all used the Sheraton Long Island as home base when work brings them to the area. Politicians Alphonse D'Amato and Jack Kemp, comedian Bob Nelson, and sports figure Bobby Nystrom are among those who have stayed or appeared at the Sheraton Long Island. •••

THE RESIDENCE INN BY MARRIOTT
Creating a Home for Visitors to Long Island
• • •

IN ENGLAND, IT WOULD BE CALLED A "HOME FROM home." Here on Long Island, however, it's not necessary to say anything more than Marriott Residence Inn in order to conjure up the image of a homelike environment available to travelers whose plans include an extended stay on Long Island.

Extended stay hotels began as a cross between the traditional hotel and an apartment. In 1974, the first Residence Inn was created in Wichita, KS and, in 1987, Marriott acquired Residence Inns. It is estimated that ten percent of all business travelers spend more than five nights in the same hotel room.

What makes the Plainview Residence Inn so unique is apparent immediately upon arrival. The hotel, nestled among beautifully land-scaped grounds, resembles an attractive condominium community far more than a hotel. Visitors enter to find a two story, atrium lobby done in welcoming blond woods and furnished with plush uphol-stered seating in intimate groupings. Here too, the ambience is more elegant private residence than bustling hotel lobby.

The Residence Inn by Marriott is one of only two hotels on Long Island to have received the American Automobile Association's coveted Four Diamond Award, according to the Inn's vice president and general manager, Kevin Moran. The award is a reflection of the hotel's commitment to quality and excellence.

APARTMENTS FEATURE HOMELIKE CONVENIENCES

The Residence Inn Plainview occupies a unique position among hotels on Long Island… as an all suite hotel, guests have the best of both worlds. Here they find the amenities and services one would expect of a full service hotel while enjoying all the comforts of home in an apartment setting. Accommodations range in size from studio suites with fully equipped kitchenettes, to spacious 2 bedroom, 2 1/2 bath apartments, containing full kitchens with dishwashers and ovens, expansive storage areas, videotape players and comfortable seating and work areas. Open the kitchen cupboards and drawers and you'll find them equipped with dishes, pots and pans, silverware, cloth napkins and matching place mats. There's even a corkscrew for your wine in the utensil drawer of every kitchen! Guests have the option of utiliz-ing the hotel's same day valet service for all their dry cleaning and laundry needs or, if they prefer, they can use the coin operated self service laundry facilities located on every floor of the hotel. There's even an iron and ironing board in the closet of every suite!

The hotel also provides a daily grocery shopping service, making it easy for guests to prepare meals in their suites. Guests leave their shopping lists at the front desk in the morning and find their gro-ceries in their suites when they return at night. There's no charge for the service; they pay only the marked price of the groceries, pur-chased at the local supermarket. The bath-rooms also reflect the facility's dedication to the needs of long term visitors; each has a full size medicine cabinet and under-the-sink vanity storage, more typical of a private home than a hotel room.

Traditional furnishings, which vary from suite to suite, another departure from standard hotel rooms, contribute to the feeling of luxury and comfort which pervades the entire property. About two thirds of the guest suites even have private balconies.

LUXURIOUS INDOOR & OUTDOOR AMENITIES

A walking trail which winds through the landscaped lawn surrounds the hotel and

The atrium lobby of the Marriott Residence Inn features many comfortable seating areas for quiet conversation.

Guests of the Marriott Residence Inn planning meetings often opt for the hotel's handsome library.

outdoor pool. Lounging at poolside or on the umbrella covered terrace is a relaxing way to spend a sunny afternoon.

Indoors, a fitness center, open 24 hours a day, features a step machine, treadmill, bicycles, free weights and a universal weight machine. A Jacuzzi and indoor lap pool adjoins the men's and women's locker rooms, each of which boasts its own sauna.

Guests can utilize the Residence Inn's wood paneled library, its meeting rooms with fireplaces, a 170-seat movie theater, self service laundry facilities, rental movies in a lobby video bank and a family game room.

GUESTS ENJOY NIGHTLY SOCIAL ACTIVITIES

Most evenings, the hotel staff plays host at a social, providing guests with an opportunity to meet and mingle.

On Tuesday evening, guests meet in the Ice Cream Parlor for the popular "Make Your Own Sundae" ice cream bar. An assortment of toppings and fixings adorn the counter along with delicious ice cream flavors from which to choose.

On Wednesday evening, guests are invited to join the hotel staff for the very popular weekly barbecue. This fun event is held outdoors on the pool terrace, weather permitting, from Memorial Day to Labor Day. The hotel staff mans the grill, cooking burgers, chicken

and hot dogs. There's lots of assorted salads, corn on the cob, watermelon, ice cold soft drinks and beer on tap.

On Thursday night, guests socialize in the Lounge, where assorted wines of different regions are highlighted, along with a variety of cheeses and crackers to sample. The hotel also boasts a "state of the art" movie theatre, so guests can enjoy feature films which are shown five nights each week. If they'd rather watch movies in the privacy of their own suite, it's easy to do. Each suite is equipped with its own video player and there's a video rental library conveniently located in the lobby of the hotel.

Lobby elevators afford access to the Inn's 165 suites, nine public conference rooms, the library and a small private dining room, available for use by guests. Although the conference rooms are, on occasion, used by outside organizations and individuals, Kevin Moran indicated that they're primarily for the use of hotel guests, as is the library where books are available for loan on the "honor system."

VARIED DINING FACILITIES OFFERED

The Terrace dining room, overlooking the outdoor pool, is the site for the Residence Inn's daily complimentary continental buffet breakfast. Guests enjoy breakfasting on juices, fresh fruit, cereals, freshly baked muffins, bagels, danish, waffles, French toast, along with assorted spreads and coffee, tea, decaf and hot chocolate. Adjacent to the dining room is the Pub, a cozy bar with inviting seating areas and the Resi Deli, a restaurant featuring a casual menu. This

A stately gazebo counterpoints the front lawn of the Marriott Residence Inn.

The Marriott Residence Inn's studio king suite is equipped with a kitchenette, king-sized bed, dining table and chairs, love seat and television/VCR combo.

The family-sized suite at the Marriott Residence Inn boasts a full kitchen and a living/dining room with a television/VCR combo. Each of the two bedrooms has a full bath and television set.

New York style "deli" has counter as well as table service. Should guests desire food services during the day, it's as easy as picking up the phone. Room service is available at the Residence Inn from 10 AM to 10 PM daily.

Guests at the Residence Inn may host private or business dinners or luncheons in several different facilities: among them are the library, where a handsome, large octagonal table is flanked by leather chairs and the Oak Room, an attractive setting for intimate dinners for up to eight people. Business travelers often use the theater, which is also a fully equipped media center, a perfect site for sophisticated corporate meetings or training sessions.

PRIVACY & LOCATION AMONG TOP LURES FOR GUESTS

Who uses the Marriott Residence Inn? "A broad cross section of the public," said Moran. Families relocating to Long Island find it an ideal place to stay while house hunting. Other guests might include visitors on temporary assignment for an extended period of time. Moran noted that some guests, former Long Islanders, now living primarily in the South, make the Residence Inn their summer headquarters. The seclusion and privacy afforded by this unique hotel has also provided a haven for the many celebrities who have been guests while performing on the Island.

Its location, in the heart of Long Island and its proximity to all major highways, shopping centers and cultural, recreational and entertainment facilities, make it the ideal place to stay, whether it be for one night or one year. Whatever the reason, travelers look with confidence to the Marriott Residence Inn as a welcoming place that spells "home" when on Long Island.   •••

The attractive outdoor pool area at the Marriott Residence Inn provides leisure time enjoyment for guests.

P.C. RICHARD & SON

• • •

P.C. RICHARD & SON IS A FAMILY-OWNED and operated business for over 86 years. It has been estimated that two-thirds of all family-owned businesses do not make it to the second generation and that 90 percent never make it to the third. However, P.C. Richard & Son is prospering under the leadership of its third and fourth generations, expanding both in product areas and in retail locations throughout Long Island, Brooklyn, Queens, Westchester, Manhattan, and New Jersey.

The company has an 86-year proven track record of steady growth and profitability, and has watched the rise and fall of over 50 competitors. Gary H. Richard, the company's president and CEO, enumerates the many appliance, electronics retailers who have come in to the market as major competitors and have gone out of business. Why has P.C. Richard & Son succeeded and grown so dramatically while others have failed? Gary says it's really simple. He explained that the company's formula for success is its dedication to a very strict culture of honesty, integrity, and reliability; and the philosophy of giving service before, during and after the sale. Customers trust P.C. Richard & Son, so they become and remain loyal customers.

This tradition of honesty, integrity, and reliability has obviously been drummed into the consciousness of each succeeding generation of the Richard family. Gary's son Gregg, who is most likely to head the company into its fourth generation of leadership, has said: "Since I'm five years old, all I've heard was 'make the customer happy, take care of your employees, and build partnerships with your vendors.' That's the philosophy that has kept us in business, and will be followed and built upon when it is time for the fourth generation to take over."

Gary's brother, Peter Richard, Sr., is executive vice president. His expertise is in the company's more than 600,000 square feet of retail space at the 37 retail locations and the massive 650,000-square-foot distribution center. He maintains and remodels existing facilities while also planning the facilities of the future. Peter explained the company's future executive organization: "My nephew Gregg will succeed to the presidency, and my son Peter, Jr. will be right next to him, helping the company grow and prosper."

When Gregg and Peter take over the reins of the company, like Peter and Gary they will have been through just about every operation, every job description at P.C. Richard & Son—including sweeping the floors! That's another company tradition that started with A.J. and continues. "Cleanliness in every location and each and every corner," said Gary. "That's how I learned the business from my father and grandfather… from the bottom up."

Six members of the fourth generation are involved in the business: Gary's three children: Gregg Richard, vice president of operations; Bonni Richard, human resources manager; and Darian Richard-Costello, computer operations; and Peter's three children: Peter Richard, Jr., warehouse distribution manager; Patty Richard-Catoir, risk management; and Kim Richard-Bohl, inventory control.

ENTREPRENEURIAL SPIRIT GUIDES COMPANY

Gary Richard speaks proudly of his family's history in the appliance, electronics, computer business—a history that began with his grandfather, Peter Christiään Richard (P.C.), an immigrant from Holland, who came to America in 1889 at age 18. He became a handyman for the customers on his milk route and slowly built an inventory of hardware, allowing him to open a hardware store in Bensonhurst, Brooklyn, in the year 1909, the

Seated left to right:
Peter, Jr., Patty, Darian,
Gregg. Standing left to
right: Kim, Peter, Sr.,
Gary, Bonni.

same year his son, Alfred J. Richard, Gary's father (A.J.), was born. Since the family lived upstairs from the hardware store, at age six and seven A.J. was always helping around the store. As he grew, so did the family business, moving in 1919 to Ozone Park, Queens.

The real beginning was in 1924 when A.J. Richard, chairman of the board, added appliances to the hardware store inventory. Westinghouse sent a salesman to the hardware store to show A.J. its new iron, which sold for $4.95 at retail.

A.J. found out that he couldn't sell them for $4.95, which was a lot of money in those days, unless he did something different. Finally, a customer came in whom A.J. knew did a lot of ironing, since she had five children. He tried to sell her the iron, but she told him she couldn't afford it. Out of nowhere he said, "Well, just pay me 50 cents a week. Take the iron, use it, and in a few days either bring the iron back or bring in 50 cents." It worked! That was the beginning of A.J.'s deferred payment plan and the opportunity for P.C. Richard & Son to enter the major appliances business.

Because he had won so many national contests selling Westinghouse irons and had earned the reputation of being an excellent merchandiser, A.J. was appointed a franchised dealer when Westinghouse introduced a spinner washing machine in the late 1920s. The spinner washing machines were very difficult to sell at first, despite their obvious advantages over handscrubbing, washboards, and wringer washers. They weren't as portable as irons, but he knew if women would try them, they would tell their friends, neighbors, and relatives, and sales would be radiated by word of mouth.

His first sale was made by convincing a customer to try the washing machine for three days. He said he would give her $5.00 if she did not like it. He delivered the washing machine to her home in a borrowed truck and demonstrated its use. When the three days were up, there was no way she would let him take it out.

That $5.00 offer helped him sell more washers than any other dealer in the eastern market. He bought six of those washers, then a dozen, then a truckload, and then a freightcar load. He hired salesmen who went door-to-door ringing bells, putting washers into homes on trial and on a time payment plan arranged with Banker's Commercial and CIT Corporation, which gave up to three years to pay.

A.J. also set P.C. Richard & Son apart from its many competitors when he launched the very first nonmanufacturer's service department in 1935. The service center, which was started to meet the needs of the boom in home radios, is now a major component of P.C. Richard & Son. More than 1,500 electronics products are repaired each week by 50 technicians at the company's Central Islip service center.

At 86 years of age, A.J. is only "semiretired." Though he spends most of the winter at his Florida residence, he's always at work answering customers' comments and overseeing the service center. When he's in New York, he enjoys visiting the showrooms chatting with, encouraging, and giving sales tips to the employees. At the corporate

Gary in the Farmingdale
warehouse.

offices in Farmingdale, he has created a veritable museum of P.C. Richard & Son's history. His office walls are covered with memorabilia—photos documenting the family's long business history and numerous awards made to the company over the years.

BUSINESS EXPANDS THROUGHOUT THE REGION

Since 1978, Gary and Peter have presided over the company's remarkable expansion in product lines and locations. In 1982, two years after Gary became president and Peter became executive vice president, there were 11 P.C. Richard & Son locations; today there are 37. The first P.C. Richard & Son free-standing drive-in store, pioneered by A.J. in Bellmore in 1951, was 10,000 square feet. At the time, the average neighborhood appliance store was about 3,000 square feet. But it was only the beginning of larger showrooms for P.C. Richard & Son. Now there are showrooms up to 40,000 square feet.

Under Gary's leadership, P.C. Richard & Son entered the computer age in 1979 with the purchase of an IBM System 34. Today, the company is managed with a state-of-the-art IBM Management Information System that captures all customer and historical data originating from a point-of-sale system, and tracks inventory and automatically replenishes merchandise in the warehouse as well as at all 37 showroom locations.

The tradition continues of making it economically feasible for customers to acquire appliances and electronics. Since 1986, the company has its own credit card, administered by Bank One of Dayton, Ohio, that offers customers a 90-days no-interest benefit. The company has over 600,000 credit card customers.

The company does all of its advertising in-house—creative, radio, TV, print, and promotional material. The company owns and operates its own distribution center with 128 employees who receive over 30 trailers of new merchandise from manufacturers daily. In addition, the company owns and operates its own delivery department with a fleet of 50 trucks manned by it's own personnel, making approximately 700 to 1,000 customer home deliveries a day, seven days a week.

The company has a Wholesale and Builder Division that sells to landlords, builders, and major developers in the tristate area. Though they won't take over for awhile, the fourth generation has already begun to make its mark on P.C. Richard & Son. Gregg Richard is credited with putting the company into the businesses of car audio sales and installation, and 35-millimeter cameras.

P.C. Richard & Son has demonstrated its commitment to its business, but is equally committed to the communities in which it serves. The company has established the P.C. Richard Foundation that supports the Marty Lyons Foundation, South Nassau Communities Hospital, North Shore University Hospital, Our Lady of Consolation Geriatric Care Center, Northville Long Island Golf Classic, Anti-Defamation League, United Jewish Appeal, American Cancer Society—Long Island Division, Long Island Cares, and many other civic, charitable, and nonprofit organizations.

Gary Richard was the recipient of Long Island's Ernst & Young LLP 1993 Entrepreneur of the Year Award. He is on the Board of Directors of the Long Island Association, Fleet Bank Long Island Regional Board, and he belongs to many other associations. Gary has said that it is a commitment of the company to be involved to enhance the communities we serve because we can make a difference for our neighbors to have a better quality of life.

In today's intensely competitive appliance, electronics retailing environment, one which has been impacted in recent years by the entry of national companies, Gary is confident that P.C. Richard & Son's winning culture of: "86 years of honesty, integrity and reliability" and "Taking care of the customers before, during and after the sale" will carry the company forward into the future just as successfully as it has in the past 86 years.

Gary always emphasizes to the P.C. Richard & Son 1,500 employees: We can make a difference and must remain: "One team quicker and better than anyone in our industry." He also says; "If you have a dream and vision, you have to execute it well to be successful. In the retail business, you have to be able to accept change and adapt to it quickly. Better, better, best, don't settle for less until better is best." Richard is Reliable—Est. 1909.　•••

After a morning at the service center in Central Islip, A.J. heads into the Farmingdale Executive offices and warehouse. Photo by Richard Liebert.

KING KULLEN GROCERY CO., INC.
Long Island's Own Supermarket
• • •

FOR GENERATIONS OF LONG ISLANDERS, A TRIP to the supermarket has meant a trip to King Kullen. In fact, when one considers the number of people who have pushed shopping carts down its aisles over the past 66 years, King Kullen has probably touched the lives of more Long Islanders than any other local company.

Just as impressive is the central role King Kullen has played in the history of modern America. During the darkest days of the Depression, a young man named Michael J. Cullen came up with a revolutionary concept that forever changed the way Americans—and the world—shopped for food.

"Before my father," noted current King Kullen CEO John B. Cullen, "people had to visit three or four different stores just to buy the day's groceries, meats, and produce. It was my father who came up with the idea of a 'super market' where customers could get everything they needed under one roof, without having to ask a clerk for assistance. That is how King Kullen became America's First Supermarket."

A VITAL PRESENCE

Were he alive today, Michael Cullen would also be impressed by the transformation of his grocery business into a closely-held corporate giant. At a time when the majority of supermarkets are owned by large out-of-state corporations or foreign conglomerates, King Kullen remains family operated—a Long Island institution that has stayed true to its roots while embracing the future.

Under the direction of Cullen and his cousin, President Bernard D. Kennedy, King Kullen Grocery Company operates 46 stores from the East End of Long Island to Staten Island, averages more than $700 million in sales annually, and is one of Long Island's largest companies. King Kullen is a more vital presence today than ever, thanks to an aggressive—and highly successful—expansion program overseen by Cullen and Kennedy.

"The willingness to change is essential in the supermarket industry," explained Kennedy, the nephew of founder Michael Cullen. "When I started working here in 1949, King Kullen was operating 29 stores. Not one of those stores is around today. We are constantly expanding and improving to meet the changing needs of our customers and to take advantage of new technology. It's a very dynamic business."

From automated check-out scanners and electronic coupons to the presence of international gourmet foods and self-service cheese and salad bars, today's King Kullen supermarket is a distant cousin to Michael Cullen's original store—a vacant garage leased in Jamaica, Queens. The typical King Kullen supermarket now averages 45,000 square feet, offers customers nearly 40,000 different items, features a seafood department, pharmacy, florist, bakery, and full-service delicatessen with catering services, and provides an enjoyable, pleasant shopping experience in state-of-the-art surroundings.

CHANGE AND INNOVATION

Perhaps it is because King Kullen was born out of change and innovation that Cullen and Kennedy have always welcomed it. In addition to its primary supermarket business, King Kullen in 1990 inaugurated a successful diversification program that saw the company enter several new arenas, including marketing and advertising, real

(top photo) King Kullen revolutionized the way Americans shop for food with facilities like this early 1930 supermarket.

Supermarket shopping has seen landmark changes since this 1940 King Kullen store opened its doors.

Wide aisles and abundant displays of food are typical of modern King Kullen supermarkets.

estate and construction, trucking, and non-foods distribution and warehousing. The company continues to diversify as opportunities are identified in the marketplace. Aware of a growing trend towards whole foods and natural products, King Kullen in 1995 opened Wild by Nature, a wholly-owned subsidiary, Long Island's first natural foods supermarket.

But John Cullen and Bernard Kennedy are quick to point out that the company's greatest asset has always been its people. With thousands of employees representing every walk of life—from part-time students to retirees who welcome the chance to return to work—King Kullen enjoys its reputation as one of the Island's largest employers. It can point with pride to many families within its ranks where children have followed in their parents' footsteps. Nowhere is this more evident than within the Cullen and Kennedy families themselves, with third generation members having moved up the ranks and proved themselves worthy of leadership roles through years of active, hands-on work in all areas of store operations.

SERVING LONG ISLAND'S NEEDS

"As a family controlled business," explained Kennedy, "the concept of family has always been important to us." Serving the needs of the greater Long Island population has also been of paramount importance. King Kullen believes in supporting a wide variety of not-for-profit organizations and chari-

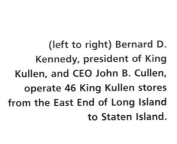

(left to right) Bernard D. Kennedy, president of King Kullen, and CEO John B. Cullen, operate 46 King Kullen stores from the East End of Long Island to Staten Island.

ties, particularly those that benefit the majority of its customers and the communities in which they live.

"As a successful business, we feel a responsibility to our neighbors," Cullen added. "That includes making a major commitment to support the work of Long Island hospitals, as well as groups like The Nature Conservancy and Family Service of Nassau and Suffolk Counties." Each summer, King Kullen makes a significant donation to benefit camp programs run by Family Service for underprivileged children.

King Kullen is also a long-time benefactor of Little Flower Children's Services of New York, an orphanage based in Wading River with several locations in New York City. Since holding the first annual James A. Cullen Memorial Golf and Tennis Outing in 1983, more than $1 million has been raised by King Kullen for Little Flower.

The company's concern for the less fortunate can be traced directly to its founder. While building the world's first supermarket, Michael Cullen was also laying the groundwork for King Kullen's tradition of corporate giving. "My father devoted large amounts of time, effort, and money to charitable institutions," concluded John Cullen. "He considered it both a duty and a privilege to assist the needy."

Under the leadership of John Cullen and Bernard Kennedy, King Kullen Grocery Co., Inc. has become an important, positive force on Long Island. The company provides an exceptional shopping experience for tens of thousands of people daily, employs a significant segment of the Nassau-Suffolk workforce and, through its charitable endeavors, makes a meaningful difference in the lives of the region's less fortunate families. As the 21st Century approaches, King Kullen is well positioned to meet the challenges that lie ahead and continue its unyielding commitment to the people of Long Island. •••

SEAMAN FURNITURE COMPANY, INC.
"The Sensible Way to A Beautiful Home"
• • •

LIKE THE BEST OF STRATEGIES, SEAMAN'S ARE simple and logical. First, take the hassle out of furniture shopping by having professionals match fabrics and coordinate a collection of items. Second, offer the package at a great price. Third, always have the furniture available for quick delivery, and, last, advertise—always and everywhere.

These distinctive merchandising and marketing strategies, originated in the 1970s, underlie the profitability and strong growth of the Seaman Furniture Company. The largest regional specialty furniture retailer in the Northeastern United States, with double the market share of its nearest competitor in the New York Metropolitan area, Seaman's now has 38 stores, nine of them added in the last fiscal year.

Five of the stores are on Long Island, in Holbrook, Smithtown, Carle Place, Farmingdale and Valley Stream, as is corporate headquarters. In fact, Seaman's is synonymous with furniture for many Long Islanders who can join right in with the jingles—"See Seaman's First," and, "The Sensible Way to a Beautiful Home"—used in the company's successful ads.

Seaman's maintains its headquarters in Woodbury, in a 40,000-square-foot facility, and employs more than 350 Long Islanders. The company has been generous in its support of local and national charities and relief efforts. It has donated furniture to the local Fund for the Homeless, and sent truckloads of furniture to victims of the flooding in the Midwest and of the Florida hurricanes.

Publicly traded on the NASDAQ exchange, under the symbol "SEAM," the company enjoyed revenues of over $250 million in fiscal year 1996. Its selection of quality living room, bedroom, dining room and other home furniture and accessories in contemporary, traditional, country and casual styles, at excellent prices, make its showrooms a shopping destination.

FOUNDED IN BROOKLYN

Julius Seaman founded the furniture chain that bears his name in 1933, in Brooklyn. For 20 years, his enterprise remained as a neighborhood retailer. But in the mid-1970s, his sons Morty and Carl originated the merchandising concepts that transformed their business.

They decided to carry and display in their stores a variety of furniture styles and models in a carefully limited selection of fabrics, colors and finishes preselected by Seaman's buyers. This "narrow and deep" merchandising allowed the company to purchase in large quantities at substantial savings that could be passed on to the consumer.

They also pioneered and trademarked "The Package"® which encourages consumers to purchase a collection of complementary furniture items at real savings over buying the pieces individually. This increased the company's average ticket sales.

Saturation advertising, in print, on radio and TV, successfully brought in buyers, and resulted in double-digit revenue increases from the mid-1970s to mid-1980s. In 1985, the company went public, and its stock doubled within a year. This attracted the attention of affiliates of Kohlberg Kravis Roberts & Co., who took Seaman's private in a leveraged buy-out.

In what Peter McGeough, Chief Administrative and Financial Officer of Seaman's,

(top) Most leather packages are in stock and available for quick delivery.

(left) Seaman's is one of the largest furniture importers in the U.S. An Italian bedroom set is shown here.

Seaman's carries a large variety of styles to satisfy the discerning customer.

now calls, "a lesson of the 80s," the company suddenly found itself staggering under huge debt. The real estate market had peaked and consumers had stopped filling new homes with rooms of furniture. In 1992, Seaman's filed for Chapter 11 bankruptcy, but quickly traded equity for debt, brought back a team of former senior managers, and resumed the strategies that had made it successful.

BEYOND THE NORTHEAST

The company has reentered and opened six stores in the Philadelphia area, and, for the first time, expanded beyond its traditional Northeast marketing area with five new stores in Ohio, four of them in Cleveland.

Senior management is now made up of President and CEO Alan Rosenberg, who has served at Seaman's since the early 1970s; Steven Halper, a veteran of Seaman's since 1968, Chief Operating Officer; and McGeough.

The new management, according to McGeough, believed that Seaman's should continue its saturation advertising, but that concentrating on yelling "Sale!" had tarnished the company's image in the eyes of many consumers. To upgrade the company's image, and reassure consumers of the quality of Seaman's merchandise, the company began offering a one-year complete warranty, and a five-year structural warranty, and worked more on corporate image advertising.

"The Package"® in addition to representing great value, coordinates a complete room for the customer.

Seaman's also instituted its "no/no/no" promotional campaign, under which qualified consumers could receive the "Seaman's Plus"® credit card and buy furniture with little or no money down, no payments for several months, and no interest for that initial time period. Interest on the credit card purchases also adds to company revenues, while the credit card itself serves to promote repeat business. Seaman's spends about $25 million annually on advertising, more than any other Metro New York furniture retailer.

A REWARDING EXPERIENCE

Seaman's also makes furniture shopping a rewarding experience for consumers by delivering the merchandise they buy generally within two weeks, and sometimes within a few days. This is possible because of the "narrow and deep" strategy, and the fact that the company stocks everything it sells in three large warehouses, one located in Central Islip. Seaman's suppliers are also chosen because of their ability to respond quickly to orders. In fact, Seaman's top 30 suppliers, most located in the United States and Canada, supply 70 percent of Seaman's merchandise.

The company also boasts one of the quickest merchandise "turns" in the industry—six times a year—and sales per square foot in the high $300s, with the industry average less than half of that.

Unlike many American industries, furniture retailing is still dominated by local, "Mom & Pop" stores. The top 100 retailers account for about 40 percent of sales. Seaman's believes the trend is toward consolidation, and intends to take advantage of that opportunity.

"The excellent companies will survive, grow and prosper," says Alan Rosenberg, Seaman's President. "We believe that Seaman's belongs with those companies who with foresight, financial strength, excellent management, reliable resources, savvy customers, a proven concept, and a well conceived plan will represent the dominant players and the future of our industry." •••

PALANKER CHEVROLET-GEO, INC.
Exceeding Customers' Expectations Every Day
• • •

THE TRI-STATE AREA' LARGEST CORVETTE RETAILER, and one of the top 100 businesses in retail sales, Palanker Chevrolet-Geo provides its facilities twice a year to host a very worthy cause. Several thousand Corvette owners showcase their collections of vintage models, featuring classics from yesterday and the most current models available now. Corvette owners throughout the tri-state area and beyond come to Palanker Chevrolet in West Babylon on Montauk Highway between Route 110 and Route 109. The thousand or more attendees look around, shop the market, compare their own prized auto with others, enter their beloved Corvettes in various competitions, and also raise money for charity. The events are sponsored by the Long Island Corvette Owners Association and, through registration fees, funds are raised for the Marty Lyons Make A Wish Foundation, which grants wishes to critically or terminally ill children. So next time the papers report a sick youngster being whisked off to a much longed-for trip to Disney World, it was probably funds raised at Palanker Chevrolet that made the trip possible.

Why West Babylon? And why Palanker Chevrolet? Because Palanker has carved out a real specialty of a niche market with the only world-class, luxury sports car manufactured in America. At any given time, at least 100 of these dream machines are in stock at Palanker. So wide is Palanker's reputation among Corvette owners that calls often come into the West Babylon dealership from around the country and even Europe inquiring about specific types of vehicles.

Of course, Palanker Chevrolet, one of Long Island's top dealerships in terms of sales volume, is also

a source for more family-oriented automobiles. Palanker carries the Chevrolet and Geo brand names which include a full range of sub-compact, compact, mid-sized and luxury cars as well as vans and other luxury recreational vehicles. In fact, Palanker is seen by many as just as much a specialist in luxury vans as it is in Corvettes.

Palanker's deep roots in serving Long Island's car buying market go back to the 1950s when the dealership was established as Booth Chevrolet. From the beginning, the dealership's hallmarks have been servicing and caring for its customers. During the early 1980s Richard Palanker bought out the company which then assumed his name. In 1994, Palanker was purchased by William Adkins who has chosen to retain the Palanker identity for his business.

Adkins came to the Long Island Chevrolet firm with years of experience gained in Ohio and California dealerships. He has not only adhered to Palanker Chevrolet's longtime reputation for service, he has added to it with many new levels of service designed to meet the needs of new generations of Chevrolet and Geo buyers. Adkins said: "We offer a caring environment where we try to exceed a customer's expectations. It's not just a buying experience; it's like inviting someone into our home as a guest."

Palanker's customers may buy or lease new or used vehicles. For those who choose to buy rather than lease, Palanker sales personnel administer promotional incentive programs offered by General Motors and also seek out the most favorable sources of financing. The best financing may be found within a General Motors Acceptance Corporation (GMAC) program, or it may be at a local bank with which

(top) In 1994 Richard and Claire Palanker (left) pass the torch of Palanker Chevrolet to William and Pauline Adkins (right).

With its extensive programs of support, Palanker Chevrolet has demonstrated that it is a good neighbor to the West Babylon community.

Palanker Chevrolet is the tri-state leader in Corvette sales.

Palanker has built a relationship over the years.

According to Adkins, leasing is a very important aspect of his business—fully 51 percent last year. So his sales team is highly trained to assist customers with the details of currently available leasing programs. Leasing programs are available at Palanker for previously owned as well as new vehicles. Adkins cited as particularly attractive to customers "vehicles coming off lease after two or three years and still under factory warranty." He said that this type of purchase represents a really good

Twice a year, East Coast Corvette owners gather at Palanker Chevrolet to compare autos, enter competitions and raise money for charity.

finds itself taking care of repair items that most companies would probably charge for. For instance, under Palanker's Service Plus policy certain parts bought and installed by the dealership's service department are guaranteed for as long as the client owns the vehicle. According to Adkins, his service department goes the extra mile because "we want our customers for life, and we'll do what it takes to retain them." Further explaining his liberal service guidelines Adkins noted "if we're there for them, they'll

value as the vehicle is likely to have low mileage and is an excellent buy for those wishing to avoid the initial depreciation.

If the vehicle had originally been leased from and serviced by Palanker, an additional advantage is that the vehicle's maintenance records are available. Adkins also noted that extended service contracts are available for these previously owned vehicles, as well as new vehicles.

Adkins regards his used vehicle division as "an important service to our customers." Most used vehicles come to the dealership through trade ins and others are privately purchased. By maintaining a used vehicle division, Adkins said, "we enable buyers to use their trade ins as equity in gaining a new one." The new vehicle thus gained by the buyer may be the latest year's model fresh off the showroom floor, or it may be a recent model just acquired by the dealership through another trade in or through the end of a lease.

At Palanker Chevrolet's service department, Adkins said, "we try to understand our customers' needs and are here to satisfy them." Because of this service-oriented philosophy, Palanker often

come back and recommend family and friends to us."

Palanker Chevrolet is also there for the community it serves. The dealership supports local school and youth programs and works with the Town of Babylon providing contributions and services for programs geared to meet the needs of senior citizens. Area soup kitchens and Toys for Tots programs enjoy Palanker support as does the West Babylon Fire Department and the school district's PTA. When local youngsters compete in the Special Olympics, it's quite likely that their participation was made possible through support from Palanker Chevrolet.

Casting his thoughts toward the future of his company, Adkins remarked that while some automobile dealers just won't be around in the years to come, others will become larger through expansion and acquisition. It's clear which category he sees for Palanker Chevrolet. Adkins said: "I look toward our business expanding as long as we continue to exceed our customers' expectations. We want to keep creating win-win situations for our customers, our team members, and our community."

•••

THE GARDEN CITY HOTEL
Long Island's World-Class Hostelry
• • •

IT'S WHERE THE VANDERBILTS AND WHITNEYS MARRIED and spent their leisure time. Today it's still the number one choice for Long Islanders planning events that call for celebration on the grandest of scales. Over more than a century, the Garden City Hotel has maintained its status as Long Island's most prestigious location for personal and corporate parties. Be it gala private occasions or top level corporate affairs, the unchallenged choice is the Garden City Hotel, Long Island's only four-star hotel. Business travelers, too, look to the Garden City Hotel for its exceptional executive accommodations.

Located in the heart of the village of Garden City, a planned community of broad, tree-lined avenues, the Hotel's roots go deep into Long Island's history. First established late in the 19th century, the Garden City Hotel quickly assumed an identity as a playground for the wealthy who had built summer "cottages" across Long Island. Vanderbilt Parkway, Long Island's first concrete road, was built by William K. Vanderbilt who was an enthusiast of one of the newest inventions of the age—the automobile. Vanderbilt built his parkway right up to the doors of the Garden City Hotel so that he and his friends could party in style following a day of motoring. In 1927 when Charles Lindbergh made aviation history with his historic flight to Paris, it was the Garden City

Hotel that hosted him prior to the brave feat. A series of fires destroyed the old building, so in 1930 a completely new Garden City Hotel was unveiled to great acclaim. The present-day Garden City Hotel opened its doors in 1983. As in 1930, the 1983 reopening was a major event for Long Island and was widely marked.

A sophisticated business center serving major corporations, the Garden City Hotel's suburban setting is just 45 minutes from New York City. Major parkways are nearby and a Long Island Railroad station is steps away from the Hotel's front door. Four airports—JFK, LaGuardia, Islip MacArthur and Republic—are within 45 minutes or less travel time.

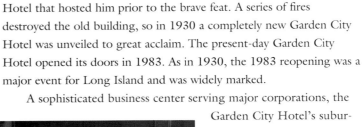

The welcome of the Garden City Hotel begins with the elegant appointments of a comfortable lobby seating area.

Within walking distance of the Garden City Hotel is one of Long Island's most elegant shopping hubs. Often called "The Fifth Avenue of Long Island," Garden City's shopping attractions include such stores as Saks Fifth Avenue and Lord & Taylor.

The elegance of the surrounding community is reflected throughout the Garden City Hotel's opulently decorated public areas, guest rooms and restaurants. A favored gathering spot for Long Island's governmental and corporate leaders, the Hotel is the site for the most powerful of Long Island's "power" breakfasts and lunches. The Polo Grill, acclaimed for its fine contemporary cuisine

Fresh flowers, priceless antiques and original art create individual personality in a Garden City Hotel penthouse suite.

Diners flock to the Polo Grill for its handsome setting and fine American contemporary cuisine.

and fresh baked goods prepared each day in the Hotel's own patisserie, is open seven days a week for breakfast, lunch, dinner and Sunday Brunch. A newer dining facility, The Dallenger Bar & Restaurant offers a casual family menu. Diners enjoy the sporting events shown on the restaurant's large screens. Wednesday, Friday and Saturday nights, however, those screens project entirely different types of images. That's when the room is transformed into The Dallenger—the Garden City Hotel's nightclub, an intimate dance club where lights, sounds, visuals and music all combine to create an excitement of contrasting moods.

Long Island's corporate event planners look to the Garden City Hotel's expert Conference Service staff to mastermind every detail of meetings and conferences. The Hotel offers 16 separate meeting room spaces which range in capacity from 10 to 650 people. Larger spaces are subdivided into smaller rooms, as needed. A full range of audio-visual equipment is always available to conferees.

The Hotel's Banquet Staff, noted for beautifully garnished, extravagant buffets and sit-down dinners, is particularly celebrated. Bridal couples seeking the ultimate in lavish weddings and special event planners organizing the most prestigious social and corporate affairs, opt for the Garden City Hotel. The Hotel offers no standard event package; each menu is custom styled according to the client's specialized preferences.

The Hotel's 280 exquisitely-appointed guest rooms include nine executive suites designed with the needs of the business traveler in mind, three grand suites, and four penthouse suites offering such amenities as working fireplaces and terraces. Each guest room features two telephone lines, oversized towels, turndown service, clock radios and color television sets equipped with Spectravision which allows guests to select their own movies. Guests enjoy the conveniences of a beauty shop and a fully-equipped gym with a 32-foot pool, sauna, whirlpool, a masseuse staff trained in both Swedish and Shiatsu massage and a personal trainer. Business guests are pleased with such in-room amenities as modem hookups, faxes, and voice mail phone systems with direct dial. They also welcome the services of an in-house business center with typing, faxing and computer services and the availability of private work stations.

The Garden City Hotel maintains a 24-hour room and concierge service. Among the many guest services offered by the Hotel's concierge staff are arrangements for tickets for theaters and other events on Long Island and in New York City, and assistance with baby-sitting services and travel arrangements. But those are just everyday services for the concierge staff. It's when guests have special needs that the Garden City Hotel staff really shines. For a bereft family, evacuated from its home at holiday time, the concierge staff provided some home-like cheer by buying and decorating a Christmas tree for the family's suite. They've collaborated with gentlemen planning a marriage proposal or couples marking a special anniversary by garbing suites in the most romantic of decorations. For travelers who've forgotten some crucial items of equipment or clothing, the concierge staff's personal buying service can be heaven-sent.

From its chandeliered lobby, to its specialty boutiques, restaurants, dance club, public and guest rooms, and total emphasis on guest service, the Garden City Hotel has set an unmatched standard of grandeur. •••

Magnificent hand-painted murals set an atmosphere of old-world charm in a public area of the Garden City Hotel.

ROSA KASPEROVICH FUNERAL SERVICE
Personal Attention at a Family's Most Difficult Time
• • •

FUNERAL HOMES ARE TYPICALLY FAMILY-RUN operations and, almost invariably, they're headed up by men. Then there's Rosa Kasperovich. In a male-dominated industry, one in which she did not benefit from any previous family involvement, Kasperovich has not only flourished; she's prevailed.

She credits her success to the degree of personal attention families find when they turn to the Rosa Kasperovich Funeral Service. "Everyone's been touched by death," said Kasperovich. She went on to explain, "The important thing is to make people feel comforted."

The Kasperovich "difference" starts right from the first telephone call. Revealing just how far she'll go to reach out with comfort, Kasperovich doesn't ask the family to come to her. Instead, she sets a time when she'll come to the family. While she acknowledges that "it's very unusual" for funeral directors to pay a personal house call, Kasperovich said that being able to consider all of the options in their own home is highly comforting to those who need to make final arrangements for loved ones. She brings with her all the necessary forms and information.

Capable of handling everything from simple cremations to elaborate burials, Kasperovich presents her clients with itemized choices so they know just what they are selecting, along with the price for that selection. In a business that's often been accused of preying upon people at a time that they're least able to withstand even subtle sales pressure, Kasperovich sets a high standard by sharing information with her clients on what they will need, and then listening carefully about

Rosa Kasperovich, one of Long Island's only female funeral directors, personalizes funerals for each family's needs.

what they want. She depends heavily upon her training as a grief counselor. Recognizing that she's functioning as both a counselor and as a businesswoman, Kasperovich maintained "you have to reach out to people—but not so much as to alienate or intimidate them." She elaborated, "They've experienced a loss, and there are financial implications to consider as well."

Most of Kasperovich's referrals come from area churches because "they're confident their parishioners will have someone sensitive to their needs." But often families she's served recommend her to other families. Unusual within an industry that she describes as highly segregated, Kasperovich, who is African-American, runs her business within a white-owned funeral home.

Kasperovich is the product of a large Southern family which, though poor, stressed education. She started out in a nursing program, but while still in school, one of her advisors suggested mortuary science as a career. Her reaction was "Wow. Women don't go into that field." But deciding to try it anyway, she switched her nursing credits over to SUNY-Farmingdale's mortuary program. Following graduation, she worked for several other funeral homes. It was what she recognized as her "strong people skills" that encouraged her to start her own business; so "I could personalize it the way I wanted to."

Kasperovich emphasized that the result of running the funeral business her way is "I give, but a lot of families give back to me. Usually they become a sort of friend, with follow-up calls, notes, and the formation of a lasting relationship." • • •

Rosa Kasperovich (center) meets with clients in her homelike conference room.

LONG ISLAND 7-ELEVEN STORES
Convenience Shopping Pioneer Upgrades and Expands
• • •

LONG ISLANDERS SURE LOVE 7-ELEVEN COFFEE. THE 146 7-Eleven stores on Long Island post the highest volume of coffee sales anywhere in the nation for this worldwide chain.

The pioneer in the operation, franchising and licensing of convenience stores, 7-Eleven's parent company, the Southland Corporation, was founded in 1927. The 7-Eleven name harks back to a time when the retail outlets were open from 7 am to 11 pm. Today, the majority of 7-Eleven stores are open 24 hours a day. The company has gone far beyond its early offerings of milk, bread, eggs and other staples. Now, shoppers now count on 7-Eleven around the clock for a vast array of items such as Oscar Mayer's "Big Bite" hot dogs, nachos, pastries, the famous "Slurpee" semi-frozen soft drink, sandwiches, salads, produce and such customer conveniences as automated teller machines (ATMs), money orders, copiers, fax machines, long-distance pre-paid phone cards, and, in some locations, lottery tickets.

Throughout the United States and Canada, there are more than 5,400 7-Eleven stores serving some six million customers each day. Approximately half are operated by franchise owners. Varying in size from 2,400 to 3,000 square feet, the customer-friendly outlets typically stock up to 3,000 different items. The familiar red, orange and green striped facade is a welcoming beacon for shoppers at home or away. Easy to find, 7-Eleven stores are usually located on busy corners for high visibility and easy access.

Beyond its North American stronghold, 7-Eleven is an established presence throughout the Far and Near East, Europe, Scandinavia, Asia, and South America.

Providing a clean, safe and swift shopping environment, 7-Eleven's Long Island market is part of the Northeast Division, which is headquartered in Melville. The market's stores have recently been upgraded with increased interior and exterior lighting, standardization of the three-stripe facade, open fresh food display cases, improved product layout and signage, wider aisles, and in locations where gasoline is sold, upgraded gasoline equipment. Additionally, new closed-circuit TV surveillance systems have been installed as part of 7-Eleven's ongoing crime-deterrence program.

In another move to bolster both product quality and customer service, 7-Eleven stores on Long Island inaugurated a daily delivery system for dairy products, packaged pastries, fresh-baked goods, fresh fruit and fresh-made sandwiches. This centralized delivery system works to reduce product cost while assuring optimum product freshness.

A good corporate neighbor, the Southland Corporation and the 7-Eleven stores are highly regarded for community service. For the past 20 years Southland and 7-Eleven have been a top corporate sponsor of the Muscular Dystrophy Association. The company also assists Mothers Against Drunk Driving in its national public awareness campaigns. In recent years, Southland has committed many of its resources to programs which promote literary. Through its People Who Read Achieve grant program, the company has awarded more than $1.5 million in grants to grass-roots literacy organizations.

On Long Island, 7-Elevens' 34 corporate employees and more than 2,000 franchise employees have focused their philanthropic support on the issues of literacy, individuals with disabilities, education and minority economic development. During 1995, approximately $95,000 was awarded by Long Island 7-Eleven stores to 110 schools, libraries, shelters, community service groups, church organizations and day-care establishments. • • •

(top) 7-Eleven stores on Long Island typically stock more than 3,000 different items.

(left) The familiar red, orange and green striped facade calls out welcome and convenience to Long Island shoppers here and across the world.

HOME DEPOT

Servicing Homeowners with Expert Knowledge

• • •

LONG ISLAND'S DO-IT-YOURSELFERS HAVE COME to view an orange apron as a bright beacon of help. That's because Home Depot, where all the sales personnel are garbed in the distinctive aprons, has established a unique level of customer service. Home Depot salespeople on the floor can respond to a customer's query because there s on-the-spot access to a professional— a plumber, electrician, carpenter, painter, nurseryman, even interior designers and certified kitchen planners—who can offer expert advice.

It's this stress on giving homeowners the knowledge they need, combined with an extraordinary array of home improvement supplies—more than 35,000 different kinds of building materials are available in each store—that has allowed Home Depot to establish its reputation on Long Island and throughout the nation.

Headquartered in Atlanta, Home Depot is the brainchild of Chairman Bernie Marcus and President Arthur Blank. Their concept of wielding together name brand building materials and a low price policy with an experienced, full-time salesforce was first launched in 1978. There are now more than 400 Home Depots in 32 states and in Canada; the stores generate more than $12 billion dollars in sales and employ more than 95,000 people.

The "secret" behind Home Depot's success, the factor that spells the Home Depot difference, is the company's intensive employee training program. From an entry level salesperson through to corporate vice presidents, everybody is trained to work with customers on the salesfloor. Reflecting the company's underlying philosophy, the central theme at all levels of training is: "How does this affect the customer?"

For the customer whose needs call for more than help on the salesfloor, Home Depot sponsors free clinics in just about every aspect of home improvement. A typical week's offerings include classes in installing vinyl siding, resealing and repairing driveways, pouring cement, maintaining and establishing lawns, and building decks.

Long Islanders who lusted after the Home Depots they saw in other parts of the country, had their appetites satisfied in 1989 when the area's first Home Depot opened in East Meadow. Twelve more followed. There are now Home Depot locations in Bay Shore,

Intensive employee training underlies the success of Home Depot, in its Georgia home, on Long Island, and throughout the U.S. and Canada.

Copiague, Commack, Elmont, Farmingdale, Flushing, Freeport, Ozone Park, Patchogue, Selden, Valley Stream and Westbury. The most recent entry, Expo in Carle Place, represents a different kind of initiative for Home Depot. Staffed by design professionals, Expo is totally devoted to home decorating.

While some may have been concerned about the local impact of this big Atlanta-based retailer, Home Depot has demonstrated that it has a commitment to all of the communities in which it does business. On Long Island, Home Depot has been especially supportive of affordable housing, providing both supplies and manpower for non-profit organizations such as Habitat for Humanity. Locally and on a nationwide basis, the company has been notable for its support of programs for at-risk youth. Home Depot also sponsors a matching gifts program in which its employees set the agenda for charitable giving. • • •

The 13 Home Depots on Long Island and Queens each offer more than 35,000 different kinds of home improvement products.

BIBLIOGRAPHY
• • •

Bookbinder, Bernie. Long Island: People and Places, Past and Present. New York, NY: Harry N. Abrams, Inc., 1983.

Heisler, Bob, ed. Newsday's Long Island User's Guide '95. Melville, NY: Newsday, Inc., 1994.

Heyen, William. Long Island Light: Poems and a Memoir. New York, NY: The Vanguard Press, Inc., 1979.

Hostek, Albert. Native and Near Native, An Introduction to Long Island Plants. Ronkonkoma, NY: The Environmental Centers of Setauket-Smithtown, Inc., 1983.

Kushner, Harvey W., Ph.D. Analysis of Factors Generating Nassau County's Low Crime Rate. A report for The Office of the District Attorney, Nassau County, NY from C.W. Post Campus/Long Island University. 1995.

Long Island Book of Lists. A supplement to Long Island Business News. Ronkonkoma, NY: *Long Island Business News*, 1995-1996.

Long Island Forum, The Magazine of Long Island's History and Heritage. Muttontown, NY: Friends for Long Island's Heritage, 1994-1995.

Long Island Leisure Guide. A supplement to Long Island Business News. Ronknonkoma, NY: *Long Island Business News*, 1995.

Long Island, The Official Magazine of the Long Island Association. Volumes 8-9. Commack, NY: 1994-1995.

Long Island Travel Guide. Uniondale, NY: Long Island Convention and Visitors Bureau, 1993-1996.

Newsday. Long Island, NY: Newsday, Inc, 1940-1996.

1995 LI Almanac. A supplement to Long Island Business News. Ronkonkoma, NY: *Long Island Business News*, 1995.

Spinzia, Raymond E., Judith A. and Kathryn E. Long Island: A Guide to New York's Suffolk and Nassau Counties. New York, NY: Hippocrene Books, 1991.

Sterling, Dorothy. The Outer Lands, Revised Edition. New York, NY: W.W. Norton and Co., Inc., 1978.

Suffolk County: A Place In Time. Catalog of a photo exhibit placed by Suffolk County Tercentenary Commission. Suffolk County, NY: Cedar Graphics, 1983.

The First Forty Years 1947-1987. Upton, NY: Brookhaven National Laboratory, 1987.

The Long Island Country House 1870-1930. A catalog of an exhibition at the Parrish Art Museum, Southampton, NY, May 15-July 10, 1988. Los Angeles, CA: Perpetua Press, 1988.

The Long Island Historical Journal. Volumes 6-8. Stony Brook, NY: State University of New York at Stony Brook, 1994-1996.

The 1995 Fun Book. A supplement to *Newsday*. Melville, NY: Newsdsay, 1995.

Wood, Simeon. A History of Hauppauge, Long Island. Hauppauge, NY: Jack Marr Publishing Co., 1981.

ENTERPRISES INDEX

● ● ●

INDEX

• • •